D1029907

The Targum of Ruth

The Targum of Chronicles

THE ARAMAIC BIBLE
• THE TARGUMS •

PROJECT DIRECTOR
Martin McNamara, M.S.C.

EDITORS
Kevin Cathcart • Michael Maher, M.S.C.
Martin McNamara, M.S.C.

EDITORIAL CONSULTANTS
Daniel J. Harrington, S.J. • Bernard Grossfeld

The Aramaic Bible

Volume 19

The Targum of Ruth

*Translated, with Introduction,
Apparatus, and Notes*

BY

D.R.G. Beattie

The Targum of Chronicles

*Translated, with Introduction,
Apparatus, and Notes*

BY

J. Stanley McIvor

A Michael Glazier Book
THE LITURGICAL PRESS
Collegeville, Minnesota

First published in 1994 by The Liturgical Press, Collegeville, Minnesota 56321.

Library of Congress Cataloging-in-Publication Data

Bible. O.T. Ruth. English. Beattie. 1994.
    The Targum of Ruth / translated, with introduction, apparatus and notes by D.R.G. Beattie. And, The Targum of Chronicles / translated, with introduction, apparatus, and notes by J. Stanley McIvor.
      p.   cm. — (The Aramaic Bible ; v. 19)
    "A Michael Glazier book."
    Includes bibliographical references and indexes.
    ISBN 0-8146-5455-X
    1. Bible. O.T. Ruth. Aramaic—Translations into English. 2. Bible. O.T. Ruth. Aramaic—Criticism, Textual. 3. Bible. O.T. Chronicles. Aramaic—Translations into English. 4. Bible. O.T. Chronicles. Aramaic—Criticism, Textual. I. Beattie, Derek Robert George. II. McIvor, J. Stanley. III. Bible. O.T. Chronicles. English. McIvor. 1994. IV. Title. V. Title: Targum of Chronicles. VI. Series: Bible. O.T. English. Aramaic Bible. 1987 ; v. 19.
BS709.2.B5 1987 vol. 19
[BS1313]
222′.35042—dc20
                                          93-36872
                                              CIP

Logo design by Florence Bern.
Typography by Graphic Sciences Corporation, Cedar Rapids, Iowa.
Printed and bound in the United States of America by Edwards Brothers, Inc., Ann Arbor, Michigan.

EDITORS' FOREWORD

While any translation of the Scriptures may in Hebrew be called a Targum, the word is used especially for a translation of a book of the Hebrew Bible into Aramaic. Before the Christian era Aramaic had in good part replaced Hebrew in Palestine as the vernacular of the Jews. It continued as their vernacular for centuries later and remained in part as the language of the schools after Aramaic itself had been replaced as the vernacular.

Rabbinic Judaism has transmitted Targums of all books of the Hebrew Canon, with the exception of Daniel and Ezra-Nehemiah, which are themselves partly in Aramaic. We also have a translation of the Samaritan Pentateuch into the dialect of Samaritan Aramaic. From the Qumran Library we have sections of a Targum of Job and fragments of a Targum of Leviticus, chapter 16, facts which indicate that the Bible was being translated in Aramaic in pre-Christian times.

Translations of books of the Hebrew Bible into Aramaic for liturgical purposes must have begun before the Christian era, even though none of the Targums transmitted to us by Rabbinic Judaism can be shown to be that old and though some of them are demonstrably compositions from later centuries.

In recent decades there has been increasing interest among scholars and a larger public in these Targums. A noticeable lacuna, however, has been the absence of a modern English translation of this body of writing. It is in marked contrast with most other bodies of Jewish literature for which there are good modern English translations, for instance the Apocrypha and Pseudepigrapha of the Old Testament, Josephus, Philo, the Mishnah, the Babylonian Talmud and Midrashic literature, and more recently the Tosefta and Palestinian Talmud.

It is hoped that this present series will provide some remedy for this state of affairs.

The aim of the series is to translate all the traditionally-known Targums, that is those transmitted by Rabbinic Judaism, into modern English idiom, while at the same time respecting the particular and peculiar nature of what these Aramaic translations were originally intended to be. A translator's task is never an easy one. It is rendered doubly difficult when the text to be rendered is itself a translation which is at times governed by an entire set of principles.

All the translations in this series have been specially commissioned. The translators have made use of what they reckon as the best printed editions of the Aramaic Targum in question or have themselves directly consulted the manuscripts.

The translation aims at giving a faithful rendering of the Aramaic. The introduction to each Targum contains the necessary background information on the particular work. In general, each Targum translation is accompanied by an apparatus and notes. The former is concerned mainly with such items as the variant readings in the Aramaic texts, the relation of the English translation to the original, etc. The notes give what explanations the translator thinks necessary or useful for this series.

Not all the Targums here translated are of the same kind. Targums were translated at different times, and most probably for varying purposes, and have more than one interpretative approach to the Hebrew Bible. This diversity between the Targums themselves is reflected in the translation and in the manner in which the accompanying explanatory material is presented. However, a basic unity of presentation has been maintained. Targumic deviations from the Hebrew text, whether by interpretation or paraphrase, are indicated by italics.

A point that needs to be stressed with regard to this translation of the Targums is that by reason of the state of current targumic research, to a certain extent it must be regarded as a provisional one. Despite the progress made, especially in recent decades, much work still remains to be done in the field of targumic study. Not all the Targums are as yet available in critical editions. And with regard to those that have been critically edited from known manuscripts, in the case of the Targums of some books the variants between the manuscripts themselves are such as to give rise to the question whether they have all descended from a single common original.

Details regarding these points will be found in the various introductions and critical notes.

It is recognized that a series such as this will have a broad readership. The Targums constitute a valuable source of information for students of Jewish literature, particularly those concerned with the history of interpretation, and also for students of the New Testament, especially for those interested in its relationship to its Jewish origins. The Targums also concern members of the general public who have an interest in the Jewish interpretation of the Scriptures or in the Jewish background to the New Testament. For them the Targums should be both interesting and enlightening.

By their translations, introductions and critical notes the contributors to this series have rendered an immense service to the progress of targumic studies. It is hoped that the series, provisional though it may be, will bring significantly nearer the day when the definitive translation of the Targums can be made.

Kevin Cathcart   Martin McNamara, M.S.C.   Michael Maher, M.S.C.

The Targum of Ruth

Translated, with Introduction, Apparatus, and Notes

BY

D.R.G. Beattie

About the Translator:

Derek Beattie has been Head of the Department of Semitic Studies at the Queen's University of Belfast since 1985. He read Hebrew and Semitic Languages at Trinity College, Dublin, where his interest in Ruth and her Targum was first aroused, and received his Ph.D. from the University of St Andrews, having written a thesis on Jewish Exegesis of the Book of Ruth.

FOR TIM

TABLE OF CONTENTS

ABBREVIATIONS

Aram.	Aramaic
b.	Babylonian Talmud
B. B.	Baba Bathra
Ber.	Berakhoth
B. M.	Baba Meşi'a
Cant	Song of Songs
Chr	Chronicles
Deut	Deuteronomy
Erub.	Erubin
Esth	Esther
Gen	Genesis
Heb.	Hebrew
Hor.	Horayoth
IBS	Irish Biblical Studies
JJS	Journal of Jewish Studies
Judg	Judges
JSOTS	Journal for the Study of the Old Testament Supplement Series
Kgs	Kings
Lam	Lamentations
LXX	Septuagint
m.	Mishnah
Meg.	Megillah
Men.	Menaḥoth

MT	Massoretic Text
Num	Numbers
Onq.	Onqelos
Pes.	Pesaḥim
Ps.-J.	Pseudo-Jonathan
R.	Rabbah (midrash)
Shab.	Shabbath
Sam	Samuel
San.	Sanhedrin
Soṭ	Soṭah
Tg(s).	Targum(s)
Vg.	Vulgate
y.	Palestinian Talmud
Yeb.	Yebamoth

Sigla employed in the Apparatus are defined on p. 13.

INTRODUCTION

I. THE TARGUM AND ITS MANUSCRIPTS

In the Jewish liturgical tradition the Book of Ruth is read at the festival of Shavuot, or Pentecost, and it may be conjectured that the Targum originated in conjunction with this practice. If the practice is an ancient one, the Targum could be very old, but the earliest record of the practice is in the post-Talmudic tractate *Sopherim* 14:3. The custom of reading the Targum along with the Hebrew text at that festival is certainly well attested among Yemenite communities, but here, again, the date of origin of the custom is not known. No Yemenite manuscript of Tg. Ruth can be dated earlier than the fourteenth or fifteenth century.

The earliest citation of Tg. Ruth is by Nathan ben Jehiel of Rome (1035–ca. 1110) in his Talmudic dictionary, the *Arukh,* completed in 1101. Nathan's contemporary, Rashi (1040–1105), in his commentary on *b. Meg.* 21b, denied the existence of a Targum of the Hagiographa, so it would appear that in the eleventh century the Targum of Ruth was, like the Palestinian Targum of the Pentateuch, known to the Jewish scholars of Italy, Spain, and Provence, but not to those of northern France and Germany.

The Targum of Ruth exists in a large number of manuscripts, of which twenty-one have been examined during the time that this work has been in preparation, although only eight have been utilized for the critical apparatus. These eight, which are identified below, range in date from the twelfth to the fifteenth century and, with the exception of British Library *Or.* 2375, which is Yemenite, are of European provenance. They all contain essentially the same text with only minor variations and in several places agree together against the text found in printed editions.

Thirteen further manuscripts, eleven of which are of Yemenite provenance and all of which are located in the library of the Jewish Theological Seminary of America, New York, were examined when the major part of the present work had already been completed. Ten of the eleven Yemenite manuscripts (L471, L472a, L472c, L472d, L472e, L474, L474a, L475, L475a, L611), which date from the eighteenth and nineteenth centuries, display notable similarities to the text found in printed editions from which they undoubtedly derive. They also display some points of difference in relation to the printed texts and earlier manuscripts, which may be explained as resulting from attempts to improve the Aramaic. Such a process is clearly demonstrated in L475a, where marginal notes have the effect of changing readings in agreement with the earlier manuscripts to conform with those found in the other late Yemenite manuscripts. The one sixteenth-century Yemenite manuscript in this collection (L431) shows many similarities to *Or.* 2375 and the European manuscripts. Both it and the two non-Yemenite manuscripts (L125, fourteenth-century Germanic, and L610, fragmentary fifteenth-century Italian) belong comfortably in company with the manuscripts on which the present work focuses hereafter.

While the present work was in the press, further study of Targum manuscripts led to the conclusion that the thirteenth-century manuscript *Solger* 6.2° of the Stadtbibliothek, Nürnberg, is the sole source of the text found in the printed editions. See D.R.G. Beattie, "The Textual Tradition of Targum Ruth," in D.R.G. Beattie and M. McNamara (eds.), *The Aramaic Bible: Targums in Their Historical Context.* Proceedings of the Royal Irish Academy Conference on the Aramaic Bible, Dublin, 1992 (Sheffield: Sheffield Academic Press, forthcoming).

The language of the Targum is a mixture of Palestinian Aramaic and "official" or Babylonian forms such as are characteristic of the Targum of Onqelos. As the apparatus which accompanies the translation below shows, Palestinian forms predominate in the manuscripts, particularly the earlier ones, while Onqelos-type forms occur more frequently in the later (fifteenth century) manuscripts and in the printed texts. However, no text adheres exclusively to one tradition or the other, and even in the earliest manuscripts some Onqelos-type forms are encountered. It might thus be surmised that Tg. Ruth, like Onqelos itself, had its origin in Palestine and its language was modified to some extent in the course of its transmission. Those changes which would appear to have occurred during the period covered by the manuscripts utilized in this study were probably occasioned directly as a result of familiarity with the language of Onqelos. However, no detailed study of the language of the Targum has yet been undertaken, and much careful work needs to be done before any secure conclusion may be pronounced.

II. THE CONTENTS OF THE TARGUM

Tg. Ruth contains, in addition to an Aramaic translation of the Hebrew text, a considerable quantity of additional material that expands the whole to more than twice the length of the Hebrew. The Hebrew text that underlies the Aramaic translation is clearly that which is known to us from the Massoretic Text, and the translation is on the whole literal, departing from the wording of the Hebrew only when this is necessitated by exegetical considerations of some kind. These include a fondness for passive verbs, the avoidance of anthropomorphisms and other expressions that were considered indelicate, the drawing out of hidden meanings and the accommodation of additional material, which is always integrated with the translation of the Hebrew.

There is some evidence from the manuscripts that the literalism of the Targum's translation is the result of a process that aimed to bring the Aramaic text into conformity with the Hebrew. The double translations that may be observed in the printed texts result from the addition of literal translations to earlier non-literal (often midrashic) renderings that appear alone in some or all of the manuscripts (though it should be noted that some double translations appear even in the earliest manuscripts), while differences in wording between manuscripts and printed texts sometimes reflect changes in understanding of the meaning of Hebrew words.

It would seem, too, that the Targum's additional material increased in quantity in the course of transmission. The oldest manuscript, Sassoon 282, which dates from the twelfth century, has the shortest text, partly in consequence of its translation, which is noticeably freer than that in other manuscripts, but also because its expansions are less verbose. However, all the substantial Targumic exegeses encountered in other texts are already present in that manuscript.

As may be seen from the translation and the accompanying notes, the exegeses contained in the Targum are broadly in tune with those found elsewhere in Rabbinic literature. Various matters in the Targum have parallels in the Talmud and Midrash. Sometimes there is agreement between the Targum and other sources, sometimes a common exegetical approach that leads to different results is displayed, and sometimes there are points of positive disagreement. In a few places the Targum displays complete independence and includes details that are without parallel elsewhere. It would thus seem to follow that the Targum represents an independent exegetical tradition that is distinct from those which found expression in the Talmud and Midrash while sharing in the same general style of exegesis as these.

The purpose of the Targum was, in a word, to expound the story in the biblical book, and so, at almost every turn, we find additions and expansions designed to answer questions that arise from the story as it appears in the Bible. In these "extra" passages, as well as in the translation of certain parts of the biblical text, it is possible to glimpse something of the mind of the meturgeman, whose chief interests may be said to have been the importance of piety and of the observance of the law. With respect to the latter, it is interesting to note that when matters of halakah are touched upon, the Targum is often out of step with statements in the Mishnah. This probably reflects the Targum's origin in the context of the synagogue rather than the academy, but it may point toward its having being composed at a date before the halakah was firmly established.

III. THE ORIGIN OF THE TARGUM

The Targum of Ruth, along with the Targums of the other Megilloth, has often been thought to be a post-Talmudic composition. The basis of this belief, in the case of Tg. Ruth, seems to be the suspicion that where its exegeses have parallels in the Talmud and Midrash, it must have used these as sources. This position has been maintained most recently by Melamed, who argued that its author often erred in his use of Talmudic sources. On the other hand, it has been pointed out, most notably by Heinemann, that the reference in 1:17 to "hanging on a tree" as a method of execution must, in view of its contradiction of the Mishnah, point to an ancient origin, at least for that part of the Targum. A variation of this approach finds the origin of Tg. Ruth among the Sadducees, or some other, unspecified, non-Pharisaic sect, but that argument, originated by Schlesinger and developed enthusiastically by Levine, lacks any secure foundation.

Among other arguments in favor of the antiquity of the Targum are the fact that the version of the aggada of the ten famines in 1:1 is demonstrably earlier than parallel versions in *Gen. R.* and *Ruth R.*, and the occurrence in 3:8 (and in 1:17 according to some manuscripts) of the pronominal use of *memra*. This usage, which occurs elsewhere in the Targums of the Writings, notably in Chronicles and Job, must be an ancient one, if only because it can hardly have developed after the word *memra* took on its theological loading.

There are good reasons to think that some elements in Tg. Ruth must be early, and it is difficult to find any that must be late. While a definitive judgment on the origin of the Targum cannot yet be pronounced, it may not be out of place of recall that the Tosafists, in contradicting Rashi's statement that there was no Targum of the Writings, observed that it was made in the time of the tannaim. That is the oldest known opinion on the origin of this Targum, and it may very well be right.

IV. THE PRESENT TRANSLATION

In the translation that follows, those parts of the text of the Targum that are translations of the Hebrew text are presented in roman type (even when the translation is, from a modern point of view, inaccurate), while all departures from the Hebrew, as well as the Targum's additional material, are presented in italic. When the Targum departs from the wording of the Hebrew or translates it in a manner different from what would be normal nowadays, an English translation of the Hebrew is given in the notes.

The question of which form of the Targum text should be adopted as a basis for translation presented certain practical difficulties that have been resolved by joining, in effect, in the tradition of the Targum and producing a new compilation of Targumic material. The translation is based on the "received" text of the Rabbinic Bibles, Lagarde and Sperber, supplemented with material from the manuscripts that have been examined and from the polyglots as recorded by Wright. While the translation, for the most part, follows the "received" text, sometimes the readings of the majority of manuscripts (or the unanimous manuscript tradition) and sometimes minority readings have been adopted. The guiding principle in any given instance has been that the fullest information should be conveyed as clearly and conveniently as possible.

At all times I have indicated in the apparatus the manuscript or other authority for the text as I have translated it, and I have attempted also to give there as complete a picture of the textual situation as is possible in the circumstances, particularly with regard to the use of words that are distinctive to certain Aramaic dialects. Bearing in mind that the task in hand has been to produce a translation rather than a critical edition of the Aramaic text, variant readings that do not affect the translation have not, in general, been noted. Thus many minor differences in orthography or syntax have been ignored, as have obvious corruptions, although some such items are mentioned in conjunction with items that do affect the translation. Variants are given as far as possible in English translation, but have occasionally been presented only in transliterated Aramaic, in order to indicate the existence of lexical variants, in cases where no different translation is possible or satisfactory.

The following sigla are used in the apparatus:

(a) *Manuscripts**:

- A — Rome, Angelica, *Or.* 72 (1326)
- Bo — Oxford, Bodleian, *Hunt.* 399 (15th cent.)
- Br — [Breslau] Wroclaw University, M1106 (1238)
- D — Dresden, 14th-century MS collated by Wright, from whom readings are derived, now extant only as a carbon block
- H — Hamburg, Staats- und Universitätsbibliothek, *Levi* 19 (1310)
- K — Copenhagen, Kongelige Bibliotek, *Cod. Hebr.* 11 (1290)
- M — London, British Library, *Or.* 2375 (15th cent.)
- S — Sassoon 282 (12th cent.)
- U — Vatican, *Urbinas Ebr.* 1 (1294)

With the exception of D, these sigla are the same as in Levine, but there are many errors in Levine's readings. It should be noted that M is seriously defective: 1:5–2:3 and 2:13-22 are missing in their entirety, while 1:2-4; 2:11; 3:9, 11, 14, 16 and 4:10 have all suffered some damage.

(b) *Printed texts*:

- R   — the "received text" of the Rabbinic Bibles, Lagarde and Sperber
- W   — Walton's Polyglot (1656), text as reprinted in Wright
- Ant. — Antwerp Polyglot (1570)
- P   — Paris Polyglot (1629)

The term "printed texts" is employed where the "received text" and the polyglot Bibles are in agreement, while "texts" includes both manuscripts and printed texts.

In order to avoid the need for long lists of sigla, the abbreviation "MSS" is used to indicate all the manuscripts that have been examined; similarly, "most MSS" or "most texts," when preceded or followed by citation of a few manuscripts or printed texts, indicates all manuscripts, or all texts, other than those specified.

For the "Jewish parallels" quoted in the notes, attention has been focused on pre-medieval sources, principally the Talmuds and the midrash *Ruth Rabbah*. Exegeses that are unique to the Targum are not always identified explicitly. The absence of any reference to other sources or the citation only of divergent ideas may be taken to indicate that no parallel comment is known to exist, at least in early sources.

---

*I am grateful to the Institute of Microfilmed Hebrew Manuscripts in the Jewish National and University Library, Jerusalem, for allowing me the use of their facilities and providing me with prints from their microfilms of the manuscripts listed here. I am grateful too to the Bodleian Library, Oxford, for permitting me to have a print made from the microfilm of MS *Hunt.* 399.

V. BIBLIOGRAPHY

EDITIONS OF THE ARAMAIC TEXT

Lagarde, P. de. *Hagiographa Chaldaice.* Leipzig, 1873.

Levine, E. *The Aramaic Version of Ruth.* Analecta Biblica 58. Rome, 1973.

Neuhausen, C. S. "The Targum of the Scroll of Ruth" (Heb.). *Hatsofeh leḥokhmat yisrael* 14 (1930) 33–52.

Sperber, A. *The Bible in Aramaic,* Vol. IV A: *The Hagiographa.* Leiden, 1968.

Wright, C.H.H. *The Book of Ruth in Hebrew and Chaldee.* London, 1864.

ENGLISH TRANSLATIONS

Crane, O. T. *The Targums on the Books of Ruth and Jonah.* New York, 1886.

Levey, S. H. *The Targum to the Book of Ruth: Its Linguistic and Exegetical Character.* Thesis, Hebrew Union College, Cincinnati, 1934. Pp. 35–47.

Levine, E. *The Aramaic Version of Ruth.* Analecta Biblica 58. Rome, 1973.

Saarisalo, A. "The Targum to the Book of Ruth." *Studia Orientalia* II (1928). Pp. 88–104. Reprinted in B. Grossfeld, ed., *The Targum to the Five Megilloth.* New York, 1973. Pp. 3–19.

OTHER WORKS DEALING WITH THE TARGUM OF RUTH

Beattie, D.R.G. *Jewish Exegesis of the Book of Ruth.* JSOTS 2. Sheffield, 1977.

_____. "The Targum of Ruth—A Sectarian Composition?" *JJS* 36 (1985) 222–229.

_____. "Towards Dating the Targum of Ruth." In J. D. Martin and P. R. Davies, eds., *A Word in Season: Essays in Honour of William McKane.* JSOTS 42. Sheffield, 1986. Pp. 205–222.

_____. "Ancient Elements in the Targum of Ruth." Proceedings of the Ninth World Congress of Jewish Studies, Division A: The Period of the Bible. Jerusalem, 1986. Pp. 159–165.

_____. "The Textual Tradition of Targum Ruth: Some Preliminary Observations." In D.R.G. Beattie and E. A. Russell, eds., *Essays in Honour of Professor Jacob Weingreen on the Occasion of His 80th Birthday.* IBS 10 (1988) 12–23.

_____. "The Yemenite Tradition of Targum Ruth," *JJS* 41 (1990) 49–56.

Churgin, P. *Targum Ketuvim* (Heb.). New York, 1945.

Díez-Merino, L. "El Targum de Rut, Estado de la Cuestion y Traduccion Castellana." In V. Collada and E. Zurro, eds., *El Misterio de la Palabra.* Madrid, 1983. Pp. 245–265.

Heinemann, Y. "The Targum of Exod 22:4 and the Ancient Halakah" (Heb.). *Tarbiẓ* 38 (1968–69) 294–296.

Melamed, E.-Z. "The Targum of the Scroll of Ruth" (Heb.). *Bar Ilan, Annual of Bar Ilan University* I (1963) 190–194.

Schlesinger, A. "The Targum to the Book of Ruth—A Sectarian Composition" (Heb.). In *Writings of Akiva Schlesinger.* Publications of the Israel Society for Biblical Research 9. Jerusalem, 1962. Pp. 12–17.

The Targum of Ruth

Translation

CHAPTER 1

1. It happened in the days of the judge of judges*[a]*[1] that there was a *severe*[b] famine in the land of *Israel. Ten severe famines*[2] *were ordained by Heaven to be in the world, from the day that the world was created until the time*[c] *that the king Messiah should come, by which to reprove the inhabitants of the earth. The first famine was in the days of Adam, the second famine was in the days of Lamech, the third famine was in the days of Abraham. The fourth famine was in the days of Isaac, the fifth famine was in the days of Jacob, the sixth famine was in the days of Boaz, who is called Ibzan*[3] *the Righteous, who was from Bethlehem, Judah.*[d] *The seventh famine was in the days of David, king of Israel, the eighth famine was in the days of Elijah the prophet,*[e] *the ninth famine was in the days of Elisha in Samaria. The tenth famine is to be in the future,*[f] *not a famine of eating bread nor a drought of drinking water,*[g] *but of hearing the word of prophecy from before the Lord.*[4] *And when that famine was severe in the land of Israel,*[5] *a great* man *went out* from Bethlehem, Judah, *and* went[h] to live in the country of Moab, he and his wife and his two sons. 2. The name of the man was Elimelech, and the name of his wife was Naomi, and the names of his two sons were Mahlon and Chilion. [They were] Ephrathites,[i] lords,[6] from Bethlehem, Judah, and they came to the land of Moab and they were *governors*[7] there.

Apparatus, Chapter 1

[a] Reading *ngyd ngydy'* with most texts. W *mgd ngydy'* = MT. S *"in the days of the judges."*

[b] *"severe"* omitted by S, Br, and H.

[c] *"the time"* omitted from the printed texts but in all MSS.

[d] *"Judah"* only in R and W.

[e] *"the prophet"* omitted by M.

[f] *"in the future"* (*'tyd*) omitted by S, Br.

[g] Printed texts, H and M have *my'*; all other MSS have the distinctively Palestinian *mwy.* At 2:9 all texts have *mwy.* At 3:3 all texts have *my'.*

[h] K omits *"and went."*

[i] *"Ephrathites"* only in R and W.

Notes, Chapter 1

[1]MT: "judging of the judges." The earliest occurrence elsewhere of Tg.'s interpretation of the Hebrew consonantal text is in Samuel Uceda (b. 1540), who attributed it to Shemariah ha-Ikriti (1275–1355). The "judge of judges," or judge par excellence, is intended as a reference to Boaz, who is identified with Ibzan.

[2]A similar list of ten famines is found in *Gen. R.* 25:3; 40:3; 64:2, *Ruth R.* 1:4, and in later midrashim. Tg. Cant. 1:1 has a list of ten songs, and Tg. Esth. II 1:1 a list of ten kings.

[3]*b. B.B.* 91a: *"Ibzan is Boaz."* For the spelling Abzan, which is normal in printed texts of Tg. Ruth, as opposed to Ibzan, which is found in MSS, as in MT Judg 12:8, 10, cf. LXX and Vg. *ibid.*

[4]Amos 8:11. The quotation is not identical to the version in Tg. Amos.

[5]Peshitta adds, at end of verse 1, "because the famine was severe in the land."

[6]In the manuscripts "lords" (Aram. *rbnyn*) clearly represents MT "Ephrathites," which is added in some printed texts. On the interpretation of the Hebrew *'prtym* as indicating rank, cf. *Ruth R.* 2:5. Elimelech and his sons are described as leading citizens in Bethlehem in *b. B.B.* 91a and *Ruth R.* 1:4.

[7]*rwpylyn*, i.e., Latin *rufuli.* Nowhere else is it said that the family held high office in Moab. The idea may have originated in an attempt to give some purpose to the statement "they were there."

3. Elimelech, Naomi's husband, died and she was left *a widow* and her two sons *fatherless.* 4. *They transgressed against the decree of the Memra of the Lord and* they took[j] for themselves *foreign*[8] wives *from the daughters*[k] *of Moab.* The name of one was Orpah and the name of the second was Ruth, *the daughter of Eglon, king of Moab,*[9] and they dwelt there for about ten years. 5. *And because they transgressed against the decree of the Memra*[l] *of the Lord and intermarried with foreign peoples,*[10] *their days were cut short* and both Mahlon and Chilion also died *in the unclean land,* and the woman was left *bereaved*[m][11] of her two sons and *widowed*[11] of her husband.

6. She arose, she and her daughters-in-law, and returned from the land of Moab, for *it was announced*[12] in the land of Moab *by an angel*[13] that the Lord had remembered[14] his people, *the house*[n] *of Israel,* to give them[o] bread *on account of the merit of Ibzan the judge and his prayers which he prayed before the Lord,*[p] *that is Boaz the Pious.* 7. She set out from the place where she was,[q] her two daughters-in-law with her, going on the way to return to the land of Judah.[r]

8. Naomi said to her two daughters-in-law, "Go, return, each to her mother's house. May the Lord deal faithfully with you as you have dealt with *your husbands who are dead, in that you have refused to take husbands after their death,*[s][15] and with me, *in that you have sustained and supported me.* 9. The Lord *has given*[16] you

---

Apparatus, Chapter 1

[j] Most texts: *nṭlw;* S: *nsybw,* the normal Aramaic word for taking in marriage. M defective.

[k] S, Br, K, H, A: *"house."*

[l] *"the Memra of"* omitted by K.

[m] Br: *"mourning."*

[n] S: *"children."*

[o] *"them"* omitted by Br, U, and K.

[p] H omits *"before the Lord."*

[q] For "where she was" H has "there."

[r] The second half of v. 7 (from "going") is omitted by R and W, but is present, with slight variations, in Ant., P and all MSS.

[s] *"in that ... death"* omitted by S, K.

Notes, Chapter 1

[8] MT: "Moabite."

[9] *b. Soṭ.* 47a; *b. San.* 105b; *Ruth R.* 2:9 (where Orpah, too, is said to have been Eglon's daughter). According to *b. Nazir* 23b; *b. Hor.* 10b, Ruth was Eglon's granddaughter.

[10] *Ruth R.* 2:9 has a similar explanation for the death of Mahlon and Chilion, but *b. B.B.* 91a sees their death, like that of Elimelech, as a punishment for leaving Palestine unnecessarily.

[11] The addition of *"bereaved"* and *"widowed"* may have stemmed from a lack of understanding of the privative use of *min.* That is clearly the case in the commentary attributed to the Karaite Salmon ben Yeroham, where a similar expansion is made.

[12] MT: "she heard."

[13] *Ruth R.* 2:11: "she heard from peddlers going around in the cities."

[14] MT: "visited."

[15] The reference to "the dead" is taken literally. *Ruth R.* 2:14 explains that Ruth and Orpah had attended to the provision of shrouds for Mahlon and Chilion.

[16] MT: "May the Lord grant." The expansion which follows shows that the Hebrew *ytn* has been construed rather as "give." Peshitta also felt the need for an object and added "kindness" (*ḥsd'*).

a perfect[t] reward for the kindness which you have done to me,[u] and through that reward[v] you will find rest, each one in the house of her husband." She kissed them, and they raised their voices and wept.

10. They said to her, *"We will not go back to our people and our god,*[w][17] but *rather* we will go with you to your people[18] *to become proselytes."*

11. Naomi said, "Go back, my daughters,[x] why would you go[y] with me? Have I yet children in my womb who may be husbands to you? 12. Go back, my daughters, *from after me.*[z] Go to your people, for[aa] I am too old to be *married* to a man. If[bb] I said, *if*[cc] I were a young woman, 'I have hope'; even if I were *married*[dd] to a man tonight and even if I bore sons; 13. would you wait for them until they grew up, *as a woman who waits for a minor brother-in-law to take her as a husband?* Would you remain tied on their account, so that you would not be *married* to a man? *Please,*[19] my daughters, *do not embitter my soul,* for it[ee] is more bitter to me than you, for *the blow*[20] *from before* the Lord has gone out against me."

14. They raised their voices and wept again, *another time,* and Orpah kissed her mother-in-law, *and went on her way,*[ff][21] but Ruth clung to her.

15. She said, "Look, your sister-in-law has gone back to her people and her gods, go back after your sister-in-law *to your people and your gods."*

16. Ruth said, "Do not urge me to leave you, to go back from after you for *I desire to be a proselyte."*

Naomi said,[22] *"We are commanded to keep*[gg] *Sabbaths and holy days so as not to walk beyond two thousand cubits."*

Ruth said, "Wherever you go, I will go."

Naomi said, *"We are commanded not*[hh] *to lodge together with gentiles."*

Apparatus, Chapter 1

[t] *šlym* in printed texts and most MSS; D and U *ṭb šlym,* lit. *"good perfect,"* probably a conflate reading.

[u] So printed texts and Bo; Br, K, U, H, A, D: *"with me."* S omits.

[v] *"and through that reward"* omitted by Ant. and P.

[w] P omits *"and our god."*

[x] Br omits "my daughters."

[y] So R, W. All MSS, Ant., and P have present tense, *"why are you going."*

[z] Ant. and P omit *"from after me."*

[aa] S, K and printed texts: *'ry;* Br, U, H, A, D, Bo have the Palestinian *'rwm.*

[bb] "If" (*'rwm*) omitted by Br, U, H, A. S, K: *'ry.*

[cc] "If" (*'ylw*) omitted by D and U.

[dd] "to a man ... *married"* omitted by K.

[ee] Bo: *"my heart."*

[ff] *"and went on her way"* omitted by R and W.

[gg] Bo omits *"to keep."*

[hh] H adds *"to engage in idolatry."*

Notes, Chapter 1

[17]This expansion stems, perhaps, from the feeling that *kî,* which in MT must be construed as corroborative, implies a contrast with something said previously. Peshitta inserts "no."

[18]Peshitta "to your land and your people."

[19]MT: "no."

[20]Or, perhaps, "plague" (*mḥ'*). MT: "the hand of the Lord." According to *Ruth R.* 2:19, the expression "the hand of the Lord" invariably means pestilence (*mkt dbr*).

[21]LXX: "and she returned to her people." Peshitta: "and she turned and went away."

[22]The catechism in verse 16f is paralleled closely in *b. Yeb.* 47b and, less closely, in *Ruth R.* 2:22-24.

Ruth said, "Wherever you lodge I will lodge."

Naomi said, "We are commanded to keep six[ii] hundred and thirteen precepts."

Ruth said,[jj] "What your people[kk] keep I will keep[ll] as if they were my people *from before this.*"

Naomi said, "We are commanded not to engage in idolatry."[mm]

Ruth said, "Your god is my god."

17. *Naomi said,* "We have four death penalties[nn] *for the guilty,* stoning with stones, burning with fire, execution by the sword[oo] and crucifixion."[pp][23]

Ruth said, "By whatever means[24] you die, I will die."

Naomi said, "We have a cemetery."[qq][25]

Ruth said, "And there will I be buried. *And do not say any more.* May the Lord do[rr] thus to me and more *to me,* if even death shall separate me[ss] and you."

18. When she saw that she was determined to go[tt] with her, she ceased speaking to her.[uu] 19. So the two of them went on until they came to Bethlehem. And when they came to Bethlehem,[vv] all the *inhabitants of the* town *were* excited[ww] about them and the women said, "Is this Naomi?"

20. She said to them, "Do not call me Naomi, call me Bitter *of Soul,*[xx][26] for Shaddai has made me very bitter. 21. I went out full *of my husband and my sons*[yy] and the Lord has brought me back empty *of them.* Why do you call me Naomi, when *from before* the Lord *my sin* has *been* testified against me,[zz] and Shaddai has brought calamity upon me?"

Apparatus, Chapter 1

[ii] H: *"three."*

[jj] Bo omits *"Ruth said."*

[kk] S omits "your people."

[ll] U and D have a double reading *'nṭwr 'h' nṭr'*; all other texts: *'h' nṭr'*; A, D, Bo and printed texts add *'n'.*

[mm] Lit.: *"to worship foreign worship."* H adds *"to idols" (lṭ'wwt').*

[nn] Most texts: *dyny mwt'.* U: *myny mwt', "kinds of death"*; so, too, D, but *dyny* in margin.

[oo] K omits "by the sword."

[pp] *wṣlybt qys',* lit. *"and hanging on a tree."*

[qq] S adds (erroneously) *"three cubits."*

[rr] H: "the Lord *said."*

[ss] For *byny,* "me," Br, H, A, Bo have *byn mymry,* "my *memra,"* i.e., "myself."

[tt] Printed texts and most MSS: *lmhk*; D, U: *lmyzl.*

[uu] So printed texts, S, Bo; Br, K, U, H, A, D: "with her."

[vv] K, D omit "and when they came to Bethlehem."

[ww] Reading *w'rgyšw* with R, W, and all MSS; Ant. and P: *w'knyšw,* "gathered."

[xx] Ant. and P omit "of soul."

[yy] Bo omits "of my husband and my sons."

[zz] *'sthyd by*, H: *'yst'r by,* "has been visited upon me."

Notes, Chapter 1

[23] *m. San.* 7:1; *Ruth R.* 2:24: "strangulation."

[24] Not a departure from, but rather an interpretation of, MT: *b'šr,* "where."

[25] Aram.: *byt qbwrt'. m. San.* 6:5; *b. Yeb.* 47b; *Ruth R.* 2:24: "two graves."

[26] So too Peshitta.

22. So Naomi returned, and Ruth the Moabite, her daughter-in-law, with her, who returned from the country of Moab. They came[aaa] to Bethlehem *on the eve of Passover,*[27] *and on that day the children of Israel were beginning to harvest*[28] *the Omer of the heave-offering, which was* of barley.

CHAPTER 2

1. Now to Naomi there was known through her husband a powerful man, *strong in the Law,*[a1] of the family[b] of Elimelech, and his name was Boaz.

2. Ruth the Moabite said to Naomi, "I will go, now, to the field and glean among the ears behind him in whose eyes I find favor."

She said to her, "Go, my daughter."

3. So she went, and she arrived and gleaned in the field behind the reapers and, as chance befell, the field belonged to Boaz, who was of the family of Elimelech.

4. Boaz came from Bethlehem and said to the reapers, "May *the Memra of* the Lord be *your sustenance.*"[2]

Apparatus, Chapter 1

[aaa] So R, W; all MSS, Ant., and P have forms of the verb "enter."

Notes, Chapter 1

[27]According to *m. Men.* 10:3, the *Omer* was reaped after nightfall on the first day of the Passover festival, but to facilitate this, agents of the Beth Din would go out on the eve of the festival and tie the barley in bundles while it was still uncut. Tg. has interpreted MT's "the beginning of the barley-harvest" as referring to these preparations. *Ruth R.* 3:6 says that Naomi and Ruth arrived in Bethlehem on the day of the reaping of the *Omer,* since it is said (*ibid.* 4.2) that every occurrence of the words "barley-harvest" should be understood as referring to the reaping of the *Omer.*

[28]MT: "at the beginning of the harvest."

Apparatus, Chapter 2

[a] S, Br, K, U, H omit *"in the Law."*

[b] U has a double translation: *mzr'wy mn yyḥws,* "*of the seed of the family.*"

Notes, Chapter 2

[1]For the explanation of *gibbôr ḥayil* as meaning a Torah scholar, cf. *m. San.* 16:18; *b. San.* 93b; *Ruth R.* 4:3.

[2]MT: "The Lord be with you." Peshitta: "Peace be with you." *m. Ber.* 9:5 prescribes, on the basis of Boaz's words in MT, that the divine name should be used in greetings. According to *Ruth R.* 4:5, this rule was instituted by "Boaz and his Beth Din."

They said to him,*c* "The Lord bless you."

5. Boaz said to his servant, who was appointed *chief*[d] over the reapers, *"Of what nation*[3] is this girl?"

6. The servant, who was appointed *chief* over the reapers, replied and said, "The girl is *from the people of Moab.*[4] She is the one who came back, *and became a proselyte,*[5] with Naomi from the country of Moab. 7. She said, 'I will gather, now, and glean *ears* among the sheaves, *whatever is left on the ground*[e] behind the reapers.' She came and stood *and has remained here*[f] from early morning until just now. It is but a short time that she has sat in the house for a little."

8. Boaz said to Ruth, "Now listen to me,*g* my daughter. Do not go to glean *ears* in another field and do not pass on from here *to go*[h] *to another nation,* but stay here with my girls. 9. Look at[6] the field where they are reaping and follow them. Have I not commanded the young men not to molest you? And *at the time* when you are thirsty *for water,* go to the vessels and drink from*i* *the water*[7] which the young men draw."

10. She fell on her face and bowed to the ground and said to him,*j* "Why have I found favor in your eyes, that you should befriend me, when I am *from a* foreign *people, from the daughters of Moab,*[k] *and from a people*[l] *who are not*[m] *permitted to enter the congregation of the Lord?"*[8]

11. Boaz replied and said to her, "It has surely been told to me*n* *about the word of the sages that, when the Lord*[o] *made the decree*[p] *about you,*[q] *he did not make it with reference to females,*[r] *he made it*[s] *only with reference to men,*[19] *and it is said to*

---

me[u][10] *by prophecy that hereafter kings and prophets shall proceed from you on ac-count of all*[v] *the kindness* that you have done for your mother-in-law, *in that you supported her*[w] after your husband died and you forsook *your god and your people, your father and your mother,*[x] and the land of your birth and went to *be a proselyte and to dwell among a people*[y] *who were not known to you*[11] in former times.

12. "May the Lord repay you[z] *a good recompense in this world* for your *good* deeds and may your reward be perfect *in the next world* from *before* the Lord, God of Israel, under *the shadow of whose glorious Shekinah,*[12] you have come *to become a proselyte and* to shelter,[aa] *and by that merit you will be saved from the judgment of Gehenna, so that your portion*[bb] *may be with Sarah, and Rebekah, and Rachel, and Leah."*

13. She said, "Let me find favor in your eyes,[cc] sir, for you have comforted me *by deeming me worthy*[dd] *to be admitted to the congregation of the Lord,* and you have spoken *consolation* to the heart of your maidservant *in that you have assured me of possessing the next world in*[ee] *righteousness,* when I *have* not *merit to have a share in the next world,*[ff] *even with* one of your maidservants."[13]

14. At mealtime Boaz said to her, "Come here[gg] and eat bread[hh] and dip your food in the *broth which is cooked in* vinegar." She sat beside the reapers and he passed to her *flour of* parched corn.[ii] She ate, and was satisfied, and had some left over.[jj]

15. When she got up to glean *ears,* Boaz instructed his young men, "Even among the sheaves let her glean, and do not embarrass her.[kk] 16. You might even let some

---

Apparatus, Chapter 2

[u] M: *"to us."*

[v] *"all"* only in Ant. and P.

[w] S, M omit *"in that you supported her."*

[x] So R, P, W; Br, U, H, A, D, Bo, Ant., P: *"and the house of* your father and your mother"; M: *"and the house of* your father and *the house of* your mother"; K: *"and the house of* your father"; S omits.

[y] For *"to be a proselyte . . . people"* U and D (only) read *"to a people."*

[z] H omits *"you."*

[aa] Br, U, H, A, D, M, R, W: *l'thb'h*; Bo, Ant., P: *l'tks'h*; S, K: *l'yths'h*.

[bb] S omits *"your portion."*

[cc] So printed texts, Bo; all other MSS: *"before you."*

[dd] Reading *l'ksrwtny* with Br, K, U, H, A, D and Bo; W: *w'ksrtny,* "and have deemed me worthy." S omits.

[ee] Reading *bsdqwt'* with Br, K, U, H, R; S, D, W: *ksdqwt'*; A, Bo: *ksdqyt', "as righteousness."*

[ff] Bo omits *"in the next world."*

[gg] Bo, Ant., P omit "here."

[hh] Br, K, U, H, A, D omit "and eat bread."

[ii] *qmh qly*; K, U: *qmh wqly, "flour and parched corn."*

[jj] S, K, H, A, D: *wsyyrt*; Bo, Ant., P: *w's'rt*; R, W: *w'st'rt*; U: *wsyyrt w'st'rt* (double reading); Br: *wsyyrt w's'rt hylwp* (double verb plus noun "remainder").

[kk] K: *tskpwnh, "discourage"*; all other texts: *tkspwnh.*

Notes, Chapter 2

[10]The double announcement is precipitated by the consonantal duplication in MT: *hugēd hugad.* In *Ruth R.* 5:3 this is explained as indicating that Boaz was told twice about Ruth.

[11]MT: "whom you did not know."

[12]MT: "whose wings."

[13]MT: "and I shall not be as one of your maidservants."

fall [14] from the pitchforks [ll] [15] for her, and leave it for her to glean. Do not reproach her."

17. She gleaned [mm] *ears* in the field until evening. Then she beat out *the ears* which she had gleaned, and *they amounted to* [16] about *three seahs* [nn] [17] of barley.
18. She took it, and went into the town. Her mother-in-law saw [oo] what she had gleaned, and she took out *of her bag,* and gave to her, that *food* which she had left over when she was satisfied.

19. Her mother-in-law said to her, "Where did you glean today, [pp] and where have you been *occupied in* working? May the man who befriended you be blessed!"

She informed her mother-in-law with whom she had been *occupied in* working, and said, "The name of the *great* [qq] man with whom I was *occupied* [rr] in working [ss] today is *called* Boaz."

20. Naomi said to her daughter-in-law, [tt] "Blessed be he by *the holy mouth of* the Lord, [uu] who has not failed in his kindness to the living and the dead."

Naomi said to her, "The man is related to us, he is one of our redeemers."

21. Ruth the Moabite said, "He also said to me 'You shall remain with my young men, until *the time when* they have finished all my harvest.'"

22. Naomi said to Ruth her daughter-in-law, [vv] "It is good, my daughter, that you go out [ww] with his girls, so that no one will molest you in another field." 23. So she joined Boaz's girls in gleaning [xx] until the barley harvest and the wheat harvest were finished, and she stayed with her mother-in-law.

Apparatus, Chapter 2

[ll] Reading *'try'* with MSS, Ant., P; R, W: *'syry',* "bundles, sheaves."

[mm] Ant., P: *wlqṭṭ*; all other texts: *wṣbrt*.

[nn] "seahs" omitted by U; in D it is supplied in the margin.

[oo] Printed texts and Bo have the verb *ḥz'*; all other MSS have the Palestinian *ḥm'*.

[pp] H omits "today."

[qq] "great" only in S, U, A, D.

[rr] H omits *"in working . . . occupied."*

[ss] *"in working"* omitted by S, Br, H, A, R, W. Bo omits *"May the man . . . working."*

[tt] Bo omits "to her daughter-in-law."

[uu] In place of "the Lord," H repeats *"blessed be he"* (bryk hw').

[vv] Br, K, H, A omit "her daughter-in-law."

[ww] H: *"remain."*

[xx] Br, K, M, R, W: *lmṣbr*; U, D: *lmlqṭ* ; H: *llqṭ'*; Bo: *lm'bd,* "in working"; S, A omit.

Notes, Chapter 2

[14] MT: "pull some out." The hapaxlegomenon *šl tšlw* has been related to the root *nšl*, rather than *šll*, and translated by Aram. *ntr.*

[15] MT: "bundles." The biblical hapaxlegomenon *ṣbtym* occurs also in *m. Erub.* 10:1, and it is explained from there by Rashi.

[16] MT: "it was."

[17] MT: "an ephah." The ephah is equated with three seahs in *m. Men.* 7:1.

CHAPTER 3

1. Naomi her mother-in-law said to her, "My daughter, *I swear that I shall not rest until the time that* I shall[1] seek for you a rest,[a] that it may be well with you. 2. Now, is there not Boaz, *who is* our friend, with whose girls you were *in the field?* He is winnowing at the barley threshing-floor *in* the night *wind.*[b] 3. So wash yourself *with water,* anoint yourself *with perfumes,* put on your *jewelry,*[2] and go down to the threshing-floor. Do not make yourself known to the man until *the time that*[c] he has finished eating and drinking. 4. *At the time* when he lies down,[d] note the place where he is lying and go and uncover his feet and lie down. *You shall ask advice from him* and he will tell you *in his wisdom*[e] what you should do."

5. She said to her,[f] "I will do all that you say to me." 6. She went down to the threshing-floor and acted according to all her mother-in-law's instructions.

7. Boaz ate and drank and his heart was merry. *He blessed*[3] *the name of the Lord who had accepted his prayers and removed the famine from the land of Israel,* and he went to lie down beside the heap of grain. *Ruth*[4] came in quietly, uncovered his feet, and lay down.

8. In the middle of the night the man was startled, and he was afraid,[5] *and his flesh became soft like turnip from fear. He saw*[g][6] a woman lying at his feet, *but he restrained*[h] *his desire and did not approach her, just as Joseph the Righteous did, who refused to approach*[i] *the Egyptian woman, the wife of his master, just as Paltiel*

Apparatus, Chapter 3

[a] S, D omit "a rest."
[b] U, D: *"in the wind until morning (of)* the night."
[c] Bo, M, R, W omit *"the time that."*
[d] R, W have two synonymous verbs: *mškbyh dmkyh*; S, Br, U, H, D, M read only *dmkyh*; K, A, Bo, Ant., P read only *mškbyh*.
[e] U: *"according to his wisdom"* (*kḥkmtyh*); all other texts: *bḥkmtyh*.

[f] D omits "to her."
[g] Bo, printed texts: *wḥz', "and he saw";* Bo, Ant., P add *wh', "and behold";* all other MSS have the Palestinian verb *wḥm'* and also add *wh'.*
[h] S: *wtqp,* perhaps meaning *"(his desire) grew strong";* all other texts: *wkbš.*
[i] H: *"to lie with"* (*lmškb*); other texts: *lmqrb.*

Notes, Chapter 3

[1] MT: "shall I not."
[2] MT: "your garment (Kethibh), garments (Qere)," which, according to *Ruth R.* 5:12; *b. Shab.* 113b, refers to Sabbath garments.
[3] According to *Ruth R.* 5:15, Boaz was in good heart because he recited grace after his meal.
[4] MT: "she."
[5] Or "trembled" (Aram.: *rtt*). MT: *wayillāpēt.* This verb is otherwise found only in Judg 16:29 and Job 6:18, and the Targum proposes to explain it from *lepet* (Aram.: *lypt'*), "turnip," the connection between "turnip" and "fear" or "trembling" (*rtyt'*) being made in the following words. *b. San.* 19b explains "his flesh became like turnip-heads."
[6] So too Peshitta. MT: "and behold."

bar^j Laish the Pious did, who placed a sword between himself^k and Michal daughter of Saul, wife of David, whom he refused to approach.[17] 9. "Who are you, *my daughter?*"^l he asked.

"I am Ruth your maidservant," she said. *"Let your name be called*[8] over your maidservant *by taking me in marriage,* for you are a redeemer." ^m

10. He said, "May you be blessed *from before*[9] the Lord, my daughter. You have made your latter good deed better than your former one, *the former^n being that you became a proselyte and the latter that you have made yourself^o as a woman who waits for^p a little^q brother-in-law until the time that he is grown up,* in that you have not gone after young men *to commit fornication with them,* whether poor or rich. 11. Now, my daughter, do not fear, all that you say *to me*[10] I will do for you,^r for *it is known before*[11] all^s *who sit at* the gate *of the great Sanhedrin*[12] of my people that you are a *righteous* woman [13] *and there is in you strength to bear the yoke of the commandments of the Lord.*

12. "Now, while^t it is true that I am a redeemer, there is also *another^u* redeemer, *for whom it is more fitting^v than for me*[14] to act as a redeemer. 13. Stay the night, and in the morning, if Tob,^w[15] *for whom it is fitting^v to redeem you according to the Law,* will redeem you, good! Let him redeem *with good fortune.* But if he is not

---

Apparatus, Chapter 3

^j S, H, M: *"ben."*
^k U and D: *bsryh,* lit. *"his flesh"*; all other MSS and printed texts *mymryh,* lit. "his *memra."*
^l S, K, R, W omit *"my daughter."*
^m S, K: *'ry pryq 't*; all other texts *'rwm pryq '(n)t,* with the distinctively Palestinian form of the conjunction.
^n S, H, D, M omit *"the former."*
^o S omits *"yourself."*
^p Reading *dntr' lybm* with most MSS; Bo and printed texts read *dntr' ybm,* "who keeps a brother-in-law."

^q S, Br, U, H, D omit *"little."*
^r Bo omits *"for you."*
^s M omits "all."
^t H omits "while" *('rwm).*
^u *"another"* only in Bo and printed texts.
^v K, Bo, R, W: *dhzy lyh*; all other MSS: *dhmy lyh,* using the distinctively Palestinian verb, but K: *dhzy* (verse 12) *dhmy* (verse 13).
^w Reading *twb,* which should be understood as a proper name, with S, Br, K, U, H, D; Bo, R, W: *gbr', "the man"*; A: *tb gbr'*; M: *twb gbr'.*

Notes, Chapter 3

[7]Boaz is compared with Joseph and Paltiel in *b. San.* 19b.
[8]MT: (as vocalized) "spread your wings." The consonantal text may be read "spread your skirt."
[9]MT: "by."
[10]So too Peshitta.
[11]MT: "all the gate of my people knows."
[12]"Gate" is interpreted several times in the Targums as referring to the "court" or "Sanhedrin." Cf. Tgs. Onq., Ps.-J. Deut 17:5; 25:7; Tg. Lam 5:14; Tg. Esth I 2:21; Tg. 2 Chr 23:5.
[13]MT: *'ešet hayil,* lit. "a woman of worth."
[14]MT: "nearer than I."
[15]MT: "he," included in the verb "he will redeem you." The reading adopted here originates in taking the Hebrew *tôb* ("good") as the subject of the verb. This exegesis is also attested in *Ruth R.* 6:3.

willing[x] to redeem you,[y] then I will redeem you. *I say with an oath before the Lord,*[16] *as I have spoken to you*[z] *so will I do.*[17] Lie down until the morning."

14. She lay at his feet until *the time of*[aa] the morning, and she arose *at dawn*[18] before a man could recognize his companion *because of the darkness,* and he said *to his servant,* "Let it not be known *to any man*[bb] that[cc] the woman came to the threshing-floor."[19]

15. Then he said, "Bring the scarf which you are wearing and hold it." She held it, and he measured out six *seahs*[20] of barley and put them on it. *Strength and power*[dd] *were given*[ee] *to her from before the Lord*[ff] *to carry them, and immediately it was said to her*[gg] *prophetically that there would descend from her six of the most righteous men of all time, each of whom would be blessed with six blessings: David, Daniel and his companions, and the king Messiah.*[21] Then *Boaz*[22] went to the town.

16. She came to her mother-in-law *at dawn,*[hh] and she asked, "Who[ii] are you, my daughter?" She told her all that the man[jj] had done for her. *According to the prophecy*[kk] *which was revealed to him, he acted toward her.*[ll]

Apparatus, Chapter 3

[x] H omits "to redeem ... willing."
[y] A adds "according to the law, good! Let him redeem."
[z] S, Br, K, U, D omit "to you."
[aa] "the time of" only in Bo.
[bb] "to any man" only in Bo and printed texts. H omits "his companion ... to any man."
[cc] R, W and most MSS have the Palestinian 'rwm; M, Ant., P: 'ry; D, U: 'rwm 'l d.
[dd] Printed texts omit "and power."

[ee] Printed texts: w'yyty, "there was brought"; MSS: w'tyhyb, "there was given."
[ff] Bo omits "the Lord."
[gg] R, W omit "to her."
[hh] H omits "at dawn."
[ii] K: "where."
[jj] H omits "the man."
[kk] So U, H, D; S, Br, K, A, Bo: "according to the word of prophecy"; R, W: "according to the word from before prophecy." M defective.
[ll] For "he acted toward her," H has "the man" (gbr').

Notes, Chapter 3

[16]MT: "by the Lord's life."

[17]A different application of Boaz's oath is found in *Ruth R.* 6:4, according to which Boaz swore that he would not give in to the incitement of his *yeṣer ra'* to have intercourse with Ruth.

[18]So too Peshitta, adding "when it was still dark."

[19]Peshitta: "she said to him, 'Let no one know that I came down to you at the threshing-floor.'" According to *Ruth R.* 7:1, Boaz's words were spoken in prayer to God.

[20]Peshitta: "measures." In *Ruth R.* 7:2 and *b. San.* 93ab it is argued that six seahs would be too much for a woman to carry, and so the reference was understood to be to six grains given specifically as a symbol.

[21]The same six descendants, Daniel's companions being specified individually by name, are mentioned in *b. San.* 93b and in *Num. R.* 13:1, where they are descendants of Nahshon. In *Ruth R.* 7:2 the list is extended to include Hezekiah and Josiah, and a list of six blessings for each is also included.

[22]MT: "he," but many Hebrew MSS and Peshitta have "she."

17. She said, *"The man[mm23]* gave me these[nn] six *seahs of* barley, for he said to me, 'Do not go back empty-handed to your mother-in-law.'"

18. She said, "Stay, my daughter, *with me in the house* until *the time[oo]* that you know *how[pp] it will be decreed from heaven and* how the matter will be resolved, for[qq] the man will not rest but he will resolve the matter *for good* this day."

CHAPTER 4

1. Boaz went up to the gate[1] *of the court[a] of the Sanhedrin* and sat there *with the elders.* When the redeemer, of whom Boaz had spoken *to Ruth,* passed by, he said, "Come here and sit down, *O man whose paths are modest."*[2] He turned aside and sat down. 2. Then he[b] took ten of the elders of the town and said, "Sit here." They sat down.

3. He said to the redeemer, "Naomi, who has come back from the country of Moab, has sold the piece of land which belonged to our kinsman Elimelech.

4. I thought I would *warn you,[c] and* inform you, and say, 'Buy!'[d] in the presence of those who sit[e] *in the gate[f] of the court of the Sanhedrin* and in the presence of the elders of my people. If *it is your wish to*[3] redeem, redeem, and if *it is* not *your wish to*[4] redeem[g] tell me, so that I may know, for there is no one apart from you *who is*

Apparatus, Chapter 3

[mm] Bo omits *"the man."*
[nn] S, K omit "these."
[oo] S, Br, K, U, H, D omit *"the time."*

[pp] Reading *'ykdyn* with A, Bo, M, R, Ant., P, W; other MSS: *'byt dyn(').*
[qq] U, D omit "for" (*'rwm*), D supplies in margin.

Notes, Chapter 3

[23]MT: "he."

Apparatus, Chapter 4

[a] Bo adds *"of the place."*
[b] A, K: *"Boaz."*
[c] R, W omit *"warn you, and."*
[d] R, W: *qnh,* "acquire"; MSS, Ant., P: *zbn,* "buy."

[e] S omits "those who sit."
[f] *"gate"* only in R, W.
[g] R, W omit "to redeem."

Notes, Chapter 4

[1]Peshitta adds "of the city."
[2]MT: "so-an-so" (Heb.: *pĕlōnî 'almōnî*). The same expression is translated "hidden and concealed" (Aram.: *ksy wtmyr*) in Tg. 1 Sam 21:3; Tg. 2 Kgs 6:8, the two words having been connected, respectively, with the roots *pl',* which was taken to mean "to be hidden," and *'lm,* "to be silent," which was sometimes equated with *'lm,* "to hide." Tg. thus derives its translation from the concept of "one doubly hidden." The same understanding of the Hebrew probably underlies LXX "O hidden one." "Ploni Almoni" was sometimes treated as a proper name (*b. B.B.* 91a; *Ruth R.* 7:7).
[3]MT: "you will."
[4]MT: "if he will not."

entitled[h] to redeem *before you and who lives as close as you. I am more distant[i] than you[j] and[k] I will be redeemer* after you."

He said, "I will redeem."[l]

5. Boaz said, "On the day that you buy the field from the hand of Naomi and from *the hand of* Ruth the Moabite, wife of the deceased,[m] *you are obliged to redeem*[n5] *and required[o] to act as her brother-in-law and to marry her*[p6] in order to raise up the name of the deceased[m] upon his inheritance."

6. The redeemer said, *"In such circumstances I am*[7] not able to redeem for myself. *Because I have a wife, I have no right to marry another in addition to her*[8] *lest there be*[q] *contention in my house and* I destroy my inheritance. You, redeem *my inheritance*[r9] for yourself, *for you have no wife,*[s] for I *am*[7] not able to redeem."

7. This *custom was observed* in former times in Israel, *at times when people were transacting business, or*[10] redeeming, or exchanging *one with*[t] another, or establishing anything.[u] A man took off his *right-hand glove*[11] and *with it conveyed ownership*[v12] to the other party. *The house of Israel was accustomed thus to make purchases*[w] one from another, before witnesses.[13] 8. So the redeemer said to Boaz, *"Stretch out your hand for the symbol of ownership and*[x] take possession[y] for

---

Apparatus, Chapter 4

[h] *"who is entitled"* only in R, W.

[i] Reading *'r'*, lit. "inferior" (cf. Dan 2:39), with Neuhausen, p. 49 note 4. Many printed texts read *'d'*, "I will know."

[j] S, Br, U, H, D, Bo, M omit *"before you ... than you."*

[k] A, K omit "tell me ... and."

[l] Br omits "He ... redeem."

[m] All MSS, R, W, *myt'*, *"dead"*; Ant., P: *škyb'*, *"sleeping."* A omits *"you are ... deceased."*

[n] So R, W; MSS, Ant., P: *"you will be acquiring."*

[o] So R, W; MSS, Ant., P omit *"and required."*

[p] So R, W; MSS, Ant., P omit *"and to marry her."*

[q] So R, W, Bo; all other MSS add *"to me."*

[r] Printed texts omit *"my inheritance."*

[s] U, D omit *"for you have no wife,"* which is present in other MSS, R, W; K: *"for you have a wife."*

[t] Printed texts, M: *"from"*; all other MSS: *"with."*

[u] So R, W: *wmqyymyn kl md'm*; all other texts omit *"or establishing anything."* S adds *"before witnesses."*

[v] Bo omits *"ownership."*

[w] M omits *"to make purchases."*

[x] H omits *"Stretch ... and."*

[y] H: *zbn*, "buy," other texts: *qny*.

Notes, Chapter 4

[5]MT: "I have acquired" (Kethibh) or "you have acquired" (Qere). LXX: "you must acquire her."

[6]The Targum is here at odds with Rabbinic exegesis, which did not consider Ruth's second marriage to be a case of levirate marriage. The Karaites, however, who interpreted the levirate law of Deut 25:5f. as applying not to an actual brother but to a more distant relative, found in Ruth an example of the practice exactly as they understood it. (See the commentary attributed to Salmon ben Yeroham, 4:10.)

[7]MT: "shall be."

[8]There was no Rabbinic legislation against polygamy before ca. 1000 C.E. (and thereafter only among Ashkenazim), but *b. Pes.* 113a recommends, "Do not marry two women; if you do marry two, marry a third."

[9]MT: "my (right of) redemption."

[10]MT: "concerning."

[11]MT: "shoe." "Glove" appears elsewhere only in the commentary attributed to David Kimchi.

[12]MT: "gave it."

[13]MT: "this was attestation in Israel."

yourself."[z] *Boaz*[aa][14] drew off his *right-hand*[bb] glove[15] and took possession for himself.[cc]

9. Then Boaz said to the elders and *to*[16] all the people, "*Be*[17] witnesses *for me* this day, that I have acquired all that belonged to Elimelech and all that belonged to Chilion and Mahlon[dd] from the hand of Naomi. 10. And also Ruth the Moabite, the wife of Mahlon, I have acquired for myself in marriage *in order* to raise up the name[ee] of the deceased upon his inheritance, and so that the name[ff] of the deceased[gg] may not disappear from among his kinsmen and from the gate of *the Sanhedrin which is in* his place. You are witnesses *for me*[hh] this day."

11. All the people who were in the gate *of the Sanhedrin*[ii] and the elders said, "*We are*[18] witnesses. May the Lord make this woman who is coming into your house[jj] *sound in luck*[kk] like Rachel and Leah, the two of whom built the house of Israel *our father with twelve tribes.* May you prosper in Ephrath and be renowned in Bethlehem. 12. May your house be *prosperous* as the house of Perez,[ll] whom Tamar bore to Judah, from the offspring which the Lord will give you by this young woman."

13. Boaz took Ruth and she became his wife. He went in to her, and the Lord gave her conception, and she bore a son.

14. The women said to Naomi, "Blessed be *the name of* the Lord, who has not withheld from you a redeemer this day. May his name be called *among the righteous of*[19] Israel. 15. May he be to you a restorer of life, and a sustainer of your old age *with delights,* for your daughter-in-law who loves you has borne him, who was better to you[mm] *in the time of your widowhood* than *many*[20] sons."

16. Naomi took the child, and laid him in her bosom, and she became his nurse.

Apparatus, Chapter 4

[z] Br omits "and take possession for yourself."
[aa] H, Bo: "he."
[bb] H, Ant., P omit *"his right-hand."*
[cc] So R, Ant., P, W; all MSS: *"from him."* H omits *"and took possession for himself."*
[dd] S omits "and Mahlon."
[ee] S, Br, K, U, H, D omit "the name."
[ff] K omits "the name."

[gg] A omits "upon ... deceased."
[hh] S, Br, K, U, H, D omit *"for me."*
[ii] H omits *"of the Sanhedrin."*
[jj] So printed texts, Bo; other MSS omit "who ... house."
[kk] So all MSS; printed texts omit *"sound in luck."*
[ll] M omits "of Perez."
[mm] U, D omit "to you."

Notes, Chapter 4

[14]MT: "he," probably referring to the redeemer, but the Rabbis were divided as to the identity of the subject (*Ruth R.* 7:12; *b. B.M.* 47a).
[15]MT: "shoe."
[16]So too Peshitta.
[17]MT: "you are."
[18]So too Peshitta.
[19]MT: "in."
[20]MT: "seven."

17. The neighbors gave him a name saying, "A son has been born to Naomi." They called him Obed. He was the father of Jesse, the father of David.

18. These are the descendants of Perez. Perez fathered Hezron. 19. Hezron fathered Ram, and Ram fathered Aminadab. 20. Aminadab fathered Nahshon, *and Nahshon was*[nn] *the head of a family of the house of Judah.* Nahshon fathered Salma *the Righteous, that is Salma*[oo] *from Bethlehem and Netophah, whose sons*[pp] *did away with the guardposts*[21] *which Jeroboam the Wicked placed on the roads, and the deeds of the father and sons were beautiful*[qq] *as balm.*[22]

21. Salmon fathered *Ibzan*[rr] *the judge, that is* Boaz *the Righteous,*[ss] *through whose merit the people,*[tt] *the house of Israel,*[uu] *were freed from the hand of*[vv] *their enemies, and on account of whose prayers*[ww] *the famine passed away from the land of Israel.* Boaz fathered Obed, *who served the Lord of the World wholeheartedly.*

22. Obed fathered Jesse, *who was called Nahash*[23] *because no sin or fault was found in him that he should be delivered into the hand of the Angel of Death to take his life from him. He lived many days until there was remembered before the Lord the advice which the serpent gave to Eve, the wife of Adam, to eat of the fruit of the tree,*[xx] *the fruit of which those who eat are wise to know*[yy] *good and evil. Through that advice all who dwell on earth were condemned to death,*[zz] *and for that sin* Jesse[aaa] *the Righteous died, that is* Jesse who fathered[bbb] David, *the king*[24] *of Israel.*

Apparatus, Chapter 4

[nn] *"and Nahshon was"* only in printed texts.
[oo] A omits *"the Righteous ... Salma,"* restored in margin.
[pp] S, Br, K, U, H, D omit *"his sons."*
[qq] H omits *"beautiful."*
[rr] So, H, Bo, R, W; S, Br, K, A, M: *"Boaz Ibzan"*; U, D: *"Boaz and Boaz (is) Ibzan."*
[ss] H omits *"that ... Righteous."*
[tt] H omits *"the people."*

[uu] So A, Bo, M, R, W; for *"people ... Israel"* S, Br, K, U, D have *"the children of Israel."*
[vv] So R, W; MSS omit *"the hand of."*
[ww] S: *"merit."*
[xx] All MSS: *"the fruit of the tree"*; R, W omit *"the fruit of."*
[yy] *"to know" (lyd')* only in printed texts.
[zz] H, Bo omit *"death."*
[aaa] S omits *"Jesse."*
[bbb] So most texts; W "and Jesse fathered."

Notes, Chapter 4

[21] *przd'wwn*, from Latin *praesidia*.
[22] Aram.: *nṭwp'*. A similar account of the deeds of Salma's sons is found in Tg. 1 Chr 2:54, on which see J. S. McIvor, p. 71.
[23] The identification is rooted in 2 Sam 17:25 read in conjunction with 1 Chr 2:16. The aggada then explains why Jesse should have been known as "snake" (Heb.: *nāḥāš*). In *b. Shab.* 55b; *b. B.B.* 17a, Jesse is said to be one of four men who died only on account of the snake.
[24] So too Peshitta.

INDEXES

BIBLICAL TEXTS
Hebrew Bible

Deuteronomy			2 Samuel			Job	
23:4	23		17:25	32		6:18	26
25:5f.	30						

Judges			Amos			1 Chronicles	
12:8, 10	18		8:11	18		2:16	32
16:29	26						

Septuagint

Judges			Ruth	
12:8,10	18		1:14	20
			4:1	29
			4:5	30

Peshitta

Ruth							
1:1	18		2:4	22		4:1	29
1:9	19		2:9	23		4:9	31
1:10	20 (bis)		3:8	26		4:11	31
1:14	20		3:11	27		4:22	32
1:20	21		3:14	28 (bis)			
			3:15	28 (bis)			

Vulgate

Judges	
12:8, 10	18

TARGUMS
Targum Onqelos

Deuteronomy	
17:5	27
25:7	27

Targum Pseudo-Jonathan

Deuteronomy	
17:5	27
25:7	27

Palestinian Talmud

Midrashim

MEDIEVAL COMMENTATORS

MODERN AUTHORS

The Targum of Chronicles

Translated, with Introduction, Apparatus, and Notes

BY

J. Stanley McIvor

About the Translator:

Stanley McIvor taught Scripture in Magee Theological College, Londonderry, and now teaches Old Testament in Union Theological College, Belfast.

In memory of my parents
JAMES AND FLORENCE McIVOR
and my eldest sister
FLORENCE MARGARET

My sincere thanks

To Reverend Martin McNamara, M.S.C., and his
Editorial Board for their invitation to play a part in this
enterprise and for their patience in waiting for results;

To Alan Thompson, my brother-in-law, who introduced
me to the thrills and spills of word processing;

To Pat, my wife, and Louise, our younger daughter, who
helped to transfer the handwritten words onto disks and
to constantly reshape them.

J. S. McIvor

TABLE OF CONTENTS

ABBREVIATIONS

Alexander	P. S. Alexander, *The Toponomy of the Targumim with Special Reference to the Table of the Nations and the Boundaries of the Land of Israel.* Ph.D. dissertation. Oxford, 1974.
AS	A. Sperber, *The Bible in Aramaic.* Vol. IVA. Leiden, 1968, pp. 3–119 (= Sperber's edition of Tg. Chr).
BDB	F. Brown, S. R. Driver, and C. A. Briggs, *A Hebrew and English Lexicon of the Old Testament.* Oxford, 1906.
BHS	*Biblia Hebraica Stuttgartensia.* Ed. K. Elliger and W. Rudolph. Stuttgart: Württembergische Bibelanstalt, 1967–77.
Braun	R. L. Braun, *1 Chronicles.* Word Biblical Commentary. Waco, Tex., 1986.
C	Cambridge manuscript of Tg. Chr. (See Introduction, p. 15).
Churgin	P. Churgin, *The Targum to the Hagiographa.* New York, 1945. (In Hebrew).
Dillard	R. B. Dillard, *2 Chronicles.* Word Biblical Commentary. Waco, Tex., 1987.
E	Erfurt manuscript of Tg. Chr. See Introduction, p. 15.
EJ	*Encyclopaedia Judaica.* Ed. C. Roth. Jerusalem, 1971.
Ginzberg	L. Ginzberg, *The Legends of the Jews.* Vols. I–VII. Philadelphia, 1909–38.
GK	A. E. Cowley, *Gesenius' Hebrew Grammar.* Oxford, 1910.
ICC	E. L. Curtis and A. A. Madsen, *The Books of Chronicles.* International Critical Commentary. Edinburgh, 1910.

JL	J. Levy, *Chaldäisches Wörterbuch über die Targumim.* Vol. I, 1866; Vol. II, 1867; rpt. Darmstadt, 1966.
L	Paul de Lagarde, *Hagiographa Chaldaice.* Leipzig, 1873, pp. 270–362 (= de Lagarde's edition of Tg. Chr).
Le Déaut	R. Le Déaut and J. Robert, *Targum des Chroniques.* 2 vols. Rome, 1971.
MJ	M. Jastrow, *A Dictionary of the Targumim, the Talmud Babli and Yerushalmi, and the Midrashic Literature.* New York, 1903; rpt. in one volume, 1967.
MT	Massoretic Text as found in *BHS* (see above).
Myers	J. M. Myers, *I Chronicles, II Chronicles.* Anchor Bible. New York, 1965.
Rudolph	W. Rudolph, *Chronikbücher.* Tübingen, 1955.
Rosenberg-Kohler	M. Rosenberg and K. Kohler, "Das Targum zur Chronik," *Jüdische Zeitschrift für Wissenschaft und Leben* 8 (1870) 72–80; 135–163; 263–278.
Schürer	E. Schürer, *The History of the Jewish People in the Age of Jesus Christ.* Rev. and ed. by G. Vermes, F. Millar, and M. Black. 3 vols. Edinburgh, 1973–87.
Smolar and Aberbach	L. Smolar and M. Aberbach, *Studies in Targum Jonathan to the Prophets.* New York and Baltimore, 1983.
V	Vatican manuscript of Tg. Chr. See Introduction, p. 14.
Williamson	H. G. M. Williamson, *1 and 2 Chronicles.* New Century Bible. London, 1982.

RABBINIC SOURCES

Talmudic

m.	Mishnah. H. Danby, *The Mishnah.* Oxford, 1933.
b.	Babylonian Talmud. L. Goldschmidt, Vols. 1–12. Rpt. Berlin, 1965. London: Soncino, 1935.
y.	Jerusalem Talmud. Krotoschin, 1866.
Ab. Zar.	Abodah Zarah
B.B.	Baba Bathra
B.Ḳ.	Baba Ḳama
B.M.	Baba Meṣia
Ber.	Berakhot

Bikk.	Bikkurim
Erub.	Erubin
Giṭ.	Giṭṭin
Ḥag.	Ḥagigah
Hor.	Horayoth
Ḥul.	Ḥullin
Ker.	Kerithoth
Keth.	Ketuboth
Ḳid.	Ḳiddushin
Meg.	Megillah
Men.	Menahoth
M.Ḳ.	Moed Ḳatan
Pes.	Pesaḥim
San.	Sanhedrin
Shab.	Shabbath
Soṭ.	Soṭah
Suk.	Sukkah
Ta'an.	Taanith
Tem.	Temurah
Yeb.	Yebamoth
Yom.	Yoma
Zeb.	Zebaḥim

Tannaitic Midrashim

Mekilta	J. Z. Lauterbach, *Mekilta de-Rabbi Ishmael,* Vols. I–III. Philadelphia, 1933.
Sifre Num.	H. S. Horovitz, *Siphre ad Numeros Adjecto Siphre Zutta.* Leipzig, 1917; rpt. Jerusalem, 1966. English: P. R. Levertoff. New York, 1926.

Midrash Rabbah	English edition by H. Freedman and M. Simon. London, 1951.
Gen. R.	Genesis Rabbah
Exod. R.	Exodus Rabbah

Lev. R.	Leviticus Rabbah
Num. R.	Numbers Rabbah
Ruth R.	Ruth Rabbah
Est. R.	Esther Rabbah

Other Sources

Midr. Teh.	W. G. Braude, *The Midrash on Psalms.* Vols. I–II. New Haven, Conn., 1959.
PRE	G. Friedlander, *Pirke de Rabbi Eliezer.* London, 1916; rpt. New York, 1970.

Targums

A. Sperber	*The Bible in Aramaic.* Vols. I–IV. Leiden, 1959–73.
Frg. Tg.	M. L. Klein, *The Fragment-Targums of the Pentateuch According to Their Extant Sources.* 2 vols. Rome, 1980.
Tg. Neof.	A. Díez Macho, *Neophyti Targum Palestinense MS de la Biblioteca Vaticana.* Madrid-Barcelona, Vols. I–V, 1968–78; Vol. VI, Appendices, 1979.
Tg. Ps.-J.	D. Rieder, *Pseudo-Jonathan, Targum Jonathan ben Uzziel on the Pentateuch.* Jerusalem, 1974.
Tg. Chr	Targum of Chronicles. For manuscripts and editions, see Introduction, p. 14–15.

Some material from an unpublished dissertation supervised by Dr. A. P. Hayman, *A Study of the Targum and Peshitta Texts of Selected Chapters of the Book of Chronicles* (University of Edinburgh, 1977) has been used in this work.

INTRODUCTION

I. THE STATUS OF CHRONICLES IN JUDAISM

In the Babylonian Talmud, in the tractate *Baba Bathra*,[1] Chronicles is placed last in the Writings, after Ezra–Nehemiah, even though it contains details of the period *before* Ezra–Nehemiah. Later on in the same tractate we are given some information on authorship: "Ezra wrote the book that bears his name and the genealogies of the book of Chronicles up to his own time."[2] Thus Ezra wrote some of it, and a few lines further on there is a comment noting that it was Nehemiah who finished it.

These statements have led to considerable debate, not just on authorship but also on the status of the book, raising questions such as: Why was Chronicles accepted into the canon, and why does it appear at the end? One suggestion is that if Chronicles was originally one with Ezra–Nehemiah, the Ezra–Nehemiah section had no difficulty in achieving recognition because this was the basic document that told how God had worked for his people at a particular time, but since the period that Chronicles dealt with had already been adequately covered in Samuel–Kings, Chronicles may have been seen as redundant. 1 Chr 1–9, however, because of its genealogical data, was then seen as necessary, and along with the part entered also the whole, aided perhaps by the Davidic emphasis.

This approach, which tends to regard Chronicles as a not altogether vital component in the canon and which may also indicate that the acceptance of Chronicles came rather late, would represent the view of e.g., Rosenberg-Kohler,[3] and while it seems a reasonable approach, should be balanced by the comment of H. E. Ryle, who, having outlined a similar approach, adds: "We have nothing further to go upon than probability in assuming that . . . Song of Songs, Ecclesiastes, Esther, and Chronicles, were accepted into the Canon at a later date than the other writings of the Hagiographa."[4]

When we try to learn more of the status of Chronicles from an examination of its use in public worship, we find we have very little evidence to work on. While the Scrolls (the Megilloth) gradually found a guaranteed place in the liturgy because of their link with certain festivals, no such good fortune came the way of Chronicles. We are aware

---

[1] *b. B.B.* 14b.
[2] *b. B.B.* 15a.
[3] Rosenberg-Kohler, 135–140.
[4] H. E. Ryle, *The Canon of the Old Testament* (London, 1892), 141f.

from a tractate in the Mishnah, *m. Yoma* 1.6, that Chronicles—along with Ezra, Job, and Daniel—had the doubtful privilege of having selections from it read to a high priest who was not versed in reading the Scriptures, apparently to try to keep him awake, before he took part in the ceremonies of the Day of Atonement. *b. Shab.* 116b suggests that in at least one center of Judaism, Chronicles may have had a part in public services: in Nehardea there was a reading from the Hagiographa as a kind of *hapthtarah* at *minhah* on the Sabbath. But this possibility is made more remote by J. Mann's comment that the whole passage in *b. Shab.* "refers to study at the Bet Hammidrash and not to the service in the synagogue as had been rightly pointed out by R. Isaiah di Trani. . . ."[5] S. Z. Leiman states: "There is no evidence that the books of Proverbs, Job, Daniel, Ezra, Nehemiah and Chronicles were recited publicly in the cult or read during the synagogue service."[6]

This rather gloomy picture, however, is brightened by the fact that in some quarters there was a little more enthusiasm for Chronicles. In the commentaries on the Pentateuch and other books, found in the Great Midrash, *Midrash Rabba,* we note a statement in the commentary on Leviticus, *Lev. R.* 1:3 (cf. *Ruth R.* 2.1), a statement attributed ultimately to Rab: "The Book of Chronicles was given only to be expounded midrashically." Whether such a saying had a certain derogatory tone, implying that there was little else one could do with the book, or whether it was meant to give Chronicles a high rating by allotting to it this kind of interpretation, or whether Chronicles' names and lists had already become the source of much popular exegesis and this statement was an attempt to acknowledge the fact and to provide official approval is difficult to say. But the very existence of such a statement, attached to a weighty name, allows us to conclude that at some time Chronicles was used in this way, and it seems that there was a collection of such midrashic interpretations based on Chronicles, e.g., *b. Pes.* 62b: "Since the day that the Book of Genealogies was hidden, the strength of the Sages has been impaired, and the light of their eyes has been dimmed. Mar Zutra said, Between '*Azel*' and '*Azel*' [i.e., between 1 Chr 8:38 and 9:34] they were laden with four hundred camels of exegetical interpretations!" We find a hint as to the nature of this exegetical approach in *b. Meg.* 13a, where an exegesis of 1 Chr 4:18, an exegesis in which names of various people and the meaning contained within these names are all taken and applied to Moses, is prefaced with the comment: "All thy words are one, and we know how to find their inner meaning," which suggests that names of different people can be regarded as referring to the same person when exegetical comments are required.

When we look at the *pesiḳtas,* homilies delivered in the synagogue, we note that both in the *Pesiḳta de Rab Kahana* (compiled in the fifth century) and in *Pesiḳta Rabbati* (compiled in the sixth to the seventh centuries), passages from Chronicles feature in the exposition, though a glance at the indices reveals that the number of passages dealt with

---

[5]J. Mann, "Changes in the Divine Service of the Synagogue due to Religious Persecutions," *Hebrew Union College Annual* IV (1927), 283 n. 88.

[6]S. Z. Leiman, *The Canonization of Hebrew Scripture: The Talmudic and the Midrashic Evidence* (Hamden, Conn., 1976), 139 n. 21.

and referred to is not nearly so great as for Samuel and Kings. Thus, while Chronicles found no place in the passages read in the synagogue, gradually some of its material had infiltrated the synagogue by a different route.

This estimate of Chronicles—at first not very popular, but later being allowed to play a specific interpretative role—is in complete contrast to the view put forward by A. Spiro.[7] In an attempt to show that Pseudo-Philo based his work on the model of Chronicles as he tried to do for the earlier period what Chronicles had done for the later one, Spiro stresses that up to the second century C.E., Chronicles held a much more exalted place than Samuel–Kings in Jewish thinking. (Spiro dates the Baraita in *b. B.B.* 14b as second century C.E.) According to him, Samuel–Kings was much larger and more difficult to handle; it contained some questionable material, and for these and other reasons Chronicles came to be "regarded as the authorised version of the history of Israel."[8] A shift in exegetical emphasis allowing offensive parts of Samuel–Kings to be so interpreted as to reveal hidden and higher meanings helped to rehabilitate Samuel–Kings, and this, coupled with the fact that it could claim prophetic authorship, had a detrimental effect on the status of Chronicles, which was then given "the last place in the Hagiographa as a useless and repetitious book."[9] One assumes that the same shift of emphasis opened up new interpretative horizons for Chronicles also (perhaps this is what *Lev. R.* 1:3 is referring to), but apparently the lack of prophetic authorship weighed heavily against it. At any rate, for Spiro the change of fortune for Chronicles is reflected in the "Baraitha, in *TB* Baba Bathra 14b, which degraded Chronicles to the last rung of the third-rate collection of Hagiographa. . . ."[10]

It is difficult to say if the position in which a book appears in a list is necessarily an indication of the status of that book. In *b. B.B.* 14b, Chronicles comes at the end of the Hagiographa, and, as has been noted, this position does raise certain queries, because that which precedes it in position follows it in time. But even if there was an initial uncertainty, there is no reason why the book should carry this label for all time. C. D. Ginsburg notes that in the St. Petersburg Codex, dated 1009 C.E., Chronicles occupies first place in the Hagiographa; the twelfth-century work *Adath Deborim* describes this order as the Palestinian practice, "and the order which places Chronicles or Esther at the end of this division as the Eastern and Babylonian practice. . . ."[11] This may indeed have represented a difference in evaluation between East and West, or the position of Chronicles just before the Psalms in the St. Petersburg Codex may have been because Chronicles, in which David plays such a leading role, was regarded as a good introduction to the book attributed to him. In fact, the short discussion on the Writings in *b. B.B.* 14b does not give any grounds for suggesting that the order of the books was determined by their importance. More recent discussion in this area would bear out this approach; for example, H.G.M. Williamson remarks: "The precise reason for the position

[7]A. Spiro, "Samaritans, Tobiads and Judahites in Pseudo-Philo," *Proceedings of the American Academy for Jewish Research* 20 (1951), 303–308.

[8]Ibid., 304.

[9]Ibid., 308.

[10]Ibid., 307.

[11]C. D. Ginsburg, *Introduction to the Masoretic-Critical Edition of the Hebrew Bible* (London, 1897), 2.

of Chronicles at the end of the Hebrew Canon thus remains unexplained. . . ."[12] Roger Beckwith, however, maintains that "Chronicles is placed last as a recapitulation of the whole biblical story."[13]

Thus the status of Chronicles in Judaism is uncertain: we have no evidence for its regular use in synagogue services, and whether Spiro is right that Chronicles had once had a golden age before its eclipse by Samuel–Kings (about the second century C.E.), or whether Chronicles had always lived under its shadow, it does seem clear that at some point a special kind of interpretation was associated with Chronicles, though *b. Pes.* 62b hints that this kind of interpretation also fell out of favor.

If, then, it is unlikely that Chronicles was read in the synagogue, its chances of having a Targum are somewhat reduced, as the production of Targums was closely linked with the synagogue services, though the fact that Job had a Targum must make us cautious in tying Targum production too closely to these services. Since there exists a Targum of Chronicles, and since Chronicles does not figure in the synagogue services, we must try to explain its origin.[14]

II. MANUSCRIPTS AND EDITIONS OF TARGUM CHRONICLES

Medieval scholars seemed to be unaware of the existence of a Targum of Chronicles. Rashi (1045–1105) did not know of any Targum of the Writings.[15] David Kimchi (1160–1235) wrote commentaries on several biblical books, including the Former and Latter Prophets, as well as on Chronicles, which was his first commentary. When he is commenting on the Former and Latter Prophets, Kimchi refers constantly to the Targums of these books; yet when dealing with Chronicles, he never once mentions a Targum of Chronicles, nor does he give any hint that he is aware of the existence of any such Targum. Indeed, when discussing passages in Chronicles that have parallels in Samuel-Kings, he quotes the Targum of Samuel-Kings but does not refer to the fact that an identical interpretation of some of these passages is given also in Targum of Chronicles.[16] Elias Levita (1469–1549) has no doubts about the matter; he is on record as saying that there is no Targum of Chronicles.[17] In Brian Walton's London Polyglot of 1654–57, no Targum is printed alongside the Hebrew text of Chronicles.

We are now aware of a Targum of Chronicles, with three manuscripts in existence:

—a Vatican manuscript (V), *Cod. Vat. Urb. Ebr. 1,* dated 1294, published by R. Le Déaut and J. Robert in two volumes, with introduction, text, notes, and a French translation, *Targum des Chroniques,* Analecta Biblica 51 (Rome: Biblical Institute Press, 1971);

---

[12]H. G. M. Williamson, *1 and 2 Chronicles,* New Century Bible (London, 1982), 5.
[13]R. Beckwith, *The Old Testament Canon of the New Testament Church* (London, 1985), 159.
[14]See below, pp. 16–17.
[15]L. Zunz, *Die gottesdienstlichen Vorträge der Juden,* 2nd ed. (Frankfurt a. Main, 1892), 68 note d.
[16]AS, 70–71.
[17]Le Déaut, 1:10.

—an Erfurt manuscript (E), *Ms. or. fol.* 1210 and 1211, dated 1343, now in the Deutsche Staatsbibliothek in East Berlin. This massive manuscript, whose condition does not permit its being microfilmed, was published in two volumes, with introduction, text, notes, and a Latin translation, by M. F. Beck, *Paraphrasis Chaldaica I Libri Chronicorum* (Augsburg, 1680) and *Paraphrasis Chaldaica II Libri Chronicorum* (Augsburg, 1683);

—a Cambridge manuscript (C), *MS. Or. Ee.* 5.9, dated 1347, now in the University of Cambridge, published by David Wilkins, who completed the work begun by Samuel Clericus, *Paraphrasis Chaldaica in Librum Priorem et Posteriorem Chronicorum Auctore Rabbi Josepho Rectore Academicae in Syria . . .* (Amsterdam, 1715).

There was a fourth manuscript in Dresden, but it was destroyed in 1945.

Paul de Lagarde gives us an edition of the Targum of Chronicles based on E, assisted by C and a third codex, in his *Hagiographa Chaldaice* (Leipzig, 1873; rpt. Osnabruck, 1967), 270–362. Alexander Sperber also published an edition of the Targum in *The Bible in Aramaic,* IVA, (Leiden, 1968), 3–119. The editions of Lagarde and Sperber are almost identical.[18] In his edition Sperber gives, along with the text, some comments on "*Alter* and *Heimat* of the Targum" and, in adjoining columns, passages in Tg. Chr with their parallels in Tg. Samuel–Kings.

Le Déaut believes that the three manuscripts E, C, and V go back to a common source, though not necessarily to the same manuscript.[19] Agreements on minor matters, such as specific word formations in certain places but different forms of the same words in other places, and even the same errors, are too numerous to admit of any other conclusion. He adds, however, that closer inspection indicates a more complex relationship: C and V have more features in common with each other than either has with E. For example, for the verb "to send," C and V use *šdr,* while E prefers *šlḥ.* C and V insert alternative readings in the text, which E does not, and these readings are very similar (1 Chr 11:16; 18:31; 21:27). C and V share the same specific word formations (1 Chr 10:7; 28:9; 28:12; 2 Chr 2:11), the same vocabulary (2 Chr 4:16; 14:5), the same dittography (2 Chr 18:33), the same unusual readings (2 Chr 33:8; 36:10). But there are also notable differences between C and V: some paraphrases in V are not found in C (1 Chr 3:12; 9:40; 2 Chr 7:6; 10:7); sometimes the paraphrases are worded differently in the two manuscripts (1 Chr 2:17-18; 4:24).

III. TARGUM CHRONICLES AND OTHER TARGUMS

Tg. Jonathan of the Former Prophets. That Tg. Chr was familiar with this Targum is borne out by the number of agreements between the two Targums, suggests Le Déaut, following P. Churgin,[20] e.g., 1 Chr 10:3, 8 and 1 Sam 31:3, 8. (For a fuller list, see note 57 in Le Déaut, Vol. 1, p. 23.) He does note, however, that there are also paraphrases in

---

[18]Ibid., 1:13 n. 22.

[19]Ibid., 21f.

[20]Ibid., 23f., with references to P. Churgin, *The Targum to the Hagiographa* (New York, 1945), 263–266 (in Hebrew).

Tg. Chr not found in Tg. Jonathan and that sometimes there are variations in translation between the two. Churgin concluded that there was at one time a Targum of the
Prophets in a Palestinian recension, which the redactor of Tg. Chr had before him but
which has now disappeared, with only fragments surviving, as suggested, for example,
in certain additions found in Codex Reuchlinianus, often introduced by the words
"Jerusalem Targum."

Tg. Pseudo-Jonathan of the Pentateuch. Especially in those passages in Chronicles that
are paralleled in the Pentateuch, we are very much aware of the presence of Tg. Ps.-J. in
the background. We find this especially in 1 Chr 1 and 2. See, for example, the close
links between Tg. Ps.-J. Exod 35:26 and Tg. 1 Chr 2:18.

IV. THE PLACE OF ORIGIN OF TARGUM CHRONICLES

From what has been said above, it is clear that there is a strong Palestinian emphasis
in Tg. Chr. Le Déaut quotes the comment of P. Churgin that Tg. Chr was composed in
Palestine, the homeland of all the Targums, and that the Aramaic language of this
Targum is the language of the Targums of Jerusalem.[21] This view had already been put
forward by L. Zunz, who stated that ". . . the Targum of Chronicles shows itself in language, style and haggadic paraphrase, to be a Jerusalem Targum."[22] He adds that this
was why, like the Palestinian Targum of the Prophets, it remained almost completely
unknown. In this connection, Churgin draws attention to the significance of the presence of loan words in Tg. Chr that do not appear in Jewish literature emanating from
outside Palestine.[23] Sperber regards the loan-word argument as decisive. He sees the
context of Tg. Chr as an area where people still spoke Aramaic in their everyday collo-
quial speech and thus required a Targum to understand the Bible. "But they also lived
under the spell of the contemporary surrounding civilisation, which in this case must
have been Graeco-Latin." These same people, however, were often obliged in public
converse to use "foreign words" that inevitably made their way gradually into daily
speech.[24] Obviously the land most likely in question here is Palestine.

Rosenberg-Kohler also accept the position that in Tg. Chr we are dealing with a Palestinian Aramaic dialect.[25] Le Déaut finds this argument strengthened by the interest
shown in Tg. Chr in Palestinian toponomy, in the scholarly institutions and the
haggadah we are familiar with in the Palestinian Targums.[26]

While there is general agreement on the country of origin, there is less certainty on
the actual *Sitz im Leben* of Tg. Chr. As the synagogue is an unlikely institution from
which it would spring (see the discussion above on the status of Chronicles in Judaism,

---

[21]Le Déaut, 1:16.
[22]*Die gottesdienstlichen Vorträge*, 84.
[23]Le Déaut, 1:16.
[24]AS, 71.
[25]Pp. 263f., 276.
[26]Le Déaut, 1:18, where he also gives a list of typical Palestinian linguistic and grammatical forms found in Tg.
Chr.

pp. 11–14), the most likely alternative institution would be the Beth Hammidrash, unless we introduce a further possibility, the area of private study, which, by its very nature has an esoteric quality and is very difficult to document. One cannot fail to notice in Tg. Chr the great emphasis on the study of Torah and the praise heaped on those who were disciples of the Law or who were leaders of the Academies or who were transformed from "mighty men of valor" in the Massoretic Text to "experts in Torah" in Tg. Chr. It does not seem at all unlikely, then, that the Tg. Chr should arise out of such a background. It is to the "house of study" that Rosenberg-Kohler allot all the activity that resulted in Targum production. "Wir müssen uns nach einer umfassenden Lehrthätigkeit umsehen, die sich über die Erklärung der ganzen Bibel erstreckte."[27] The center of this *Lehrthätigkeit* they find in the Beth Hammidrash, the school.

There are those, however, who wish to be more precise and—to match the Pentateuch and the Prophets—to find a specific author for the Targums of the Writings. Both Beck and Wilkins find this author in Rab Joseph. Wilkins locates him on his title page in the Academy in Syria, which Rosenberg-Kohler regard as an error for the Academy in Sura.[28] Rab Joseph "the Blind," who died in 325, is credited in *b. B.K.* with a reputation as an expositor, but it does seem unlikely that a Babylonian Amora would be the author of a Targum with such a strong Palestinian emphasis. Rab Joseph's authorship of the Targums of the Writings was challenged already in the Middle Ages and was rejected by Elias Levita.[29] On the evidence available, Le Déaut's conclusion seems to be the most reasonable. He suggests that we are dealing in Tg. Chr with something which was composed gradually and which is the work of generations of interpreters in the schools and Jewish Academies, transmitted orally for a long time, enriched with glosses and haggadic creations, and finally committed to writing.

V. THE DATE OF TARGUM CHRONICLES

In light of the last sentence in the preceding section, it would seem unwise, indeed hazardous, to try to assign a date to this work. This is an area where certainty is rarely attained. One general comment, however, may be made at the outset: in reading through Tg. Chr, one often has a sense of "lateness," a feeling that we are dealing with the last term in the series. For example:

1) With regard to Tg. 1 Chr 2:18, in the traditions behind the expansion in this verse in *b. Shab.* 74b and 99a and in Tg. Ps.-J. Exod 35:26, there is a certain ambiguity as to how the preposition *'l* is to be interpreted, an ambiguity reflected in the variant reading *mn*. Tg. Chr, by adding *kdl' gzyn*, "without being shorn," makes it absolutely clear that *'l* is the reading and that it means exactly what it says.

2) Occasionally Tg. Chr seems to be one stage further away from the original biblical stimulus, e.g., 1:43, where Tg. Chr had an opportunity to use *bl'*, "to swallow up," in the Bela-Balaam context, as had been done in Tg. Ps.-J. Num 22:5, but he uses another

[27]Rosenberg-Kohler, 274.

[28]Ibid., 271.

[29]Le Déaut, 1:28, with reference to P. Churgin, *The Targum to the Hagiographa*, 236.

verb instead, which may suggest that Tg. Chr had moved away from the original "foundation-pillars" of the expansion. In 2:54 a rich background of outwitting-the-enemy traditions by various ruses is condensed into a one-word allusion, *bṣn'*, "secretly," an indication perhaps that the stories were now so far in the past as to be almost forgotten or that they were so well known as not to require retelling.

3) Occasionally Tg. Chr gives us a "compressed expansion," exceptionally brief but opening a window on a vast panorama of exegetical tradition, e.g., 1:24 Shem, *the great priest;* 1:44 Bela, *whom Phinehas slew in the desert;* 2:19 *Miriam who is called* Ephrath. Sometimes an extended expansion indicates that it is the last term in the series; sometimes exceptional brevity indicates the same phenomenon, the almost cryptic brevity implying that herein is a reference to a story or series of traditions so well known as to need no further elaboration.

These three suggestions, in slightly different ways, indicate a certain lateness on the part of Tg. Chr.

4) In comparing Tg. Chr with Tg. Samuel–Kings, Tg. Chr often seems to be building his expansion on the latter work; e.g., 2 Sam 5:2 and 1 Chr 11:2; 2 Kgs 15:5 and 2 Chr 26:21.[30]

But "lateness" is also a relative term, very difficult to define. However, the fact that so often the traditions adopted and/or adapted in Tg. Chr are found in the Babylonian Talmud may help to confirm this impression of "lateness," leading to some such position as, for example, that we have the beginnings of the process of development in a Palestinian context, perhaps fourth century C.E., perhaps earlier. This development continues into the post-Talmudic period, drawing heavily on the Babylonian Talmud in that process, on Tg. Samuel–Kings, on various midrashic works such as the *Pirqe de Rabbi Eliezer, Mekilta,* the *Pesiḳtas,* the *Midrash Rabba,* leading to a final redaction perhaps in the eighth century C.E. The lack of Arabisms in Tg. Chr discourages further postponement of the final redaction.[31]

VI. THE WORK OF THE TARGUMIST

1. *The Targumist makes the rough places plain.*

The Targumist takes a word or phrase that is obscure, outdated, abstract, vague, and makes it intelligible, modern, concrete and specific.

a) *Textual Matters*

1 Chr 2:18 MT: "Caleb ... became the father of Azubah, a woman and Jerioth and these were her sons...." "Her" is ambiguous, and the next verse makes it clear that

---

[30]For a fuller list, see Le Déaut, 1:24 n. 60.
[31]See Le Déaut, 1:25.

Azubah was the wife of Caleb. Tg.: "Caleb ... had children by *(mn)* Azubah *his* wife ..., and these were her sons."

2 Chr 35:21 MT: "Not against you, you (nominative) today." Tg.: "It is not against you that I have come up to wage war—for you are attacking me this day."

2 Chr 25:8 MT: "For if you go, act, be strong for the battle, God will make you stumble." Tg.: "For if you go with the tribe of the house of Ephraim, the Lord will make you stumble."

2 Chr 32:5 MT: "And he brought up upon the towers." Tg.: "and he brought up towers upon it."

There are also occasions when Tg. Chr leaves a difficult text as it is. In 2 Chr 18:17 MT: "Did I not tell you that he would not prophesy good concerning me but evil?" In MT there is an *l* before "evil." It is not found in the parallel verse in 1 Kgs, and most commentators would like to be rid of it, but it is still there in Tg. Chr.

2 Chr 3:4 in MT, with its complex set of measurements, is just as confusing in Tg. Chr.

b) *Out-of-date Expressions*

The Targumist takes a word or phrase whose original significance is forgotten and updates it:

1 Chr 11:15 MT: "The Rephaim," pre-Israelite inhabitants of Canaan, become "the warriors."

1 Chr 18:17 MT: "The Cherethites and the Pelethites" become "the archers and the slingers."

1 Chr 11:20 and 12:19 MT contain references to "the three" and "the thirty," problematic groups who had a special relationship with David but whose denotation is often puzzling: in Tg. Chr they become "the warriors."

1 Chr 29:5 MT: "Who will offer willingly to fill his hand today for the Lord?" "To fill his hand": an expression that may at one time have been used when setting apart a priest for his office becomes in Tg. Chr "to present his offering."

2 Chr 9:16 MT: "the house of the forest of Lebanon" becomes "the house of the cooling of kings," i.e., "the summer house of the kings," a term that would be understood in a Hellenistic-Roman context.

c) *Coinage*

Coins too are modernized: The daric of 1 Chr 29:7 has become a *zuz*, while the shekel of 1 Chr 21:25 has become a *sela* (both the *zuz* and the *sela* are mentioned in Rabbinic literature), while the talent of 1 Chr 29:7 is translated there and in many other places in Tg. Chr as the *centenarium*.

d) *Geographical and Ethnic Terms*

Geographical terms and names of peoples are given their modern equivalent.
1 Chr 21:2: Dan becomes Pameas.

1 Chr 18:9: Hamath becomes Antioch, though occasionally it remains Hamath (1 Chr 18:3).

1 Chr 1:38: Seir becomes Gabla, though occasionally it remains Seir (2 Chr 25:11).

1 Chr 1:9: Cush becomes Arab.

2 Chr 21:16: The Cushites become the Africans, but in 2 Chr 12:3; 14:11, 12 they remain Cushites.

1 Chr 1:29: Qedar becomes Arab.

1 Chr 27:30: Obil the Ishmaelite becomes Obil the Arab(ian).

1 Chr 1:15: The Sinites become the Orthusians.

See Tg. 1 Chr 1 for more examples of geographic and ethnic updating.

Even peoples of whose identity in MT we are uncertain present no problem to Tg. Chr. In MT 1 Chr 1:11 we have the Ludim and Anamim. For *ICC* (63), these are not yet identified; for Tg. Chr there is no difficulty: they are the Niotites and the Mareotites, both peoples linked to specific areas in Egypt.

e) *Vague or General Expressions*

Expressions that are in any way vague or general are made much more precise and specific, with little room left for ambiguity. In the examples the addition in the Targum is in italics:

2 Chr 21:17: "They came up into *the land of the house of* Judah."

2 Chr 21:12: ". . . Asa king of *the tribe of the house of* Judah."

1 Chr 23:18: "Shelomith *was appointed* head."

1 Chr 17:1: "I am living in a house of cedars" becomes "I am living in a house *which is covered with* cedar *paneling.*"

1 Chr 29:24: "All the leaders . . . pledged their loyalty to king Solomon, *to support him and to strengthen him in all his kingship.*"

1 Chr 10:1: "And they fell, killed *by the sword.*"

1 Chr 11:3: "According to the word of the Lord *which he had spoken* through Samuel."

2 Chr 22:4: "He did evil—like the house of Ahab" becomes "He did what was evil . . . just as *the men of* the house of Ahab *had done.*"

2 Chr 12:12: "And also in Judah were good things" becomes "*to those of the house of* Judah *he decided to bring* good fortune."

1 Chr 11:18: "They drew water . . . *took it* . . . carried it and came. . . ."

2 Chr 18:20: "The spirit who was to lead Ahab astray" becomes "the spirit *of Naboth.*"

2 Chr 18:33: The unnamed bowman who shot Ahab is given a name, *Naaman, the Syrian army commander.*

2 Chr 32:21: "An angel" becomes "*the* angel *Gabriel.*"

1 Chr 20:1: "At the turn of the year" becomes "at the *end* of the year . . . *during the days of the month of Nisan.*"

Such examples could be multiplied. Sometimes an ambiguity is removed, but often the addition made by Tg. Chr adds little or nothing to what is already in MT. Occasionally the Targumist's desire for precision deprives the original of some of its effectiveness. This is true especially for proverbial or parabolic expressions, which often make their impact because they are brief and cryptic. 2 Chr 25:18: The brief "thorn-cedar" parable loses much of its initial bite when its meaning is spelled out in detail. 1 Chr 29:15: "Our days upon the earth are like a shadow"—and one's imagination does the rest. But Tg. Chr deprives us of the opportunity of using that imagination by adding "(a shadow) *of a bird which flies in the air of the heavens.*" The same can be said of the re-phrasing, in a rather pedestrian way, of the proverb in 2 Chr 10:10, where "my little fin-ger is thicker than my father's loins" becomes "My *weakness* is *more powerful* than *my* father's *strength.*"

There is, however, one instance where the Targumist's love for greater precision does not emerge, namely, 1 Chr 18:4; MT's: "David hamstrung all the chariots"! (cf. 1 Chr 19:18).

2. *The Targumist answers the questions that the intelligent layperson would ask.*

1 Chr 11:13 MT: "There was a plot of ground full of barley." But what of 2 Sam 23:11, where the crop is lentils? Answer: barley in one half of the field, lentils in the other.

2 Chr 2:13 MT and 1 Kgs 7:14 seem to have different views on the origins of Hiram's mother. In the former she is of the tribe of Dan; in the latter, she is of the tribe of Naphtali. Tg. Chr resolves the problem by pointing out that her mother was of Dan, but her father was of Naphtali.

2 Chr 20:1 MT: How can one explain the last clause of the sentence: "The sons of Moab and the sons of Ammon and with them some of the Ammonites"? Tg. Chr an-swers by rewriting the last clause as "and with them some *Edomites who had allied themselves to the* Ammonites."

1 Chr 10:13 MT: "Saul did not keep the command of the Lord." When? Tg. Chr sup-plies the answer: *"When he waged war against those of the house of Amalek."*

1 Chr 21:1 MT: Satan incited David to number Israel? How can this be reconciled with 2 Sam 24:1, where "the Lord incited David"? The Targumist replies by stating that *"the Lord raised up* Satan against Israel and he incited David. . . ."

Why did such a good king as Josiah meet with such an abysmal end? 2 Chr 35:23 MT has already hinted at the reason, but Tg. Chr leaves us in no doubt.

Whether or not the Targumist's answers to these questions are satisfactory is of little consequence, but he is making a serious attempt to deal with problems that may arise.

3. *The Targumist ensures that all things are done "decently and in order," that is, in accordance with the law as currently interpreted.*

1 Chr 15:27 MT: David wears a linen ephod. Since this could be worn only by the priests, it becomes in Tg. Chr a "*sleeved* linen *tunic.*"

1 Chr 2:35 MT: Sheshan gives his daughter in marriage to his Egyptian slave. Tg. Chr ensures that the correct procedures are carried out by stating that "Sheshan *released . . .* his slave" and then gave his daughter.

1 Chr 11:18 MT: David pours out the precious water his warriors have brought him, "to the Lord." It was the priest's duty to pour out a libation, so in Tg. Chr David "*gave orders* to pour it out *before* the Lord."

Tg. 1 Chr 27:34: The troops do not go out to battle until all the proper consultations have taken place through the use of the Urim and the Thummim by the priests.

Any hint of impropriety in the priests' sanctifying themselves in the second part of 2 Chr 5:11 is removed by Tg. Chr's rewriting that part. In MT 2 Chr 9:11, Solomon makes "lyres and lutes for the singers," but in Tg. Chr those lyres and lutes are "*for the sons of Levi, who were to offer praise with them.*"

Indeed, two of the big issues in Tg. Chr center around the law and its current interpretation—the affair of "Ruth the Moabitess" (1 Chr 2:17) and the correct observance of "Hezekiah's Passover" (2 Chr 30).

VII. THE METHODS OF THE TARGUMIST

1) Translation—this is the Targumist's major technique! He is translating a work written in Hebrew into a different, though closely related language. Inasmuch as his aim in translating is to make the text understandable, and understood in such a way that his audience will be edified and the practice of their faith brought more into conformity with the current understanding of that faith, it is natural that he will from time to time, consciously or unconsciously, take some liberties with the text before him. It must be said, however, that on the whole he follows the Hebrew text faithfully, apart from what he adds to it. For various reasons, some of which are dealt with in the next section, certain words and phrases are normally translated in the same way, e.g., "God," when standing on its own in the absolute state, without suffix, becomes "The Lord"; "the house of God" becomes "the sanctuary house of the Lord"; "the man of God" becomes "the prophet of the Lord"; "to seek the Lord" often becomes "to seek instruction from before the Lord" or "to seek the fear of the Lord." When the Lord acts, we often find "the Memra of the Lord." "Peace offerings" (*šlmym*) become "sacrifices of holy things"; "to hear, listen" often becomes "to receive from"; "steadfast love" *(ḥsd)* becomes "goodness."

There are times, however, when the translation becomes rather flat. We see this especially in instances where two or more Hebrew words are translated by one Aramaic word; for example, in 2 Chr 20:18 the Hebrew verb *qdd,* "to bow," and *npl,* "to fall," are both translated by *kr',* "to bow"; in 2 Chr 20:21, the Hebrew verbs *šyr,* "to sing," *hll,* "to praise," *ydh,* "to confess, acknowledge, praise," are all translated by *šbh,* "to praise." This approach is seen most clearly in the use of the Aramaic verb *qtl,* "to kill," which often does duty for *hrg,* "to kill," 1 Chr 7:21; for Hiphil of *mwt,* "to put to death," 2 Chr 25:4; for Hiphil of *nkh,* "to strike down," 1 Chr 18:5; for *dqr,* "to pierce, stab," 1 Chr 10:4; for *ḥll,* "pierced, slain," 1 Chr 10:1; and for *šḥt,* "to destroy," 2 Chr 24:23.

2) The Targumist sometimes translates proper nouns by reproducing the Aramaic word corresponding to the meaning of the Hebrew proper noun; for example, in 2 Chr 16:6, the place name *mṣph,* "watchtower," becomes *skwt',* "watchtower"; in 1 Chr 1:30, five of Ishmael's sons are given their corresponding Aramaic name, e.g., *dwmh,* "si-

lence," is renamed *štwq'*, "silence"; in 1 Chr 4:28, Hazar*shual* becomes Hazar*tala,* the words in italics being the Hebrew and Aramaic words for "fox."

3) The Targumist makes comments or expansions, which he adds to the text.

a) Sometimes the expansion simply spells out in more detail what is already reasonably clear in the text; e.g., 1 Chr 5:22, "until the exile" becomes "until the exile *of Sennacherib.*"

b) Sometimes, paradoxically, the expansion is "compressed"[32] and serves as a key to unlock a treasure house of exegetical tradition with all kinds of ecclesiastical and political implications; e.g., 1 Chr 1:24, "Shem, *the great priest*"; 2:19, "*Miriam who is called Ephrath.*"

c) Sometimes the expansion is based on the real or apparent meaning of the Hebrew word. The notes to 1 Chr 1 and 2 refer to many such instances, e.g., 1:10: Nimrod, *mrd,* "to rebel"; 1:20: Hazar Maweth, "the courtyard of death." See especially 2:55, where several words form the basis for such expansions.

d) Sometimes the expansion is based on the meaning of an associated word; e.g., in 1 Chr 4:15 the comment on Caleb is based on his father's name, Jephunneh; in 1 Chr 1:19 the comment on Joktan *(yqtn)* is based on a word similar in appearance *qt',* "to cut off"; in 2 Chr 13:5 the reference to "a covenant of salt" leads into an expansion that speaks of the sweetening of the waters of the sea!

e) Sometimes the expansion is based on the reputation of the people mentioned, e.g., in 2 Chr 7:10, where three names are given—David, Solomon, Israel his people—each name being followed by a laudatory comment.

f) Sometimes the expansion is based on the separate syllables contained in a word; e.g., in 1 Chr 16:3 each person is given a loaf of bread and an *'špr,* a word of uncertain meaning. The Targumist takes the first syllable, *'š,* and links it with the word for "six," to which in appearance it has some resemblance, and the second syllable, *pr,* which by itself means "bull, ox," and the end result is that each person receives "one sixth of an ox"! The same technique is used in dealing with the next word in the sentence, *'šyšh.* In 2 Chr 9:16 beaten *(šhwt)* gold is used for the shields. The first syllable *š* is sometimes used as an abbreviation for *'šr,* "which," and the second, *hwt,* means "thread," giving an expansion: "refined gold *which they spun like thread.*"

g) Sometimes synonymous expressions are given two separate interpretations; e.g., in 1 Chr 28:2, where "my brethren" and "my people" lead into "my brethren *the house of Israel,* and my people, *the proselytes who are in their towns.*"

h) Sometimes the expansion is based on a variant reading; e.g., 2 Chr 33:13 MT has *wy'tr,* "and he accepted his prayer," but there is a variant reading, *wyhtr,* from the root *htr,* "to break through," which in Tg. Chr leads to an opening being made in the heavens to enable Manasseh's prayer to get through to the throne of glory, there to be considered and accepted by the Lord. A similar technique is used later on in the same verse, where the expansion is based on *yšyb* and another reading, *yšb.* A reading from elsewhere may also be used as the basis for the expansion; e.g., in MT 1 Chr 13:9 we have

---

[32]See also above, pp. 17–18, "The Date of Targum Chronicles."

"the threshing-floor of Kidon." In the parallel verse in 2 Sam 6:6 it is "the threshing-floor of Nacon," which in Tg. Sam. becomes "a place prepared," from the root behind "Nacon" *(kwn).* It is this rendering that appears in Tg. Chr.

i) Sometimes the expansion is based on "identification" or "equation." Following the instruction in *Lev. R.* 1:3 that Chronicles is to be interpreted midrashically, and the dictum in *b. Meg.* 13a: "All thy words are one and we know how to find their inner meaning," the Targumist uses many of the names in Chronicles to good effect. Often in dealing with an individual he identifies or equates him with someone else, e.g., 1 Chr 1:43, "Balaam = Laban"; 2:7, "Carmi = Zimri"; 2:19, "Miriam = Ephrath"; 2:55, "Jabez = Othniel"; 3:3, "Eglah = Michal"; 4:15, "Mered = Caleb"; 8:33, "Abiel = Ner"; 23:16, "Shebuel = Jonathan," while in 4:18 Moses is identified with six other people and given their names. All this seems strange to us, especially when in making such identifications no cognizance is taken of generation gaps. That, of course, would not have been a problem to the expositor, for as the *Mekilta* at Exod 15:9 notes again and again, ". . . no strict order as to 'earlier' and 'later' is observed in the Torah." By making the equation "x = y," he is seeking to attach to "x" a virtue or a vice or an attribute associated with "y" or linguistically derivable from the form of his name, thereby to make "x" even more praiseworthy or blameworthy or whatever than he already is. It is as though the expositor chose persons instead of adjectives to emphasize his point. Thus when he tells us that Balaam = Laban or that Carmi = Zimri, he is saying: "I am trying, through personality, to stress just how evil evil is, and rather than use several evil persons as separate illustrations, all the persons are identified, and the resultant "composite person" is shown to be exceptionally evil, and the appropriate lessons drawn therefrom.[33]

If "translation" is regarded as the Targumist's "major technique," a final note should be added to pay tribute to that skill which enabled him (or them?) to deal with the many "camel loads" of traditions available to him and to sift through them, choose, modify, and adapt them for his own particular purpose. He is surrounded but never overwhelmed by "a great cloud of witnesses" and, in a very real sense, is the filter through which the significance of these many and varied traditions was conveyed to his audience.

VIII. THE THEOLOGY AND TEACHING OF THE TARGUMIST

1. *God*

The Targumist ensures that God is God and remains "high and lifted up." He does this by the following means:

a) *By occasional paeans of praise* in which he extols God's splendor and majesty, his power in creation, his deliverance of his people, and his sovereignty over all. See, e.g., 1

---

[33]See further Z. H. Chajes, *The Student's Guide Through the Talmud* (London, 1952), chs. 21 and 22; R. Beckwith, *The Old Testament Canon of the New Testament Church* (London, 1985), 217–220.

Chr 29:11, 12; 2 Chr 2:5; 2 Chr 6:18, passages in which the short tributes in MT are elaborated on and spelled out in detail, leaving no doubt as to the transcendence of God: "Yours, O Lord, is the dominion *in the firmament* and you are exalted above all *the angels that are in heaven and above all those who are appointed* as leaders *on earth*" (last sentence of 1 Chr 29:11).

b) *By removing God from the scene of direct action or direct contact with human beings.* In Tg. Chr the divine action takes place through something that almost becomes someone, an agent, an intermediary acting for God, but so closely related to God that the recipient knows that here indeed God is at work. The word most frequently used in this connection in Tg. Chr is *Memra,* whose basic meaning is "word," from the verb *'mr,* "to say." When this expression is used, the emphasis is usually on divine action. This is especially obvious in one of the most common usages of the word: If "God helped him" or "was with him," in the sense of a supportive and helpful presence, the normal translation in Tg. Chr is: "The Memra of the Lord was in his support," e.g., 1 Chr 17:2, 8. There are also occasions when *Memra* seems to have the force of a personal pronoun, e.g., 1 Chr 21:15: "And he [the Lord] repented *in his Memra*" (or better "in himself"). The question is open to debate as to whether *Memra* is simply a reverential circumlocution for "Yahweh" or whether there is also some hint of an "intermediary." According to E. Levine, ". . . the rather prosaic truth of the matter is that God's Word *(memra')* appears throughout the targum as a substitute for the Tetragrammaton, YHWH, no more and no less . . . in the targum it conveys the *being* and the *doing* of YHWH, across the entire spectrum."[34] It is of interest that there are also instances where *Memra* is used of humans, in each case with the force of a pronoun. In Tg. 2 Chr 16:3, Asa speaks to Benhadad: "There is a covenant between *my Memra* and *your Memra*" (MT: "between me and between you"). See also 2 Chr 23:16; 25:19, and especially 32:1, where we read: "*the Lord decided in his Memra* to . . .," and later on in the same verse, "Sennacherib . . . said *in his Memra* to. . . ." There are, of course, examples where the Lord acts without the inclusion of the Memra, e.g., 1 Chr 28:4, 5: "The Lord chose"; "The Lord gave." In whichever sense *Memra* is used—either as a reverential circumlocution for Yahweh, or as possessing some "intermediary" role—its constant use is helping to place a reverential hedge around the Lord and preserve his transcendence.

The other word used in Tg. Chr in speaking of God is *Shekinah* (from *škn,* "to dwell"), signifying especially the Divine Presence. 1 Chr 17:4: "For I did not dwell in a house . . ." becomes in Tg. Chr: "For I did not *cause my Shekinah to* dwell in a house" (also in verses 5 and 6). Other words that may indicate God's presence sometimes receive similar treatment. 2 Chr 33:4: "In Jerusalem shall my name be . . ." becomes in Tg. Chr: "In Jerusalem *I shall cause my Shekinah to dwell.* . . ." 2 Chr 30:9: "He will not turn away his face from you" becomes in Tg. Chr: "He will not *take up his Shekinah* from *among* you." It is used even when God's Presence is implied even though there is no word to express it. 2 Chr 32:19: "The God of Jerusalem" becomes in Tg. Chr: "the

---

[34]E. Levine, *The Aramaic Version of the Bible* (Berlin/New York, 1988), 59f.

God *whose Shekinah dwells* in Jerusalem." The frequent use of this word allows the transcendent God to be present in a place in heaven or on earth but does not tie him to that place or in any way compromise his transcendence.

c) *By rephrasing many expressions which might suggest that there was something human about God.* This applies especially to parts of the human body transferred to God (hands, feet, mouth, eyes, ears, or the functions carried out by those parts—hearing, seeing, etc.). This happens very often in Tg. Chr, as a few of the examples quoted will indicate, but other examples will show that the Targumist is not wholly consistent.

Feet: 1 Chr 28:2: ". . . to build . . . a resting-place . . . for the stool of the feet of our God" becomes in Tg. Chr: "a resting-place . . . for the footstool of *the throne of the glory of the Lord.*"

Hand: 2 Chr 6:4: ". . . who with his hand has fulfilled" becomes in Tg. Chr: ". . . who by his *good will . . .*"; or similarly in 6:15: ". . . you spoke with your mouth and with your hand have fulfilled it . . ." becomes in Tg. Chr: ". . . *you decided by your Memra and by your will you brought it about.*" But note MT 1 Chr 28:19, "All this in a writing from the hand of the Lord," is unchanged in Tg. Chr. See also 1 Chr 29:12, 16; and note 2 Chr 25:8, where "hand" is not in MT but appears in Tg. Chr MT: "for there is power with God" becomes in Tg. Chr: "for there is power *in the hand of the Lord*"!

Mouth: 2 Chr 6:15 quoted in preceding paragraph. In 2 Chr 36:12, ". . . the prophet, who spoke from the mouth of the Lord" becomes in Tg. Chr: ". . . the prophet, who *prophesied to him* from the mouth of *the Memra of* the Lord."

Ears: 1 Chr 28:8: "In the ears of our God" becomes in Tg. Chr: *"before the Memra of the Lord,"* but the "ears" remain in Tg. 2 Chr 6:40 and 7:15.

Eyes: In the formula used to sum up the conduct of a king, MT's "(he did what was good/evil) in the eyes of the Lord" regularly becomes in Tg. Chr: ". . . *before the Lord,*" 2 Chr 14:1. Occasionally, however, the same procedure is followed with reference to people: 1 Chr 13:4: "The thing was right in the eyes of all the people" becomes in Tg. Chr: ". . . *before* all the people." See also 2 Chr 30:4, where it is used of both king and people in the same verse.[35] 2 Chr 6:20: "That your eyes may be opened toward this house" becomes in Tg. Chr: "that *there may be good pleasure before you to protect* this house"; cf. 6:40; 7:15. In 2 Chr 16:9 however, "the eyes of the Lord survey the whole earth" is found in both MT and Tg. Chr.

To express the functions of the parts of the body, Tg. Chr often uses the passive voice. 2 Chr 34:27: "I have heard" becomes *"It has been heard before me,"* but it is followed immediately by "The Lord has said"! (though it should also be noted that "hear" is very often translated in Tg. Chr by *"accept from"*—2 Chr 6:23, 25, 27, 30, 33). 2 Chr 7:12: "The Lord appeared" becomes in Tg. Chr: "The Memra of the Lord *was revealed.*" 2 Chr 12:7: "And when the Lord saw" becomes in Tg. Chr: "and when *it was revealed* before the Lord."

---

[35]See M. L. Klein, "The Preposition *qdm* ('before') a Pseudo–Anti-Anthropomorphism in the Targums," *Journal of Theological Studies* 30 (1979): 502–507.

d) *By rephrasing expressions that might imply close contact with God from the human standpoint.* "To seek the Lord" becomes "to seek *instruction from before* the Lord" (2 Chr 11:16; 1 Chr 21:30). "To return to the Lord" becomes "to return to *the fear of* the Lord" (2 Chr 6:37) or occasionally *"to his worship"* (2 Chr 6:38). "To pray to the Lord," "to give a gift to the Lord," "to offer sacrifice to the Lord"—in each of these cases the "to" is replaced by *"before,"* a preposition which, while still suggesting a certain nearness to God, lacks the directness involved in the preposition "to" (2 Chr 32:23, 24; 1 Chr 21:8; 1 Chr 21:46; 1 Chr 23:31). "To praise the Lord" also becomes "to offer praise *before* the Lord and *to the name of* the Lord" (2 Chr 5:13).

Even though some of the expressions quoted in this and the preceding section may be "common idiomatic and translational phenomena" (to use M. L. Klein's phrase, quoted in E. Levine),[36] and in spite of the fact that Tg. Chr is not always consistent in their use, it still seems possible that for Tg. Chr they are playing an anti-anthropomorphic role, helping to put before the readers something of the majesty and transcendence of God.

e) *By refusing to allow the term "God" to be used for anything or anyone other than the true God, Yahweh, Israel's God and Lord of the world.* While certain parts of MT might suggest that there are other gods but they are so useless as to be "non-entities," Tg. Chr will not allow them the credibility they might gain by being called "gods." He goes out of his way to downgrade them. The word he normally uses to describe "other gods" or "gods of the peoples" is *ṭ'wwt,* coming from a root meaning "to lead astray," and usually translated as "idols" (2 Chr 7:19, 22; 28:25; 34:25). Another word less frequently used is *dḥlt,* based on the root *dḥl,* "to fear"—"objects of fear," "objects of worship" (2 Chr 13:8). Both these words are used in 1 Chr 16:26 in the rendering of "for all the gods of the peoples are idols (lit. 'worthlessnesses')," which in Tg. Chr becomes in a literal translation "for all the *idols* of the peoples are *objects of worship which are of no use.*" Surprisingly, in the previous verse (25) he translates "gods" as *"angels"* (cf. Ps 8:6 in LXX), apparently according them some status, though the development of the theme in verse 26 shows this status to be of little consequence. The Targum uses the same approach when dealing with people and objects associated with these idols. MT uses the word *mzbḥ* for "altar," be it Yahwistic or pagan, and *khn* for "priest." Tg. Chr uses the cognate words only for legitimate altars and priests, while the words *'gwr'* ("a heap of stones") and *kwmr'* ("pagan priest") appear for pagan or non-legitimate altars and priests.

But if Tg. Chr gives us a picture of such a lofty, transcendent God, it must be stressed that such transcendence does not imply a cold deism, in which God is so remote from his people and his world that he has lost all interest in them. The Targumist also highlights the graciousness of this transcendent God. He shows us:

—God as Father (or at least like a father). Statements made on this theme in MT are taken and, while avoiding any hint of physical fatherhood, are developed in Tg. Chr in a much more tender and intimate way (1 Chr 17:13; 22:10; 28:6). For the rather blunt

---

[36]P. 61.

statement in MT 1 Chr 28:6: "I have chosen him [Solomon] to be my son and I will be his father," Tg. Chr gives us: "I have chosen him, *to love him that he should be before me beloved as a* son and I shall be to him *like* a father."

—God as merciful. This emerges very clearly in the Aqedah reference in 1 Chr 21:15, where the transcendent God shows himself to be a God who is moved by what he sees and halts the slaughter of his people.

—God as one who forgives the repentant sinner. Manasseh, the sinner par excellence, turns to God in penitence to discover that God has not only prepared the way for his return but is ready both to forgive and restore. He discovers the truth of the comment in Tg. 2 Chr 33:13 that his *"right hand is stretched out to receive the sinners who return to his fear, and who break the inclination of their heart by repentance."*

And Tg. Chr never tires of listing occasions when God (or his Memra) acted on behalf of his people for deliverance, help, and comfort (1 Chr 17:21; 1 Chr 29:11; 2 Chr 28:3).

Yet this graciousness on God's part never degenerates into sentimentality. After the "father-son" statement in 1 Chr 28:6, the Targumist loses no time in stressing that God's love is neither to be taken for granted nor trifled with. He does this by inserting an extra clause in 1 Chr 28:9: "If you seek him, he will be found by you *whenever you seek his fear and seek him.* But if you forsake him, he will reject you for ever." In the eyes of the Targumist, both Manasseh and Josiah were to know the truth of this verse.

2. *Angels*

"Angels" play quite a part in Tg. Chr. The loan word *'ngly* is used once (1 Chr 16:31); otherwise the normal Hebrew and Aramaic word *ml'k* appears. We are aware already in MT of "the angel of the Lord," sometimes helping, sometimes destroying. In Tg. Chr we have the same emphasis, though now it is "an angel *sent from before* the Lord" (1 Chr 21:18, 30). Sometimes the expression is used as a substitute for God where we might have expected the Memra (1 Chr 17:21). We also meet groups of angels, a kind of celestial host. In MT 1 Chr 12:23, "like an army of God" becomes in Tg. Chr: "like the camp *of the angels of the Lord.*" "The sound of marching in the tops of the balsam trees" that will herald God's presence in MT 1 Chr 14:15 becomes in Tg. Chr: "the sound of *the angels who are coming to help you*" (cf. Tg. Ezek 1:24). Similar groups of angels assist at Sinai in the giving of the Law (1 Chr 29:11), while in 1 Chr 16:31, *"the angels on high"* is the translation in Tg. Chr for MT's "the heavens." In 2 Chr 32:21 the names of Gabriel and Michael (cf. Dan 8:16; 12:1) are given to the angel sent to destroy the Assyrians. We thus have in Tg. Chr a more developed angelology than in MT Chr. Throughout Tg. Chr, the angel(s) are Yahweh's messengers, completely under his control, acting on his behalf. There is, however, one slight blot on the Targum's picture of the angels. In 2 Chr 33:13, when Manasseh offers his prayer of repentance, it is the angels who try to prevent it from reaching the heavenly throne. This may be the reflection of a time when the role of angels was a matter of controversy between various groups in Judaism in the early Christian centuries.

3. *The Law*

Reference has been made above to the Targumist's desire to ensure that everything is done according to the Law, "as Moses commanded."[37] In Tg. Chr the Law, its study, and its observance are thus constantly to the fore, some examples of which are listed below: Jabez (=Othniel) sets up an academy for the disciples (1 Chr 2:55), and in 1 Chr 4:9, where MT notes that "he was more honored than his brothers," Tg. Chr reproduces this as "he was more honored *and expert in the Law* than his brothers." In Tg. Chr Boaz is head of the academy in Bethlehem (1 Chr 4:22), and in the following verse it is made clear that it is the disciples of the Law who help to keep the world in place; indeed, it was for their sake that the world was created. In 1 Chr 11:2 it was David who "led us out *to battle* and brought us in *to the house of study and who taught Israel,*" while verse 11 in Tg. becomes a eulogy on his prowess in battle and in Torah, to study which he rises in the middle of the night (1 Chr 20:5). In 1 Chr 11:25 Benaiah, the warrior who in MT is put in charge of David's bodyguard, is in Tg. Chr "appointed *head of the academy, in charge of the disciples,*" having received, a few verses earlier (22), a glowing tribute as a champion of Torah. MT 1 Chr 12:33 describes the sons of Issachar as having "understanding of the times, to know what Israel ought to do." Tg. Chr, after interpreting this, describes them as "*heads of the sanhedrin . . . who were putting into practice the decrees of the Law. . . .*" In Tg. 1 Chr 24:6, Moses is called "*the great scribe,*" while in 2 Chr 24:16 Jehoiada, who in MT "had done good in Israel," in Tg. Chr "had *kept the commandments* in Israel." In 1 Chr 5:12 and 2 Chr 34:22 the *mšnh*, "second," of MT becomes, by linking it with *šnh*, in Tg. Chr: "*the house of instruction*" or "the school." In MT 2 Chr 20:20, as Jehoshaphat's army goes forth to war he urges them to "put their trust in the Lord . . . put their trust in his prophets." Between these two objects of trust Tg. Chr inserts: "*Put your trust in his Law.*" Josiah's fatal blunder is attributed in Tg. 2 Chr 35:23 to the fact that he "*had not sought instruction from before the Lord.*" Indeed, this is one of the Targumist's favorite translations of the expression "to seek the Lord"; for him it is "to seek *instruction from before* the Lord" (2 Chr 12:14; 2 Chr 15:4; 2 Chr 20:3, 4).

4. *Prophecy*

Tg. Chr, surprisingly, has many references to prophets and prophecy. Those normally called "prophets" are there, but others join the prophetic ranks: those called "the man of God" (Moses, 1 Chr 23:14; David, 2 Chr 8:14; Shemaiah, 2 Chr 11:2; one unnamed, 2 Chr 25:7); "the seer" of MT also becomes a "prophet" (2 Chr 16:7, 10), though Asaph the seer of 2 Chr 29:30 remains a seer. "The vision of . . ." in MT usually becomes in Tg. Chr "the *prophecy* of" (2 Chr 32:32). The normal prophetic formula in MT: "The word of the Lord was with . . ." becomes in Tg. Chr: "there was a word *of prophecy from*

---

[37]See above, pp. 21–22.

before the Lord with . . ." (1 Chr 17:3). The expression in MT: "The Spirit of God was upon . . ." becomes in Tg. Chr: "a spirit *of prophecy from before the Lord rested* upon . . ." (2 Chr 15:1).

These many references to prophecy, however, add little to our knowledge of how Tg. Chr understood the phenomenon. But two things may be noted:

a) In Tg. 1 Chr 2:55 a group of scribes finds one of its sources of inspiration in the fact that *"they were covered with the spirit of prophecy."* In 1 Chr 28:12 it is the spirit of prophecy that helps David plan the layout of the Temple. Such comments would suggest that one major component in "prophecy" was understanding divine wisdom, and the fact that scribes are its recipients may also indicate that Tg. Chr is following the normal Talmudic principle that the role of the prophet is to explain and clarify the teachings of God's revelation to Moses.

b) False prophecy is dealt with in Tg. Chr in more specific terms than in MT. In Tg. 1 Chr 23:16 Shebuel (= Jonathan), son of Gershom, is appointed a false prophet, a prophet of falsehood. In 2 Chr 18, in the Micaiah incident, all the "court prophets" are classified as prophets of falsehood. But the surprise comes in Tg. 2 Chr 18:20, 21, when the spirit of Naboth volunteers to be "a spirit of false prophecy in the mouth of all his prophets." While Naboth receives God's instruction to carry on, his action does cost him his place among the righteous—a not very satisfactory way of dealing with one of the difficult verses in the MT. The two false prophets Ahab and Zedekiah, who are so sternly castigated in Jer 29:21–23 and whose death by burning is to be taken as a lesson to all, are mentioned also in Tg. 2 Chr 28:3 in the roll call of those who passed through the fire. For such as them, not even the merits of a righteous man can suffice, though it would seem that Shebuel in 1 Chr 23:16 fared somewhat better, for his repentance brought him a new post!

5. *Merit*

It was inevitable that in a religion which stressed the importance and benefits of keeping the Law, a doctrine of merit should arise. In the case of Joshua, the son of Jehozadak (Tg. 2 Chr 28:3), his merit leads to his own deliverance. But the merit of exceptionally good men could also be transferred to others; as G. F. Moore puts it, "because of the Fathers God blessed their descendants."[38] While often it is the patriarchs who are in mind when "the merit of the Fathers" is discussed, Tg. Chr mentions several people whose merit has been transferred to the account of others. 1 Chr 2:55: The merit of Moses *"was of more value to them than horsemen and chariots"* (cf. Tg. Jonathan 2 Kgs 2:12). Likewise in 1 Chr 4:18, where *"he covered the house of Israel with his merit,"* and, later in the same verse, it is on his account that God forgives Israel's sins. In Tg. 1 Chr 29:18 David asks that the massive freewill offering that has been contributed for the building of the Temple be kept as eternal merit, leading to a right attitude of fear of God in the hearts of the people. It was also due to David's merit that the gates of the sanctuary house had been opened (2 Chr 7:10; cf. Tg. Ruth 4:21 and Tg. Song of Songs

---

[38]G. F. Moore, *Judaism in the First Centuries of the Christian Era* (Cambridge, Mass., 1927–30) 1:538.

2:8, where the merit benefits Israel). But Tg. Chr also gives instances where the merit of an individual can benefit another individual: 1 Chr 8:33, where the merit of Abiel, Saul's grandfather, helps Saul to become king. Eliezer (1 Chr 23:17) has only one son, Rehabiah, but because of the merit of Moses, the sons of Rehabiah increased to more than sixty myriads.

6. *The Glorification of the Great Ones in Israel*

MT Chr gives a very high place to both Moses and David. But their treatment in MT is completely overshadowed by the fulsome tributes paid to them in Tg. Chr. The merit of Moses and of David has been mentioned already. The virtues and achievements of Moses are dealt with at length in an intriguing expansion in Tg. 1 Chr 4:18, where three pairs of father-and-son names are taken, each is applied to Moses, and the meaning of each name forms the basis for a sentence of tribute to him, e.g., *"She called him Jered because he brought down manna for Israel"* (root *yrd,* "to go down"). As for David, in Tg. 1 Chr 11:2 he is skilled in battle and in Torah. In 1 Chr 17:8 God has given him a reputation "as good as that of the great *fathers of the universe who have been* on the earth," a fact that David acknowledges in Tg. 1 Chr 17:17, now that God has shown him *"that I shall stand in the ranks of the mighty ones."* But it is in 1 Chr 11:11 that Tg. Chr waxes most eloquent in his praise of David. Two names are taken and used as the basis for an expansion that paints David in the brightest colors, causing him to appear as one who is not only without blemish but outstanding in all the important areas of life, with a special mention of his skill in Torah. In 1 Chr 13:8 and 15:29 any suggestion of unseemly behavior that might lie behind the expression "making merry before the Lord" is removed by the Targum's substitution of *"offering praise before the Lord."*

Mention should also be made of others who in MT have a much smaller role than either Moses or David, but who in Tg. Chr are moved much more into the center and are shown to be making a great contribution to the life and work of God's people: Miriam (1 Chr 2:19; 4:4); Benaiah (1 Chr 11:22); Obed Edom (1 Chr 13:14).

IX. GREEK AND LATIN LOAN WORDS

The following words with their Greek or Latin "origins" appear in Tg. Chr. The appropriate references in Jastrow and Levy are given together with the reference in Tg. Chr where the word first occurs.

1) *'wyr.* "Air." Greek *aēr.* MJ—no reference to Greek origin. JL I, 15. 1 Chr 20:2.
2) *'wklwz.* "Levy of troops." Greek *ochlos.* MJ—no reference to Greek origin. JL I, 27. 1 Chr 11:6.
3) *'zmrgd.* "Smargad, emerald." Greek *smaragdos.* MJ 38. JL I, 18 and 224. 1 Chr 29:2.
4) *tymws.* "Ready, determined." Greek *etoimos.* MJ 42. JL I, 22. 2 Chr 28:3.
5) *'yqwn.* "Icon, image, likeness." Greek *eikōn.* MJ 59. JL I, 25. 1 Chr 21:15.
6) *'ngly.* "Angels, messengers." Greek *aggeloi.* MJ 80. JL I, 40. 1 Chr 16:31.

7) *'sṭbl'*. "Stable." Latin *stabulum*. MJ 1708. JL I, 45. 2 Chr 32:28.

8) *'sṭwwn'*. "Balcony" (MJ). "Pillar, column" (JL). Greek *stulos, stēlē, stoa*. MJ—no reference to Greek origin. JL I, 45. JL also suggests possibility of Persian origin. 2 Chr 23:13.

9) *'sṭrwlwgws*. "Astrologer, astronomer." Greek *astrologos*. MJ 91. JL I, 58. 1 Chr 12:33.

10) *'sṭrṭyg*. "Camp, garrison." Greek *stratēgion*. MJ 92. "Army commander." Greek *stratēgos*. JL I, 47. 1 Chr 11:16.

11) *'sṭrṭywṭ'*. "Soldier." Greek *stratiōtēs*. MJ 92. JL I, 46. 1 Chr 18:6.

12) *'spwg*. "Sponge cake, spongy bread." Greek *spoggos*. MJ 1012 thinks the Greek word may be of Semitic origin. JL I, 48. 1 Chr 23:29.

13) *'prky'*. "Prefecture, province." Greek *eparchia*. MJ 59. JL I, 56. 1 Chr 1:5.

14) *'qlyd'*. "Key, lock." Greek *kleis*. MJ 112. JL I, 59. 1 Chr 9:27.

15) *'rkwn'*. "Ruler, elder." Greek *archōn*. MJ 121f. JL I, 65. 1 Chr 11:2.

16) *'rqbt'*. "Arkafta, second-in-command." Basically a Persian word but found also in Greek *argapetēs*. MJ 73. JL I, 34, 70. JL refers to probable Persian origin but does not refer to the Greek connection. 2 Chr 28:7.

17) *bsys'*. "Base, stand, footstool." Greek *basis*. MJ—no reference to Greek origin. JL I, 103. 2 Chr 4:14.

18) *bss*. "To tread." Pael "to establish firmly, found." Greek: from noun *basis*. MJ—no reference to Greek origin. JL I, 103. 2 Chr 3:3.

19) *glp*. "To dig out, engrave." Greek *gluphō*. MJ—no reference to Greek origin. JL I, 143. 2 Chr 2:13.

20) *dwkn'*. "Platform." Greek *docheion*. MJ—no reference to Greek origin. JL I, 164. 2 Chr 7:6.

21) *dwrwn*. "Gift." Greek *dōron*. MJ 289. JL I, 188. 1 Chr 18:2.

22) *dywqn'*. "Image, likeness." Greek *duo + eikōn*. MJ 297. JL I, 170. 2 Chr 33:7.

23) *zmrgd'*. "Smargad, emerald." Greek *smaragdos*. MJ 405. JL I, 225. (See also *'zmrgd'* above.) 1 Chr 1:9.

24) *ṭymy*. "Value, worth." Greek *timē*. MJ 532. JL I, 300. 1 Chr 20:2.

25) *ṭyqs'*. "Formation, arrangement, standard." Greek *taxis*. MJ—no reference to Greek origin. JL I, 318. 1 Chr 11:11.

26) *ṭqs*. "To arrange, prepare battle, count." Greek *tassō*. MJ 549. JL I, 317. 2 Chr 13:3.

27) *ṭrygwn'*. "Triangular, triangle." Greek *trigōvos*. MJ 553. JL I, 318. 1 Chr 9:24.

28) *kyrwmnyqy'*. "Handcuffs, manacles." Greek *cheiromanika*. MJ 636. JL I, 362. 2 Chr 33:11.

29) *krdwt*. "Tunic with sleeves." Greek *cheiridōtos*. Latin *chirdota*. MJ 664. JL I, 384. 1 Chr 15:27.

30) *krwz'*. "Public announcement, herald." Greek *kērux*. MJ—no reference to Greek origin. JL I, 385. 2 Chr 24:9.

31) *lblr'*. "Copyist, scribe." Latin *librarius*. MJ 689. *libellarius*. JL I, 401. 2 Chr 20:34.

32) *mṭrwnyt'*. "Matron, lady." Latin *matrona*. MJ 770. JL II, 30. 2 Chr 35:25.

33) *mrglyt'*. "Jewel." Greek *margaritēs*. MJ 836. JL II, 66. 1 Chr 1:23.

34) *mrgnyn*. "Whips." Greek *maragna*. MJ 836. JL II, 66. 2 Chr 10:11.

35) *mrmyr*. "Marble." Greek *marmaros*. Latin *marmor*. MJ 844. JL II, 70. 1 Chr 29:2.

36) *swpysṭ*. "Sophist, scholar." Greek *sophistēs*. MJ 968. JL II, 180. 1 Chr 12:33.

37) *sn(h)dry*. "Sanhedrin." Greek *sunedrion*. MJ 1474. JL II, 175. 1 Chr 12:33.

38) *pwndq*. "Lodging house." Greek *pandokeion*. MJ 1143. JL II, 271. 1 Chr 1:20.

39) *pyṭq*. "Ballot, tablet, letter." Greek *ptukton* or *pittakion*. MJ—no reference to Greek origin. JL II, 260. 2 Chr 21:12.

40) *pyyl*. "Broad, flat bowl." Greek *phialē*. Latin *fiala*. MJ 1162. JL II, 262. 2 Chr 4:8.

41) *plṭyn*. "Palace." Greek *palation*. Latin *palatium*. MJ 1180. JL II, 269. 2 Chr 34:10.

42) *plṭyryn*. "Palace, headquarters." Greek *praitōrion*. Latin *praetorium*. MJ 1180. Greek *palation*. Latin *palatium*. JL II, 269. 1 Chr 9:18.

43) *plqt*. "Concubine." Greek *pallakē*. MJ—no reference to Greek origin. JL II, 271. 1 Chr 1:32.

44) *prgwd*. "Curtain, tunic." Latin *paragauda*. MJ 1214 thinks the Latin word is of Semitic origin. JL II, 286. 2 Chr 3:14.

45) *przd'wwn*. "Posts, guards." Latin *praesidia*. MJ 1219. *praesidiarii*. JL II, 288. 1 Chr 2:54.

46) *prs*. "Tax, tribute, gift." Greek *phoros*. MJ 1233 gives the meaning as "slaves' fare," with no reference to origin. JL II, 293. 1 Chr 18:2.

47) *prs*. "Curtain, cover." Greek *pharos*. MJ makes no reference to Greek origin. JL II, 294. 1 Chr 15:23.

48) *prqmṭyt*. "Trading woman." Greek *pragmateutēs;* MJ 1214. *pragmatikē;* JL II, 300. 1 Chr 2:3.

49) *qwls*. "Helmet." Greek *koros*. MJ—no reference to Greek origin. JL II, 364. 2 Chr 26:14.

50) *qytwn*. "Bedchamber." Greek *koitōn*. MJ 1357. JL II, 357. 1 Chr 28:11.

51) *qlpwnyn*. "With fine voices." Greek *kalliphōnos*. MJ 1381. JL II, 367 gives the meaning as "a melodious musical instrument." 1 Chr 15:20.

52) *qnt'nr*. "Centenarium." Latin *centenarius*. MJ 1389f. JL II, 371. 1 Chr 19:6.

53) *qsṭr*. "Camp, fort." Latin *castra*. MJ 1396. JL II, 374. 1 Chr 4:32.

54) *qrwnyt*. "Capital of column." Greek *korunthos;* MJ 1414. *korōnis;* JL II, 389. 2 Chr 3:15.

55) *tyq*. "Sheath." Greek *thēkē*. MJ 1665. JL II, 536. 1 Chr 21:27.

56) *tsbr*. "Treasury, store." Greek *thēsauros*. MJ 1682 believes the Greek word is of Semitic origin. JL II, 547. 1 Chr 26:20.

57) *trys*. "Shield." Greek *thureos*. MJ—no reference to Greek origin. JL II, 560. 1 Chr 12:9.

X. PRACTICAL MATTERS

For anyone wishing to study the Targum of Chronicles, there is no better guide than the two-volume work of R. Le Déaut and J. Robert, *Targum des Chroniques* (Rome,

Biblical Institute Press, 1971). My indebtedness to both these volumes can be seen on every page of what follows. My translation is based on the Vatican Manuscript, Cod. Vat. Urb. Ebr. 1,[39] as presented in Volume Two of the above work, and extensive use has been made of the Apparatus Criticus given there, with considerable assistance from David Wilkins' edition of the Cambridge Manuscript and some guidance from M. F. Beck's edition of the Erfurt Manuscript, with occasional help from microfilms of the first two manuscripts mentioned.

In the early days of this enterprise, an attempt was made to provide a translation in good modern English, but it soon became clear that while to follow this line might produce a "good translation," the Aramaic flavor of the original work would have disappeared in what would inevitably be "a targum of a targum." It is hoped that the final product, though more literal in its emphasis than first intended, has at least preserved the Aramaic emphasis, which one assumes to be one of the main intentions of the project. Occasionally, however, when forced to depart from the Aramaic style in order to avoid a translation that is too wooden, a footnote draws attention to the literal rendering of the Aramaic. Where the Targum differs from the Massoretic Text, italics are used for the translation, with a footnote indicating the reading of the Massoretic Text. If the Targum gives a straightforward addition to the Hebrew Text, that addition also is printed in italics, but without a footnote to record the fact. The abbreviation Tg. Chr is used for "The Targum of Chronicles."

Words enclosed in parentheses ( ) in the translation are not found in the Aramaic text, but have been added in the English translation in those places where a little extra help was needed to reproduce a clause or sentence in passable English.

Personal names abound in Chronicles. In dealing with these, the usage of the Revised Standard Version has been followed, even though this leads to an occasional anomaly, e.g., where ṣ usually appears as *z,* which also represents the letter *zayin.*

---

[39]See above, p. 14.

The Targum of First Chronicles

Translation

CHAPTER 1

1. *This[a] is the book of the genealogies, the Chronicles from earliest times.[1]* Adam, Sheth, Enosh. 2.[b] *Kenan, Mahalalel,[c] Jared.* 3. *Enoch, Methusaleh, Lamech.* 4. *Noah, Shem, Ham and Japheth.* 5. *The sons of Japheth: Gomer, Magog, Madai, Javan, Tubal, Meshech, and Tiras. The names[2] of their provinces[3] are: Phrygia,[4] Germania,[5] the Medes,[6] Macedonia,[d6] Bithynia,[7] Usia,[e8] and Thrace.[f9]* [*Another[g] version reads: Germania,[5] Gethia,[10] Hamdan,[6] Ephesus,[11] Bithynia,[7] Musia, and Thrace.[9]*] 6. *The sons of Gomer: Ashkenaz, Diphath,[h] and Togarmah. The names[2] of their provinces[3] are: Asia,[12] Parkevi,[i13] and Barbaria.[14]* [*Another version reads:*

Apparatus, Chapter 1

[a] C: "The Targum of Chronicles."
[b] E omits verses 2-4.
[c] In verses 2-4, V gives only the first name in each verse. Frequently V omits names that he has written already in the immediately preceding Hebrew transcription.
[d] C: *mwqdwnyy'.* E, L, AS: *mwqdwny'.*

[e] C: *mwsyyh.*
[f] E, L, AS: *trqy'.*
[g] This alternative version is found in C, but not in E, L, AS.
[h] Margin in V has *rypt,* as in many Hebrew MSS, LXX, Vg, and MT of Gen 10:3.
[i] C: *prsww':* Persians.

Notes, Chapter 1

[1] Lit.: "days of old."
[2] Lit.: "name."
[3] Tg. Chr uses the plural of *'prky',* "eparchy, prefecture, province," borrowed from Greek *eparchia* (MJ 59 and JL I, 56).
[4] *'pryqy.* A name which refers sometimes to Africa, sometimes to Phrygia. The uncertainty is mirrored in *Gen. R.* 37:1, referring to Gen 10:2, where it is translated "Africa," but a footnote adds: "this probably refers to ancient Phrygia in Asia Minor...." See also Tg. 2 Chr 21:16, where the Cushites are called *'pryq'y,* usually regarded as "Africans." P. S. Alexander (*The Toponomy of the Targumim ...,* Ph.D. dissertation, Oxford, 1974) thinks that in Gen 10:2 it is Phrygia which is intended, as Gomer's sons and brothers are all located in the North in the Targumim (106–108).
[5] *grmny'* (for Magog): Germania, sometimes Germamia. JL (I, 155) thinks of Germany in its modern sense, MJ (270) thinks also of the land of the Cimmerii. In Tg. Ezek 27:14, "Germamia" is used for Beth-Togarmah. Alexander (121–124) thinks that in the Targumim it refers to *Germania barbara,* Germany east of the Rhine.
[6] *hmd'y* (for Madai): the Medes. Another reading in the next line gives *Hamadan,* the ancient capital of Media, better known as Ecbatana. (Alexander, 124f.). *mqdwny'* (for Javan): Macedonia: the province of that name.
[7] *wytyny'* (for Tubal): Bithynia, a region in northern Asia Minor.
[8] *'wsy'* (for Meshech): Usia, thought to be Musia (cf. C), i.e., Mysia in Asia Minor (Alexander, 126f.).
[9] *trqy* (for Tiras): Thracia or Thrace, in southeastern Europe.
[10] *gytyh:* perhaps Gothia (MJ 228), the land of the Goths.
[11] *'wbysws:* Ephesus (MJ 21); Euboea, a Greek island (JL I, 13).
[12] *'sy'* (for Ashkenaz): Asia: of three possibilities Alexander (108–110) selects the Roman province of Asia, which MJ (93) defines as "embracing the Western part of the peninsula of Asia Minor."
[13] *prkwwy* (for Diphath or Riphath): Parkevi: MJ (1229) name of a country in northern Ariana; JL (II, 291)—identity of land uncertain. *Gen. R.* 37:1 Adiabene. Alexander (110–112): Hyrcania, but in Palestinian Targums of Gen 10 refers to Parthia. Cf. Tg. Lam 4:21.
[14] *brbry'* (for Togarmah): Barbaria: an expression used to refer to a barbarian land, variously identified with a region in East Africa, North Africa, or Northern Europe. In the context of Gen 10 and 1 Chr 1:6, Northern Europe is the most likely area, Alexander (113–115); *Gen. R.* 37:1 Germania; Tg. Ezek 38:6 Germamia. M. McNamara (*Targum and Testament,* Shannon, 1972, 192), a region in Asia Minor.

The sons of Gomer: Asia, [12] *Derigath, and Germanicia.* [15]] 7. The sons of *Macedon: Hellas,* [16] *Tarsos,* [17] *Italy,* [18] *and Dardania.* [j][19] [*Another version reads: Elishah, Hellas,* [16] *Tusas,* [k] *Achzia,* [k] *and Dardania.* [19]] 8. The sons of Ham: *Arab,* [20] *Mizrayim,* [21] *Allihrok,* [22] and Canaan. 9. The sons of *Arab: the Sinidians,* [123] *the Indians,* [24] *the Semarians,* [25] *the Libyans,* [26] *Mauritanus,* [26] *and the Zingites.* [27] The

Apparatus, Chapter 1

[j] E: *dwdny'.*

[k] No alternative version is found in E, but C has an alternative version similar to that in V but with three additional names: "and the sons of Javan: Elishah, Alam, Tarsis, Achzavia, Dardinaya, Ridom, Hamer, and Antioch." The last three additional names appear in an alternative version at verse 16 in V.

[l] E, L, AS: *synr'y.* cf. Tg. Ps.-J. Gen 10:7: *synyr'y.*

Notes, Chapter 1

[15] *grmnqyh* (for Togarmah): Germanicia, MJ (270) "town (and district) in the province of Commagene, near the borders of Cappadocia." *Gen. R.* 37:1 after "Germania" for "Togarmah" (see previous note), "R. Berekiah said : Germanicia."

[16] *'ls* (and *'lsw* in C and *'lm* in alternative reading in C) (for Elishah): Ellas or Hellas. JL (I, 33) suggests Aeolis, a district in northwestern Asia Minor. MJ (72) and Alexander (116f.) prefer Hellas, as Greece—for MJ, *Graecia Magna*, which has a strong Italian connection; for Alexander, the narrower area of Greece, excluding the Peloponnese.

[17] *trsws* (for Tarshish): Tarsus: MJ (555) suggests Tarentum in Italy, but prefers Tartessus in Spain, as does JL (I, 320). Alexander (117f.), with Josephus, thinks Tarsus in Cilicia is the most likely place. Tg. 2 Chr 20:36, however, seems to locate it more specifically on the coast, "on the Great Sea."

[18] *'ytlywn* (for Kittim): Italion = Italy. The Kittim of MT become sometimes Achaia, a term which covers the Peloponnese, and later they are linked very closely with Italia, Greek Italy, i.e., Southern Italy (cf. Tg. Ezek 27:6, where the term used is "Apulia," a province in southeastern Italy). And often, in the thinking of Jews, Kittim, Italy was a term which signified Rome and her imperial domination (Alexander, 118–120, and M. McNamara, *Targum and Testament,* 196).

[19] *drdny'* (for Rodanim, though many Hebrew MSS and Gen 10:4 have Dodanim. *Gen. R.* 37:1 is aware of both readings): Dardania: of three possibilities, Alexander (121) prefers a location in northwestern Asia Minor. He notes that the city of Dardanus stands at the mouth of the river Rhodius (cf. the variant readings mentioned above).

[20] *'rb* (for Cush): Arab: which could refer to an inhabitant of Arabia or to the area known as Nabataea. Alexander (127–131) thinks that the Targumist in Gen 10:4 may have had Southern Arabia in mind.

[21] *msrym:* Egypt.

[22] *'lyhrq* (for Put): Alihroq: MJ (69), name of an Egyptian eparchy, probably Heracleotes (cf. Alexander, 131). JL (I, 30), name of an African tribe.

[23] *synyd'y* (for Seba): The Sinidians: it has been suggested that these were the inhabitants of Syene in Upper Egypt, modern Aswan. But nothing more is known.

[24] *hndq'y* (for Havilah): The Indians. The river Pishon (Gen 2:11), coming out of the Garden of Eden, "which flows around the whole land of Havilah," was equated with the Indus or the Ganges. See Tg. Ps.-J. Gen 2:11 (Alexander, 132–135).

[25] *smr'y* (for Sabta): The Semarians: there is uncertainty as to their identity. Perhaps "the inhabitants of Samareia" in northern Egypt (Alexander, 135).

[26] *lwb'y* and *mwwry'tynws* (for Raama): The Libyans and Mauritanus. "Libya" was an amorphous term that could refer to the whole of Africa or to that part which we call Libya, though even this latter usage could signify various areas. Alexander suggests (136–138) Mauretania, an area in northwest Africa along the Mediterranean.

[27] *yng'y* (for Sabteca): The Zingites, living on the East African coast in an area known by the Greeks as Azania (Alexander, 135f.).

sons of *Mauritanus:*[28] *Zemargad,*[29] and *Mezag.*[m][30] 10. *Arab* became the father of Nimrod: he was the first to be a mighty man *in sin, shedding innocent blood and a rebel before the Lord.*[31] 11. Mizrayim became the father of the *Niotites,*[n][32] the *Mareotites,*[o][33] the *Libyans,*[34] the *Pentaschianites,*[35] 12. the *Pentapolitites,*[36] the

Apparatus, Chapter 1

[m] E, L, AS: *mzgg.*

[n] E, L, AS: *nṭ'y.*

[o] E, L, AS: *mr't'y.*

Notes, Chapter 1

[28]MT: "Raama."

[29]*zmrgd* (for Sheba): Zemargad: Based on a word borrowed from Greek *smaragdos,* "emerald" (MJ 405; JL I, 225). This is probably a reference to "the region known as *Mons Smaragdus . . .* a mountain not far from the Red Sea coast of Egypt, just North of Berenice, where emeralds are mined" (Alexander, 139).

[30]*mzg* (for Dedan): Mezag is a name that refers to the Mazikes, a general designation for the Berbers (Alexander, 139f.). Note that in 1:32 Sheba and Dedan and their Aramaic equivalents appear as sons of Jokshan.

[31]MT: "in the earth." In MT this verse is identical with Gen 10:8. Gen 10:9 gives more information about Nimrod: he was a mighty hunter, his reputation in this connection becoming proverbial. Tg. Onq. adds nothing further, but Tg. Ps.-J., Frg. Tg., Tg. Neof. and Tg. Neof. (M) give considerable expansions, based largely on the "mighty man" of MT and on the name "Nimrod," which could be translated as "we shall rebel," from the root *marad,* "to rebel," though current standard lexicons would tend to disagree: *BDB,* 650, "etym. and meaning wholly unknown." As Gen 10:10 includes Babel in his kingdom, it is understandable that Nimrod should become a mighty man in sin and an arrogant rebel before the Lord. Tg. Chr includes both these emphases in its expansion but introduces an additional claim to his notoriety: "he shed innocent blood." The Targums reflect some of the unfavorable traditions associated with Nimrod in Jewish literature, which depict him as the rebellious sinner par excellence, e.g., in *b. Pes.* 94 a-b, R. Johanan b. Zakkai, commenting on one of Nebuchadnezzar's more arrogant statements (Isa 14:14) addressed him as: "Thou wicked man, son of a wicked man, descendant of the wicked Nimrod, who incited the whole world to rebel against me during his reign"—cf. *b. Ḥag.* 13a; Ps.-Philo, *LAB,* IV, 7; *Gen. R.* 37:2, and Rashi, who gives a detailed treatment of Gen 10:8, 9, along these lines.

Another nail in Nimrod's coffin in Jewish tradition was his clash with Abraham. Having read Abraham's birth in the stars and knowing that Abraham would challenge his arrogance, he massacred seventy thousand innocent children, hoping thereby to prevent his survival. Later, when Abraham smashed Nimrod's idols, Nimrod tried to burn him. (In Tg. 2 Chr 23:8 God delivers Abraham from the fiery furnace into which he had been cast because of his refusal to worship an idol.) The reference to Nimrod's shedding innocent blood in Tg. Chr may be a reference to the massacre of the innocents at the time of Abraham's birth. For this expression: "he shed innocent blood," cf. also Tg. Psalms 5:7; Tg. Onq. and Tg. Ps.-J. Deut 19:13.

Oddly enough, favorable traditions about Nimrod have also survived: see Tg. Ps.-J. Gen 10:11, Ibn Ezra and some Syriac Nestorian commentators quoted in A. Levene (*The Early Syrian Fathers on Genesis,* London, 1951, 81, 200), where Nimrod's name is used as a blessing. Thus, Tg. Chr, in dealing with Nimrod gives in summary fashion, under two heads, what the Gen Targums have said at considerable length: (a) mighty in sin; (b) a rebel before the Lord. Tg. Chr then adds a further charge: (c) a shedder of innocent blood.

[32]*nywt'y* (for Ludim): Niotites: R. Le Déaut translates as Nabateans; Alexander (155f.) emends to *nyswt'y,* the inhabitants of Nesut, on the coast of Egypt.

[33]*mrywt'y* (for Anamim): Mariotites: inhabitants of Mareotis, a district to the south of Alexandria (Alexander, 156).

[34]*lywwq'y* (for Lehabim): Libyans: using the Greek loan word *Libukoi,* a reference to the inhabitants of the Libyan district of Egypt (Alexander, 156).

[35]*pnṭskyyn'y* (for Naphtukim): Pentaschianites, inhabitants of Pentaschoinon, on the road from Palestine to Egypt (Alexander, 156).

[36]In MT Gen 10:14 and 1 Chr 1:12, the three names are in the same order: Pathrusim, Casluḥim and Caphtorim. The names attached to these names in Tg. Chr are the same as those attached in Tg. Ps.-J. Gen 10:14, but the first two names are in reverse order. Nonetheless, I shall take them in the order in which they come in Tg. Chr. *pntpwlyt'y* (for Pathrusim): Pentapolitites, the inhabitants of Pentapolis, i.e., Cyrenaica (Alexander, 158).

Nasiotites[p37]—from whom came the Philistines—and the *Cappadocians.*[38]
13. Canaan became the father of *Buthnias, who built* Sidon *and was Canaan's
firstborn,*[39] of Heth, 14. of the *Jebusites,*[40] the *Amorites,* the *Girgashites,* 15. the
Hivites, the *Arkites,* the *Anthusians,*[41] 16. the *Arethusians,*[q42] the *Emesians,*[43] and
the *Antiochenes.*[r44] [*Another*[s] *version reads: Ridus,*[45] *Emesa and Antioch.*] 17. The
sons of Shem: *the Elamites,*[46] *the Assyrians, the Arpachsadites,*[t] *the Ludites, the
Aramaeans,*[u47] *the Armannians,*[48] *the Hulites,*[49] *the Gethrites, and the Mashchites.*
18. *Arpachsad*[50] became the father of Shelah; and Shelah became the father of
Eber. 19. Two sons were born to Eber: the name of one was Peleg, because in his
days *the inhabitants of*[51] the earth were divided *according to their language;*[v52] the
name of his brother was Joktan, *because in his days the years of sons of man began*

Apparatus, Chapter 1

[p] E, L, AS: *ns't'y.*
[q] E, L, AS: *ltws'y.*
[r] E, L, AS: *'ntwk'y.*
[s] No alternative version is found in C or E.
[t] C, E, L, AS: *'rpsd'y.*

[u] E, L, AS omit, perhaps because of the close similarity to the next word. Or is there one word too many in V and C?
[v] "According to their language" missing in E, L, AS. (= Tg. Ps.-J. Gen 10:25).

Notes, Chapter 1

[37]*nsywt'y* (for Casluḥim): Nasiotites: MJ (261) emends to Casiotites, as does Alexander (157): the inhabitants of Casiotis, a district east of Pelusium in Egypt.

[38]*qpwtq'y* (for Caphtorim): Cappadocians: inhabitants of Cappadocia, in Asia Minor. See also Tg. Deut 2:23 (cf. LXX) and Tg. Jer 47:4 (Alexander, 158–160).

[39]MT: "the father of Sidon, his first-born."

[40]In this and the four following Gentilic nouns, MT uses the singular (collective) form while Tg. Chr uses the plural.

[41]*'ntws'y* (for Sinim): The Anthusians, or Orthosians, "the inhabitants of Orthosia in the Lebanon" (JL I, 44). According to *Gen. R.* 37:6, Orthosia is a Phoenician seaport.

[42]*lwts'y* (for Arvadites): Probably the Arethusii (MJ 697), the inhabitants of Arethusia, between Epiphania and Emesa. See 1 Macc 15:37. Beck (see app crit) sees the origin of the word in the Greek *litosaioi*—"seafarers."

[43]*hwms'y* (for Zemarites)—the Emesians—inhabitants of *hms,* Emesa (*hms*—see also alternative version in V at verse 16), a city in Syria on the eastern bank of the Orontes (MJ 479).

[44]*'ntywk'y* (for Hamathites): Antiochenes, the inhabitants of Antioch. In almost all cases Hamath in MT becomes Antioch in Tg. Chr, e.g., 1 Chr 18:9; 2 Chr 7:8.

[45]*rydws:* Arados, on the Phoenician coast (MJ 1456).

[46]Here and in the next three words, Tg. Chr changes the name of a "person" into a plural Gentilic form, e.g., MT's "Elam" becomes "Elamites." MT: Elam, Asshur, Arpachshad; and C, E, L, AS lose Lud.

[47]MT: *'ws.* Tg. 1 Chr 1:42 has *'rmnyws* for this same Hebrew word.

[48]*'rmnyy'y.* "The Armannians" (MJ 123), inhabitants of "Armannia (Romania, New Rome, Constantinople)."

[49]In this word and in the two following words the same pattern is followed as in note 46: Ḥul, Gether, Meshech.

[50]MT: "Arpachshad." Tg. Chr has "the Arpachsadites," but as it is followed by a singular verb, I have followed MT's singular name.

[51]"The inhabitants of" is found frequently in Tg. Chr where MT has simply "the earth/land."

[52]The expansion, based on the root *plg,* "to divide," has already begun in MT and continues in Tg. Chr, which limits the division to *the inhabitants of* the earth and provides the basis on which the division was made, viz., language. Only V and C include this basis, while the Targums to Gen 10:25 omit it altogether. The mention of "language" recalls the tower of Babel and the confusion of tongues, with overtones of God's punishment on an evil and arrogant generation (Gen 11:1-9), but no hint of blame or accusation emerges in Tg. Chr unless it is implied by association in the second half of this verse. See also Josephus, *Ant.* I, 146; *Jubilees* VIII, 8–30 and X, 18–27; *Gen. R.* 37:7.

to be cut short because of their sins.[53] 20. Joktan became the father of Almodad, *who measured and divided the land with ropes,*[54] Sheleph, *who diverted the rivers to the borders,*[55] Hazarmaveth, *who prepared ambushes to kill passersby,*[56] Jerah, *who set up inns and administered a deadly*[w] *poison to everyone who came in to eat and drink, and took everything he had.*[57] 21. Hadoram, Uzal, Diklah, 22. Ebal,[x]

Apparatus, Chapter 1

[w] V and C: "killing." E, L, AS: "deadly." For the partaker the effect was the same!

[x] E adds: "where gold comes from and Havilah where jewels come from," all of which seems to have been borrowed from verse 23, and is not found in verse 23 in E.

Notes, Chapter 1

[53]R. Le Déaut (I, 40 n. 12) suggests that this expansion is based, not on the root *qṭn,* but on the similar sounding root *qṭ',* "to cut (off)," a form of which is used in the expansion *l'tqṭ'.* We have a similar emphasis in *Yashar Noah* 17a (see Ginzberg, I, 172 and V, 193 n. 70), though there is no mention of "sins" as the reason for the cutting off. In Tg. Ruth 1:5 the days of Mahlon and Chilion were also cut off because of their sin in marrying into foreign nations. In Tg. Chr there is no suggestion that Joktan's sin was very great—indeed elsewhere he is regarded as a worthy man, e.g., in *Gen. R.* 6:4; 37:7, where, starting from the root *qṭn,* "to be small," Joktan is used as an illustration of the theme: "He that humbles himself shall be exalted." Cf. Rashi on Gen 10:25. *Ps.-Philo* V, 1; VI, 1-14 depict him as a God-fearing man who helps Abraham. In Tg. Chr Joktan shares the common lot of humanity whose days are shortened because of sin, and he has the misfortune to be used by Tg. Chr as a means of dating an unfortunate occurrence, though in the next verse Tg. Chr does not present his four sons in such a happy light.

[54]This expansion is found only here and partly in Tg. Ps.-J. Gen 10:26 ("who measured the earth with ropes") and is based on the Hebrew root *mdd,* "to measure," found in the word Almodad. "Earth" or "land" would be a suitable object for this measuring. *PRE* 30, speaking of what the children of Ishmael (referring no doubt to the Arabs) will do in the land in the latter days, says that "they will measure the land with ropes." The significance of the measuring and dividing is not clear, unless such a procedure was a means of obtaining exact measurements (see *m. B.B.* 7.1), perhaps to help encourage integrity in transactions involving land, perhaps as a prelude to a levying of taxes.

[55]Reading *'wšly'* with MJ 128. The expansion is based on the root *šlp,* "to draw, pull." A literal translation would read: "he drew the rivers to the borders." Various attempts have been made to explain this. JL (II, 489) suggests: "because he drew out the rivers from their beds (and used them) as borders." R. Le Déaut (I, 40) regards "borders" as "courses," "who directed the rivers according to their courses," though this too is confusing, as rivers normally run according to their courses without any need of diversion. MJ (1587): "he drew the rivers into his domain," the implication being that he had diverted the rivers in order to irrigate his own land. But this translation involves the introduction of a suffix which has no textual support. Tg. Ps.-J. Gen 10:26 is much simpler: "who drew the waters of the rivers," with no suggestion as to the purpose of his action. If Tg. Chr was trying to make Tg. Ps.-J.'s comment a little more specific, his efforts have led only to further confusion.

[56]Not the happiest name to bless a child with, "courtyard of death," but it provides the basis for this expansion. This man prepares an ambush, which for passers-by became their "courtyard of death," the place which led to their death. *Gen. R.* 37:8, commenting on Gen 10:26, has the same morbid approach with a different emphasis: Hazarmaveth has become a place "where people eat leeks, wear garments of papyrus and hope daily for death."

[57]In Tg. Chr, Jerah has been transformed into a poisoning, robbing innkeeper (not unlike his brother Hazarmaweth), but it is difficult to see the connection between his name and his activities. (a) There does not seem to be any link between the expansion and the meaning of the name in Hebrew, "new moon, month." (b) There may be some link between Jerah and the Hebrew and Aramaic root *'rḥ,* "to journey, take lodging" (cf. Joktan and the root *qṭ'* in verse 19) linking the name with the idea of lodging, guest, etc. (c) Beck sees "Jericho" as the operative word, as it introduces the notion of a robbers' cave. Though Le Déaut is unhappy with this connection, Jericho may have been notorious as a hideout for robbers. May not this be one of the reasons why Jesus told the story of the Good Samaritan in the way he did? A. Plummer (*St. Luke, ICC,* Edinburgh, 1898, 286 n. 1) mentions that "it was near Jericho that Pompey destroyed strongholds of brigands," and he refers to Strabo, *Geogr.* xvi.2.41. (d) Le Déaut (I, 41 n. 16) links Jerah with a town of similar name, Jerakh, at the southern end of Lake Tiberias, but while the names have similar sounds, the "poisoning, robbing" element is still unaccounted for.

Abimael,[y] Sheba,[y] 23. Ophir, *where gold comes from,*[58] Havilah, *where jewels*[59] *come from,*[60] and Jobab. All these were the sons of Joktan. 24. Shem *the great priest,*[61] Arpachshad,[z62] Shelah, 25.[aa] Eber, Peleg,[bb] Reu,[bb] 26. Serug, Nahor,[bb] Terah,[bb] 27. Abram, that is, Abraham. 28. The sons of Abraham: Isaac and Ishmael. 29. These are their generations: the first-born of Ishmael, *Nebat,*[63] then *Arab,*[64] Adbeel, Mibsam, 30. *Zayetha, Shethoka, Mesobara, Harepha, Adroma,*[65] 31. [cc]Jetur, Naphish, and *Kidduma.*[66] These are the sons of Ishmael. 32. The sons

Apparatus, Chapter 1

[y] E omits.
[z] E, L, AS: *'rpsdy.* C = V.
[aa] E omits verses 25-28.
[bb] V omits.

[cc] E, L, AS reproduce the last two words of the Hebrew text of the preceding verse at the beginning of verse 31.

Notes, Chapter 1

[58]The name of Joktan's son becomes a place name. In the OT Ophir and gold are associated (cf. 1 Kgs 10:11 and Job 22:24), so it is natural, if a little superfluous, for the Targumist to record this association.

[59]Tg. Chr uses the plural of *mrglyt',* "gem, jewel, pearl," borrowed from Greek *margarites* (MJ 836; JL II, 66).

[60]This personal name has also become a place name. In Gen 2:11 it was a land famous for its precious stones. See also note 24.

[61]Shem is mentioned three times in chapter 1 (in verses 4, 17, 24), but only here is he accorded an expansion, albeit a "compressed expansion." It is generally accepted that here we have a reference to Melchizedek, whom the Gen Targums (less Tg. Onq.) of 14:18 equate with Shem, and though they do not refer to Shem as a priest, Tg. Neof. and Frg. Tg. call him "Shem the great." This may reflect an attempt by Jews to challenge Christian claims, e.g., in the Letter to the Hebrews and Church Fathers, that the priesthood of Christ was superior to the Levitical priesthood because Christ's priesthood was derived from Melchizedek's priesthood (Ps 110:4), to whom Abraham had offered a tithe (Gen 14:20), thereby acknowledging Melchizedek's superiority, and as at this point Levi was in the loins of Abraham, the priesthood of Levi was therefore inferior to that of Melchizedek. (Heb 7, esp. verses 1-10).

Melchizedek was held in high esteem by Philo (*De Abr.,* sect. 235; *Leg. Alleg.,* III, sects. 79-82), who called him "great priest"; by 11 *Q Melchizedek* (see F. L. Horton, *The Melchizedek Tradition,* Cambridge, 1976, esp. 56); and by Josephus (*War,* VI, 438 and *Ant.* I, 179-181), who on the whole regarded him as a priest, as a larger-than-life figure, and as a friend of Abraham; but when this ancestorless non-Jew became a weapon in the armory of the Christians in their attempt to discredit Jewish institutions, Judaism's reply was to equate Melchizedek with Shem, thus providing him with a genealogy (Gen 10:1; 11:10-26; *b. Ned.* 32b). J. Bowker (*The Targums and Rabbinic Literature,* Cambridge, 1969, 198): "Melchizedek, by being identified with Shem, was brought firmly inside the Jewish fold, and thus no priesthood was admitted outside Judaism" (cf. *Midr. Teh.* on Ps 37:1 and on Ps 76:3; Ephrem also refers to it: R. Murray, *Symbols of Church and Kingdom,* Cambridge, 1975, 180). But why should Melchizedek be equated with Shem? Did Shem have some "priest potential"? C. Spicq (J. Fitzmyer, 230 n. 32) finds the answer in the fact that from Adam to Levi, the cult was supposed to have been cared for by the first-born, Shem being the first-born of Noah. Gen. 38 may also be relevant in this connection. In Gen 38 the conduct of both Judah and his daughter-in-law Tamar leaves a lot to be desired, though Judah does admit that she has been more righteous than he. Tamar, however, like Melchizedek, is also without ancestry, and as she will in due course claim David among her descendants, it is important that her pedigree be "correct." This the Rabbis ensure by making Shem the father of Tamar (*b. Meg.* 10b; *Gen. R.* 85:10; *Gen. R.* 13:4). This process of priesting Shem may have been encouraged by drawing the implications of the combination of Gen 38:24 with Lev 21:9.

[62]MT: *'rpkšd.*

[63]MT: *nbywt.* Nebat, according to MJ (868) and JL (II, 85) is Nabatea, though *ICC* (72) notes: "Whether the Nebaioth were the later Nabateans is uncertain." In Tg. Ps.-J. Gen 25:13, Nebaioth also becomes Nebat.

[64]MT: "Qedar." In Tg. Ezek 27:21, Qedar becomes Nabatea.

[65]Tg. Chr gives us the five Aramaic equivalents of five Hebrew names, which mean: Listening, Silence, Burden (bearer), Sharp One, South. See also Tg. Ps.-J. Gen 25:14-15.

[66]Tg. Chr provides the Aramaic equivalent of the Hebrew word in MT, "east, or eastward."

of Keturah, Abraham's concubine:[67] she bore[dd] Zimran, Jokshan, Medan, Midian, Ishbak, and Shuah. The sons of Jokshan: *Zemargad*[ee] *and Mezag.*[68] 33. The sons of Midian: *Hawelad,*[69] Epher, Hanoch, Abida, and Eldaah. All these were the sons of Keturah. 34.[ff] Abraham became the father of Isaac. The sons of Isaac: Esau and Israel. 35.[gg] The sons of Esau: Eliphaz, Reuel, Jeush, Jalam, and Korah. 36. The sons of Eliphaz: Teman, Omar, Zephi, Gatam, Kenaz, Timna, and Amalek. 37. The sons of Reuel: Nahath, Zerah, Shammah, and Mizzah. 38. The sons of *Gebal:*[70] *the Lotites,*[71] *the Shobalites,*[72] Zibeon, Anah, *Dithon,*[73] Ezer, and *Dithan.*[hh] 39.[ii] The[jj] sons of Lotan: Hori, and Homam; Lotan's sister was Timna. 40. The sons of Shobal: Alian, Manahath, Ebal, Sheph, and Onam. The sons of Zibeon: Aiah, and Anah. 41. The sons of Anah: Dishon. The sons of Dishon: Hamran, Eshban, Ithran, and Cheran. 42. The sons of Ezer: Bilhan, Zaavan, and Jaakan. The sons of *Dithan:*[kk][74] *Armanios,*[75] and Aran. 43. These are the kings who ruled over the land of Edom before there was a king to rule over the children of Israel: *Balaam,*[76] *the Villain, the son of Beor. He is Laban, the Aramean, who allied himself with the sons of Esau, in order to destroy Jacob and his sons, and he tried to wipe them out. He ruled over Edom and* the name of his *capital* city[77] was Dinhabah, *which had been*

Apparatus, Chapter 1

[dd] E, L, AS have Aphel; V has Peal. C omits.

[ee] E, L, AS: *zmrgz.*

[ff] Verses 34 (except for "became the father of"), 35–37 missing in E.

[gg] The last four words in verse 35, the last seven words in verse 36, and the last three words in verse 37 are missing in V. Translation follows C.

[hh] E, L, AS: *dyšwn.*

[ii] E omits verses 39–42a.

[jj] The last five words in verse 39, the last four words in verse 40 and the last six words in verse 41 are missing in V. Translation follows C.

[kk] C: *dytwn.*

Notes, Chapter 1

[67] Tg. Chr uses the word *plqt*, "concubine," borrowed from Greek (JL II, 271).

[68] The same two words appear in Hebrew and in Aramaic as in verse 9, but this time they are the sons of Jokshan. See notes 29 and 30.

[69] MT: *'yph.* See Tg. Isa 60:6, where the same Hebrew word becomes *hwlk.*

[70] MT: "Seir." MJ (207) Gabla, Gabalena, "a district (and town) south or southwest of Jerusalem, occupied by Edomites." This is Tg. Chr's normal word for Seir, but note Tg. 2 Chr 25:11.

[71] MT: *lwṭn.*

[72] MT: *šwbl.*

[73] MT: *dyšn.*

[74] MT: *dyšwn.*

[75] MT: *'wṣ.* In 1:17, "Armannia" is the Aramaic rendering for this word. See note 48.

[76] MT: *bl'.*

[77] Lit.: "the city of the house of his kingdom."

given to him as a free gift.[78] 44. Bela[79] died—*Phinehas killed him in the wilderness*[79]—and Jobab, the son of Zerah, from *Butra*,[80] reigned in his place. 45. Jobab died and Husham, *who was* from the land of the *south*,[81] became king in his place. 46. Husham died, and Hadad, the son of Bedad, became king in his place; it was he who *killed*[82] the Midianites in the *fields*[ll] *of the Moabites when they*

Apparatus, Chapter 1

[ll] For "the fields of (Moab)," V, C, L, AS have *bḥqly*.
E has *bḥlqy*, alternative spelling; cf. Tg. 1 Chr 8:8 and JL I, 263.

Notes, Chapter 1

[78]Bela, the first king of Edom in MT, has in Tg. Chr become Balaam who cursed/blessed Israel, an identification which some scholars accept (see Curtis, *ICC,* 77). In the parallel passage in Gen 36:31-32, Tg. Ps.-J. in Ginsberger's edition also calls him Balaam, but Rieder insists on calling him Bela, with Balaam reduced to the status of a variant reading. Tg. Ps.-J. makes no further comment on that verse. But in Tg. Ps.-J. Num 22:5 and Num 31:8, Balaam and Laban are identified, giving a rather unpleasant composite picture similar to the expansion in Tg. Chr. In Tg. Ps.-J. Num 22:5, the expansion is based on the root *blʿ* "to swallow up": "Balaam, who sought to swallow up the people of Israel" (cf. *b. San.* 105a), though this basis is not even hinted at in Tg. Chr, the two "destructive" verbs used being entirely different. Of Balaam, Tg. Chr tells us:

a) *He was wicked.* The OT depicts Balaam in a not unfavorable light. But in Jewish tradition he becomes a shiftless, evil-minded, vicious hater of Israel. Vermes (*Scripture and Tradition in Judaism,* Leiden, 1961, 175) suggests that the Rabbis took one stratum of the Balaam story, as found in Num 31:8, 16; Josh 13:22, and used this as the basis for their very negative approach (see also *m. Ab.* 5:19; *b. San.* 105b, 106b and cf. NT references 2 Pet 2:15, 16; Jude 11; Rev 2:14). He thus becomes "the wicked Man, *par excellence*" (Vermes, 174).

b) *He was Laban the Aramean.* In Genesis, Laban, the brother of Rebecca, appears as a rather wily Oriental. The Rabbis, however, emphasized this aspect of his character so much that they depicted him as arrogant, avaricious, and cunning, summing him up anagramatically as: Laban *'rmy* (the Aramean) is Laban *rm'y* (the imposter, cheat) (*Gen. R.* 63:4 and 70:19). It is not clear just why these two were identified—perhaps because of similar unfortunate character traits or because each in his own way had tried to harm Israel.

c) *He tried to destroy Israel.* Two incidents may be in question here: Balaam's attempt, as one of Pharaoh's counsellors, to wipe out the male children (Tg. Ps.-J. Num 31:8; *Exod. R.* 27:3, 6). Thwarted in Egypt, he had incited the Amalekites (descendants of Esau) to accomplish what he had failed to achieve (*Est. R.* 7:13).

d) *He ruled over Edom:* a rather gratuitous statement, as we have been told already that he was a king of Edom, but, bearing in mind the later constant unhappy relationships between Israel and Edom, such a comment would not be reckoned to Balaam for righteousness.

e) *His capital city was Dinhabah, which had been given to him as a gift.* This expansion is an attempt to link the town with the root *yhb,* "to give." We are given no indication of the reason for this gift. But see also *Yashar Shemoth,* quoted by Ginzberg (II, 156f. and V, 372 nn. 424 and 425), where Bela, son of Beor, is Edom's first warrior-king and reigns happily for thirty years. Later (II, 159) a Balaam, son of Beor, with certain magical powers, comes on the scene. Thus some did not accept the Bela-Balaam identification nor the thought that Balaam was king of Edom.

[79]Bela has been identified with Balaam in verse 43, and one would expect the identification to appear here also in Tg. Chr. Surprisingly, it is Bela who is spoken of, not Balaam, though it is clear that now in the Targumist's mind the two are interchangeable, for the expansion which follows, telling us how Bela died, is found elsewhere in relation to Balaam. In MT Num 31:8 Balaam's death is stated quite briefly: "and they also slew Balaam the son of Beor with the sword." Tg. Ps.-J. of this verse gives us a story of aerial combat between Phinehas the priest (though *b. San.* 106b calls him "a robber") and Balaam, the latter finally meeting his end by the sword of Phinehas. The expansion may (Vermes, 171) be based on the word *'l,* "on, upon, over," of Num 31:8, "on (RSV translates "with") their slain," and here we have a compressed form of it.

[80]MT: *bṣrh.*

[81]MT: "Temanite." In Hebrew, Teman is a northern district of Edom and can also mean "south," which is how Tg. Chr takes it.

[82]MT: "who struck down Midian in the field(s) of Moab."

went forth to meet them in battle.[83] The name of his *capital* city was *Avith.*[84]
47. Hadad died and Samlah, *who was* from *Mashrekah,*[85] became king in his place.
48.[mm] Samlah died and Saul, *who was from Palyutha,*[86] *the great city which was
built on the bank of the Euphrates,*[87] became king in his place. 49. Saul died and
Baalhanan, the son of Achbor, became king in his place. 50. Baalhanan, *the son of
Achbor,*[nn] died, and Hadad[oo] became king in his place. The name of his *capital* city
was Pai,[pp] and the name of his[88] wife Mehetabel, the daughter of Matred, *who
worked*[qq] *with hunter's spear and net, and when he became rich and acquired possessions, he became proud and altered his outlook*[89] *saying: "What is silver and what is*

Apparatus, Chapter 1

[mm] E omits verses 48-49.
[nn] Missing in C, E, L, AS.
[oo] V has *hdd* as in MT, but C, L, AS have *hdr*, found
in some Hebrew MSS and Gen 36:39. It is the verb
hdr that is used in the expansion in this verse and
in verse 51.

[pp] E, L, AS have *p'w*, which is found in many Hebrew
MSS, LXX (L), Syr, Vg, and in Gen 36:39.
[qq] E has feminine.

Notes, Chapter 1

[83] A similar expansion is found in Tg. Ps.-J. of the parallel verse in Gen 36:35, but there the singular personal pronoun is retained: "when *he* went forth to meet them" (clearly "them" are "the Midianites"). Tg. Chr, however, by
shifting a clause and changing a "he" to "they," leaves some ambiguity as to the identity of "they" and "them," as to
who went out to meet whom in battle. "Hadad, who slew the Midianites in the fields of the Moabites when *they* went
out to meet *them* in battle." Rashi, at Gen 36:35, remarks that "Midian attacked Moab, whereupon Edom came to
its help and defeated Midian." Ginzberg (II, 164), relying on *Yashar Shemoth*, also refers to a battle in which
Midianites had attacked Moabites, having been let down by the Moabites in a previous battle against Hadad, and
Hadad came to the rescue of the Moabites by attacking the Midianites. From MT it is clear that some battle of
Edom against Midian in Moab lived on in the folk memory, but whether the frame which is given to this picture in
some of the traditions quoted brings us any nearer to historical reality is another matter.
[84] Tg. Chr follows Qere. Kethibh is *'ywt*.
[85] MT: *msrqh*.
[86] Reading *pltywt'* with C, L, AS for V's *plyywt'*. As the word seems to be an Aramaic version of the corresponding
Hebrew word, V's reading does not fit very well!
[87] MT has "Rehoboth of/on the River." Tg. Chr takes the meaning of the first word, "open places," and reproduces
it in an Aramaic form (cf. 1:30), Paltyutha or Pelatyutha, based on the Greek loan word *plateia*, "open place." All the
Targums of Gen 36:37 retain the Hebrew name (though Tg. Neof. replaces the whole expression with "from Mesopo-
tamia"), as do the LXX, Syr, and Vg translations of both the Genesis and Chronicles verses. Tg. Chr then takes the
second word, "the river," which sometimes in MT refers to the Euphrates and which here stands in an uncertain relationship to the previous word. Tg. Chr, like all the Genesis Targums (less Tg. Neof.) and like some English translations of this Chronicles verse, specifies "the river" as the Euphrates (though not all commentators on the MT would
agree; see *ICC*, 78) and removes the relationship ambiguity by inserting *"which was built on the bank of."* It is interesting that the Syriac translators do not seem to have been aware of the existence of this large town, though the
Levenne Nestorian Commentary identifies a similar expression in Gen 10:11 with Arbel or perhaps Adiabene. The
Vulgate has a translation not unlike that of Tg. Chr: "de Rooboth quae iuxta amnem sita est."
[88] MT: "his wife." Only V lacks "his."
[89] Lit.: "went around."

gold?"[90] 51. *Hadar*[91] died *and the kingdom ceased from them because the land was conquered by*[92] *the children of Esau.* The princes of *the Edomites,*[93] *rulers in the land of Gebala,* were prince *Timnath,*[rr][94] prince Alwah,[95] prince Jetheth, 52.[ss] prince Oholibamah, prince Elah, prince Pinon, 53. prince Kenaz, prince Teman, prince Mibzar, 54. prince Magdiel, prince Iram. These were the princes of *the Edomites.*[93]

Apparatus, Chapter 1

[rr] V: *tmnt.* C, E, L, AS: *tmn'* (= MT).

[ss] Verse 52 after first word and all of verse 53 are missing in E.

Notes, Chapter 1

[90] The parallel verse in Gen 36:39 has an expansion in all four Targums, three of which, Tg. Ps.-J., Frg. Tg. and Tg. Neof., are quite similar to Tg. Chr. In Tg. Chr there are three pillars on which the expansion rests:

i) *Matred:* he became wealthy by using his *matredutha* ("hunting spear") and net.

ii) *Hadar:* as a verb this word means "he turned around"—his new wealth altered his whole outlook, and now he treats it with contempt.

iii) *Mezahab:* though originally meaning "waters of gold," it is seen to mean "What is gold (and silver)?"—either an expression of disdain or an indication that he knew the value of money.

There are certain peculiarities in this and the other expansions:

i) Hadad and Hadar seem almost interchangeable as the king's name, though it is Hadar which is used in the expansion (Beck uses Hadad and Frg. Tg. uses Hazar, bearing out the truth of Vermes' comment that "a combination of variant readings in the interpretation of a text is a characteristic of midrashic exegesis" (160).

ii) Apart from Frg. Tg. (and perhaps Beck), Matred has become male, though in MT of both Genesis and Chronicles she is clearly female. This gender problem is reflected in Pesh.

iii) "Hunter's spear" is Jastrow's translation of *matredutha.* JL, however, gives a different translation, *Beschäftigung:* "weil er bemüht war mit Beschäftigung" (II, 30). A similar emphasis is found in D. Wilkins' translation of MS C and in M. L. Klein's translation of Frg. Tg. (MS P): "trade" (II, 24).

One can see how these expansions could be used homiletically to stress, e.g., (a) diligence brings prosperity; (b) prosperity may lead to pride; (c) money is not all-important; (d) only the diligent know the value of money. There are other interpretations of this verse, e.g., *Gen. R.* 73:4.

[91] MT: "Hadad." Hadad, the last king of Edom, dies rather abruptly, and MT leads straight into a list of princes. Tg. Chr smooths the transition by pointing out that the monarchy had ceased because of a takeover by the sons of Esau. Edom and Esau are often thought of as coterminous, but J. R. Bartlett (*JTS* 20 [1969] 7ff.) regards this as an oversimplification, for at times they are also regarded as quite distinct. Thus Tg. Chr seems to be saying that the Edomite monarchy ceased to exist when Edom was overrun by a group resident in Seir (Gebala), i.e., a part, not the whole, of Edom. If the two sentences in Tg. Chr are meant to be chronologically connected, the "princes of Edom" may refer to a counterrevolution by the Edomites, whose princes now are listed, or it may be a reference to appointees following a Roman takeover (see *Yashar Shemoth,* Ginzberg II, 166).

[92] Lit.: "before."

[93] MT: "Edom."

[94] MT: *tmn'.*

[95] Tg. Chr follows Qere. Kethibh is *'lyh.*

CHAPTER 2

1. *a* These are the sons of Israel: Reuben, Simeon, Levi and Judah, Issachar and Zebulun, Dan, *b* Joseph, and Benjamin, Naphtali, Gad and Asher. 2. The sons of Judah: Er and Onan and Shelah; *the* three *of them were*[1] born to him, 3. by the daughter of Shua, *the trading woman.* *c*[2] Er *and Onan were doing what was* evil *before*[3] the Lord and he killed *them because they were corrupting their ways.*[4] 4. Tamar, his daughter–in–law, also bore him Perez and Zerah. The sons of

Apparatus, Chapter 2

a E omits verses 1-29.
b DW, L, and AS follow the verse division of MT.

c C, L, and AS: *prqmtyt*'.

Notes, Chapter 2

[1] MT has the singular form of verb, though one Hebrew MS has the plural.

[2] Tg. Chr has *prqmt(y)t*', borrowed from Greek *pragmateutēs* (MJ 1214) or *pragmatikē* (JL II, 300), "trader." MT has *hkn'nyt*, "the Canaanitess," though in Hebrew this word has also a non-ethnic meaning, "trader, merchant" (Job 40:30; Zeph 1:11; see BDB 489); cf. Tg. Ps.-J. Gen 38:2: "the daughter of a man, a merchant." Is it possible that, as in Ps.-J., Tg. Chr, by making Bathshua "a trading woman," is making it clear that the ancestors had not been in breach of the later law which forbade marriage with Canaanites, e.g., Exod 34:16; Deut 7:3? It is interesting that MT Gen 38:2, "the daughter of a man, a Canaanite, whose name was Shua," has become in MT 1 Chr 2:3 "the daughter of Bath Shua, the Canaanitess."

[3] MT: "in the eyes of."

[4] MT: "And Er, the first-born of Judah, was evil in the eyes of the Lord and he put him to death." The inclusion of Onan in Tg. Chr may give credence to Rudolph's suggestion (p. 15 and *app. crit.* of BHS) that the reference to Onan, which is found in the parallel verse in Gen 38:10, may have failed to appear in 1 Chr 2:3 because of homoioteleuton. ICC (84), however, does not think that the omission here is accidental, as the Chronicler sometimes gives only part of the story, assuming that his readers are familiar with the complete story—in this case, Onan's sin of making his semen ineffective. In MT there are four references to this incident: Gen 38:7-10; 46:12; Num 26:19; 1 Chr 2:3, but only in the first passage is Onan's sin specifically mentioned. In Gen 38:9 it is described thus: *wšḥt 'rṣh*, lit. "And he corrupted/spoiled earthwards," which is usually interpreted, e.g., *BDB* (1008): "he spoiled (it) upon the ground, made it ineffective . . . ," the "it" referring to semen (cf. Vg). Tg. Ps.-J. and Tg. Neof. translate this clause using the same wording: "he destroyed his works upon the ground" (following McNamara's translation of Tg. Neof. in Díez Macho, *Neophyti 1* [Madrid, 1968] 602), each using the root *ḥbl* as the operative verb.

What, then, of Er's sin in Gen 38:7? Only Tg. Ps.-J. tells us what this was—that he did not perform his marital duty to his wife, obviously similar to Onan's sin. The same Targum to Gen 46:12 and to Num 26:19, by speaking of the deaths of Er and Onan and their wickedness in the same breath, seems to regard both of them as guilty of similar, if not identical, sins. Cf. *b. Yeb.* 34b: "Er and Onan indulged in unnatural intercourse." There is no problem about Onan's guilt, but how can the same be attributed to Er? *b. Yeb.* goes on: "R. Nahman b. Isaac replied: It is written, *and he slew him also*, he also died of the same death," "also" being the operative word, in accordance with the first of the "two and thirty Middoth" ascribed to Eliezer ben Jose Ha-gelili, as given by H. L. Strack, *Introduction to the Talmud and Midrash*, 1931, 96: "*Ribbui*. The particles *'af, gam, 'eth* indicate an inclusion or amplification." Nahmanides, however, simply notes: "His sin is not indicated, save that he died for his own sin . . ." (A. Cohen, ed., *The Soncino Chumash*, 237).

In Gen 38:9, Tg. Onq. has a different approach. Speaking of Onan, it uses the same verb as Tg. Ps.-J. and Tg. Neof., *ḥbl*, but supplies a different object. Instead of "he destroyed his works upon the ground," Tg. Onq. has: "he destroyed/corrupted his way upon the ground." In a sense, Tg. Chr brings Tg. Ps.-J. and Tg. Onq. together: it regards Er and Onan as equally guilty (one assumes of the same sin), but the expression used to denote it is very close to Tg. Onq.: "because they were corrupting their ways." Before making a claim that there is a link here between Tg. Onq. and Tg. Chr, one should remember that the expression in Tg. Onq. is very similar to that used in Gen 6:12, both in MT and in the various Targums: "for all flesh had corrupted (Heb: *šḥt*; Aram: *ḥbl*) its way upon the earth." In due

Judah—five in all. 5. The sons of Perez: Hezron and Hamul. 6. The sons of Zerah: Zimri, Ethan, Heman, Calcol, and Dara: *d* all of them *officials upon whom the spirit of prophecy rested*[5]—*there were* five *of them*. 7. The sons of Carmi, *that is, Zimri:* Achar, *that is, Achan,* who troubled Israel *when they fled and fell before the men of Ai because*[6] he had acted deceitfully in the matter of the devoted thing. 8. The sons

Apparatus, Chapter 2

d C, L, and AS: *drd'*, as many Hebrew MSS, Syr;
and MT of 1 Kgs 5:11 (EVV 4:31).

Notes, Chapter 2

course this expression was interpreted with a specifically sexual emphasis, e.g., *b. Ab. Zar.* 23b; *b. San.* 108a; *Gen. R.* 27:8; *PRE* (p. 162), which actually links Gen 6:12 with Gen 38:9. Thus while Tg. Chr regards Er and Onan as equally guilty and though he speaks in general terms of the sin of Er and Onan in the first part of the verse, the very expression he uses in the second part of the verse makes it clear that he is in no doubt as to the nature of their sin.

[5]The seeds of this expansion must lie in the inherent abilities of the group even though there may be some uncertainty as to the actual identity of all the names. 1 Kgs 5:11 (EV 4:31) refers to Ethan the Ezrahite, along with Heman, Calcol, and Darda. In 1 Chr 2:6, Ethan becomes the son of Zerah, the same transformation taking place in Tg. Jonathan to 1 Kgs 5:11. It seems reasonable that Tg. Chr, aware of what had happened in his text and had also happened in Tg. Jonathan, and aware of the link with officialdom (Heman, the king's seer—1 Chr 25:5; Tg. Chr: the king's prophet), temple music (Heman and Ethan, singers—1 Chr 15:17; Heman's sons to prophesy with musical instruments—1 Chr 25:1; Heman and Ethan—psalm titles: Pss 88 and 89; Zimri, perhaps originally Zabdi, but now with a very musical name, root *zmr*, "to make music"), wisdom (Ethan, Heman, Calcol, Darda—1 Kgs 5:11) with all this potential, Tg. Chr has no hesitation in pouring on them all "the spirit of prophecy," indeed calling them *'mrkwlyn*, written more usually as *'mrklyn*, a term denoting officers of considerable status on the Temple staff. (MJ 79 lists the *Amarkal* as "one of the seven Temple trustees superintending the cashiers." See also JL I, 38–39, *Num. R.* 6:1 and *Schürer*, rev. ed., II, 282–283: "The *amarkelin* . . . also probably belong to the category of officers of the treasury" (282). See also references in Tg. Chr.) The sons of Zerah are highly esteemed in various Jewish traditions, e.g., *Pes. R.* 14:9; *Seder Olam*, sect. 21, where they are prophets in Egypt; see Ginzberg II, 283 and V, 407.

[6]In Josh 7:24, 25, 26, Achan is the name mentioned, though the etymological references clearly presuppose "Achar." In MT 1 Chr 2:7, Achar is the name used, fitting in neatly with the "troubler" aspect (verb *'kr*), but Tg. Chr also brings in a qualifying identification with the better-known name "Achan" from Josh 7, and to this is added an abbreviated history of Achan's misdeeds and their effects. The identification between Carmi and Zimri is more complex. It may be that the identification was made originally on "occupational grounds": Carmi may be connected with *krm*, "vineyard," and the three occurrences of II *zmr*, "to trim, prune" (see *BDB*, 274) in Lev. 25:3, 4, and Isa 5:6, each refer to pruning a vineyard.

There are two Zimris in question here:

a) The Zimri of Num 25 (esp. v. 14), who brings a Midianite woman into the camp with disastrous consequences and is slain by Phinehas. This Zimri became well known in Jewish tradition as a rebellious apostate, "a symbol for the worst rebellion against God and his Torah" (*EJ*, Vol. 16, 1027), a man who flouted God's and Moses' commandment, brought a massacre on his people and a shameful death on himself and his "bride." Even Aprahat and Ephrem refer to him with horror. Saul, a Simeonite, is identified with him in Tg. Ps.-J. Exod 6:15: "that is, Zimri, who lent himself to debauchery like the Canaanites." Cf. *b. San.* 82a and b; Tg. Ps.-J. Gen 46:10; Tg. 1 Chr 4:24; *Num. R.* 20:24; 1 Macc 2:26.

b) Zimri, son of Zerah. If Carmi is identified with this Zimri, then Zimri becomes the father of Achan. This introduces a problem of relationships, for elsewhere in Rabbinic traditions, (e.g., *b. San.* 44a-b; *Lev. R.* 9:1) Zimri and Achan are identified, and sometimes it is the Zimri of Num 25 that is being referred to and sometimes the Zimri of 1 Chr 2:7. Such complications did not worry the Jewish exegetes. When a homiletical point is being made, tribal, family, and generation barriers are completely disregarded. It may be, then, that the intention in Tg. 1 Chr 2:7 is to portray Achar in the worst possible light. Tg. Chr does this by giving us *after* Achar the identification with Achan, followed by an abbreviated history of Achan's misdeeds and their consequences, and then by unobtrusively placing Zimri, with all the memories which this name would call up in the believer's mind, *before* Achar—he has thus succeeded in thoroughly "evilizing" Achar.

of Ethan: Azariah. 9. The sons of Hezron, who *were*[7] born to him *in Timnath:*[8] Jerahmeel, Ram, and Chelubai. 10. Ram became the father of Amminadab, and Amminadab became the father of Nahshon, leader of *the clan of*[9] the sons of Judah. 11. Nahshon became the father of *Shalma;*[10] *Shalma*[10] became the father of Boaz. 12. Boaz became the father of Obed; Obed became the father of Jesse. 13. Jesse[e] became the father of Eliab, his first-born; Abinadab, the second; Shimea, the third; 14. Nethanel, the fourth; Raddai, the fifth; 15. Ozem, the sixth; David, the seventh; 16. Their sisters were Zeruiah and Abigail. The sons of Zeruiah: Abishai, Joab, and Asahel, *the* three *of them men.*[11] 17. Abigail bore Amasa, and the father of Amasa was Jether, *the Israelite;*[12] *they called him Jether, the Ishmaelite, however, because he girded his loins with a sword to help David, like an Arab,[f] when Abner tried to exclude David and the whole of Jesse's family, so that they would not be eligible to enter the congregation of the Lord because of the affair of Ruth, the Moabitess.*[13] 18. Caleb, the son of Hezron, had children[14] by[15] his[15]

Apparatus, Chapter 2

[e] C, L, and AS: *yšy.* V: *'yšy,* which is the reading of MT.

[f] For *hy k'rb'h,* "like an Arab," C, L, and AS have *b'rk'h.* Both MJ and JL prefer the latter reading. MJ (1119) translates the noun *'rk'h* as "registration of legitimacy, citizens' list," giving in this verse the meaning "to assist David in establishing his legitimacy of citizenship." JL (II, 245) translates the noun as *Obrigkeit,* giving the translation "um dem David behilflich zu sein bei der Obrigkeit." DW actually translates the C reading as "cum Arabibus."

Notes, Chapter 2

[7]MT has singular form of verb. Cf. note 1.

[8]Tg. Chr locates the birthplace of the three sons of Hezron, son of Perez, son of Judah, by rounding off with an adverbial expression a rather clumsy relative clause. The Old Testament does not tell us that these sons were born in Timnath. Possibly we have here a reference to the Timnah to which Judah was traveling when he was waylaid by his daughter-in-law Tamar, who, as a result, bore him Perez and Zerah. The site of Timnah is uncertain, and the Rabbis were unsure if it was the same Timnah where Samson was born (Judg 14:1). See *b. Soṭ.* 10a and *y. Soṭ.* 17a. *Gen. R.* 85:6 regards Timnah as important because of a kingly connection, the suggestion being that the Rabbis assumed Perez, the ancestor of David, was born there, and it would seem that Tg. Chr regarded his grandchildren as being born there too.

[9]LXX has "the house of."

[10]V and C. MT: "Salma."

[11]Translating according to the vowels of V and C. A slight change in pointing would give the more satisfactory translation "mighty men," as with Le Déaut.

[12]MT: "Ishmaelite," but one Hebrew MS, MT, and the Targum of 2 Sam 17:25 have "Israelite."

[13]This expansion is based on the fact that in the Hebrew text before him Tg. Chr saw "Jether the Ishmaelite," which he altered to "Jether the Israelite" and justified his alteration in his expansion, which has five components: Jether the Israelite/Ishmaelite; Jether the swordsman and supporter of David; the Arab connection; Abner the exclusivist; and Ruth the Moabitess. Bearing in mind the prohibition of Deut 23:4, did Ruth, the Moabitess (and, by extension, David) have any right to be part of the congregation of Israel? Ruth 2:10-12 is unaware of any problem, but Tg. Ruth is very much aware of it and solves it by stating that Deut 23:4 applied only to males, cf. m. Yeb. 8.3: "An Ammonite or a Moabite is forbidden and forbidden for all time (to marry an Israelite) but their women are permitted forthwith" (Danby). This halakah surfaces again and again, e.g., *b. Ḳid.* 67b; *Keth.* 7b; *Ḥul.* 62b; *Yeb.* 69a; 76b; 77a; *y. Yeb.* 9c; *Ruth R.* 4:1; *Midr. Teh.* 9.11. Sometimes different emphases appear: e.g., *b. Yeb.* 76b and 77a,

wife, Azubah. *Now, why do they call her Azubah? Because she was barren and despised.*[g] *But her humiliation was made known before the Lord, and she was blessed with children; she gloried in wisdom and skillfully*[16] *she spun goats' hair upon the goats'*[h] *bodies without shearing them, for the curtain of the Tabernacle.*[17] These were her sons: Jesher, Shobab, and Ardon. 19. Azubah died, and Caleb married *Miriam,*

Apparatus, Chapter 2

[g] V: *k' ywt*, which, by switching two letters, could be *k' wyt*, "as a pointed out one," i.e., an object of scorn. C: *bzywt*. L and AS: *bzyt*, meaning "despised," which fits in well with the preceding adjective "barren" and is the reading followed.

[h] Reading *'yzy*, with Le Déaut's footnote. V, L, and AS: *'zy*. C: *'wy*.

Notes, Chapter 2

where Jether girds on his sword "like an Ishmaelite" to mete out justice to those who would not observe this halakah; in *y. Yeb.* 9c, however, Jether the Ishmaelite came to be called "the Israelite" because he burst into the house of study where Jesse was expounding the Scriptures and experienced a dramatic conversion, though the alternative view is also referred to.

In 2 Sam 17:25 "Ishmaelite" seems to be the more likely original reading, on the ground that it would be odd in this context to refer specifically to an Israelite as an "Israelite" (see J. Mauchline, *1 and 2 Samuel*, NCB, London, 1971, 282). But the final editor/scribe of MT Sam did not wish to have a sister of David linked with an Ishmaelite and made the necessary alteration. The Chronicler, however, did not share his alarm, but Tg. Chr felt it necessary to "correct" the reading (though one Hebrew MS and LXX A have "the Israelite") and place David beyond all reproach by his "Ruth the Moabitess" reference and by removing the Ishmaelite taint from the marriage arrangements of David's sister. The various Talmudic references use the expression "like an Ishmaelite," but Tg. Chr updates this, "like an Arab." Cf. Tg. 1 Chr 27:30. In Tg. Chr, Abner is the one who tried to exclude David, though in the fierce controversy described in *b. Yeb.* 76b and 77a Abner is very strongly on David's side. Perhaps *Gen. R.* 82:4 provides evidence for the fact that Abner is an opponent of David.

[14]Lit.: "became a father."

[15]Not in MT. Syr also has "by" and "his."

[16]Lit.: "with wisdom."

[17]That the MT of this verse presents serious difficulties to both translator and commentator is confirmed by the fact that there are almost as many solutions to its problems as there are commentators. MT states: "And Caleb, the son of Hezron, became the father of Azubah, a woman, and Jerioth; and these are her sons: Jesher and Shobab and Ardon." But, if Azubah is Caleb's daughter, what of the next verse, which makes her his wife? Some Hebrew MSS and the Versions try to improve things, usually by omitting or substituting words. Tg. Chr gives us as the basic text: "Caleb, the son of Hezron, became a father BY HIS wife Azubah; these are her sons: Jesher and Shobab and Ardon" (cf. partly Keil 63, Rudolph 23 and 12, and NEB). The name "Jerioth" of the MT has disappeared but remains as a common noun, "curtains," and becomes, with Azubah (meaning "forsaken"), a pillar for Tg. Chr's expansion. Azubah, forsaken, becomes the launching pad for a flight of fancy where, at first barren and abandoned, she is blessed by the Lord with children and wisdom. We return to the Massoretic rails, as it were, when we find her, endowed with this wisdom, spinning goats' hair for the curtains of the Tabernacle. The incredible thing, however, is that she spins the goats' hair "upon the bodies of the goats without shearing them," which would require considerable wisdom! We find a similar comment in Tg. Ps.-J. Exod 35:26, where the women are spinning the goats' hair "upon their bodies and hackling them while they were still alive." This may be Tg. Ps.-J.'s way of drawing out the significance of the ambiguous statement in MT which says that "with wisdom they were spinning the goats." As ambiguity is regarded as a means of hiding something special, and as wisdom is required in this context, the "something special" is interpreted here by Tg. Ps.-J. as doing the work on their bodies while they were still alive. Tg. Chr follows a similar pattern, but for him the spinning is done on the bodies of the goats, without shearing them—in either case, a pretty formidable task! See further *b. Shab.* 74b; 99a; *b. Soṭ.* 11b; *Exod. R.* 1:17.

who was called[18] Ephrath; she bore him Hur. 20. Hur became the father of Uri, and Uri became the father of Bezalel. 21. Later, Hezron *seduced*[19] the *virgin* daughter of Machir, the father of Gilead, and he took her *in marriage;* he was sixty–*six*[20] years old[21] *when* she bore him *Shegub*. 22. *Shegub*[22] became the father of Jair; he had twenty-three towns in the land of Gilead. 23. But *the Geshurites*[23] *and the Arameans*[24] took from them the villages[25] of Jair, Kenath and its villages:[26] sixty towns, all of which *belonged to*[27] Machir, the father of Gilead. 24. After this Hezron died in *the home of his son* Caleb, *in* Ephrath.[28] Hezron's wife, Abijah, *the*

Notes, Chapter 2

[18]This is one of Tg. Chr's "compressed expansions" (cf. Shem, 1:24). Miriam is identified with Ephrath, an identification found also in 4:4 and 4:17. This opens a window on a vast expanse of theological and political discussion emerging, e.g., in *b. Soṭ.* 11b; *Exod. R.* 1:17; 40:4; *Sifre Num.* Underlying these is the story in Exod 1:15-21, where God made "houses" for the two midwives, Shiphrah and Puah, who had ensured that the children of Israel were not wiped out in Egypt: Shiphrah is identified with Jochebed, Moses' mother, and Puah with Miriam, Moses' sister. (*Exod. R.* 40:4 sees the ground for the identification of Miriam and Ephrath in the root underlying Ephrath, *prh*, "to bear fruit." Puah (= Miriam) made sure that the children of Israel bore fruit—and survived. See also *Exod. R.* 1:17.) Priestly and Levitical families come from Jochebed, via Moses and Aaron; but a *royal* family comes from Miriam, because David is descended from Miriam, a conclusion which follows from taking 1 Chr 2:19 and 1 Sam 17:12 together. (The allocation of "houses" is dealt with also in the Targums of Exod 1:15-21, less Tg. Onq., though one MS of Frg. Tg, MS P, reverses this allocation: "Jochebed obtained the crown of kingship and Miriam the crown of high priesthood.")

These seemingly innocuous lineages assume considerable importance at times when the nature of Messiahship is hotly debated, whether the question at issue is a kingly Messiah able to exercise a priestly function or a priestly Messiah who could also be king. While such arguments may have arisen in controversies between Hasmoneans and anti-Hasmoneans (V. Aptowitzer, for example, felt that "the bulk of the Rabbinic and sectarian references to the priestly Messiah reflects the political struggles of the Hasmonean era, especially under John Hyrcanus and Alexander Jannaeus," in M. D. Johnson, *The Purpose of the Biblical Genealogies,* Cambridge, 1969, 131), their use was not necessarily confined to that period.

[19]MT: "came to." A puzzling addition to the character of Hezron, who, apart from being a connecting link, plays very little part in either Old Testament or later Jewish literature. In the Tg. Ps.-J. version of the Book of the Covenant, at Exod 22:15, the same verb is used ("if a man *seduces* a virgin . . ."). It is puzzling to see Hezron described in such unflattering terms. As Hezron is mentioned in the genealogies of Jesus in both Matt (1:3) and Luke (3:33), is there perhaps in Tg. 1 Chr 2:21 the trace of an anti-Christian tendency, an attempt to downgrade one who featured in the line of descent of the Christian Messiah?

[20]MT: "sixty." Perhaps dittography has produced the Tg. Chr figure. LXX has "sixty-five."

[21]In MT this clause precedes the semicolon.

[22]MT: "Segub." C = MT.

[23]MT: "Geshur."

[24]MT: "Aram."

[25]Reading *kprny,* with C, L, and AS, for *kwprty.* In MT this word is usually construed as the first part of a proper noun. Tg. Chr takes it as a common noun.

[26]MT: "daughters," i.e., dependent towns, villages.

[27]MT: "the sons of." LXX has "to the sons of."

[28]MT: "After the death of Hezron in Caleb Ephrathah." The Versions are unhappy with this, perhaps because with such a recent mention of Caleb as a person, it does not seem right to treat him as a place, though we have a similar type of place name in Mic 5:1, "Bethlehem Ephrathah," and they deal with it in varying ways: Tg. Chr as above; Syr: "And after these things, Hezron died in the land of Caleb, in Ephrath"; LXX, Arm. Vg: "Caleb came to Ephratha," regarding, apparently, the preposition *b* as an abbreviation for *b*; "he came" (cf. *Exod. R.* 40:4), leaving open the question whether Ephratha is a person or a place. Perhaps Tg. Chr regarded the preposition as an abbreviation for *byt,* "the house of."

daughter of Machir, was left pregnant,[29] and she bore him[i] Ashhur, *the leader of the Tekoaites.*[30] 25. The sons of Jerahmeel, the first-born of Hezron, were: Ram, the first-born, then[31] Bunah, Oren, Ozem, and Ahijah. 26. Jerahmeel had another wife, whose name was Atarah, the[32] mother of Onam. 27. The sons of Ram, the first-born of Jerahmeel, were: Maaz, Jamin, and Eker. 28. The sons of Onam were: Shammai and Jada. The sons of Shammai: Nadab and Abishur. 29. The name of Abishur's wife was Abihail, who bore him Ahban and Molid. 30. The sons of Nadab: Seled and Appaim; Seled died without sons. 31.[j] The sons of Appaim: Ishi. The[k] sons of Ishi: Sheshan. The sons of Sheshan: Ahlai.[k] 32. The sons of Jada, Shammai's brother: Jether and Jonathan; Jether died without sons. 33. The sons of Jonathan: Peleth and Zaza. These were the sons of Jerahmeel. 34. Now Sheshan had no sons, only daughters. But Sheshan had an Egyptian slave,[l] whose name was Jarha. 35. *Sheshan released*[m][33] Jarha, his slave, and gave him his daughter in marriage; she bore him Attai. 36.[n] Attai became the father of Nathan; Nathan became the father of Zabad. 37. Zabad became the father of Ephlal; Ephlal became the father of Obed. 38. Obed became the father of Jehu; Jehu became the father of Azariah. 39. Azariah became the father of Helez; Helez became the father of Eleasah.[o] 40. Eleasah[o] became the father of Sismai; Sismai became the father of Shallum. 41. Shallum became the father of Jekamiah; Jekamiah became the father of Elishama. 42. The sons of Caleb, the brother of Jerahmeel: Mesha, his first-born, who was *the leader of the Ziphites;*[34] and the sons of Mareshah, the father of Hebron. 43.[p] The sons of Hebron: Korah, Tappuah, Rekem, and Shema. 44. Shema became the father of Raham, the father of Jorkeam; Rekem became the father of Shammai. 45. The son of Shammai: Maon; and Maon, the father of Bethzur. 46. Ephah, Caleb's concubine, bore Haran, Moza and Gazez; Haran became the father of Gazez. 47.[q] The sons of Jahdai: Regem, Jotham, Geshan, Pelet,

Apparatus, Chapter 2

[i] C, L, and AS add: "after his death."
[j] E omits verse 31.
[k-k] Following C. V omits.
[l] E: "an Egyptian slave *went* to Sheshan."
[m] E omits.

[n] E omits verses 36-41.
[o] C has Eleashah.
[p] E omits verse 43.
[q] E omits verse 47.

Notes, Chapter 2

[29] Tg. Chr makes explicit what is already implicit in the next clause.
[30] MT: "the father of Tekoa."
[31] Lit.: "and."
[32] V omits the personal pronoun "she" of MT.
[33] It would have been inappropriate for a freeborn daughter to marry a slave. Following the instructions in *b. Pes.* 113a, the slave is first emancipated: "Free thy slave and give her to him."
[34] MT: "the father of Ziph"; cf. 2:24.

Ephah, and Shaaph. 48. Maacah, Caleb's concubine, bore[35] Sheber[36] and Tirhanah. 49. And Shaaph[37] bore the father of Madmannah and *Sheba,*[38] the father of Machbenah and the father of Gibea. Caleb's daughter was Achsah.[r] 50. These were the sons of Caleb,[39] the son of Hur, the first-born of *Ephrath:*[40] Shobal, the *leader of those* of[41] Kiriath-jearim, 51. *Shalma,*[42] the *leader of those of*[41] Bethlehem, and Hareph, *the leader of those* of[41] Bethgader. 52. Shobal, the *leader* of[41] Kiriath-jearim, had sons: *they were the disciples and priests who were worthy to distribute the offerings.*[43] 53. The families *who were living in* Kiriath-jearim *were the Levites, the sons of Moses, whom Zipporah bore to him,*[s] the *Jithrites,*[44] the *Puthites,*[44] the *Shumathites,*[44] and the *Mishraites.*[44] From these came *the disciples of the prophets of Zorah* and *of Eshtaol.*[45] 54. The sons of

Apparatus, Chapter 2

[r] C: *'ks'.* V, L, and AS: *'ksh* = MT.

[s] E: "she bore" for "Zipporah bore to him."

Notes, Chapter 2

[35]Tg. Chr uses the feminine form of the verb, along with several Hebrew MSS listed by de Rossi, where MT has the masculine.

[36]Tg. Chr inserts *yt,* the object marker, before "Sheber."

[37]MT of the first part of this verse is difficult, largely because of the uncertainty of the identity of Shaaph, but one possible translation is: "She also bore Shaaph, the father of Madmannah. . . ." Tg. Chr, by inserting an object marker before "the father of Madmannah," alters the roles of the participants: "And Shaaph bore the father of . . . and . . ." (cf. Arm). Even if this sounds awkward, it seems more correct than Le Déaut's translation: "Puis elle enfanta Shaaph, le père . . ." (cf. DW's translation).

[38]Tg. Chr: *šb'.* MT: *šw'.*

[39]In 2:19 Hur is the son of Caleb. Here Hur is the father of Caleb. The problem is eased if a full stop is inserted in 2:50 after "Caleb." "These were the sons of Caleb" then becomes a summary of what has gone before in 2:42-49. LXX, Vg, Arm adopt this solution, as does Le Déaut in his translation, though V does not give him any ground for so doing.

[40]MT: *'prth.*

[41]MT: "the father of"; cf. 2:24, 42, 51, 52.

[42]MT: "Salma" = C.

[43]MT: "Haroeh, half of the Menuhoth." Tg. Chr takes the basic meaning of the root of the last three Hebrew words in the verse and clothes it in Aramaic dress: *r'h,* "to see" becomes *hzy,* whose passive participle also means "worthy"; *hsy,* "half," "to divide, distribute," becomes *plg; mnhh,* "gift, offering," becomes *qrbn'.* (Tg. Chr interpreted the last word, not as in MT, where it is a plural of "resting-place," but as the plural of *mnhh,* "gift, offering.") *ICC*'s comment (97) on these three words in MT is: "This passage is utterly obscure." Tg. Chr removed the obscurity by supplying a subject for the sentence, "the disciples and priests," whom he then made sons of Shobal, thereby enhancing considerably Shobal's reputation!

[44]MT: singular.

[45]MT: "the Zorathite and the Eshtaolite." Kiriath-jearim, a person in MT, has become a place in Tg. Chr, and in it dwell various groups of Levites (who apart from this verse are otherwise unknown in MT), from whom emerge prophetic disciples. The basis for the expansion may lie in "the Jithrite." But the connection here is unlikely to be with Jether (2:17; cf. 2 Sam 17:25) for however we regard him, it would be difficult to find a Levitical connection in his family. A more likely candidate for the post is Jethro (*ytrw*), for Zipporah, who is mentioned in Tg. Chr, was his daughter. Note also that in 1 Chr 23:14f. the two sons of Moses, Gershom and Eliezer, are made "honorary Levites." Zorah and Eshtaol were two towns in the Shephelah (Jos 15:33), and it was between these two towns that the Spirit of the Lord began to stir Samson (Judg 13:25). It may be that the "prophetic link" is to be found in a variant reading in the Targum of Judg 13:25, from a Geniza fragment (Sperber, II, 76), where, for "a spirit of power from before the Lord" (which is the rendering of the Targum for "the spirit of the Lord"), we have "a spirit of prophecy." See Ginzberg, III, 76, for the other names in this verse. Verse 54 makes a further reference to Zorah.

Shalma[42] *who were from* **Bethlehem**, *righteous*[1] *men whose reputation was as good as balm, because they had done away with the guardposts*[46] *which Jeroboam had set up on the road so that the first fruits might not reach Jerusalem. The sons of Shalma used to decorate the first fruits in baskets and transport them secretly to Jerusalem. They would split the wood, make ladders and bring them up to Jerusalem so that they could prepare a place in which they could burn the offerings.*[47] *They came from the family of* **Joab**, *the son of* **Zeruiah**. *Some of them were priests who distributed what was left over of the offerings in Jerusalem, and the disciples of the prophets who were from Zorah.*[48] 55. *The family of Rehabiah, the son of Eliezer, the son of Moses:*

Apparatus, Chapter 2

[1] V and C: *ṣdyqy*. E, L, and AS: *ṣdyqym*.

Notes, Chapter 2

[46]Tg. Chr has *prwzdw'wwn*, borrowed from Latin: "an adaptation of *praesidia*, posts, guards" (MJ 1219); from "*praesidiarii*, Wachen, die zur Aufsicht dienen" (JL II, 288).

[47]Lit.: "the fireplace for the offerings."

[48]The literal translation of MT is: "The sons of Salma: Bethlehem and the Netophathite, Atrothbethjoab, and half of the Manahathite, the Zorite." Tg. Chr is not very interested in the identity of the people listed in this verse. He has taken the words of MT, or words of similar appearance or sound, and used them in their Aramaic dress as stepping-stones in his narrative. *slm'* becomes *swlm'*, "ladder"; *ntwpty* ("Netophathite") becomes *ntwp*, "balm"; *'trwt*, "garlands of," becomes *m'tryn*, "were decorating," from the Aramaic I *'tr*, "to decorate"; *the house of Joab* becomes "the family of Joab"; *ḥṣy*, from the same root, "to divide," becomes *mplgyn*, "were dividing," from *plg*, "to divide" (cf. 2:52 n. 43); *mnḥty*, "the Manahathite" is linked with the plural of *mnḥḥ*, "gift, offering," whose corresponding word in Aramaic is *qwrbn'*, "offering"; *ṣr'y (Zorite)* becomes the corresponding place name *(from) Zorah*.

There are various interrelated factors in this expansion:

i) Jeroboam, son of Nebat, is alleged to have set up guardposts to prevent the people of the Northern Kingdom from going to Jerusalem to worship (deduced from 1 Kgs 12:25-33; see *b. Ta'an.* 30b).

ii) Hoshea ben Elah, last king of Israel, removed these guardposts—deduced, perhaps, from his name, with its link with salvation, deliverance, and from 2 Kgs 17:2, where the implication is that there was some good in him, the "good thing" perhaps referring to his removal of the guardposts (see *b. Giṭ.* 88a; *b. M.Ḳ.* 28b, where Abijah is credited with removing them).

iii) In *m. Ta'an.* 4,5 and *t. Ta'an.* 4, 7, we hear of pestle smugglers and fig pressers and ladder carriers, all of whom used their native wit to outsmart the occupying power ("the kings of Greece") which had set up roadblocks on the way to Jerusalem. They covered the first fruits in the basket with figs, and, carrying basket and pestle, led the guards to believe that they were on their way to make cakes of dried figs in a mortar which lay beyond the guardpost. Safely through the cordon, they decorated the first fruits (*m'tryn*; see *m. Bikk.* III,3) and brought them to Jerusalem. A similar ruse, involving the carrying of a ladder by the sons of Salma, the Netoṣathite, on the pretense of fetching down some imaginary pigeons from a dove cote somewhere beyond where the guards were stationed, ensured that the wood reached Jerusalem (see also *b. Ta'an.* 28a). In the references given under (iii) above, the setting up of the guardposts is compared with similar activity on the part of Jeroboam.

iv) In *y. Ta'an.* 68b we have a very similar narrative, but the incident referred to (figs, etc.) is not compared with the Jeroboam incident—it *is* the Jeroboam incident. In Tg. Chr also it *is* the Jeroboam incident, and the leading role is played by the sons of Salma: they remove the guardposts of Jeroboam; they decorate the first fruits in baskets; they bring the wood in ladder form; some were priests (perhaps because for Tg. Chr only priests could divide the surplus of the offerings), and some were prophets from Zorah (see 2:53). Tg. Chr does not describe in detail the stratagems used to outwit the guards, either because he was unaware of them as stratagems or because he regarded them as so well known as to make narration unnecessary.

Tg. Ruth 4:20 has a similar story: "And Nahshon became the father of Salma the Righteous. He was Salma of Bethlehem and Natophah, whose sons did away with the guardposts which Jeroboam the guilty had set up on the

the disciples of Jabez, *who is Othniel, the son of Kenaz. He was called*[49] *Jabez, because,* [u] *by his counsel, he set up an academy for the disciples. They were called*[50] Tirathim, [u] *because when they sang praises, their voice was like a trumpet blast;* Shimeathim, *because they looked with favor*[51] *on the traditional laws;*[v] Sucathim, [w] *because they were covered*[x] *with the spirit of prophecy. These are the Shalmaites,*[y] *the sons of Zipporah, who were enrolled with the family of the Levites, because* they came *from the descendants of Moses, the leader of Israel, whose merit was of more value to them than*[z] horsemen and chariots.[52]

Apparatus, Chapter 2

[u-u] E omits, probably through homoioteleuton.
[v] E: singular.
[w] E: *swbtym.*
[x] C: Ithpaal; V, E, L: Pael. AS: "speaking" (*mmllyn* for *mṭllyn*).

[y] C: "Salmaites."
[z] C: initial letter is *l* instead of the expected *m.*

Notes, Chapter 2

roads. And the deeds of father and sons were as pleasant as balm." While there are some differences of detail, it is Salma and/or his sons who actually remove the guardposts, i.e., in both Targums Jeroboam's guardposts are not being used simply as an object of comparison.

There is however, an apparent contradiction in Tg. Chr: we are told that the guardposts were removed, *then* we hear of the ruses used to outwit the guards. *Either* that is the correct order, in which case there was still danger involved after the removal of the posts in getting the materials to Jerusalem. *Or* Tg. Chr is unaware that the incidents he refers to were part of the ruses used to get past the guards. *Or* he knows there is a contradiction and simply sets down the two statements beside each other. *Or* the sons of Salma both outsmarted the guards and, as well, at some later point physically removed the guardposts. *Or* (and this seems most likely) the use of participles preceded by the verb "to be" in the second and third sentences in 2:54 ("they were decorating . . . transporting . . . splitting . . . making . . . bringing . . .") may indicate that the events described in these sentences, taking place obviously before the removal of the guardposts, actually helped to "do away with" the posts. Some scholars suggest that the incident referred to in Tg. Chr may reflect conditions following the imperial edict by Hadrian forbidding access by the Jews to Jerusalem after the failure of the Bar Cochba revolt in 135. (See J. A. Fitzmyer, *Essays on the Semitic Background of the New Testament*, London, 1971, 351f.)

[49]Lit.: "they were calling him."

[50]Lit.: "They were calling them."

[51]Le Déaut suggests, following MJ (952), that we read Aphel for Pael, but MJ also gives a Pael meaning, as used in the translation above.

[52]MT: "The families also of the scribes that dwelt at Jabez: the Tirathites, the Shimeathites, and the Sucathites. These are the Kenites who came from Hammath, the father of the house of Rechab." In Talmud and Midrash this verse is quoted frequently, often with Judg 1:16 or Num 24:21 or 1 Chr 4:9f., showing the link between Rechabites, Kenites, Jethro, Jabez, and usually with reference to Torah-centered scribal activity and the role of proselytes within Judaism. There are seven significant words in the verse—two pairs of two, separated by a block of three.

a) Group of two: "Scribes" (*sprym*) and "Jabez" (*yʿbṣ*). Jabez is also dealt with in 4:9, 10, and any relevant comments on those verses will be noted here. In Tg. Chr two comments are made about Jabez: (i) In 2:55 and 4:9, 13, he is identified with Othniel, perhaps because each was regarded as a champion of Torah, and in *b. Tem.* 16a this identification is followed by a composite word play which bears out this emphasis: "Jabez (*yʿbṣ*) because he gave advice (*yʿṣ*) and spread (*rbyṣ*) Torah in Israel," while 4:9 notes that he was "more skilled in Torah than his brethren." Tg. 2 Chr 2:55 tells us (also using the composite wordplay just referred to) that "He was called Jabez, because by his counsel (*yṣtyh*) he set up an academy (*trbyṣ*) for the disciples." The basic biblical stimulus here may lie in MT 2:55, where Jabez and "scribes" (*sprym*) are adjacent to each other. Othniel finds himself in the same high-powered group because it was he who captured Kiriath Sepher (*spr*), Josh 15:15ff.; Judg 1:11ff.; and he was regarded in *b. Tem.* 16a as responsible for restoring many teachings which had been forgotten after the death of Moses. (ii) The prayer of

CHAPTER 3

1. These were the sons of David, who were born[1] to him in Hebron: the first-born Amnon, by Ahinoam, *who was from Jezreel;*[2] *the*[3] second Daniel, *that is, Chileab, who resembled his own father in every way,*[4] by Abigail, *who was from Carmel;*[5] 2. the third Absalom,[a][6] the son of Maacah, the daughter of Talmai, king of Geshur; the fourth Adonijah, the son of Haggith; 3. the fifth Shephatiah, by

Notes, Chapter 2

Jabez in Tg. 1 Chr 4:10 has a more explicit theological reference than in MT. In Tg. Chr he asks for all the "right things"—sons, disciples, divine help in debate, like-minded companions to prevent the provocation of the evil inclination.

b) The block of three. The MT names of the three families of scribes are given, followed by a brief Aramaic comment based on the root meaning of the Hebrew word involved, each comment heaping further theological praise on the disciples of Jabez. The TIRATHIM: *trw'h,* "the trumpet blast," and the late Hebrew root *tr'*, "to sound the alarm, to blow the Shofar at public services" (MJ 1700); the SHIMEATHIM: *šm't'* (from *šm'*, "to hear"), "what was heard, oral decision, traditional law"; the SUCATHIM: *skk,* "to cover with boughs," *especially to cover the festal booth* (MJ 990), but this time they are covered (*mt/llyn*) with the spirit of prophecy (see also *Mekilta,* Amalek IV and *Sifre Numbers,* 73).

c) Group of two: The Kenites and Rechab. In Tg. Chr both names have disappeared. Instead of the "Kenites" we have the "Shalmaites" (see *b. B.B.* 56a, and cf. Judg 11:16, where the Targum makes a similar substitution). They have been highly commended in verse 54 and now, through Zipporah, like the Kiriath-jearim group of verse 53, are taken into the Mosaic family and become part of the Levitical structure. "Rechab" reappears in "chariots," the last word of the verse—the Hebrew word for "chariot" having the same root letters as Rechab (*rkb*). The "merit of Moses" is referred to also in Tg. 1 Chr 4:18; 23:17. In 2:55 we have an expression similar to what is found in the departure of Elijah story in 2 Kgs 2:12 and Elisha's comment on it, as given in Tg. Jonathan: "My master, my master, who was of more value to Israel by his prayer than chariots and horsemen." In Tg. 1 Chr 23:17, the family of Rehabiah, mentioned in 2:55, grew exceedingly large, sixty myriads, because of the merit of Moses.

Apparatus, Chapter 3

[a] C adds another "the third" after "Absalom."

Notes, Chapter 3

[1] MT: singular verb.

[2] MT: "the Jezreelitess."

[3] MT omits definite article.

[4] In the parallel passage in 2 Sam 3:2 the name is Chileab; here it is Daniel. Rudolph (27) suggests that "Chileab" was a complimentary nickname, implying "like father, like son." This is the line developed by Tg. Chr as he splits the word in half: *kl-'b,* meaning "all father," thus stressing that Daniel-Chileab was indeed his father's son, because the resemblance between son and father was total. This approach may have been used to counteract a suggestion that Daniel was not David's son, having been conceived already by Abigail from Nabal, her first husband, before she met David. Tg. Chr is affirming that he is so like his father that there could be no doubt whatever as to parentage. See also *b. Ber.* 4a. A similar attempt to establish that Isaac is indeed Abraham's son is found in Tg. Ps.-J. Gen 21:2.

[5] MT: "the Carmelitess."

[6] MT has *l* before "Absalom," which may have been inserted because of the two occurrences of this preposition in the previous verse. Many Hebrew MSS and the Versions omit *l*.

Abital; the sixth Ithream, by his wife Eglah, *who was Michal, Saul's daughter.*[7]
4. Six[b] were[8] born to him in Hebron, where he reigned for seven years and six
months. Thirty-three years he reigned in Jerusalem. 5. These were born to him in
Jerusalem: Shimea, Shobab, Nathan and Solomon—*the* four *of them* by Bath-
shua,[9] *who was Bathsheba,*[10] the daughter of Ammiel; 6.[c] then[11] Ibhar, Elishama,
Eliphelet, 7. Nogah, Nepheg,[d] Japhia,[d] 8. Elishama, Eliada, and Eliphelet—nine.
9. All *these* were the sons of David, besides sons of concubines, and Tamar their
sister. 10. Solomon's son was Rehoboam, Abijah was his son, Asa his son,
Jehoshaphat his son, 11.[e] Joram his son, Ahaziah his son, Joash his son,
12. Amaziah his son, Azariah, *who was Uzziah,*[f][12] his son, Jotham his son,
13. Ahaz his son, Hezekiah his son, Manasseh his son, 14. Amon his son, Josiah
his son. 15. The sons of Josiah: the first-born Johanan, the second Jehoiakim, the
third Zedekiah, the fourth Shallum, *in whose days the kingdom*[g] *of the house of
David came to an end.*[13] 16.[h] The sons of Jehoiakim: Jeconiah his son, Zedekiah

Apparatus, Chapter 3

[b] V and C: *'šth.* E, L, and AS: *šyt'.*

[c] E omits verses 6–8.

[d] Following C. Missing in V.

[e] E omits verses 11–14.

[f] This expansion is missing in C, L, and AS.

[g] E, L, and AS have *mlkwtyh*, "its kingdom," using
the anticipatory suffix followed by *d*—an alternative way of expressing the genitive relationship.

[h] E omits verses 16–23.

Notes, Chapter 3

[7]Jewish tradition took a kinder view of Michal, David's first and later estranged wife, than the Old Testament.
Here she is identified with Eglah, perhaps because, since Eglah is the only one in this section to be called "his wife,"
it was thought that this must refer to his first wife, i.e., Michal. Therefore Eglah = Michal. This identification is
found, e.g., in *b. San.* 21a; *Midr. Teh.* 59.4; *Gen. R.* 82:7; *Ps. Jerome* on 2 Sam 3:5 (col. 1347), all of them seeing the
point of identification as somehow linked with the name Eglah, *'glh*, whose meaning is "young cow," succinctly
stated in *Ps. Jerome* on 1 Chr 3:3: "Egla interpretatur vitula, quam nonnulli putant Michol filiam Saul." A. Sperber
draws attention to a marginal comment in Codex Reuchlinianus on 2 Sam 3:5, where instead of "by Eglah, the wife
of David," we have "Michal, the wife of David."

[8]MT: singular verb; cf. note 1.

[9]One Hebrew MS and Vg: *bt šb'.*

[10]Only here in MT is David's wife Bathsheba given the name Bath-shua. *šw'* has become *šb'*, "a phonetic variation
arising from the similar sound of *bh* and *w*" (*ICC*, 99). See 1 Chr 2:49, where *šw'* in MT becomes *šb'* in Tg. Chr. Tg.
Chr is ensuring that the Bath-shua in the text before him would not be confused with the Bath-shua who had played
a considerable part in earlier history and he simply added the explanatory note "i.e., Bathsheba."

[11]Lit.: "And."

[12]Tg. Chr is noting, for the sake of clarity, the other name, "Uzziah," by which Azariah was known and which MT
prefers to use in 2 Chr 26.

[13]This is a puzzling expansion. In Jer 22:10-12 Jehoahaz and Shallum are identified. But if this is the same
Shallum referred to in 1 Chr 3:15 we know that the kingdom did not end with Jehoahaz, that, in fact, the last king
was Zedekiah. *b. Ker.* 5b and *b. Hor.* 11b state that Zedekiah was the last king, and they identify Shallum with
Zedekiah. Perhaps the Rabbis saw an ideal opportunity here to link up Zedekiah with Shallum (from the root *šlm*,
"to come to an end"), especially since Shallum is the last name in the list of the sons of Josiah in this verse, and thus
imprint on a pupil's mind: Zedekiah = Shallum—*FINIS*. Tg. Chr takes over almost verbatim one of the two comments made on Shallum in the Talmudic references listed above: "in whose days the kingdom of the house of David
came to an end." The Talmud made this comment in a "Zedekiah = Shallum" context. In Tg. Chr, however, where
Zedekiah immediately precedes Shallum with no suggestion of identification, and where the expansion is simply attached to Shallum, those who read or listened to this expansion must have been left with the impression that
Shallum was the last king of Judah.

his son. 17. The sons of Jeconiah: Assir [14] *his son,* Shealtiel his son, 18. Malchiram, Pedaiah, Shenazzar,[i] Jekamiah, Hoshama, and Nedabiah.[i] 19. The sons of Pedaiah: Zerubbabel and Shimei. The son of Zerubbabel: Meshullam and Hananiah and Shelomith, their sister. 20. And Hashubah, Ohel,[j] Berechiah, Hasadiah, and Jushabhesed—five.[j] 21. The son[k] of Hananiah: Pelatiah and[l] Jeshaiah, and the sons of Rephaiah, the sons of Arnan, the sons of Obadiah, the sons of Shecaniah.[l] 22. The sons of Shecaniah: Shemaiah; the sons of Shemaiah: Hattush, Igal, Bariah, Neariah, and Shaphat—six. 23. The *sons*[15] of Neariah: Elioenai, Hizkiah, and Azrikam—three. 24. The sons of Elioenai: Hodaviah,[16] Eliashib, Pelaiah, Akkub, Johanan, Delaiah, and Anani—*he is the king Messiah who will be revealed*[17]—*in all,* seven.

CHAPTER 4

1.[a] The sons of Judah: Perez, Hezron, Carmi,[b] Hur, and Shobal.[b] 2. Reaiah, the son of Shobal, became the father of Jahath, and Jahath became the father of

Apparatus, Chapter 3

[i-i] Following C. Missing in V.
[j-j] Following C. Missing in V.

[k] C, L, and AS have "the sons of," as in some Hebrew MSS, LXX, Syr. V, however, agrees with MT.
[l-l] Following C. Missing in V.

Notes, Chapter 3

[14]Bearing in mind Jeconiah's captive status, an alternative translation of MT is possible: "Jeconiah, prisoner, Shealtiel his son...."
[15]MT: "son," though some Hebrew MSS and LXX have "sons."
[16]Tg. Chr follows Qere. Kethibh: *hdywhw.*
[17]The operative word here is Anani (*'nny*), which can be linked with Dan 7:13, where Daniel saw visions, "and behold with the clouds (*'nny*) of heaven there came one like a son of man...." Debate on this is reflected in *b. San.* 98a, in which Isa 60:22 is also examined, leading to a discussion as to when the Messiah would come: at the appointed time or speedily. Zech 9:9 is also discussed, for there the Messiah is to be "humble (*'ny*) and riding on an ass." If people were worthy, he would come "with the clouds of heaven," i.e., speedily; if they were not worthy, he would come "humble and riding on an ass," i.e., at the appointed time. See also S. H. Levey, *The Messiah: An Aramaic Interpretation,* Cincinnati, 1974, 162, who regards the Talmudic discussion on the "clouds of heaven" as possibly the origin of our Targumic statement.

Apparatus, Chapter 4

[a] E omits verse 1.

[b-b] Following C. Missing in V.

Ahumai and Lahad. These were the families of *Judah who lived in Zorah.*[1]
3. These were the *princes*[c] *who lived in*[2] Etam: Jezreel, Ishma and Idbash; and the
name of their sister was Hazlelponi. 4. And Penuel was the father of Gedor, and
Ezer the father of Hushah. These were the sons of Hur, the first-born of *Ephrath,*[3]
who was Miriam,[4] *and he was appointed leader in*[5] Bethlehem. 5. Ashhur, the
leader of[6] Tekoa, had two wives, Helah and Naarah. 6. Naarah bore him Ahuzzam,
Hepher, Timeni, and *Ahashtari.*[7] These were the sons of Naarah. 7.[d] The sons of
Helah: Zereth, Izhar,[ef] Ethnan, and *Koz.*[f8] 8. Koz became the father of Anub,
Zobebah,[9] and the family of *Aharel,*[10] *who was Hur,*[g] *the first-born of Miriam.*[11]
9. Jabez, *who was Othniel,*[12] was more honored *and expert in the Law* than his
brothers; his mother had called his name Jabez, "for," she said,[h] "I gave birth *to
him* in pain." 10. Jabez *prayed*[13] to the God of Israel, saying: "O that you might indeed bless me[i] *with sons,* and extend my territory *with disciples!* O that your hand
might be with me *in debate,*[j] and that you[14] *might provide me with companions like*

Apparatus, Chapter 4

[c] E, L, and AS omit "the."
[d] E omits verse 7.
[e] Tg. Chr follows Kethibh. Qere is *wṣḥr.*
[ff] Following C. Missing in V.
[g] Missing in E.
[h] Missing in C, E, L, and AS.

[i] E: "us."
[j] V has *bmšql wmkr'.* C, E, L, and AS have
bmšql wmṭr', which is an expression used to
describe the give and take of negotiating or
debating (MJ 552). (JL II, 511f.).

Notes, Chapter 4

[1]MT: "The Zorathite."
[2]MT: "These the father of Etam," which most commentators regard as difficult (*ICC,* 105: "meaningless"): some
follow LXX and translate "father" as "sons." Tg. Chr's rendering, though it does change what appears to be a person
into a place, is as helpful as most: "These were the *rbny'*" [the "leaders," which I have taken as "princes" where DW
prefers "doctores"] "who lived in Etam."
[3]MT: "Ephrathah." E, L, and AS follow MT. See 2:50.
[4]See 2:19, note 18.
[5]MT: "the father of." Tg. Chr thus sidesteps the problem thrown up by MT of 2:51, where Salma is the father of
Bethlehem, though it does leave uncertain the identity of the "he" who was appointed leader in Bethlehem.
[6]MT: "the father of." E, L, and AS follow MT.
[7]MT: "Ha Ahashtari," which could be translated "the Ahashtarite."
[8]"And Koz." Not in MT. Rudolph (*BHS*) regards it as originally in MT but dropped out through haplography;
others (e.g., Braun) see it as "in harmony with the Targum's tendencies to harmonize and conflate" (38).
[9]MT: *hṣwbbh.*
[10]MT: *ḥrḥl* which is followed by C, E, L, and AS.
[11]MT: "the son of Harum." Hur is designated the first-born of Miriam (Ephrath) as in 2:19, 4:4, but the basis for
the identification of Aharhel and Hur is uncertain.
[12]For comment on verses 9 and 10, see Tg. 1 Chr 2:55, note 52.
[13]MT: "called."
[14-14]MT is difficult. Literally it reads: "Oh that you might do/make from evil . . ." (*w'śyt mr'h*), often translated as
"Oh that you might keep me from evil." Tg. Chr has taken these two words as the basis for his expansion. "Oh that
you would *make* for me companions like myself so that the *evil* inclination. . . ."

myself, so that *the evil inclination* [14] may not provoke me!" [k] And *the Lord* [15] brought about what he had asked for. 11. Chelub, the brother of Shuhah, became the father of *Perug,* [16] who was the father of Eshton. 12. Eshton became the father of Beth–Rapha, Paseah, and Tehinnah, the father of Irnahash. These were the men of *the Great Sanhedrin.* [l] [17] 13. The sons of Kenaz: Othniel, *who was Jabez,* [18] and *Sheraiah;* [19] the sons of Othniel: Hathath. 14. Meonothai became the father of Ophrah; *Sheraiah* became the father of Joab, *chief* [20] of the Valley of the Craftsmen, [21] for craftsmen they were. 15. The sons of Caleb, the son of Jephunneh, *who was Hezron. They called him Caleb, the son of Jephunneh, because he had refused to accept the advice* [m] *of the spies."* [22] *These were his sons:* Iru, Elah, and Naam. The sons of Elah: Kenaz. [23] 16. [o] The sons of Jehallelel: Ziph, [p] Ziphah, Tiria, and Asarel. [p] [24] 17. The son of Ezra: [25] Jether, Mered, Epher, and Jalon, and

---

Apparatus, Chapter 4

[k] Reading Aphel with C and E.
[l] V and C: *snhdryn*; E, L, and AS: *snhdry.*
[m] E: *'ṣt* for *'yṭt* of V, C, L, AS.

[n] Reading *m'lly'* with C. V: *m'lyy'.*
[o] E omits verse 16.
[p-p] Following C. Missing in V.

Notes, Chapter 4

[15] MT: God.

[16] MT: *mḥyr,* "price." Tg. Chr has taken the meaning of the Hebrew word and reproduced it in its Aramaic form (*pyrwg,* "price").

[17] The Great Sanhedrin, consisting of seventy-one members including its high priestly president, was regarded as having its origin in the group of seventy elders in Num 11:16, appointed to assist Moses. It emerges in more recognizable form in the Persian period, and even more clearly in Maccabean times, wielding considerable power in matters religious, judicial, and administrative. It disappeared after the fall of Jerusalem in 70 C.E. There was also the Small or Lesser Sanhedrin with twenty-three members (see Schürer, II, 199–226).

Obviously the basis for this expansion is to be found in "the men of Recah" (*rkh*), but the link is not absolutely clear. *b. B.B.* 4a is thought to provide the clue. In an attack on Herod, he is told: "Though you strut with your sword, your genealogy is here; you are neither a *reka* nor the son of a *reka*" (*l' rk' wl' br rk'*). A question is posed as to the meaning of *rk'* and the answer is found: (i) in 2 Sam 3:39: "I am this day *rak* and anointed king." The meaning of *rk* as "*tender*" is extended to "*noble, royal.*" (ii) In Gen 46:43: "and they cried before him Abrek," interpreted as "father of the king." It is assumed that *rkh,* thus linked with *rk* and its extended meaning of "noble, royal," must refer to those who were part of the nobility, wielding aristocratic power in the Great Sanhedrin. Cf. MJ (1474). JL (II, 175) also quotes *b. B.B.* 4a, but in addition sees a connection between *rkh* and the Greek *archē,* with the meaning not only of "*beginning*" but also of "*power.*"

[18] See Tg. 1 Chr 2:55, note 52.

[19] MT: "Seraiah." V = C.

[20] MT: "father."

[21] Usually regarded as a place name and in most English versions the Hebrew is reproduced as "Ge-harashim." Tg. Chr gives the meaning of the Hebrew in Aramaic form.

[22] Lit.: "because he had turned his heart from the advice of the spies." The spies whom Moses sent to explore Canaan brought back a depressing report. Caleb, however, presented a glowing picture of the land and recommended that they go forward. In Tg. Chr, Caleb's non-conformity is stressed, but the basis for it is found, not in his name, but in the name of his father, Jephunneh, from the root *pnh,* "to turn." There has always been some debate about the number of Calebs in the Old Testament. By identifying Jephunneh and Hezron, Tg. Chr makes it clear that there is only one, the son of Jephunneh, i.e., Hezron.

[23] MT: "and Kenaz." Tg. Chr is shared with a few Hebrew MSS, LXX, Vg.

[24] C: Asharel. MT: Asarel.

[25] MT: *'zrh*; V: *'zr'.* C, E, L, and AS = MT.

she conceived[q] *by him* Miriam,[r] *who was Ephrath, Shammai, and Ishbah, the father of Eshtemoa. 18. His wife, Jehuditha,[s] brought up Moses after she had drawn him up[t] out of the water. She called his name* Jered, *because he brought down manna for Israel; chief*[26] *of Gedor, because he rebuilt the ruins of Israel;[u] Heber, because he united Israel with their father who is in heaven; chief*[26] *of Soco,*[27] *because he covered the house of Israel with his merit; Jekuthiel, because in his days Israel waited forty years in the wilderness for the God who is in heaven; chief*[26] *Zanoah, because on his account, God forgave Israel's sins.* These *names* Bithiah, the daughter of Pharaoh, *called him by the spirit of prophecy. She became a proselyte,* and Mered, *who was Caleb, married her, for he had opposed*[28] *the advice of the spies.*[29] 19. The sons of the wife of Hodiah, the sister of *Zeath,*[30] *the leader*[31] *of Keilah, who was from Garam,*[32] *and Eshtemoa, who was from Maacah.*[33] 20.[v] *The sons of Shimon:*

Apparatus, Chapter 4

[q] V, C, and L: *"dy't* (Aphel). E and AS: *'dy't* (Pael).

[r] C, E, L, and AS, by omitting the object marker of MT and V, have transformed Miriam into the subject of the verb: "Miriam ... conceived by him ..."

[s] E: *yhwdyt.*

[t] E: *šlḥtyh*: "she had sent him."

[u] E omits.

[v] E omits verse 20.

Notes, Chapter 4

[26]MT: "father."

[27]MT: *šwkw.*

[28]Lit.: "rebelled against."

[29]Verses 17 and 18 in MT perplex most commentators, who often resort to shifting sections of text to try to bring some coherence to the passage. As verse 18 stands, we learn that his Jewish wife bore three children. The second part of the verse informs us that the wife concerned is Bithiah, the daughter of Pharaoh, and the husband Mered. Tg. Chr, however, finds no difficulties in this verse. The Jewish wife is the one who draws Moses out of the water and rears him, giving him six names (the names of the three children mentioned as well as the three names of their children). The Hebrew root meanings of the six names then form the basis for six brief comments extolling the virtues and achievements of Moses. The daughter of Pharaoh becomes a proselyte, and Mered, who is identified with Caleb, marries her. Tg. Chr is very similar to *b. Meg.* 13a and to *Lev. R.* 1:1, where some further virtues are added to Moses. The root of the whole expansion is probably found in the expression "the daughter of Pharaoh," which immediately calls to mind the drawing out of the water and the rearing of Moses, and this leads on to his various virtues.

Below is a summary of the relevant passage in *b. Meg.* 13a. The similarities and differences can be seen when it is set alongside Tg. Chr: JERED from *yrd,* "to go down": "because manna *came down* for Israel in his days"; GEDOR from *gdr,* "to fence in, wall up": "because he *fenced in* the breaches of Israel"; HEBER from *ḥbr,* "to join": "because he *joined* Israel to their father in heaven"; SOCO from *swkh,* "booth": "because he was like a *sheltering booth* for Israel"; JEKUTHIEL from *qwh,* "to wait for, hope," and *'l,* "God": "because Israel *trusted in God* in his days"; ZANOAH from *znḥ,* "to remove": "because *he made* Israel *abandon* their iniquities." The name MERED comes from *mrd,* "to rebel," and, as Caleb had rebelled against his fellow spies, Mered and Caleb are identified: "The Holy One, blessed be he, said: 'Let Caleb who *rebelled* against the plan of the spies come and take the daughter of Pharaoh who rebelled against the idols of her father's house.'" (See also *b. San.* 19b for the Mered/Caleb equation.) As with Sheshan releasing his slave before allowing his daughter to marry him (see 2:35, note 33), Tg. Chr also does things correctly: Bithiah becomes a proselyte before Mered marries her.

[30]MT: *nḥm.* E: *dy n't.*

[31]MT: "father."

[32]MT: "the Garmite."

[33]MT: "the Maachathite."

Amnon, Rinnah, Barhanan and *Tilon.*[34] The sons of Ishi: Zoheth and Barzoheth. 21. The sons of Shelah, the son of Judah: Er, the father of Lecah, Laadah, the *leader*[w 35] *of* Mareshah and the families of the linen works, *whose kingly and priestly garments were entrusted*[x] to the house of Ashbea.[36] 22. *And the prophets and*[y] *scribes who came from the descendants of Joshua, and the Gibeonites who were made servants in the sanctuary house because they had lied to the princes of Israel;* and Joash, *who was Mahlon,* and Saraph, *who was Chilion,* who *took wives from the daughters of* Moab, *and Boaz, leader of the sages of the academy of Bethlehem, who were engaged in (the study of) the words*[z] *of the Ancient of Days.*[37] 23. *These were the disciples of the Law, for the sake of whom the world was created, who sit in judgment and establish*[aa] *the world, who build up and restore completely the ruins of the house of Israel, along with the Shekinah of the king of the world, by the service of the Law, by the intercalation of months and by*[bb] *the fixing of the beginnings of years*

Apparatus, Chapter 4

[w] E: *'b'.* V, C, L, and AS: *rb'.* E = MT.
[x] V has *msyryn* (plural). C, E, L, and AS have *msyr'* (singular). If we follow the latter reading, we would require some such translation as "the making of whose kingly and priestly garments was entrusted to...."

[y] E: "of." Confusion of *d* ("of") and *w* ("and").
[z] C omits.
[aa] V: *mysby.* C: *myysbyn yt.* E, L, and AS: *mysbyn yt.*
[bb] C, E, L, and AS omit.

Notes, Chapter 4

[34]Tg. Chr follows Qere. Kethibh: *twlwn.*
[35]MT: "father."
[36]*Ruth R.* 2:1 links this verse to Josh 2:6, 12, where Rahab hid the spies in the flax and asked them to swear to her. Ashbea = *'šb'* and the root of the verb "to swear" is *šb'. Ruth R.* 2:2, however, sees the "linen connection" as relating to David "who busied himself with the curtain (of the Ark)." Other interpretations are also found in the same section of *Ruth R.* relating to verses 21–23, but few of them are reflected in Tg. Chr.
[37]MT: "and Jokim, and the men of Cozeba, and Joash and Saraph, who ruled in Moab, and Jashubi-Lehem: the matters/words are ancient." In the expansion we have a fusion of biblical and later traditions in a Joshua–Ruth context. The treatment of this verse in *b. B.B.* 91b has clearly made an impact on Tg. Chr: JOKIM (*ywqym*) is Joshua, because he kept (*hyqym*) his oath to the Gibeonites (Josh 9:15, 26). The men of COZEBA (*kzb'*) are the Gibeonites who lied (*kzb*) in order to ensure their future but who, on being found out, were sentenced to be hewers of wood and drawers of water for God's house (Josh 9:23). The reference to Moab later in the verse helps to introduce Mahlon and Chilion, with whom JOASH and SARAPH are identified, it would appear because Mahlon and Chilion were doomed not only because of their doom-laden names (from the root *ḥll,* "to profane," and from the root *klh,* "to destroy") but also because they left their land (*b. B.B.* 91a: "... even the merit of one's ancestors is of no avail when one leaves the land for a foreign country"). Joash (*yw'š*) has no hope because he lost hope (*y'š,* "to lose hope") in the messianic redemption of Israel; Saraph's (*śrp*) future was equally hopeless because he was condemned to be burned (*śrp,* "to burn"). WHO RULED IN MOAB, that is, they married wives of the women of Moab, as the verb *b'l* means both "to rule" and "to be a husband." JASHUBI-LEHEM "refers to Ruth the Moabitess, who returned and kept fast by Bethlehem of Judah" (*šwb,* "to return"). This line however, is not followed by Tg. Chr, which instead highlights Boaz, the mighty man in Torah, as leader of the Bethlehem academy. THE THINGS ARE ANCIENT: these things were said by the Ancient of Days (Dan 7:9, 22), which suggests that all that has happened was preordained by God. Tg. Chr's approach is not quite so forceful, though we are left with the picture of intense Torah activity in the academy of Bethlehem.

and appointed times: they[cc] *were allowed to* sit there, *and there was agreement*[cc] *in heaven with their opinions, in the days of Ruth, the mother of the kingdom*[dd] *and up to the days of king Solomon.*[38] 24. The sons of Simeon: Nemuel, Jamin, Jarib, Zerah, Shaul—*who was Zimri*[ee]—*who handed over his body for punishment.*[39] 25.[ff] Shallum was his son, Mibsam his son, Mishma his son. 26. The sons of Mishma: Hammuel[gg] his son, Zaccur his son, Shimei his son.[gg] 27. Shimei had sixteen sons and six daughters. His brothers, however, did not have many sons; as a result, their whole family did not have as many *sons* as the sons of Judah. 28. They lived in Beersheba, Moladah, *Hazartaalah,*[40] 29.[hh] in Bilhah, in *Etam,*[41] in Tolad, 30. in *Bethel,*[42] in Hormah, in Ziklag, 31. in *Uryawat Artikaya,*[43] in *Darath*

Apparatus, Chapter 4

[cc-cc] Missing in E.
[dd] C: "kingdoms."
[ee] E: *smry.* L and AS repeat "Saul" after "Zimri." C adds a variant reading: *š'wl š'yl gwpyh lpwr'nwt'* ("Saul, his body was requested for punishment").

[ff] E omits verses 25 and 26.
[gg-gg] Following C. Missing in V.
[hh] E omits verses 29 and 30.

Notes, Chapter 4

[38]MT: "These were the potters and the inhabitants of Netaim and Gederah; they dwelt there with the king for his work." The expansion here gives us an ideal picture of the lofty status and important role of those who love Torah; in this context one assumes he has in mind such as those over whom Boaz presided in the academy of Bethlehem. Each statement has a link with MT.

i) For them the world was created. MT: "potters": root *yṣr,* "to form," used in the creation story in Gen 2:7, 8, 19.

ii) They judge and establish the world. MT: "the inhabitants of Netaim": roots *yšb:* "to sit"; *nṭ':* "to plant, establish."

iii) They build up and restore the ruins of Israel. MT: "Gederah": root *gdr:* "to fence in, wall up" (a similar comment, based on Gedor, was made in verse 18).

iv) With the Shekinah of the king of the world. MT: "with the king." Shekinah is often used of God with emphasis on the notion of the divine presence.

v) By the service of the law, by the intercalation. MT: "in his work." It was of utmost importance that the festivals and all set times be held at the correct time. It was important, therefore, to know when the month/year began and, because of the difference between solar and lunar year, to know when to insert a day or a month. (See *PRE* ch. 7, 47, "... the intercalation is introduced to equalize the days of the solar year with the days of the lunar year.") Intercalation was so important that its principle was handed down from God to Adam and then passed on through the generations. (See, e.g., *PRE,* ch. 8.)

vi) They were allowed to sit there. MT: "they sat there." The reference to Ruth as the mother of the kingdom is an echo of *b. B.B.* 91b: Ruth, "who saw the kingdom of Solomon ...," on the basis of 1 Kgs 2:19: "and (Solomon) caused a throne to be set up for the king's mother," which R. Eleazar interpreted as "to the mother of the dynasty." Perhaps the most significant comment in this "manifesto" is the statement to the effect that heaven set its seal on all that they did, obviously because it was in line with the divine will.

[39]In *Num. R.* 21:3 the wicked Zimri is called Saul, "because he lent himself (*hish'il*) to transgression." Here Saul is identified with Zimri in slightly different terms.

[40]The second half of the place name is changed from *šw'l* (= "fox," Hebrew) to *t'l'* (= "fox," Aramaic).

[41]MT: *'ṣm,* followed by C, L, and AS.

[42]MT: *btw'l,* followed by L and AS.

[43]MT: "In Beth-Marcaboth, in Hazar-Susim." I have treated these as proper nouns in line with the other place names in the verse. These are in fact the approximate Aramaic equivalents of the Hebrew names, meaning: "the stables of the chariots," "the enclosures of the horses."

Susaya,[43] in Beth Biri, and in Shaaraim. These were their towns until David became king. 32. Their *camps*[44] were: Etam and Ain *and*[45] Rimmon and Tochen, and *Etan*[46]—five towns, 33. and all[ii] their *camps*[44] which were around these towns as far as Baal. This was their area of residence and they were officially registered for these places. 34. And *from Shobab,*[47] and Jamlech, *Jutah,*[48] the son of Amaziah, 35.[jj] Joel, Jehu the son of Joshibiah, the son of *Sheraiah,*[49] the son of Asiel, 36. Elioenai, Jaakobah,[kk] Jeshohaiah, Asaiah, Adiel, *Jeshimiel,*[50] Benaiah,[kk] 37. Ziza, the son of Shiphi, the[ll] son of Allon, the son of Jedaiah, the son of Shimri, the son of Shemaiah.[ll] 38. Those who came, *set apart* by name as officers in the *families of*[51] their clans, became very numerous. 39. They went to the *entrances*[52] of Gedor, to the east of the valley, to look for *a place suitable for* pasture for their flocks. 40. They found *a place suitable for* pasture, fat and good, and[mm] a land that was *rich and* spacious,[53] both peaceful and secure, for the people who had been resident there *from* of old belonged to *the sons of* Ham.[nn] 41. Those who had been *set apart*[54] by name came in the days of Hezekiah, king of *the tribe of* Judah. They struck down their tents and the *dwellings*[55] which *they* found there. They destroyed them completely, as is still the case today, and they settled in their place because it was an *area suitable for the* pasture of their flocks. 42. Some of them, five hundred men belonging to the sons of Simeon, went to the mountain of *Gebala;*[56] Pelatiah, Neariah, Rephaiah, and Uzziel, the sons of Ishi, *had been appointed*[oo][57] as *army commanders,* at their head. 43. They struck down the remainder of the survivors who belonged to *those of the house of* Amalek, and they have lived there to this day.

Apparatus, Chapter 4

[ii] E: "and in all."
[jj] E omits verses 35–37.
[kk-kk] Following C. Missing in V.
[ll-ll] Following C. Missing in V.
[mm] L and AS omit.

[nn] C omits "Ham."
[oo] V has singular form of verb, but C, L, and AS have plural. E has plural, albeit with a rearrangement of the consonants, which Beck corrects.

Notes, Chapter 4

[44] Borrowed from Latin, *castra,* "camp," in Aramaic form *qstr'* (C has *qstr'*). MJ 1396; JL II, 374. MT: "villages."
[45] Only V has "and." MT, C, E, L, and AS omit "and," giving the possibility of one place name: "Ain-Rimmon."
[46] MT: *'sn,* followed by C, E, L, and AS.
[47] MT: "Meshobab" (*mswbb*). The *m* in MT is understood as "from" (a shortened form of *mn*) in Tg. Chr.
[48] MT: *ywsh,* followed by C, E, L, and AS.
[49] MT: *sryh.*
[50] MT: *ysym'l.*
[51] MT: "in their families; and their clans increased greatly." Tg. Chr, by running "families" and "clans" together, has clearly made "those who came" the subject of the final verb.
[52] MT: singular.
[53] Lit.: "fat and wide of borders" for MT's "wide of (on) both hands, i.e., in both directions" (*BDB,* 390).
[54] MT: "those who were written by names."
[55] Following C, L, and AS. MT: "the Meunim" (Qere). V and E have "rebels" (*mrwdy*). Beck, however, recommends "dwellings," *habitacula, mdwry',* which is found in L, AS, and possibly also C. The Qere, *m'nym,* may have been construed as the plural of *m'wn,* "dwelling," even though the plural form is not found in the Old Testament.
[56] MT: "Seir." Cf. 1 Chr 1:38.
[57] V has singular form of verb, but there is clearly a plural reference.

CHAPTER 5

1. The sons of Reuben, the first-born of Israel: he was indeed the first-born, but when he desecrated *his sanctity by going up to* his father's bed, his birthright[a] was *taken away*[b] *from him and* given to the sons of Joseph, the son of Israel, so that *the sons of Reuben* would not be enrolled for the birthright. 2. Because Judah was the strongest of his brethren, *the kingship was taken away from Reuben and given to Judah, for he was a man*[c] *and it is from him that the kingship* comes. *As for Levi, he was a godly man, and (the Levites) did not act sinfully in the affair of "The Calf,"*[1] *so the high priesthood was taken away from the sons of Reuben and, because of them, from all their first-born,*[2] *and given to Aaron and his sons, the sacred service (was given) to the Levites,* but the birthright went to Joseph.[3] 3.[d] The sons of Reuben, the first-born of Israel: Hanoch, Pallu, Hezron, and Carmi. 4. The sons of Joel: Shemaiah his son, Gog his son, Shimei his son, 5. Micah his son, Reaiah his son, Baal his son, 6. Beerah his son, *who was Beerah the prophet,*[4] whom *Tiglath*[5]

Apparatus, Chapter 5

[a] V, C, E: *bkyrwtyh.* L and AS: *bkwrwtyh.* No difference in meaning.

[b] E: *'stlqt,* "was taken up," though in the next verse (2) he has the same reading as V.

[c] Though V points this as "man," *gbr'* (cf. also V's similar pointing in Tg. 1 Chr 1:10), C's reading of *gybr'* (mighty man) seems more acceptable, bearing in mind the context and Gen 49:8-12.

[d] E omits verses 3–5.

Notes, Chapter 5

[1] See Exod 32:25-29.

[2] The assumption is that before the inauguration of the levitical priesthood the cult was in the hands of the first-born (see discussion at 1:24 on Shem "the great priest"). Le Déaut notes how in Exod 24:5, in some of the Targums, "the young men" of MT who offer burnt offerings, etc., are replaced by "the first-born sons" (see also *b. Zeb.* 115b).

[3] The story of Reuben's sin—how he slept with his father's concubine, Bilhah—is narrated in Gen 35:22. The effects of that sin are recorded in Gen 49:3, 4, where it is stated that, as first-born, Reuben should have the preeminence, but "you shall not have preeminence because you went up to your father's bed." This sin, its effect, and its repentance are referred to again and again in later Jewish writings. From our point of view, of special interest are *b. Shab.* 55b, the Genesis Targums, especially of 49:3, 4, and *Gen. R.,* e.g., 97. In these documents the preeminence is spelled out in three ways: that his should have been the birthright, priesthood, and kingship; but because of his sin the birthright was passed to Joseph, the priesthood to Levi, and the kingship to Judah. (In Frg. Tg. of Deut 33:17, both birthright *and* kingship pass to Joseph.) It must be stated, however, that in these documents there is a strong element of compassion, e.g., forgiveness is promised Reuben, while in *b. Shab.* and Tg. Ps.-J. he is absolved of even committing the offence stated, but because he moved his father's bed, it was reckoned to him *as if* he had slept with his father's concubine; in Frg. Tg. and Tg. Neof. the words that describe the sinful act are not translated into Aramaic. Tg. Chr does not introduce the compassionate note: obviously the Targumist is less interested in Reuben than in the reallocation of the offices and the reasons for their reallocation to particular groups, e.g., the priesthood is passed to Levi because when the children of Israel worshiped the calf, Levi was faithful, and the kingship is passed to Judah because he was a mighty man.

[4] Beerah is identified with "Beerah the prophet," a reference, one assumes, to Hos 1:1, where Hosea is called "the son of Beeri." Beeri can also be regarded as a prophet, in line with *Lev. R.* 6:6: "wherever a prophet's own name is specified and his father's name also, he is a prophet, the son of a prophet."

[5] MT: *tlgt* = C. Many Hebrew MSS, LXX A, Syr have *tglt.*

Pilneser, the king of Assyria, took *into exile:* he was an officer of the *tribe of Reuben.*[6] 7. His brothers, by *their*[7] families, as registered in their family records,[8] *who were appointed as their* leaders:[9] Jeiel, Zechariah,[e] 8. and Bela, the son of Azaz, the son of Shema, the son of Joel: he lived in Aroer and as far as Nebo and *as far as the plain of*[10] Meon. 9. To the east his territory extended[11] to the edge of the desert *and*[12] from the river Euphrates, for their herds had increased in the land of Gilead. 10. In the days of Saul they waged war against the *Hongrites,*[f][13] who fell by their hands;[14] then they occupied their tents in the whole of the eastern part of Gilead.[15] 11. The sons of Gad, facing[16] them, lived in the land of *Buthnan*[g][17] as far as *Seleucia.*[18] 12. Joel was the president *of the Sanhedrin,*[19] Shapham[h] the *prin-*

Apparatus, Chapter 5

[e] C: "Zebadiah," confusion between two consonants of almost identical appearance *d* and *r.*
[f] V and C: *hwngr'yy.* E, L, and AS: *hwngr'y.*

[g] E: *bmtnn.*
[h] C: *špm;* L and AS: *špṭ* (LXX Saphat kai Saphan).

Notes, Chapter 5

[6]MT: "the Reubenite(s)."
[7]MT: "his," but LXX(L) and Syr have "their."
[8]MT: "according to their generations."
[9]Lit.: "who were appointed over them as the head." MT gives the impression that Jeiel was leader, followed by those listed. In Tg. Chr, however, Jeiel and those listed are the leaders.
[10]Sometimes in a place name the Targumist substitutes "plain" for the word "baal" (5:23; 14:11; Josh 11:17; 13:5; 2 Sam 5:20). But in Josh 13:17, two place names which have "baal" as a component part remain unchanged.
[11]Lit.: "he dwelt."
[12]MT: "*l*" "to," "for." E = MT.
[13]MT: "The Hagrites": a tribe located probably in North Arabia, as would seem to be suggested here. It is thought that there is some connection between their name and that of Hagar. In Ps 83:6 they are linked with Ishmaelites and Moabites as traditional enemies of Israel. Tg. Onq. and Tg. Ps.-J. identify Shur, near the Egyptian border, with Hagra (e.g., Gen 16:7), and as the Hebrew word Shur means "wall," the link may have been that of a wall for protection in a border area. *Num. R.* 13:2 also locates it in the south ("I shall bring back the captivity of Teman and that of the Hagrites and the entire south...."). Exactly whom Tg. Chr had in mind in 5:10, 19, 20; 27:31 is uncertain. MJ (339) calls the *hungr'y* "the inhabitants of Hagra," and Hagra is "an Arabian district" (332). JL (I, 203) calls them "die Ungaren," the Hungarians. R. Le Déaut calls them "the inhabitants of Hagrah," and he notes that Rashi regarded Hungary as "eretz Hagra"; he feels that the presence of the *Nun* in the Aramaic word points also in this direction.
[14]MT: "hand."
[15]By omitting the *l* prefixed to Gilead in MT, Tg. Chr shifts the emphasis from "the area east of Gilead" to "the eastern area of Gilead."
[16]Lit.: "opposite."
[17]Usual translation of Hebrew "Bashan" in Palestinian Targums: "Batanaea." In Tg. Onq. and Tg. Jonathan "Bashan" becomes "Mathnan," e.g., Josh 12:4.
[18]MT: *slkh.* Tg. Chr: *slwwky'.* Seleucia in northeastern Palestine, "an anachronistic adaptation of *slkh*" (MJ 994).
[19]Joel as "head" must be head of the most important body, the Sanhedrin.

cipal of the school,[i20] and Janai,[j] *the judge*[k21] in *Buthnan.*[l17] 13. Their brothers, according to their clans were: Michael, Meshullam, *Shema,*[22] Jorai, Jacan,[m] Zia, and Eber—*the* seven *of them rulers.* 14.[n] These were the sons of Abihail, the son of Huri, the son of Jaroah, the son of Gilead, the son of Michael, the son of Jeshishai, the son of Jahdo, the son of Buz. 15. Ahi, the son of Abdiel, the son of Guni, *was appointed* head[o] of their clans. 16. They lived in Gilead, in *Buthnan,*[p23] and in its villages,[24] and in all the outlying areas of *the plain*[25] right to their extremities. 17. All of them were registered in the days of Jotham, king of *the tribe of the house of* Judah, and in the days of Jeroboam, king of Israel. 18. The sons of Reuben and Gad[26] and the half tribe of Manasseh: some of their mighty warriors, men who carried shields[27] and *were equipped with* swords,[28] and who drew the bow and were trained in warfare—forty four thousand, seven hundred and sixty, ready for military service. 19. They waged war against the *Hongrites*[13] and Jetur, Naphish and Nodab. 20. *Their*[q] brethren, the house of Israel,[q] gave them assistance[r28] and the *Hongrites*[13] and all who were with them were delivered[s] into their *hands*[29] because they had *prayed before the Lord*[30] during the battle. He *had received their prayer,*[31]

Apparatus, Chapter 5

[i] E: "his schools."
[j] E: *yy't.* C: + *špt.*
[k] C: "judges."
[l] E: *bbmtnn.* C: *bmtnn.*
[m] C, E, L, and AS: *y'bn.*
[n] E omits verse 14.
[o] Missing in E.
[p] C: *mtnn.* E: *bmtnn;* cf. 1.

[q-q] Missing in E.
[r] V and C use a form of the verb *sy':* E, L, and AS of the verb *s'd,* both verbs meaning "to help, assist."
[s] V and C use a form of the verb *msr,* "to hand over"; E, L, and AS of the verb *yhb,* "to give" (= MT).

Notes, Chapter 5

[20]MT: *hmšnh* (Ha Mishneh), "the second." This word comes from the root *šnh,* "to repeat, do a second time." From the same root comes *Mishnah:* "repetition, verbal teaching by repeated recitation, traditional law, collection of oral laws," eventually known as "the Mishnah." The verb *šnh* also came to mean "to study the Mishnah," then a general word, "to study, to teach." "Shapham the second" thus becomes "Shapham, the principal of the school." See also Tg. 2 Chr 34:22.

[21]MT: *špt,* "Shaphat"; in Tg. Chr this word has had a change of vowels, *dyyn'* in Tg. Chr presupposing "Shophet" = judge, in MT.

[22]MT: *šb',* followed by C, L, and AS.

[23]MT: "Bashan."

[24]MT: "daughters," i.e., dependent villages.

[25]MT: "Sharon." The change from *šrwn* to *myšr,* Le Déaut suggests, may have taken place because of a similarity of consonants, or because "Sharon" was regarded as *the* plain par excellence, or because both words go back to the same basic sort, *yšr.*

[26]MT: "Gadite."

[27]MT: singular.

[28]MT: "They were assisted against them."

[29]MT: singular.

[30]MT: "cried to God."

[31]MT: "he was entreated by them" or "he let himself be entreated by them" = "he granted their request."

because they had trusted in *his Memra.*[32] 21. They carried off their livestock: their fifty thousand camels,[i] two hundred and fifty thousand sheep, two thousand asses, along with one hundred thousand people.[33] 22. For many fell slain, because the battle was from *before*[u] *the Memra of the Lord,*[34] and they dwelt in their territory until the exile[v] *of Sennacherib, the king of Assyria.* 23. The sons of the half–tribe of Manasseh dwelt in the land from *Buthnan*[35] to *the plain of*[36] Hermon[w] and the mountain of *the stinking fruits*[37] and Mount Hermon. They were numerous. 24. These were the heads of their clans: Epher,[38] Ishi, Eliel, Azriel, Jeremiah, Hodaviah, and Jahdiel—men who were mighty warriors, men of renown, *appointed*[x] heads of their clans. 25. But they were unfaithful to the God of their fathers, and they went astray after the *idols*[39] of the peoples of the land whom *the Lord*[40] had destroyed from before them. 26. Then *the Memra of* the God of Israel aroused the *vehemence*[41] of Pul,[y] the king of Assyria,[z] and the *vehemence*[41] of[y] Tilgathpilneser,[aa] the king of Assyria, and *they*[42] took them into exile—the *tribe of Reuben,*[43] the *tribe of Gad,*[44] and the half–tribe of Manasseh, and *they*[42] brought

Apparatus, Chapter 5

[i] C, E, L, and AS: "their livestock and their camels fifty thousand...." V (= MT) lacks the *Waw* "and," suggesting that the animals following "livestock" are meant to be taken in apposition to that word.
[u] Missing in C.

[v] C, E, L, and AS: "until the time of the exile."
[w] Missing in E.
[x] E, L, and AS: "and appointed."
[y-y] Missing in E, probably by homoioteleuton.
[z] C: "Aram."
[aa] C: "Tiglathpilneser."

Notes, Chapter 5

[32]MT: "in him."
[33]MT: Lit.: "soul of man" (*npš 'dm*). V: Lit.: "soul of the sons of man." C, E, L, and AS: Lit.: "souls of the sons of man."
[34]MT: "from God."
[35]MT: "Bashan." C = MT. E: "which was in Mathnan." L and AS: "which was from Buthnan."
[36]MT: "Baal." See note 10.
[37]MT: *śnyr*. Deut 3:9 gives two alternative names for Hermon: Sirion and Senir. Tg. Chr seems to have taken over and applied to Senir the explanation given for "Sirion" in *Tg. Ps.-J.* and *Frg. Tg.* (V) of Deut 3:9 and in the Targum of Ps 29:6: *msry pyrwy*, based on the verb *sry*, "to stink." Aph. "to make stink." Thus, "a mountain causing its fruits to stink" (See JL II, 190). MJ (1026) suggests *mśyr pyrwy*, a mountain "that drops its fruit," from *nšr*, "to drop." Beck reads E as a proper noun, "the mountain of Mesre Parzi." (Waw has become zayin in the second word.) L and AS have *mysr przy*, "the mountain of the plain of Parzi."
[38]MT: "And Epher." The other versions also omit "and," whose presence in MT may indicate that an earlier name has dropped out.
[39]MT: "gods." In MT "Elohim" is normally translated "God," but in certain contexts is better translated "gods" (of the nations, etc.). Tg. Chr, however, will not dignify such non-entities by allowing the divine name to be used to describe them. The word often used to describe them is *ṭ'wt*, lit., "going astray" or "idol" (from *ṭ'y*: "to go astray").
[40]MT: "God."
[41]MT: "spirit."
[42]MT: "he." V seems to have thought of Tilgathpilneser and Pul as two separate people, but E, C, L, and AS agree with MT.
[43]MT: "the Reubenite(s)."
[44]MT: "the Gadite(s)."

them to Hala and Habor, *the mountains of darkness,*[45] and the river of Gozan, to this day. 27.[bb] The sons of Levi: Gershon,[cc] Kehath, and Merari.[cc] 28. The sons of Kehath: Amram,[dd] Izhar, Hebron, and Uzziel.[dd] 29. The sons[46] of Amram: Aaron,[ee] Moses and Miriam; the sons of Aaron: Nadab, Abihu, Eleazar, and Ithamar.[ee] 30. Eleazar became the father of Phinehas, Phinehas became the father of Abishua, 31. Abishua became the father of Bukki, Bukki became the father of Uzzi, 32. Uzzi became the father of Zerahiah, Zerahiah became the father of Meraioth, 33. Meraioth became the father of Amariah, Amariah became the father of Ahitub, 34. Ahitub became the father of Zadok, Zadok became the father of Ahimaaz, 35. Ahimaaz became the father of Azariah, Azariah became the father of Johanan, 36. Johanan became the father of Azariah—it was he who was *appointed as priest*[47] in the house which Solomon built in Jerusalem. 37.[ff] Azariah became the father of Amariah, Amariah became the father of Ahitub, 38. Ahitub became the father of Zadok, Zadok became the father of Shallum, 39. Shallum became the father of Hilkiah, Hilkiah became the father of Azariah, 40. Azariah became the father of *Sheraiah,*[48] *Sheraiah*[48] became the father of Jehozadak. 41. Jehozadak went *into exile* when the Lord took *the men of* Judah and *the inhabitants of* Jerusalem into exile by the hand of Nebuchadnezzar.

Apparatus, Chapter 5

[bb] E omits verses 27-35.
[cc-cc] Following C. Missing in V.
[dd-dd] Following C. Missing in V.

[ee-ee] Following C. Missing in V.
[ff] E omits verses 37-40.

Notes, Chapter 5

[45]MT: "Hara." "Hara" is a place name like Hala and Habor, but perhaps because of its similarity to the Hebrew word for "mountain" (*har*), Tg. Chr uses it to stress the horror of exile by shrouding both places in darkness. Le Déaut refers to Tg. Jer 13:16.

[46]"sons" may seem out of place with the inclusion of "Miriam" in the list. To alter it, however, might give the impression that a different word is used in the original text, either Hebrew or Aramaic. This is not the case.

[47]MT: "who acted as priest" (verb).

[48]MT: "Seraiah." L = V.

CHAPTER 6

1.*^a* The sons of Levi: Gershom, Kehath, and Merari. 2. These are the names of the*^b* sons of Gershom: Libni and Shimei.*^b* 3.*^c* The sons of Kehath: Amram,*^d* Izhar, Hebron, and Uzziel.*^d* 4. The sons of Merari: Mahli and Mushi. These are the families of the Levites according to their fathers. 5.*^e* Of Gershom: Libni his son, Jahath his son, Zimmah his son, 6. *and* Joah his son, Iddo his son, Zerah his son, and *Atherai*[1] his son. 7. The sons of Kehath: Amminadab his son, Korah his son, Assir his son, 8. Elkanah his son, and *Abiasaph*[2] his son and Assir his son, 9. Tahath his son, Uriel his son, Uzziah his son, and Shaul his son. 10. The sons of Elkanah: Amasai*^f* and Ahimoth.*^f* 11. Elkanah: *the sons of*[3] Elkanah: Zophai his son and Nahath his son, 12. Eliab his son, Jeroham his son, Elkanah his son. 13. The sons of Samuel*^g* the first-born Vashni and Abijah. 14. The sons of Merari: Mahli; Libni his son, Shimei his son, Uzzah his son, 15. *Shimeah*[4] his son, Haggiah his son, Asaiah his son. 16. These are the men whom David appointed to be in charge of the singing of the *sanctuary* house*^h* of the Lord, *when* the Ark was deposited *in it.* 17. They ministered with songs before *the tent,* the tent of meeting,[5] until Solomon had built the *sanctuary* house of the Lord in Jerusalem. They carried out their service in accordance with the rules laid down for them.[6] 18. Those who served, *they and* their sons: From the sons of *Kehath:*[7] Heman the singer, the son of Joel, the son of Samuel, 19. the son of Elkanah, the*ⁱ* son of Jeroham, the son of Eliel, the son of Toah,*ⁱ* 20.*^j* the son of Zuph,[8] the*^k* son of Elkanah, the son of Mahath, the son of Amasai,*^k* 21. the son of Elkanah, the*^l* son of Joel, the son of Azariah, the

---

Apparatus, Chapter 6

^a E omits verse 1.

^{b-b} Missing in E.

^c E omits verse 3.

^{d-d} Following C. Missing in V.

^e E omits verses 5-15.

^{f-f} Following C. Missing in V.

^g C inserts "Elqanah" before Samuel, as do L and AS. It is of note that in spite of the difficulties MT presents in this verse, V follows MT rigidly.

^h After "house" C inserts an alternative reading: "tent."

ⁱ⁻ⁱ Following C. Missing in V.

^j E omits verses 20-23.

^{k-k} Following C. Missing in V.

^{l-l} Following C. Missing in V, in verse 21 and in verse 22.

Notes, Chapter 6

[1]V has read yod as waw. The other witnesses follow MT and read *y'try.*

[2]MT: "Ebiasaph." V = C.

[3]V follows Qere, but C, L, and AS adopt the Kethibh: "his son."

[4]MT: *šm'.* C, L, and AS follow MT.

[5]MT: "the tent of the tent of meeting."

[6]Lit: "They stood, as was proper for them, upon/by their service."

[7]MT: "the Kehathite(s)."

[8]Tg. Chr follows Qere. Kethibh is *ṣyp.*

son of Zephaniah,[l] 22. the son of Tahath, the[l] son of Assir, the son of *Abiasaph,*[9] the son of Korah,[l] 23. the son of Izhar, the son of Kehath, the son of Levi, the son of Israel. 24. And his brother Asaph, who stood[m] at his right hand; *he* was Asaph, the son of Berechiah, the son of Shimea, 25.[n] the son of Michael, the[o] son of Baaseiah, the son of Malchijah,[o] 26. the son of Ethni, the son of Zerah, the son of *Azariah,*[10] 27. the son of Ethan, the[p] son of Zimmah, the son of Shimei,[p] 28. the son of Jahath, the son of Gershom, the son of Levi. 29. The sons of Merari, their brethren, were on the left: Ethan, the son of Kishi,[q] the son of Abdi, the son of Malluch, 30.[r] the son of Hashabiah, the[s] son of Amaziah, the son of Hilkiah,[s] 31. the son of *Amai,*[11] the[t] son of Bani, the son of Shemer,[t] 32. the son of Mahli, the son of Mushi, the son of Merari, the son of Levi. 33. Their brethren, the Levites, were put in charge of all the service of the tent of the *sanctuary* house of *the Lord.*[12] 34. But Aaron and his sons *were offering up sweet-smelling incense*[13] upon the altar of the burnt offering and upon the altar of incense, for all the service of the Holy of Holies and[u] to make atonement for Israel, according to all that Moses the servant of *the Lord*[12] had commanded. 35.[v] These are the sons of Aaron: Eleazar his son, Phinehas his son, Abishua his son, 36. Bukki his son, Uzzi his son, Zerahiah his son, 37. Meraioth his son, Amariah his son, Ahitub his son, 38. Zadok his son, Ahimaaz his son. 39. These are their places of residence, according to their *villages*[14] within their borders: to the sons of Aaron who belonged to the family of Kehath—for *this was the share assigned to them by* lot[15]— 40. To them they gave Hebron in the land of *the house of* Judah, and its common land round about it,[w] 41. but the fields belonging to the town and its hamlets they gave to Caleb, the son of Jephunneh. 42. To the sons of Aaron they gave the cities of refuge—Hebron, Libnah and its common land, Jattir,[x] Eshtemoa and its common land, 43.[y] *Helen*[16] and its common land, Debir and its common land, 44. Ashan

Apparatus, Chapter 6

[m] C, by rearranging the consonants *dq'ym,* giving *d'qym,* has "whom he appointed."

[n] E omits verses 25-28.

[o-o] Following C. Missing in V.

[p-p] Following C. Missing in V.

[q] E: "Kushi."

[r] E omits verses 30-32.

[s-s] Following C. Missing in V.

[t-t] Following C. Missing in V.

[u] C, L, and AS omit "and."

[v] E omits verses 35-38.

[w] E, L, and AS: *shwr ḥzrnwth'.*

[x] Missing in E.

[y] E omits verses 43 and 44.

Notes, Chapter 6

[9] MT: "Ebiasaph"; cf. verse 8.

[10] MT: "Adaiah" = C, L, and AS.

[11] MT: "Amzi" (*'mṣy*) = C, L, and AS.

[12] MT: "God."

[13] Lit.: "offered up incense of spices." The Hebrew uses simply the Hiph. of *qṭr,* "to make sacrifices smoke, to offer incense."

[14] MT: "encampments," "settlements."

[15] MT: "for to them was the lot."

[16] MT: "Hilez" (*ḥylz*), though many MSS have *ḥyln.* C, L, and AS have *ḥlyn.*

and its common land, Beth Shemesh and its common land. 45. And from the tribe of Benjamin, Geba and its common land, Alemeth[z] and its common land, Anathoth and its common land. All their cities throughout their families were thirteen cities. 46. To the sons of Kehath who remained over from the family of the tribe, from the half-tribe of Manasseh,[17] ten towns *assigned to them* by lot. 47. To the sons of Gershom according to their families, thirteen towns (were allotted) from the tribe of Issachar, from the tribe of Asher, from the tribe of Naphtali, and from the tribe of Manasseh in *Buthnan*.[18] 48. To the sons of Merari according to their families, twelve towns from the tribe of Reuben and from the tribe of Gad and from the tribe of Zebulun *were assigned* by lot. 49. So the children of Israel gave the Levites the towns and their common lands. 50. They also gave, *assigned* by lot, from the tribe of the sons of Judah, from the tribe of the sons of Simeon, and from the tribe of the sons of Benjamin, these towns which they designated by name. 51. Some of the families of the sons of Kehath had towns of their territory from the tribe of Ephraim. 52. To them they gave the cities of refuge: Shechem and its common land in the hill country of[aa] Ephraim, Gezer and its common land, 53.[bb] Yokmeam and its common land, Beth Horon and its common land, 54. Aijalon and its common land, Gath Rimmon and its common land. 55. And from the half-tribe of Manasseh, Aner and its common land, *Jobleam*[19] and its common land, for the families *of* the sons of Kehath who were left over. 56. To the sons of Gershom (they gave) from the family of the half-tribe[cc] of Manasseh, Golan in *Buthnan*[18] and its common land and Ashtaroth and its common land. 57. From the tribe of Issachar, Kedesh and its common land, Daberath and its common land, 58. Ramoth and its common land, *Anam*[20] and its common land. 59. From the tribe of Asher: Mashal and its common land, Abdon and its common land, 60. Hukkok and its common land, Rehob and its common land. 61. From the tribe of Naphtali: Kedesh in Galilee and its common land, Hammon and its common land and Kiriathaim and its common land. 62. To the sons of Merari who remained over (they gave) from the tribe of Zebulun: Rimmon and its common land *and*[21] Tabor and its common land. 63. And on the other side of the Jordan, *opposite*[22] Jericho, on the east of the Jordan, from the tribe of Reuben: Bezer in the wilderness and its common land, Jahzah and its common land, 64.[dd] Kedemoth

Apparatus, Chapter 6

[z] C: "Alamoth."
[aa] C adds "the house of."
[bb] E omits verses 53 and 54.

[cc] Missing in C.
[dd] E omits verse 64-66.

Notes, Chapter 6

[17] This verse in MT is very difficult. Tg. Chr tries to tidy it up, by omitting "half" from before "of Manasseh."
[18] MT: "Bashan." C, E, L, and AS: "Mathnan."
[19] MT: "Bileam (*bl'm;* V has *ybl'm*). Cf. Josh 17:11.
[20] MT: "Anem" = C.
[21] "And" missing in MT, C, E, L, and AS.
[22] Tg. Chr prefixes *d* to "Jericho," and "opposite" seems to be implied; hence the translation. See also Josh 20:8.

and its common land and Mephaath and its common land. 65. From the tribe of Gad: Ramoth in Gilead and its common land, Mahanaim and its common land, 66. *Hushbanah*[23] and its common land and Jazer and its common land.

CHAPTER 7

1.[a] The sons[1] of Issachar: Tola, Puah, *Job,*[2] and Shimron—four. 2. The sons of Tola: Uzzi, Rephaiah, Jeriel, Jahmai, Ibsam,[b] and Samuel, *appointed* heads *over* their clans, *called by the name of* Tola *their leader,* mighty warriors, according to their family lists; their total[c] number during the days of David was twenty two thousand, six hundred. 3. The sons of Uzzi: Izrahiah. The sons of Izrahiah: Michael, Obadiah, Joel and Isshiah. All five of them *were appointed as* heads. 4. As well as them, military units ready for battle *were established* according to their family lists, according to their clans,[d]—thirty-six thousand, for they had many wives and sons. 5. Their brethren, who belonged to all the families of Issachar, were eighty-seven thousand mighty warriors, and all of them were enrolled. 6. *The sons of*[3] Benjamin: Bela, Becher, and *Jedaiah*[4]—three. 7. The sons of Bela: Ezbon, Uzzi, Uzziel, Jerimoth and *Iro;*[5] the five *of them* were heads of clans, *placed in*

Notes, Chapter 6

[23]MT: "Heshbon." Heshbon was a city of Moab, held by the Amorites, captured by the Israelites, and assigned eventually to the Levites. It is mentioned in a ballad in Num 21:27-30. The root behind the word is *ḥšb,* "to think, consider, count, calculate." In the treatment of this passage in Tg. Num, which becomes an exhortation to calculate the effects of good and evil actions, the righteous are seen as those who are able to make such a calculation (*ḥwšbn'*). *b. B.B.* 78b also has a discussion, based on the same passage in Numbers, on the theme that good and evil actions bring their own reward. It is assumed that Tg. Chr, in using this word *ḥwšbn'* to replace the name "Heshbon," was aware of the traditions behind Tg. Num 21 and *b. B.B.* 78b.

Apparatus, Chapter 7

[a] E omits verse 1.
[b] E: "Ibsham."

[c] C, L, AS: "their number." E omits.
[d-d] Missing in E.

Notes, Chapter 7

[1]Both MT and Tg. Chr have "and to the sons of." LXX(A), Syr, Vg have "the sons of."
[2]MT: Qere *yšwb*; Kethibh *yšyb*. Tg. Chr's reading is found in the MT parallel passage. Gen 46:13.
[3]"The sons of": missing in MT, perhaps through haplography.
[4]MT: "Jediael"; C, L, and AS = MT. In E the whole verse except for the final word is missing.
[5]MT: "Iri." C, E, L, and AS = MT.

charge of the mighty warriors, and they were enrolled *in charge of* twenty-two[e] thousand and thirty-four. 8.[f] The sons of Becher: Zemirah, Joash, Eliezer, Elioenai, Omri, Jeremoth, Abijah, Anathoth, and Alemeth. All these were the sons of Becher. 9. They were enrolled, according to[g] their family lists, heads of their clans—twenty thousand two hundred mighty warriors. 10.[h] The sons of Jediael: Bilhan. The sons of Bilhan: *Jeush,*[6] Benjamin, Ehud, Chenaanah, Zethan,[i] Tarshish, and Ahishahar. 11. All these, the sons of Jediael, became the heads of *their* clans, mighty warriors, seventeen thousand two hundred, ready for active service. 12.[j] Shuppim and Huppim, *who dwelt in the town of*[7] Hushim, were sons of Aher. 13. The sons of Naphtali: *Jahzeel,*[8] Guni, Jezer, and *Shillem,*[9] the sons of Bilhah. 14. The sons of Manasseh: *Ashriel,*[10] whom his Aramaean concubine bore; she was *also*[11] the mother of Machir, the father of *the Gileadites.*[12] 15. Machir took a wife *from the Hushites and the Huphites.*[k][13] Their[14] sister's name was Maacah. The name of the second was Zelophehad, and Zelophehad had daughters. 16. Maacah, the wife of Machir, bore a son and she called his name Peresh and his brother's name Sheresh, and his sons were Ulam and Rakem. 17.[l] The sons of Ulam: Bedan. These were the sons of Gilead, the son of Machir, the son of Manasseh. 18. His sister, who was queen,[15] bore Ishhod,[m] Abiezer and Mahlah.[m] 19.[n] The sons of Shemida were Ahian, Shechem, Likhi and Aniam. 20. The sons of Ephraim: Shuthalah, Bered his son, Tahath his son, Eleadah his son, Tahath his son, 21. Zabad his son, Shuthelah

Apparatus, Chapter 7

[e] Missing in E.
[f] E omits verse 8.
[g] E has "and."
[h] E omits verse 10.
[i] C, L, and AS: *dytn.*

[j] E omits verses 12 and 13.
[k] C has: "from the Huphites and the Hushites."
[l] E omits verse 17.
[m-m] Missing in E.
[n] E omits verses 19 and 20.

Notes, Chapter 7

[6]Follows Qere. Kethibh = *y'yš.*

[7]Tg. Chr treats what in MT seems to be a person's name, *'yr,* as a common noun meaning "city." V regards it as being in the construct state, giving the translation above, while C, L, and AS take it as being in the absolute state: "S and H, who dwelt in a town; Hushim, the sons of Aher."

[8]MT: "Jahziel" (*yhṣy'l*). V's reading is found in some Hebrew MSS and in Gen 46:24; Num 26:48. C, L, and AS agree with MT.

[9]MT: "Shallum" (*šlwm*). V's reading is found in a few Hebrew MSS and in Gen 46:24; Num 26:49. C, L, and AS agree with MT.

[10]MT: "Asriel."

[11]Missing in MT. (C = MT). E, L, and AS have *d* instead of *w* (as in V). As both these consonants have a similar appearance, there may have been some confusion. The *d* would have to be translated as either "who" or "for."

[12]MT: "Gilead."

[13]MT: "for Huppim and Shippim."

[14]MT: "his."

[15]Translating V, in spite of the vowel pointing, as "who reigned/became queen," in line with the feminine participle of the same verb in MT.

his son, and Ezer[o] and Elead. *They were the officers of the house of Ephraim who had calculated the fixed time from the hour that the word of the Lord of the universe had been communicated to Abraham between the pieces. But they had made a mistake, for it would have been more correct if they had made the calculation from the day that Isaac was born. Thus they had gone out from Egypt thirty years before*[p] *the time appointed because it was thirty years before Isaac was born that the word of the Lord of the universe had been communicated to Abraham between the pieces. When they went out from Egypt there were with them two hundred thousand men with weapons of every kind from the tribe of Ephraim.* The men of Gath, who had been born in the land *of the Philistines,* killed them, because they had come down to raid[16] their herds.[17] 22. Their father, Ephraim, mourned *for them* many days and *all* his brothers came to comfort him. 23. Then he went in to his wife; she conceived and bore a son. He[q] called his name Beriah,[18] because (he was born) in the misfortune which was in his house. 24. His daughter was Sheerah, *who survived the massacre;*[19] she built lower Beth-Horon and upper *Beth-Horon,* as well as Uzzan *of* Sheerah. 25.[r] Rephah was his son, Resheph *his son,*[20] Telah his son, Tahan his son, 26. Ladan his son, Ammihud his son, Elishama his son, 27. Non his son, Joshua his son. 28. Their inheritance and *the area of their settlement*[21] were Bethel and its

Apparatus, Chapter 7

[o] Missing in E.

[p-p] Missing in E. Homoioteleuton.

[q] C, E, L, and AS: "She called," as in a few Hebrew MSS and Syr.

[r] E omits verses 25-27.

Notes, Chapter 7

[16]MT: "to take."

[17]In Exod 13:17 God led his people out, not by way of the Philistines, the reason being that they might see the bodies of the Ephraimites on that road, take fright and return to Egypt. These Ephraimites, two hundred thousand of them, had been killed because they were raiding the cattle of the men of Gath (1 Chr 7:21). They had been driven to this because of hunger on their premature journey from Egypt. This premature departure came about through a computing error: they had miscalculated the departure date. According to Gen 15:13, they were to leave the land after four hundred years; but it was intended that the counting of the four hundred years should begin with the birth of Isaac, "until four hundred years after seed shall be granted to thee" (*Gen. R.* 44:18). They, however, made their calculation starting from the making of God's covenant with Abraham, i.e., thirty years earlier. They left, therefore, before the fixed time, with disastrous consequences: "the children of Ephraim, who, having left Egypt thirty years before the appointed time had arrived, fell into the hands of the Philistines ... and were killed" (Tg. Song of Songs 2:7). Their bones were the dry bones which God restored to life through Ezekiel. See, e.g., the Palestinian Targums of Exod 13:17; *b. San.* 92b; *PRE* 48; *Exod. R.* 20:11.

[18]The word play in MT between the name "Beriah" (*bry'h*) and the expression "with misfortune" (*br'h*) is not carried over into the Tg. Chr because the Aramaic word for "misfortune" comes from a different root.

[19]Lit.: "who was left over from those slain." The name "Sheerah" (*š'rh*) comes from the root in Hebrew and Aramaic *š'r*, "to remain, be left over," and on this meaning the expansion is based.

[20]Missing in MT, though a few Hebrew MSS have it. C, L, and AS = MT.

[21]MT: "their settlements."

villages,[22] to the east *Naadan,*[23] to the west Gezer and its *villages,*[22] Shechem and its *villages,*[22] *Adaiah*[s] and its *villages,*[22] 29. and *on the border*[24] *of* the sons of Manasseh, Beth-Shean and its *villages,*[t22] Taanach and its *villages,*[22] Megiddo and its *villages,*[22] and *Dor*[25] and its *villages.*[t22] In these dwelt the sons of Joseph, the son of Israel. 30.[u] The sons of Asher: Imnah, Ishvah, Ishvi, Beriah and their sister, Serah.[v] 31. The sons of Beriah: Heber and Malchiel who was the father of Birzaith.[26] 32. Heber became the father of *Jiphlet,*[27] Shomer, Hotham, and their sister, *Shuthah.*[28] 33. The sons of Japhlet: Pasach, Bimhal and Ashvath. These were the sons of Japhlet. 34. The sons of Shemer: Ahi, Rohgah, *Hubbah*[29] and Aram. 35. The son of Helem his brother: Zophah, Imna, Shelesh and Amal. 36. The sons of Zophah: *Savvah,*[30] Harnepher, Shual, Beri, Imrah, 37. Bezer, Hod,[w] *Shammah,*[x] Shilshah, Ithran and Beera.[w] 38. The sons of Jether: Jephunneh,[y] Pispa and Ara.[y] 39. The sons of Ulla: Arah,[z] Hanniel and Rizia.[z] 40. All these were the sons of Asher, heads of clans, chosen men, mighty warriors, the leaders of the officers: they were enrolled as fit for military service;[31] their total number was twenty-six thousand men.

Apparatus, Chapter 7

[s] C, L, and AS: *'d 'zh,* which is found also in many Hebrew MSS, LXX(A), Vg. E has *'d 'yh.*

[t-t] Missing in E, probably through homoioteleuton.

[u] E omits verses 30-39.

[v] V and MT: *śrḥ.* C, L, and AS: *srḥ*

[w-w] Following C. Missing in V.

[x] C, L, and AS: *šmh.* MT *šm.'*

[y-y] Following C. Missing in V.

[z-z] Following C. Missing in V.

Notes, Chapter 7

[22] MT: "daughters," dependent villages.

[23] MT: "Naaran." C, E, L, and AS = MT.

[24] MT: "on the hands."

[25] MT: *dwr.* C, L, and AS = MT.

[26] Tg. Chr follows Qere. Kethibh: *brzwt.*

[27] MT: Japhlet = C.

[28] MT: *šw''* = C, L, and AS.

[29] MT: V follows Qere. C, L, and AS follow Kethibh, (*yḥbh*).

[30] MT: "Suah" (*swḥ*). In V the *w* is a doubled consonant. C = MT.

[31] Lit.: "in the army, in the battle."

CHAPTER 8

1.[a] Benjamin was the father of Bela his first-born, Ashbel *second*,[1] *Ahara*[2] the third. 2. Nohah the fourth and Rapha the fifth. 3. Bela had sons: Addar, Gera, Abihud, 4. Abishua, Naaman,[b] Ahoah,[b] 5. Gera, *Shephupham*[b3] and[b] Huram.[b] 6. These were the sons of Ehud—they were heads of clans of the inhabitants of *Gibatha*,[4] and they were deported[5] to Manahath, *to the land of the house of Esau*: 7. Naaman, Ahijah and Gera[6]—it was *they* who led them into exile—and he was the father of Uzza and Ahihud. 8. Shaharaim had children in the land[7] of Moab after he had divorced *and then remarried*[8] his wives Hushim and Baara. 9. From *Baara*,[c] *that is, Hodeshah*,[9] his wife—*for a novel interpretation of the law was established through her marriage*[d10]—he became the father of Jobab, Zibea, Mesha, Malcam, 10. Jeuz, *Shabiah*[11] and Mirmah. These were his sons, heads of clans.[e] 11. By Hushim *his wife*[f] he became the father of *Ahitob*[12] and Elpaal. 12. The sons of Elpaal: Eber, Misham and *Shamer*.[13] *It was Elpaal* who built Ono and Lod and

Apparatus, Chapter 8

[a] E omits verses 1-5.
[b] Following C. Missing in V.
[c] C: *b'rt*.
[d] V: *bnśw'h*. E, L, and AS split this into two words, *bny sw'h*, giving what JL (II, 131) calls a meaning-

less translation: "because he restored the sons of Sua."
[e] E: "their clans."
[f] Missing in E.

Notes, Chapter 8

[1] MT: "the second."
[2] MT: *ḥrḥ*. V: *ḥr'*. C, L, and AS = MT.
[3] MT: "Shephuphan," though a few MSS have "Shephupham." L and AS = C.
[4] MT: "Geba." See 6:45 where it remains Geba in Tg. Chr.
[5] Lit.: "and they deported them."
[6] MT suggests that Gera was the one who led them into exile. Tg. Chr implies that the three men named were involved in this exercise, which raises the question as to who is the subject of the next verb "and he became the father of." The simplest solution is to put the "exile" clause in parenthesis and to regard the last named, viz., Gera, as the subject of the next verb.
[7] Lit.: "fields."
[8] This addition alters the sense of MT, which suggests that these two wives are divorced, and then in the next verse children are born to a different wife. The addition in Tg. Chr necessitates the retention of Baara in verse 9 as an alternative name for Hodesh.
[9] MT: "Hodesh."
[10] Following the translation of MJ (909), who, in line with *y. Yeb.* 9C supplies the word *halakah* as the something new referred to. It is assumed that Baara was a Moabitess, and the new interpretation of Deut 23:4 made plain that an Ammonitess and a Moabitess were not affected by the prohibition in that verse. (See 2:17, note 13, on the question of Ruth the Moabitess.)
[11] MT: *škyh*, but many Hebrew MSS and LXX have *šbyh*.
[12] MT: "Abitub," = C, E, L, and AS, though some Hebrew MSS and Syr have "Ahitub."
[13] MT: "Shamed," though many Hebrew MSS, LXX, and Syr have "Shamer."

its *villages*[14] *which the children of Israel devastated and burned with fire when they fought against the tribe of Benjamin at Gibatha.* 13. Also Beriah and Shema—they were heads of the clans of the inhabitants of Aijalon, they *were the warriors*[g] *who in battle* put to flight the inhabitants of Gath. 14.[h] Ahio, Shashak and Jeremoth, 15. Zebadiah, Arad, Eder, 16. Michael, Ishpah[i] and Joha were the sons of Beriah. 17. Zebadiah, Meshullam, Hizki, Heber, 18. Ishmerai, Izliah and Jobab were the sons of Elpaal. 19. Jakim, Zichri, Zabdi, 20. *Elionai,*[j] Zillethai, Eliel, 21. Adaiah, *Beraah*[k] and Shimrath were the sons of Shimei. 22. Ishpan, Eber, Eliel, 23. Abdon, Zichri, Hanan, 24. Hananiah, Elam, Anthothijah, 25. Iphdiah and Peniel[l][15] were[m] the sons of Sheshak.[m] 26. Shimsherai, Shehariah,[n] Athaliah,[n] 27. Jaareshiah, Elijah[o] and Zichri were the sons of Jeroham.[o] 28. These were heads of clans, according to their families, heads: these lived in Jerusalem. 29. *The princes*[16] *of* Gibeon[p] lived in Gibeon and the name *of Gibeon's*[16] wife was Maacah. 30.[q] His first-born son was Abdon, then[17] Zur, Kish, Baal, Nadab, 31. Gedor, Ahio[r] and Zecher.[r] 32. Mikloth was the father of Shimeah. They, too, facing their brethren, lived in Jerusalem with their brethren. 33. Ner, *who was called Abiel,* became the father of Kish. *They called him Ner because he used to light the lamps in the schools and synagogues, and this merit enabled Saul, his grandson, to become king, for king-*

Apparatus, Chapter 8

[g] C: "men."

[h] In verses 14-24 V gives in each verse, in unpointed form, only the first name in his text. Translation follows C. E omits verses 14-27.

[i] MT: *yšph.* Tg. Chr *yšp'.*

[j] MT: *'ly'ny.* V: *'lyw'yny.* C, L, AS: *'lyw'ny.*

[k] MT: *br'yh.* Tg. Chr *br'h.*

[l] V follows Kethibh. C, L, and AS follow Qere.

[m-m] Following C. Missing in V.

[n-n] Following C. Missing in V.

[o-o] Following C. Missing in V.

[p] Missing in C.

[q] E omits verses 30-31.

[r-r] Following C: Missing in V.

Notes, Chapter 8

[14]MT: "daughters," i.e., dependent villages. In Judg 19 and 20 we have the sordid story of how a group of Benjaminites ravish the concubine of a man who is being given overnight lodging in a house in Gibeah, which belongs to Benjamin. The concubine dies, and an incensed Israel assembles to deal with Benjamin. After a fierce battle, the Israelites defeat the Benjaminites and "all the towns which they found they set on fire" (20:48). In a discussion in *b. Meg.* 49 on 1 Chr 8:12, a query is raised as to how the sons of Elpaal could have built three towns which were assumed to have been in existence since Joshua's day. The answer is that they *were* in existence since Joshua's day, but "they were laid waste in the days of the concubine of Gibeah; and Elpaal came and rebuilt them." The assumption clearly is that these three towns were among those destroyed in Judg 20:48.

[15]V follows Kethibh; C, L, and AS follow Qere.

[16]MT: "In Gibeon lived the father of Gibeon." In Hebrew the verb is plural, even though the subject is singular. Tg. Chr deals with this problem by substituting "the princes of" for "the father of." But because of this plural substitution, Tg. Chr has to bring in "Gibeon" later in the verse to take account of the *"his"* wife in MT, even though it means a shift of a generation. A similar problem appears in the duplicate verse 9:35, but even though the solution there is also clumsy, it is less awkward because in MT "the father of Gibeon" is given a name, Jeiel, thus avoiding the identity problem of "his" later in the verse.

[17]Lit.: "and."

ship is compared to a lamp.[s][18] Kish became the father of Saul, and[t] Saul became the father of Jonathan, Malchishua, Abinadab and Eshbaal.[t] 34.[u] The son of Jonathan, Merib Baal, and Merib Baal became the father of Micah. 35. The sons of Micah: Pithon,[v] Melech, Tarea and Ahaz.[v] 36. Ahaz became the father of Jehoadah; Jehoadah became the father of Alemeth, Azmaveth and Zimri; Zimri became the father of Moza. 37. Moza became the father of Binea; Raphah his son, *Eleashah*[19] his son, Azel his son. 38. Azel had six sons and these were their names: Azrikam *his first-born,*[20] Ishmael, Sheariah, Obadiah and Hanan. All these were the sons of Azel. 39. The sons of Eshek[w] his brother: Ulam his first-born, Jeush his second and Eliphelet the third. 40. The sons of Ulam were men who were mighty warriors, *mastering their desires like a man* who draws the bow *with skill; it was for this reason that* they had many sons and grandsons; *their family* numbered one hundred and fifty. All these were from the sons of *the tribe of* Benjamin.

Apparatus, Chapter 8

[s] The whole expansion is missing in C.
[t-t] Missing in E.
[u] E omits verse 34-39.

[v-v] Following C; missing in V.
[w] C "Esek."

Notes, Chapter 8

[18]In MT 1 Sam 9:1, Abiel is the father of Kish; in 1 Chr 8:33, Ner fulfills that role. *Lev. R.* 9:2 points out that his real name was Abiel, but the fact that he used to light lamps for the public in the dark passages between his house and the house of study had two results: (i) he was given the friendly nickname Ner = "lamp"; (ii) the merit acquired by such an altruistic act spilled over to the benefit of Saul, helping to make him king. Tg. Chr brings (i) and (ii) together by reminding us of the link between "lamp" and "kingship," a link that is implicit in MT 2 Sam. 21:17; 1 Kgs 11:36; 15:4; 2 Chr 21:7, and explicit in the Targums of each of these verses, where the word "lamp" is in each case replaced by "kingdom"/"kingship."

[19]MT: *'l'sh.* C: *'l'sh.* L and AS = MT.

[20]MT: *bkrw (Bocheru).* V, C, L, and AS: *bwkryh,* "his first-born," which is also the reading of some Hebrew MSS, LXX, and Syr. DW regards it as a name and translates it as "Bucreh."

CHAPTER 9

1. Thus all *the Israelites*[1] were enrolled and behold they were recorded in the book of the kings of *the house of*[a] Israel and *the kings of the house of* Judah; *and they*[2] *went off* into exile in Babylon because of their *acts of* unfaithfulness. 2. *Those who* were first to settle in their property in their towns were Israel, the priests, the Levites and the Nethinim.[3] 3. And in Jerusalem there dwelt some of the sons of Judah, some of the sons of Benjamin, some of the sons of Ephraim, and *some of the sons of*[b] Manasseh: 4.[c] Uthai, the son of Ammihud, the son of Omri, the son of Imri, the son of Banemin, *from* the sons of Perez,[d4] the son of Judah. 5. From *the tribe of Shiloh:*[e5] Asaiah *his* first-born and his sons. 6. From the sons of Zerah: Jeuel,[f] and their brethren, six hundred and ninety. 7.[g] From the sons of Benjamin: Salu, the son of Meshullam, the son of Hodaviah, the son of *Saneah;*[h6] 8. Ibneiah, the son of Jeroham; *Elai,*[7] the son of *Uzzai,* the son of Michri, the son[8] and Meshullam, the son of Shephatiah, the son of Reuel, the son of Ibneiah, 9. and their brethren according to their families, nine hundred and fifty-six. All these men were heads of clans, according to their clans. 10.[i] From the priests: Jedaiah, Jehoiarib, *Jamin,*[j9] 11. Azariah, the son of Hilkiah, the son of Meshullam, the son of Zadok, the son of Meraioth, the son of Ahitob, director in charge of the *sanctuary* house of *the Lord.*[10] 12. And Adaiah, the son of Jeroham, the son of Pashhur,

---

Apparatus, Chapter 9

[a] "the house of" missing in E.
[b] E, L, and AS omit: "some of the sons of," in agreement with MT.
[c] E omits verses 4 and 5.
[d] L and AS follow Qere. "the son of Bani from ..." C has "the son of Benjamin, the sons of. ..."

[e] C: "Shelah."
[f] E, L, and AS. "Jeiel," cf. LXX A.
[g] E omits verses 7 and 8.
[h] C, L, and AS = MT (*hsnh*).
[i] E omits verses 10–12.
[j] C, L, and AS: Jakim (= MT).

Notes, Chapter 9

[1] MT: "all Israel." Tg. Chr has "All of them Israel." Hence the translation above.
[2] In MT the subject of the verb apparently is "Judah": "And Judah was taken into exile. . . ."
[3] "Nethinim," lit.: "the given ones," the descendants of the Gibeonites who tricked the Israelites (Josh 9:27) and who were allocated menial duties in the sanctuary and who possibly continued to carry out such duties. (See Schürer, II, 290–291.)
[4] Qere: "son of Bani, from the sons of Perez." Kethibh: "son of Banemin the sons of Perez." Tg. Chr combines K and Q by retaining the "Banemin" of K and the "from" of Q.
[5] MT: "the Shilonite."
[6] MT: *hsn'h.*
[7] MT: "Elah."
[8] The copyist in V, so accustomed to writing "son of" (*bar*) apparently had written it on this occasion before he realized that it was not in his text.
[9] MT: "Jakim."
[10] MT: "God."

the son of Malchijah, and Maasai, the son of Adiel, the son of *Jehuran,*[k11] the son of Meshullam, the son of *Meshillemeth,*[l12] the son of Immer, 13. and their brethren *were appointed* heads of their clans—one thousand seven hundred and sixty warriors, *put in charge* of the service of the worship of the *sanctuary* house of *the Lord.*[10] 14.[m] From the Levites: Shemaiah, the son of Hashshub, the son of Azrikam, the son of Hashabiah, of the sons of Merari, 15. and Bakbakkar, Heresh, Galal and Mattaniah, the son of *Micah,*[n13] the son of Zichri, the son of Asaph, 16. and Obadiah, the son of Shemaiah, the son of Galal, the son of Jeduthun, and Berechiah, the son of *Asaph,*[o14] the son of Elkanah, who lived in the towns of the *Netophathites.*[p15] 17. The gatekeepers: Shallum, *Akkob,*[q16] Talmon, Ahiman and their brother Shallum who *was appointed* head. 18. Up until now they have been in the eastern gate of the king's *palace.*[17] They are the gatekeepers for the camps of the sons of Levi. 19. Shallum, the son of Kore, the son of Abiasaph,[r] the son of Korah, and his brethren who belonged to his clan, the Korahites, were in charge of the service of worship, the guardians of the thresholds of the tent, and their fathers were *put in charge* of the camp of the Lord, the guardians of the entrance. 20. Phinehas, the son of Eleazar, had been their director from the beginning,[18] *from the day that the tent of meeting was set up in the wilderness,* and *the Memra of* the Lord was *in support of him.*[19] 21. Zechariah, the son of Meshelemiah, *was put in charge of the gate*[20] of the tent of meeting. 22. All these were chosen as gatekeepers at the thresholds: there were two hundred and twelve of them. They were in their *towns,*[21] enrolled *in the* twenty four *courses*[22] *which* David and Samuel the

Apparatus, Chapter 9

[k] C, L, and AS: *yhzrh* (= MT).
[l] C, L, and AS: *mslmyt* (= MT).
[m] E omits verses 14 and 15.
[n] C, L, and AS: *myk'* (= MT).
[o] C, L, and AS: *'s'* (= MT).

[p] Most of verse 16 missing in E, except for the last three words: "who lived in the towns of the Netophathite(s)."
[q] C = "Akkub" (= MT).
[r] E, L, and AS: *'by'sp.* V and C: *'bysp.*

Notes, Chapter 9

[11] MT: *yhzrh.* V: *yhwrh.*
[12] MT: *mslmyt.* V: *mslmt.*
[13] MT: *myk'.* V: *mykh.*
[14] MT: *'s'.* V: *'sp,* with many Hebrew MSS and Syr.
[15] MT: singular.
[16] MT: "Akkub."
[17] Tg. Chr has *pltyryn,* borrowed from Greek and Latin, MJ (1180), *praitorion* and *praetorium;* JL (II, 269), *palation* and *palatium:* "palace, residence, headquarters."
[18] MT: "in time past."
[19] Lit.: "in his support." In the Targum, "The Memra of the Lord was in support of him" is a regular way of translating MT: "The Lord was with him," etc.
[20] MT: "was gatekeeper at the entrance."
[21] MT: "settlements" or "villages" (*ḥṣr*).
[22] Corresponding to the number of priestly courses which, according to the Chronicler (1 Chr 24:7–18), were set up by David. (See Schürer, II, 245–250.)

prophet[23] had set up on account of their faithfulness.[24] 23. They and their sons *were put in charge* of the gates of the *sanctuary* house of the Lord and were to be a guard for the *sanctuary* house.[25] 24. *They*[26] *were* on the four *sides*[s][27]—*six guards* on the east, *six guards* on the west, *six guards* on the north, *six guards* on the south. 25. And their brethren who were in their towns had to come in (to serve) with them for a seven[t] day period from time to time. 26. For the four chief gatekeepers *were*[u] serving faithfully. They were Levites and they were *put in charge* of the chambers and the treasuries[v] *in*[28] the *sanctuary* house of *the Lord.*[29] 27. They spent the night in the precincts of the *sanctuary* house of *the Lord,* for it was their responsibility to mount the guard, and they *were put in charge of the keys*[30]—*to shut and to open* every morning *at the proper time.* 28. Some of them *were put in charge* of the vessels used in worship, bringing[w] in the correct number and taking out the correct number.[31] 29. Some of them were put in charge of the utensils and all[x] the holy vessels and the fine flour *of the meal offering* and the wine[32] *of the libation* and the frankincense *of the memorial offering* and the spices *of the incense offering.*[33] 30. But it was some of the sons of the priests who *were*[34] *skilled in the manufacture of incense, made fragrant with perfumes for* the spices.[34] 31. Mattithiah, one of the

Apparatus, Chapter 9

[s] C, L, and AS add: "they were appointed in charge of the gates."

[t] C, E, L, and AS: *ywmyn.* V: *ywmy.*

[u] C, preceded by "they entered."

[v] For V's *tmbry'* read *tsbry'* with C, L, and AS.

[w] See note 31. "for" = *mṭwl d* (V and C), *'rwm* (L and AS).

[x] Missing in C.

Notes, Chapter 9

[23] MT: "the seer."

[24] Or "on account of their faithfulness." In MT "David and Samuel ... established them in their office of trust," following *GK* 135a, n. 1, where *hmh* is taken as an accusative. With the addition in Tg. Chr of "twenty-four courses which," it is difficult for the relative pronoun to refer to anything other than the twenty-four courses. Does Tg. Chr wish to imply that David and Samuel established the courses, or did they establish them in the courses? The translation in the text follows the first alternative. Another possibility is to regard "twenty-four courses" as parenthetical. Thus: "They were in their towns and were enrolled; they (twenty-four courses) whom David and Samuel had established in their office of trust (because of their faithfulness)."

[25] MT: "for the house of the tent."

[26] MT: "The gatekeepers."

[27] For *rwḥwt*: "winds, sides," Tg. Chr has the plural of *trygwn*: "corner, side," borrowed from the Greek: *trigōnos,* "triangular, triangle" (MJ, 553; JL I, 318).

[28] MT: "of."

[29] MT: "God."

[30] MT: singular. Tg. Chr has the plural of *'qlyd',* borrowed from the Greek word *kleis, -dos,* "key" (MJ, 112; JL I, 59). MT: "and they were in charge of the key/opening and for every morning."

[31] Lit.: "For by number they were bringing them in and by number they were bringing them out."

[32] Tg. Chr omits "the oil" of MT.

[33] Tg. Chr is being very specific, ensuring that each commodity is linked to the appropriate offering.

[34-34] MT: Lit.: "the blenders of the mixture for the spices."

Levites—he was the first-born of Shallum, who [35] was *from the family of Korah* [35]—because of his loyalty was *put in charge* of the production of the offering which was prepared on the pan. [y] 32. Some of the sons of *Kehath* [36] *and* some of their brethren were *put in charge of* the shewbread, to have it ready *on the table* every Sabbath. 33. These were the singers, the heads of the clans of the Levites, (living) in the chambers and [37] exempt [z][38] from other service, because they were on duty day and night. 34. These were heads of the clans of the Levites, *the* heads according to their families. They lived in Jerusalem. 35. In Gibeon lived *the fathers* [39] of *the Gibeonites,* [aa][40] Jeiel, [41] and his wife's name was Maacah. 36. And his first-born son, Abdon, then [42] Zur, Kish, Baal, Ner, Nadab, 37. Gedor, Ahio, Zechariah [bb] and Mikloth. [bb] 38. Mikloth became the father of Shimeam. They, however, facing their brethren, lived in Jerusalem with their brethren. 39. [cc] Ner became the father of Kish, Kish became the father of Saul, Saul became the father of Jonathan, Malchishua, Abinadab and Eshbaal. 40. The son of Jonathan was Meribbaal, and Meribbaal became the father of Micah. [*Another reading.* The son of Jonathan was Meribbaal. *He is Mephibosheth. He was called Meribbaal because he had had a controversy with the Lord of the universe over the fact that David had returned in peace but had not repaid the good deed to him as he had sworn to Jonathan his father.* [dd][43]

Apparatus, Chapter 9

[y] C: plural.
[z] C, L, and AS have *ptwryn*: "(in the chambers of) release/exemption," or if we can treat it as a verbal form, "(in the chambers of) those exempted." E has *lškt ṭwnyn*: "in the chamber of ropes"; cf. 1 Kgs 6:18, where the same He-

brew word (*ptwrym*) in its construct form is also translated by "ropes."
[aa] L and AS: "Gibeon" (= MT).
[bb-bb] Following C: missing in V.
[cc] E omits verses 39–45.
[dd] Another reading found only in V.

Notes, Chapter 9

[35-35] MT: "The Korahite."
[36] MT: "The Kerahite(s)."
[37] Lit.: "who."
[38] V has *ptwrym*, a Hebrew word, "released" (plural masc.). See Apparatus.
[39] MT: singular.
[40] MT: "Gibeon."
[41] Tg. Chr follows Qere. Kethibh: *y'wl*.
[42] Lit.: "and."
[43] In 2 Sam he is Mephibosheth; in 1 Chr we know him as Meribbaal, the lame son of Jonathan. Tg. Chr brings the two names together and bases the expansion on Meribbaal, meaning originally "Baal contends." For Tg. Chr, Meribbaal is so called because he had a dispute with the Lord because of David's failure to keep his promises. David had promised that for the sake of his father Jonathan, Mephibosheth would receive Saul's land, and that he would be looked after by Saul's servant, Ziba and his family (2 Sam 9:6-13). Following David's return from his flight from Absalom (2 Sam 19:24-30), he upbraided Mephibosheth for his failure to accompany him, then modified his earlier promise, taking away half of Saul's land from Mephibosheth and giving it to Ziba. In the Talmud this wrong is not forgotten. Mephibosheth is regarded as David's teacher, and in *b. Yom.* 22b the punishments meted out to David for some of his sins are listed, one of which is that he listened to slander against Mephibosheth, the punishment for which lies still in the future. "At the time when David said to Mephibosheth: 'I say, Thou and Ziba divide the land,' a heavenly voice came forth to say to him: Rehoboam and Jeroboam will divide the kingdom." Thus the founder of the united kingdom would be responsible for its division.

41. The sons of Micah: Pithon, Melech, Tahrea *and Ahaz.*[ee][44] 42. Ahaz became the father of *Jadah;*[45] *Jadah*[45] became the father of Alemeth, Azmaveth and Zimri; Zimri became the father of Moza. 43. Moza became the father of Binea; Rephaiah was his son, Eleasah[ff] his son, Azel his son. 44. Azel had six sons and these were their names: Azrikam, *his first-born,*[46] then Ishmael, Sheariah, Obadiah and Hanan. These were the sons of Azel.

CHAPTER 10

1. Now the Philistines *waged war*[1] against Israel, and the men of Israel fled from before[a] the Philistines and they fell, *killed*[b][2] *by the sword,* on the mountain of Gilboa. 2. The Philistines overtook Saul and his sons, and the Philistines struck down Jonathan, Abinadab and Malchishua, the sons of Saul. 3. *Those making war pressed hard*[3] upon Saul, and the archers, *expert in drawing the bow,* found him, and he was *afraid*[4] of the archers. 4. And Saul said to his armor-bearer: "Draw

Apparatus, Chapter 9

[ee] Following C, the four sons are missing in V.   [ff] C: Eleashah."

Notes, Chapter 9

[44]Missing in MT, but found in the main versions and thought to have fallen out of MT through haplography.
[45]MT: "Jarah," though some Hebrew MSS have "Jadah."
[46]MT: *bkrw (Bokru),* which most commentators regard as a proper noun; cf. 8:38, where we have the same form in the MT, but there some Hebrew MSS, LXX, Tg., and Syr read "his first-born."

Apparatus, Chapter 10

[a] Missing in C.   [b] V has *d* (of); C, L, and AS: *b* (by).

Notes, Chapter 10

[1]Tg. Chr often translates *nlḥm,* "to fight," by *'gyḥ qrb',* "to wage war."
[2]MT: Lit.: "pierced."
[3]MT: "The battle was heavy."
[4]MT: "and he was in agony." Tg. Chr either misread *wyḥl* as *wdḥyl* ("and he was afraid"), words very similar in appearance, or, not quite certain of the word before him, it supplied a word which would represent the natural reaction in battle conditions.

your sword and *kill*[5] me with it, lest these uncircumcised come and mock[c] me."
But his armor-bearer[6] was unwilling for he was terrified. So Saul took the sword
and *threw himself*[7] upon it. 5. When his armor-bearer[6] saw[d] that Saul was dead, he
too *threw himself*[7] on the[e] sword and died. 6. Thus Saul died; his three sons and
all *the men of* his house *who were there*[f8] died together. 7. When all the men of Israel who were in the valley saw that they had fled and that Saul and his sons were
dead, they left their towns[9] and fled. Then the Philistines came and dwelt in them.
8. On the next day the Philistines came to strip the *slain*,[10] and they found Saul
and his *three* sons, *slain, lying*[11] on the mountain of Gilboa. 9. They stripped him,
cut off[12] his head and his armor and sent[g] throughout the land of the Philistines to
give the news *to the house of*[13] their idols and to the people. 10. Then they placed
his weapons in the house of their *idols*,[14] but his[h] skull they *raised on a pole facing
the idol of* Dagon.[15] 11. When all *the men of* Jabesh Gilead heard all that the Philistines had done to Saul, 12. they arose, *every single man of them*,[i16] and they took
the body of Saul and the bodies of his sons and they brought them to Jabesh, and
they buried their bones under the terebinth of[j17] Jabesh and fasted for seven days.
13. So Saul died because of his unfaithfulness, in that he had acted unfaithfully
against *the Memra of* the Lord, because[k] of the word of the Lord[k] which he had not

Apparatus, Chapter 10

[c] E, L, and AS: *yt'lbwn* (= some Tg. Sam. MSS); V:
    ytl'bwn. No difference in meaning.

[d] V: *ḥz'*. C, E, L, and AS: *ḥm'*.

[e] E, L, and AS: "his."

[f] E omits "who were there."

[g] C has *šd'*, or *šr'*, which may be a scribal error for
    šdrw, as in all the other witnesses.

[h] E: "their."

[i] C: "every valiant man" (*kl gbr gybr*).

[j] C, L, and AS: "which was in."

[k-k] E omits, perhaps through homoioteleuton.

Notes, Chapter 10

[5]MT: "pierce."

[6]Twice in this verse and once in verse 5 we have the expression "armor-bearer." In MT this is in each case "the
bearer of his weapons." In Tg. Chr the first occurrence has "the bearer of his weapons," the second "the bearer of his
weapon," which is the case also in verse 5.

[7]MT: "fell."

[8]Tg. Chr answers the question implicit in MT's statement ". . . and all his house died together": what about 2 Sam
2:8f., where Ishbosheth, Saul's son, is still alive?

[9]Following C, L, and AS. V has "town."

[10]Lit.: "the killed ones." MT uses the more expressive *ḥllym*, "the pierced ones, the slain." See note 2.

[11]Lit.: "cast." MT: "fallen."

[12]MT: "lifted up."

[13]Not in MT but found in some Hebrew MSS and Syr. Found also in MT and Tg. 1 Sam. 31:9.

[14]MT: "gods."

[15]MT: "they impaled (in) the house of Dagon."

[16]MT: "every valiant man."

[17]MT: "in."

observed *when he waged war against those of the house of Amalek*, [18] and, as well, because he had consulted *necromancers*, [19] seeking *instruction from them*; [20] 14. but he had not sought *instruction* from *before* the Lord [21] *through the Urim and the Thummim, because he had killed the priests who were at Nob.* [22] So *the Lord killed* [23] him and transferred the kingdom to David, the son of Jesse.

CHAPTER 11

1. All Israel gathered together to David at Hebron, saying: "We are indeed [1] your *kinsfolk* [2] and your flesh. 2. In times past, [3] even when Saul was king, you were the one who led us out *to battle,* and who brought *us* in *to the house of study and who taught* Israel. The Lord your God said to you: "*You will be leader and you will have authority over* my people *and* you will *govern* [4] Israel; it is you who will be ruler [5] over my people Israel. 3. Then all the elders of Israel came to the king at Hebron; David made [6] a covenant with them at Hebron before the Lord, and they anointed

Notes, Chapter 10

[18]Tg. Chr answers the question implicit in MT: When did Saul act unfaithfully? See 1 Sam 15 for the Amalekite incident.

[19]MJ (140): "fictions, lying oracles, conjurers." JL (I, 81) *die Todtenbeschwörer,* for MT *'wb:* "necromancer," which the Palestinian Targums always reproduce as *bydyn.*

[20]"To inquire," especially of God, is normally expressed in Tg. Chr by "to seek instruction from."

[21]MT: "But he had not sought/inquired of the Lord."

[22]Tg. Chr is a little concerned by the comment in MT that Saul had not sought the Lord, because elsewhere (1 Sam 28:6) it is stated that he *had* sought the Lord. Tg. Chr is at pains here to stress that Saul had not sought him in the correct way, i.e., using the correct liturgical aids, the Urim and the Thummim. And why not? Because he had killed the priests who were at Nob (1 Sam 22), and only the priests could use the Urim and the Thummim. Tg. Chr is in fact confirming the Chronicler's argument that Saul's ruin was complete long before his death; it was complete, says Tg. Chr on the day that he killed the Lord's priests and thereby cut himself off from the Lord.

[23]MT: "And he put him to death."

Notes, Chapter 11

[1]MT: "Behold."

[2]MT: "bone."

[3]MT: Lit.: "Both yesterday and three days (ago)." Tg. Chr: "Both from yesterday and from the beginning."

[4]MT: "shepherd."

[5]Tg. Chr has *'rkwn,* borrowed from Greek *archōn,* "ruler": MJ (121f.), JL I, 65.

[6]MT: "cut."

David[a] king over Israel according to the word of the Lord *which he had spoken through*[7] Samuel. 4. David and all Israel went to Jerusalem, that is, Jebus; the *Jebusites,*[8] the inhabitants of the land were there *up to that time*. 5. The inhabitants of Jebus said to David: "You will not come in here." But David captured the fortress of Zion, that is, the city of David. 6. Now David had said: "Whoever *kills*[b9] the Jebusite *and captures the city*[10] will be *appointed* head *of the army* and leader *of the troops.*"[c11] Joab, the son of Zeruiah, was the first to go up, so he became chief *of the army*. 7. David took up residence in the fortress, so they called it "The City of David." 8. He built up the city all around from the *mound*[12] to the area round about it, while Joab *administered*[13] the rest of the city. 9. David went from strength to strength, and *the Memra of* the Lord of hosts[14] was *in support of him*.[15] 10. Now these were the chiefs of the warriors who *were with* David,[16] who, along with Israel,[17] strongly *supported*[d] him in his kingship, in order to make him king, according to the Word of the Lord concerning Israel. 11. These are the total numbers[18] of the warriors who were with David, *the warrior,*[19] *the leader of the camp, sitting on the judgment seat, anointed with holy oil, with all the prophets and wise men round about him. When he went forth to battle he received help from on high; when he sat down to give instruction in the Law, the correct decision came to his mind;* select *and* fastidious, *handsome in his appearance and comely in looks,*[e] *skilled in wisdom, intelligent in counsel, mighty*[19] *in strength, head of the academy, with a pleasant voice, an outstanding singer,*[20] *officer in charge of all the warriors, equipped with weapons, carrying a spear on which was hung the sign of the formation*[21] *of the camp of Judah, going forth on the instruction*[22] *of the spirit of ho-*

Apparatus, Chapter 11

[a] C: "him."
[b] Following C, which has imperfect.
[c] V: *'wklwz*. C: *'wklwn*. L, AS: *'wklws*.

[d] V: *mtwqpyn*. L, AS: *mtqpyn*. Ittaphal and Ithpaal, both with the same meaning.
[e] C: "his looks."

Notes, Chapter 11

[7]MT: Lit.: "by the hand of." Tg. Chr: "by the hands of."
[8]MT: singular.
[9]MT: "strikes down."
[10]MT: "first."
[11]Tg. Chr has *'wklwz*, "levy of troops," borrowed from Greek *ochlos*, "crowd": JL I, 27.
[12]MT: "Millo." Tg. Chr uses a word based on the same root, *mly*, "to fill (up)": *mlyt*, "mound, rampart."
[13]MT: "restored."
[14]Tg. Chr retains Hebrew word: *ṣb'wt*.
[15]MT: "with him."
[16]MT: "David's warriors."
[17]MT: "with all Israel."
[18]MT: "the number."
[19]Reading "warrior" with C. V has "man."
[20]Lit.: "master in songs."
[21]Tg. Chr has *tyqs*, "arrangement of (troops), formation, banner," from Greek *taxis*, JL I, 318.
[22]Reading *pm* (C) or *pwm* (AS). V has *ps*. Lit.: "going forth according to the command of the voice of."

liness, he was victorious in battle and *with the spear cut down*[23] three hundred men slain at the one time. 12. After him was Eleazar, the son of *his uncle,*[f24] *the son of Ahohi.*[25] He was among the three warriors. 13. He was with David at Pas-Damim, where the Philistines had gathered, *drawn up ready* for battle. There was a plot of ground, full of *crops, half of it in lentils, half of it in* barley.[26] And the people fled from before the Philistines. 14. They took up their position in the middle of the plot, saved[g] it and *killed*[27] the Philistines. Thus *through them* the Lord wrought a great deliverance. 15. Three[28] *warriors,* from *the warriors of the heads of the camp,*[28] went down to the rock to David, to the cave of Adullam, while a regiment[29] of the Philistines was encamped in the valley of the *warriors.*[30] 16. At that time David was in the fortress, while the garrison[h31] of the Philistines was in Bethlehem. 17. And *the soul of* David was filled with longing and he said: "Who will give me a drink of water[32] from the cistern of Bethlehem which is at the gate?" 18. Then the three *warriors*[i] *took courage* and broke their way through the camp of the Philistines, drew water from the cistern of Bethlehem which was at the gate, *took it,* carried it and came[33] to David. But David was unwilling to drink it and

Apparatus, Chapter 11

[f] C: "the son of Dodo" (variant reading, "his uncle").

[g] E, L, AS: *šyzbwt,* "rescue, deliverance." Just one letter of difference from V, C, AS: *šyzbwh,* "saved it."

[h] V and C have a variant reading "*'stryg,* variant reading *'strtyg.*" E, L and AS: *'ystrtyg.* The Hebrew word used here, *nṣyb,* means "garrison," but it can also mean "governor."

[i] L, AS have *gbryn.*

Notes, Chapter 11

[23]MT: "Jashobeam, son of Hachmoni, was chief of the thirty. He wielded his spear against...." In Tg. Chr, Jashobeam, son of Hachmoni, has disappeared and has become the basis for a eulogy on David so extravagant that it reads more like a modern obituary. Le Déaut sees the eulogy as being built on the two words: "Jachobeam," meaning "he presides over the people" (though *BDB* 1000 prefers a different derivation) and "Hachmoni," related to the word for "wisdom." Tg. 2 Sam. 23:8 provides a similar but briefer eulogy. In Tg. Chr, David emerges as most excellent in every aspect of life—as a leader, civilian or military, a scholar, a warrior; indeed it is he, not Jashobeam, who slays the three hundred!

[24]MT: "Dodo," a proper noun, which means "his uncle."

[25]MT: "the Ahohite."

[26]In 2 Sam 23:11 the field is full of lentils; in MT 1 Chr 11:13, it is full of barley. The Rabbis were aware of the problem arising and put forward various solutions to it: that there were two fields, or that there was one field but two years were involved; some also saw a legal dimension to it that if the Philistines were hiding in the lentils, was it legitimate to burn the field, etc.? (See *b. B.Ḳ.* 60b; *Ruth R.* 5:1.) Tg. Chr reconciles the two passages and has the best of both worlds: that there was one field with two halves.

[27]MT: "struck down."

[28-28]MT: "Three from the thirty heads ..." ("heads" is singular in MT).

[29]Lit.: "the camp."

[30]MT: "Rephaim," a name given to pre-Israelite inhabitants of Palestine, but unknown as an ethnic group outside the Old Testament.

[31]Tg. Chr has *'stryg,* with variant reading *'strtyg.* This word is borrowed from Greek: *stratēgion,* "camp, regular garrison" (MJ 92) or *stratēgos:* "army commander" (JL I, 47).

[32]Lit.: "Who will give me to drink water...?"

[33]MT: "brought," though one MS and LXX have "came."

gave orders [34] to pour it out *before* [35] the Lord. 19. And he said: "Far be it from me from *before the Lord* [36] that I should do this! Could I *possibly* drink, *as it were,* [37] the blood of these men [38] *who went* [39] in *danger of* their *life*? [40] For it was *in exchange* for their *life* [40] that they brought it." So he was unwilling to drink it. These *mighty acts* the three warriors did. 20. *Abishai,* [41] the brother of Joab—he was the chief of *the warriors.* [42] It was he who wielded his spear against three hundred *whom he killed,* [43] and *he had* a reputation [44] among the three *warriors.* 21. Of the three, he was more honored than the (other) two, and he became their leader, but he did not attain to three *mighty acts.* [j][45] 22. Benaiah, the son of Jehoiada, the son of a warrior, *dreaded sins* and had *good* deeds to his credit. He was from Kabzeel. He killed the two *princes* of Moab *who were like two strong lions;* he went down and *killed* a lion in the middle of a pit on a snowy day. *He was a righteous man, great beyond compare in both the First Temple and the Second Temple. One day, when he stepped on a lizard which was dead, he went down to Shiloah, broke a piece of ice* [46] *and washed himself. He then went up and expounded the Sifra debe Rab, that is, the Book of the Law of the priests, during a short winter's day, the tenth of the month Tebeth.* [47] 23. It was

Apparatus, Chapter 11

[j] E: *gwbryn.*

Notes, Chapter 11

[34]Lit.: "said." *'mr* can also mean "to promise." In either case, Tg. Chr is ensuring that David is not contravening any regulations by pouring it out himself (a task for the priests) or by doing it outside the sanctuary at Jerusalem (see Smolar and Aberbach, 19).

[35]MT: "to."

[36]MT: "from my God."

[37]Reading *k'lw* with C, E, L, AS for *b'lw* of V.

[38]Reading *gwbryyh* or *gwbry'* (E, L, AS) for *gwbryh* of V and C.

[39]Reading *'zlw* with all other witnesses for V's *'zly.*

[40]MT: plural.

[41]MT: *'bšy.*

[42]MT: "the three."

[43]MT has *ḥll,* "pierced, slain."

[44]Tg. Chr follows Qere. Kethibh: "no reputation." Probable confusion of *lw* and *l'.*

[45]MT: "the three."

[46]MJ (230): "broke a hole in the ice."

[47]Already in MT, Benaiah is a doughty warrior. In Tg. Chr he is great beyond compare in his abhorrence of sin and his performance of good deeds, reinforced by his scrupulous observance of the precepts of the Torah. The expansion develops from three statements (the first two are found also in Tg. 2 Sam 23:20):

i) He was the son of a valiant man, an *'yš ḥyl:* the last word resembles *dḥyl,* "to fear." Thus "he fears sins."

ii) He was "great in deeds"; in Tg. Chr "he was great in *good* deeds."

iii) "He struck down two Ariels of Moab, and a lion in a pit on a snowy day." The "Ariel" is of uncertain meaning; it may have meant "princes," "foreign emissaries," or "altar hearths." The Rabbis, taking the last meaning, regarded these altar hearths as referring to the two temples, bearing in mind David's descent from Ruth, the Moabitess. The first part of the word contains the word for "lion," *'ry,* and it is this lion-like emphasis which dominates the rest of the expansion: lion-like in his meticulous observance of the law (see Lev 11:29-31) in his ice-breaking project, lion-like in his ability to master in a short time (a winter's day) the halachic commentary on Leviticus (the *siphra debe Rab*), which had been produced in the school of Rab (Rab was head of the Academy of Sura, at the beginning of the third century).

he who *killed*[48] the Egyptian man, a huge man, whose height was five cubits *in royal cubits*. In the Egyptian's hand was a spear, as *thick* as a weaver's beam. But he went down to him with a staff, *seized him,* wrenched the spear from the hand of the Egyptian and killed him with his spear. 24. These *mighty acts* did Benaiah, the son of Jehoiada, and he had a reputation among the three warriors. 25. Of the three[k][49] *warriors* he was *more* honored *than the (other) two,* but he did not attain to three *mighty acts.*[l] David appointed him *head of the academy,* in charge of *his disciples.*[50] 26. Also the mighty men *among the warriors:*[51] Asahel, the brother of Joab, Elhanan, the son of Dodo, *who was* from Bethlehem; 27.[m] Shammoth, *who was from Haror,*[52] Helez, *who was from Pelan;*[53] 28. Ira, the son of Ikkesh, *who was from Tekoa,*[54] Abiezer, *who was from Anathoth;*[55] 29. Sibbecai, *who was from Hushath,*[56] Ilai, *who was from Ahoah;*"[57] 30. Maharai, *who was from Netophath,*[58] Heled, the son of Baanah, *who was from Netophath;*[58] 31. *Ittai,*[59] the son of Ribai, *who was from Miggibeah,*[60] of Benjamin,[61] Benaiah, *who was from Pirathon;*[62] 32. Hurai, *who was* from the wadies of Gaash, Abiel, *who was from Arbath;*[63] 33. Azmaveth, *who was from Baharum,*[o][64] Eliahba, *who was from Shaalbon;*[65] 34. the sons of Hashem, *who was from Gizon,*[66] Jonathan, the son of *Shage,*[67] who

Apparatus, Chapter 11

[k] L, AS: "thirty" (= MT). L, AS also omit "warriors" (= MT).
[l] C omits: "mighty acts."

[m] E omits verses 27–31.
[n] C, L, AS: "From those of the house of Ahoah."
[o] C: "Barahum."

Notes, Chapter 11

In 2 Sam 8:18 in MT, Benaiah is in charge of "David's bodyguard, the Cherethites and the Pelethites," who in Tg. Sam become "the archers and the slingers"; in the parallel verse in Tg. 1 Chr 18:17 they also become "the archers and the slingers," but as well they make up the two Sanhedrins, the Greater Sanhedrin and the Lesser Sanhedrin (see 18:17, note 27; 27:34, note 49; *b. Ber.* 4a, 18b).

[48] MT: "struck down."
[49] MT: "thirty."
[50] MT: "bodyguard."
[51] Tg. Chr: Lit.: "the mighty men of those making war." MT: "the mighty men of the armies."
[52] MT: "The Harorite."
[53] MT: "The Pelonite."
[54] MT: "The Tekoite."
[55] MT: "The Anathothite."
[56] MT: "The Hushathite."
[57] MT: "The Ahohite."
[58] MT: "The Netophathite."
[59] MT: *'yty.* Tg. Chr = 2 Sam 23:29.
[60] The *min* has been duplicated in error. Read "Gibeah."
[61] MT: "the sons of Benjamin."
[62] MT: "The Pirathonite."
[63] MT: "The Arbathite."
[64] MT: "The Baharumite."
[65] MT: "The Shaalbonite."
[66] MT: "The Gizonite."
[67] MT: *šgh.* Tg. Chr: *šg'.*

was from Harar.[68] 35. Ahiam, the son of Sachar, *who was from Harar,*[68] Eliphal, the son of Ur; 36. Hepher, *who was from Mecherath,*[69] Ahijah, *who was from Pelon;*[70] 37. Hezro,[p] *who was from Carmel,*[71] Naaraai, the son of Ezbai; 38. Joel, the brother of Nathan, Mibhar, the son of *Gadda;*[q72] 39. Zelek, *who was from the sons of Ammon,*[73] Naharai, *who was from Beeroth*[74]—the armor-*bearers*[75] of Joab, the son of Zeruiah; 40.[r] Ira, *who was from Jether,*[76] Garab,[77] *who was from Jether;*[76] 41. Uriah the Hittite, Zabad, the son of Ahlai; 42. Adina,[s] the son of Shiza, *who was from the tribe of Reuben,*[78] the chief of *the tribe of Reuben,*[78] and with him thirty *warriors.* 43.[t] Hanan, the son of Maacah, and Joshaphat, *who was from Mattan;*[79] 44. Uzzia, *who was from Ashtaroth,*[80] Shama and *Jeiel,*[81] the sons of Hotham, *who was from Aroer;*[82] 45. Jediael, the son of Shimri, and Joha, his brother, *who was from Tiz;*[83] 46. Eliel, *who was from Mahawa,*[84] Jeribai and Joshabiah,[85] the sons of Elnaam, and Ithmah, *from the sons of Moab;*[86] 47. Eliel and Obed and Jaasiel, *who was* from Masobaiah.

Apparatus, Chapter 11

[p] C: "Hezrai" = Qere of 2 Sam 23:35.
[q] E: "Gera" (*gr'*); L, AS: "The Hagrite."
[r] E omits verses 40 and 41.

[s] C: '*zyn*' (V: '*dynh*).
[t] E omits verse 43.

Notes, Chapter 11

[68]MT: "The Hararite."
[69]MT: "The Mecherathite."
[70]MT: "The Pelonite."
[71]MT: "The Carmelite."
[72]MT: "Hagri."
[73]MT: "The Ammonite."
[74]MT: "The Berothite."
[75]MT: singular, but LXX(L) and the Kethibh of 2 Sam 23:37 have plural.
[76]MT: "The Jithrite."
[77]MT: "Gareb" (= C).
[78]MT: "The Reubenite."
[79]MT: "The Ashterathite."
[80]MT: "The Mithnite."
[81]Tg. Chr follows Qere. (Kethibh = *y'w'l*).
[82]MT: "The Aroerite."
[83]MT: "The Tizite."
[84]MT: "The Mahawites."
[85]MT: "Joshaviah."
[86]MT: "The Moabite."

CHAPTER 12

1. These are the men who came to David at Ziklag, while he was still under pressure from Saul, the son of Kish. They were among the warriors who were supporting *him* in the battle.[1] 2. They were *expert* bowmen, *who could shoot arrows* with *their* right hand or *their* left; *they could sling* stones and *fight*[2] with arrows *and* with the bow. From among the kinsmen of Saul, from *the tribe of* Benjamin: 3. *the one who was appointed* chief was Ahiezer, and Joash, the sons of *Shimea,*[3] *who was from Gibeatha.*[4] Then *Jeziel*[5] and Pelet, the sons of Azmaveth; Beracah and Jehu *who was from Anathoth;*[6] 4. Ishmaiah, *who was from Gibeon,*[7] a warrior among the warriors,[8] *who attained to the mighty acts of warriors.*[9] 5.[10] Jeremiah, Jahaziel, Johanan, and Jozabad, *who was from Gederah.*[11] 6. Eluzai, Jerimoth, Bealiah, Shemariah, and Shephatiah, *who was from Haroph.*[12] 7. Elkanah, Isshiah, *Azriel,*[a][13] Joezer and Jashobeam, *who were from the family of Korah.*[14] 8. Joelah and Zebadiah, the sons of Jeroham from *Gedor.*[15] 9. Some members of *the tribe of*[16] Gad also defected to David *at* the fortress in the wilderness. They were intrepid warriors, trained soldiers, prepared for combat, shields at the ready[17] and *carrying* the spear. Their appearance *in battle* was *like* the appearance of a lion, and they were speeding along like *a gazelle*[b][18] on the mountains. 10. Ezer was the leader, Obadiah the second in command, Eliab the third, 11. *Mashmannah*[19] the fourth, Jeremiah the fifth, 12. Attai the sixth, Eliel the seventh, 13. Johanan the

Apparatus, Chapter 12

[a] V: *'zry'l,* also read by a few Hebrew MSS. C, L, and AS: *'zr'l* (= MT).

[b] C: plural (= MT).

Notes, Chapter 12

[1] MT: Lit.: "helpers of the battle."
[2] Lit.: "wage war."
[3] MT: "Shimaah" (= C).
[4] MT: "The Gibeathite."
[5] Tg. Chr follows Qere. Kethibh: *yzw'l.*
[6] MT: "The Anathothite": the singular suggests that only Jehu came from Anathoth.
[7] MT: "The Gibeonite."
[8] MT: "the thirty."
[9] MT: "and over the thirty." See also 11:21, 25.
[10] Le Déaut follows versification of MT.
[11] MT: "The Gederathite."
[12] MT: Qere, "The Haruphite." Kethibh: *ḥrypy.* Tg. Chr follows the pattern of Qere.
[13] MT: "Azarel."
[14] MT: "The Korahites."
[15] MT: "The Gedor" (*hgdwr*); some MSS have *hgdwd,* "the troop"; cf. C: "from Gedud."
[16] MT: "The Gadite(s)."
[17] Lit.: "setting shields in order." Tg. Chr has the plural of *trys',* borrowed from Greek *thureos,* "shield," JL II, 560.
[18] MT: plural.
[19] MT: "Mishmannah" (= C). V's "Mashmannah" is shared by two Hebrew MSS.

eighth, Elzabad the ninth, 14. Jeremiah the tenth, Machbannai the eleventh.
15. These from the sons of Gad were commanders of the army:[c] *each* one who was
lesser[d][20] *fought with*[21] a hundred, but the *one who was* great *among them fought
with* a thousand. 16. These were the men who crossed the Jordan in the first
month, when it was overflowing all its *inlets,*[22] and who put to flight *all who lived
in* the valleys, to the east and to the west. 17. Some of the sons of Benjamin and
Judah came to David at the fortress. 18. David went out to face them and he began
to speak to them:[23] "If you have come to me in peace, to support me, I shall ensure
that our hearts are joined together *in peace;*[24] but if to deceive me *and to harass
me*[25]—even though there are no *acts of violence*[26] in my *hand*—then *let it be revealed before* the God of our fathers and let *retribution be made.*[27] 19. Then a *powerful* spirit took hold of[28] *Amasa,*[29] the chief of the *warriors,*[30] who replied:[31] "It's
for your sake that we've come, David, and *that we may be* with you, son of Jesse.
Peace be yours *both day and night,*[32] and peace be upon your *helpers,*[33] for *the
Memra of* your God *is in support of you.*"[34] David accepted them and placed them
among the leaders of *the armed soldiers.*[35] 20. Some of *the tribe of Benjamin*[36]
encamped[37] with David when he came with the Philistines *to make war* against
Saul; but they did not give them any assistance, for the *commanders*[38] of the Philistines, when they had discussed the matter,[39] sent him away, saying: "It's at the cost

Apparatus, Chapter 12

[c] C: "armies."
[d] E, L, and AS: *mn zwṭry*, "from the lesser ones." C
seems to have lost the distinction between lesser

and greater and renders the second part of the
verse as "every one fought with a thousand."

Notes, Chapter 12

[20]Reading *zwṭr'* (singular).
[21]MT, with its use of the preposition *l*, is often interpreted as "in charge of," but Tg. Chr has an equally good case
for taking it as "to" in the sense of "against," or with the idea of fighting "with."
[22]MT: "banks" (Qere).
[23]Lit: "and he answered and said unto them."
[24]Lit: "there will be to me concerning you peace a heart as one."
[25]MT: "to my enemies."
[26]MT: singular.
[27]MT: "may the God of our fathers see and rebuke."
[28]Lit.: "clothed himself with"; cf. Judg 6:34; 2 Chr 24:20.
[29]MT: *'mśy* (= L, AS). V and C: *'mś'*.
[30]MT: "thirty," following Kethibh. Qere has "officers."
[31]Not in MT, but found in main versions and 2 Chr 10:16.
[32]MT: "Peace by day and peace by night be yours."
[33]MT: "helper."
[34]MT: "has helped you."
[35]MT: "the troop, the raiding band"; cf. 12:22.
[36]MT: "Manasseh" (= E, C, L, AS). See verse 21.
[37]MT is slightly stronger: "fell to, deserted to"; cf. 2 Chr 15:9.
[38]MT: "the lords (*srn*). Tg. Chr uses the plural loan word *'sṭrṭyg'*; see 11:16, note 31.
[39]Lit.: "in counsel."

of our *heads*[40]—*by killing us*[e]—that he will (be able to) *return*[41] to his master Saul." 21. When he came to Ziklag, those who *encamped and joined forces*[42] with him from *the tribe of* Manasseh were: *Adnah,*[f][43] Jozabad, Jediael, Michael, Jozabad, Elihu and Zillethai, chiefs of the *warriors*[44] who were from *the tribe of* Manasseh. 22. They assisted David *with the supervision of the armed soldiers,*[45] for they were all mighty warriors, and they were *appointed* commanders *of*[46] the army. 23. For day in and day out men kept coming to David to support him until *they had become a camp of troops*[47] so *numerous*[g] *that they were like the camp of the angels*[h] *of the Lord.*[48] 24. These are the total numbers of the chiefs *of the army* who were equipped for active service, who came to David at Hebron to transfer to him the kingdom of Saul according to the decree *of the Memra* of the Lord. 25. The sons of Judah, bearing *shields*[49] and *spears:*[49] six thousand eight hundred armed soldiers. 26. From the sons of Simeon, mighty warriors (ready) for active service: seven thousand one hundred. 27. From the sons of the Levites: four thousand six hundred, 28. as well as Jehoiada, *an officer of the house of* Aaron, who had with him three thousand seven hundred; 29. and Zadok, a young man, a mighty warrior, whose clan had twenty two commanders. 30. From the sons of Benjamin, the *kinsfolk*[50] of Saul: three thousand; up until this time *their sons*[51] had maintained their allegiance to Saul.[52] 31. From the sons of Ephraim: twenty thousand eight hundred mighty warriors, men of reputation in their clans. 32. From the half-tribe of Manasseh: eighteen thousand who had been specifically chosen by name to come and make David king. 33. From the sons of Issachar, men who were skilled in understanding the times, *expert at fixing beginnings of years and beginnings of*

Apparatus, Chapter 12

[e] C, L, AS omit "us."
[f] V: *'dnh*. C, L, AS: *'dnḥ* (= MT).

[g] V, C: *sgy'yn*. E, L, AS: *mgy'yn?*
[h] C: singular.

Notes, Chapter 12

[40]Lit.: "head," but used obviously in a collective sense. MT: plural.
[41]MT: "fall, desert"; see note 37.
[42]MT: "who fell (deserted) to him."
[43]MT: *'dnḥ*, but some MSS have *'dnh*.
[44]MT: "thousands."
[45]MT: "against the troops/raiding band." In MT this seems to be a reference to a band of Amalekite raiders as mentioned in 1 Sam 30, but Tg. Chr regards *'l* as suggesting "over" with the sense of supervision, as in verse 19.
[46]MT: "in."
[47]Tg. Chr uses *wklwzyn*, borrowed from Greek *ochlos*. See 11:6, note 11.
[48]MT: "until there was a great camp (army), like an army of God."
[49]MT: singular.
[50]MT: "brothers."
[51]MT: "most of them."
[52]MT: "the house of Saul."

months and at intercalating the months and the years, scholars[53] *who were able to work out the beginning of the lunar cycle so that they could fix the festivals at their proper time, familiar with the solstices, astrologers*[i53] *who had knowledge of the planets and the stars and were thus able* to know what *things were right for the house of* Israel to do, their leaders, *the heads of the Sanhedrins*: two hundred, with all their brethren, *who were putting into practice the decrees of the Law and who were wise* according to *the word of* their mouth.[54] 34. From *the tribe of* Zebulun, men who were fit for military service, drawn up in battle order, with all the weapons of war: fifty thousand and playing their part with one clear purpose.[55] 35. From *the tribe of* Naphtali: one thousand commanders, and along with them, thirty seven thousand[56] with *shields* and *spears*. 36. From *the tribe of Dan,*[57] drawn up in battle order: twenty-eight thousand six hundred. 37. From *the tribe of* Asher, fit for military service, capable of fighting in battle order: forty thousand. 38. From the other side of the Jordan, from *the tribe of Reuben,*[58] from *the tribe of Gad,*[59] and from the half-tribe of Manasseh, *equipped* with all kinds of military weapons: one hundred and twenty thousand. 39. All these, men of war, *drawn up*[60] in battle formation, came with one single purpose[61] to Hebron—to make David king over all Israel. All the rest of Israel, too, had one purpose[62]—to make David king. 40. They were there with David for three days eating and drinking, for their brethren had made preparation for them. 41. As well, their neighbors as far away as Issachar, Zebulun

Apparatus, Chapter 12

[1] V: *ṣrwlwgyn*. C: *'yṣrwlwgyn*. E, L, AS: *ṣṭrwlwgyn*.

Notes, Chapter 12

[53]Reading with E, C, L, AS, *swpystyn*, plural of *swpysṭ',* borrowed from Greek, *sophistēs*: "sophist, scholar" (MJ 968; JL II, 180). For the next technical terms in the verse, "astrologers," Tg. Chr uses the plural of the word *ṣrwlwgws* (see Apparatus for variants), "astrologer," borrowed from Greek *astrologos* (MJ 91; JL I, 58). It is interesting that any role (even though in this verse that role is limited and a little ambiguous) should be given to astrologers in a religion which found its guidance through seeking instruction from the Lord and his Law. Tg. Eccl, however, has several clear references to the part played by the planets in shaping man's destiny, e.g., "time and fate befall all according to their planets" (9:11; see also 9:1, 2), and suggests that an examination of these planets will tell man something of his end (7:27). But nearer the end the Targum does stress that "he who watches the planets will not reap a reward" (11:4), and follows this with an affirmation of the sweetness of the light of the Law (11:7).

[54]The other tribes supporting David in Hebron brought men drawn up in battle formation, seasoned troops, mighty warriors. When Issachar's turn came, that tribe's contribution was a group of scholars. In Jacob's blessing, Tg. Ps.-J. Gen 49:15, Issachar bows his shoulders to labor in the Law. This is what makes Issachar a tribe of scholars, mighty in Torah. For a society that laid great stress on keeping religious observances at certain fixed times, it was of the greatest importance to have experts available who could ensure that the times chosen were indeed the correct times. It is this aspect that receives most attention in this expansion. See also *b. Meg.* 12b; *Gen. R.* 62:5.

[55]Lit.: "without a heart and a heart," i.e., not double-hearted.

[56]Reading *šb''* with C, L, AS "thirty-seven thousand." For "seven," V has "seventy."

[57]MT: "The Danite(s)."

[58]MT: "The Reubenite(s)."

[59]MT: "The Gadite(s)."

[60]MT: "helpers of," but a few Hebrew MSS and LXX have *'rky,* "drawing up the battle order."

[61]Lit.: "with a perfect heart."

[62]MT: "heart."

and Naphtali, brought bread *for them* on asses, camels, mules and oxen; provisions,[63] *portions of* pressed figs, *bunches of* grapes, wine, oil, oxen and sheep in abundance, because there was joy in Israel.

CHAPTER 13

1. David conferred with the commanders of the thousands and of the hundreds, with every officer. 2. Then David said to all the assembly of Israel: "If it is good *before*[1] you and *if it is the will of* the Lord our God, let us *act courageously*[2] and send to[3] our brethren who are left in all the districts of Israel, and with them, to the priests and the Levites in the towns where they have their common lands, so that they may come and join us. 3. And let us bring back to us the ark of our God, for we did not seek it[4] during the days of Saul." 4. The whole assembly said to do so, for the thing was right *before* all the people. 5. Then David assembled[a] all Israel from the *Nile*[5] of Egypt to the entrance[6] *to Antioch,*[7] to bring the ark of *the Lord*[8] from Kiriath Jearim. 6. And David and all Israel went up to[b] *Baal,*[9] to Kiriath Jearim, which[c] is *in*[10] Judah,[c] to bring up[d] from[e] there[e] the ark of *the Lord;*[11] he is

Notes, Chapter 12

[63]The "flour" of MT seems to have disappeared.

Apparatus, Chapter 13

[a] V, C: *knš*; L, AS: *'knš*.
[b] E, L, AS exactly as MT, including the "directive *h*." C: *lb'lh*.

[c-c] Missing in C.
[d] C, L, AS: "to bring in."
[e-e] Missing in C, L, AS.

Notes, Chapter 13

[1]MT: "upon."
[2]MT: "break through."
[3]Lit.: "for the sake of."
[4]Tg. Chr, like MT, is ambiguous. "We neglected it," "we did not inquire of it," "we did not seek him,"—all are possibilities.
[5]MT: "Shihor." Sometimes in MT Shihor clearly refers to the Nile (Isa 23:3), sometimes to the Wady el Arish (Josh 13:3); in the last reference the Targum leaves it as "Shihor." Probably the word refers to some northern branch of the Nile in the eastern delta. In Tg. Chr it has become "the Nile of Egypt," *nylws,* borrowing from the Greek *Nilos.*
[6]Reading *m'ln* (C, L, AS).
[7]The usual translation in Tg. Chr for Hamath. See 18:9.
[8]MT: "God," though some Hebrew MSS have "the Lord."
[9]MT: "Baalah."
[10]MT: "to" (= L, AS).
[11]MT: "God."

the Lord *whose Shekinah* dwells *above* the cherubs, (the Lord) *whose* name is called *over it.* 7. So they *brought down* [12] the ark [13] of *the Lord* [11] from the house of Abinadab on a new cart, with Uzza and Ahio driving the cart, 8. while David and all Israel were *offering praise* [14] before *the Lord* [11] with all their might, with [15] songs and lyres and lutes and timbrels and cymbals and trumpets. 9. When they came to *a place which had been prepared,* [16] Uzza stretched out his hand to hold the ark, because the oxen *were making it sway.* [17] 10. And the anger of the Lord *was strong* [18] against Uzza, and he struck him down because he had stretched out his hand upon the ark, and he died there before *the Lord.* [11] 11. David was annoyed [19] because the Lord had burst forth against Uzza, and he called that place "*the place where* Uzza died," [20] up to this day. 12. That day David was afraid *from before the Lord,* [21] saying: "How am I to bring the ark of *the Lord* [11] to me?" 13. So David did not remove the ark to him, to the city of David, but he removed it to the house of Obed Edom, the Gittite. 14. The ark of *the Lord* [11] remained for three months with Obed Edom in his house, and the *Memra* of the Lord blessed Obed [22] Edom *with sons and grandsons; for his wife became pregnant, as did his eight daughters-in-law; each one of them gave birth eight times in one pregnancy until, between fathers and sons they amounted to eighty-one in one day. He blessed also* everything which belonged to him *and increased it greatly.* [23]

Apparatus, Chapter 13

[f-f] Missing in C, L, AS.

Notes, Chapter 13

[12]MT: "they caused to ride, transported." V's version is in contrast to the previous verse, where they were "to bring up" the ark of the Lord.

[13]This word in V has the vocalization of a plural noun; follow C, where the vocalization is that of a singular noun.

[14]MT: "making merry." Is Tg. Chr in this translation trying to avoid attributing anything unseemly to David and to all Israel? Cf. 15:29.

[15]Tg. Chr omits "and" before "with."

[16]MT: "the threshing floor of Kidon." In MT 2 Sam 6:6 we have "the threshing floor of Nacon," which in Tg. Sam becomes "a place prepared" (from the root behind Nacon: *kwn*). It would seem that Tg. Chr has taken over this rendering verbatim.

[17]MT: "stumbled," though this is not certain.

[18]MT: "hot."

[19]MT: "it was hot to David." Tg. Chr: "it was strong to David," i.e., the anger was strong; cf. Exod 22:23.

[20]MT: "the bursting forth against Uzza." Tg. Chr manages to retain the word play "Paraṣ–Pereṣ" in the earlier part of the sentence by using the cognate *tr'– twr't*, but in this place name it is more difficult, lit.: "the bursting forth against Uzza" (*pereṣ Uzza*); so he gives a straightforward paraphrase.

[21]MT: "David was afraid of God."

[22]MT has "the house of Obed Edom."

[23]In *b. Ber.* 63b-64a there is a discussion on the importance of hospitality, in the course of which the *a fortiori* argument is brought forward: that if the Lord blessed Obed Edom and all his house because of something which did not eat or drink (the ark), how much more will he bless a man who entertains a scholar and gives him to eat and drink. The blessing experienced by Obed Edom is then described: *all* his house was blessed, which of course includes his wife, his sons, and his daughters-in-law, the end result of which is a huge household—though *b. Ber.* mentions only six children in each pregnancy. See also 26:4, 5, note 5, and 2 Chr 25:24.

CHAPTER 14

1. Huram,[1] the king of Tyre, sent[a] messengers to David with cedar trees and master[2] builders *who were skilled in the construction of* walls, and carpenters *who were expert in cutting*[b] wood *before it begins to rot*[c3] *or is split by the heat of the sun,*[2] in order to build *a palace*[4] *for him*. 2. And David knew that *the Memra of* the Lord had established him as king over Israel, *and* that *his glory* was exalted on high, and his kingship, *in order to do good*[5] to his people, Israel. 3. Once again[d] David took wives in Jerusalem, and again David became the father of sons and daughters. 4. These are the names of those who were born (and) *who grew up*[6] in Jerusalem: Shammua, Shobab, Nathan, Solomon, 5.[e] Ibhar, Elishua,[f] *Eliphelet*.[f7] 6. Nogah, *Beeliada*,[g] Nepheg, Japhia,[g] 7. Elishama, Beeliada,[h] and Eliphelet. 8. Now the Philistines heard that David had been anointed as king over all Israel, and all the Philistines came up to challenge David *to fight*.[8] When David heard he went out to meet them. 9. The Philistines came and *spread out*[9] in the valley of *the warriors*.[10] 10. And David inquired of *the Memra of the Lord,*[11] saying: "Shall I go up against the Philistines? Will you deliver them into my hand?" The Lord said to him: "Go up and I shall deliver them into your hand." 11. They came up into *the valley*[12] *of* Perazim, and David struck them down there. David said: *"The Lord*[13] has

Apparatus, Chapter 14

[a] E: *šlḥ*.
[b] C: *lmqbw'*, "to fix, appoint."
[c] V: *bylṭyt'*. C, L, AS: *mlṭyt'*.
[d] E: *'wd*.
[e] E omits verses 5-7.

[f] Following C: missing in V.
[g-g] Following C: missing in V. "Beeliada" is found only in C.
[h] C: "Eliada"; cf. 3:8.

Notes, Chapter 14

[1] Tg. Chr follows Qere, along with some Hebrew MSS. Kethibh is *hyrm*.
[2-2] MT: Lit.: "craftsmen of wall and craftsmen of wood," i.e., masons and carpenters.
[3] MJ (146, 789) and JL (I, 98; II, 38) each list two words (*bwlṭyt'* and *mlṭyt'*), both found as variants in different MSS of Tg. Chr. Each word is given the same meaning "worm-eatenness, rottenness, corrosion." Lit.: "at the time that worm-eatenness has not authority in them."
[4] MT: "house."
[5] MT: "for the sake of."
[6] MT: "who were to him," i.e., whom he had.
[7] MT: *'lplṭ*, though many Hebrew MSS have *'lyplṭ* (= Tg. Chr).
[8] Lit.: "to seek David for battle."
[9] MT uses root *pšṭ* "to strip off, make a raid." The parallel verse in 2 Sam 5:18 uses the Niphal of *nṭš*, "to roam, spread abroad." Tg. Sam uses the same verb as Tg. Chr from the root *rṭš*, in Ithpa: "to be abandoned, scattered, spread out."
[10] MT: "Rephaim."
[11] For "Memra of the Lord," MT has "God."
[12] MT: "Baal."
[13] MT: "God."

smashed[14] the enemies *of David*[i][15] like *the smashing*[14] *of an earthen vessel which is full of* water." It is for this reason that the name of that place is *"the valley*[12] *of* Perazim" *up to this day.* 12. They had left their *idols*[16] there, and on David's orders[17] they were burnt in the fire. 13. Yet again the Philistines *spread out*[9] in the valley. 14. Once more David inquired of *the Memra of the Lord.*[11] *The Lord* said to him: "Do not go up after them but make a detour round them, then come at them from the direction of the *trees.*"[18] 15. And whenever you hear the sound of *the angels who are coming to help you,*[19] then go out to battle, for[20] *an angel who has been sent from before the Lord* will have gone forth *to give success* before you[20] by killing[21] the camp of the Philistines. 16. David did as *the Lord*[11] had commanded him, and they struck down the camp of the Philistines from Gibeon to Gezer. 17. David's reputation went out into all lands, and *the Memra of* the Lord put the fear of him upon all the nations.

CHAPTER 15

1. He built[1] houses for himself in the city of David and prepared *the* place for the ark of *the Lord*[2] and pitched *the* tent for it. 2. Then David said: "No one *is permitted* to carry the ark of *the Lord*[2] except the Levites, for the Lord chose them to carry the ark of the Lord and to minister to him for ever." 3. So David gathered

Apparatus, Chapter 14

[i] V and C: "the enemies of David." E, L, AS: "my enemies in my hand" (= MT).

Notes, Chapter 14

[14]In MT there is a good example of word play: "God has *broken through (paraṣ)* my enemies in my hand like a *breaking through (pereṣ)* of water." Tg. Chr tries to preserve this by using the verb *tbr,* "to break, smash," and *tybwr* "breaking, smashing," but is unable to continue it in the last sentence of the verse, and the "Perazim" of MT is simply reproduced; cf. 13:11.

[15]V omits "in my hand" of MT.

[16]MT: "gods."

[17]Lit.: "David said."

[18]MT: "balsam trees."

[19]MT: "the sound of marching in the tops of the balsam trees."

[20-20]MT: "for God will have gone forth before you."

[21]MT: "striking down."

Notes, Chapter 15

[1]Lit.: "he made."

[2]MT: "God."

together*a* all Israel to Jerusalem to bring up the ark of the Lord to its place which he had appointed for it. 4. Then David brought together the sons of Aaron and the Levites. 5. For the sons of Kehath: Uriel the leader and his brethren—one hundred and twenty. 6. For the sons of Merari: Asaiah the leader and his brethren—two hundred and twenty. 7. For the sons of Gershom: Joel the leader and his brethren—one hundred and thirty. 8. For the sons of Elizaphan: Shemaiah the leader and his brethren—two hundred. 9. For the sons of Hebron: Eliel the leader and his brethren—eighty. 10. For the sons of Uzziel: Amminadab the leader and his brethren—one hundred and twelve. 11. Then David summoned the priests, Zadok and Abiathar; and the Levites, Uriel, Asaiah, Joel,*b*3 Eliel and Amminadab. 12. He said to them: "You are the heads of the clans of the Levites; *prepare yourselves,*4 you and your brethren and you will bring up the ark of the Lord, the God of Israel, to *the place which*5 I have appointed for it. 13. Because, on the first occasion, *before you were present,*6 the Lord our God broke forth against us, because we had not consulted in the correct manner. 14. So the priests and the Levites *prepared*7 themselves to bring up the ark of the Lord, the God of Israel. 15. And the sons of*c* the Levites carried the ark of *the Lord*2—as Moses had commanded in accordance with the word of the Lord—with poles on their shoulders.*8* 16. David also told the leaders of the Levites *to bring up*9 their brethren, the singers,*d* with instruments of praise— lutes, lyres, and cymbals—sounding forth as they raised a joyful sound. 17. So the Levites appointed Heman, the son of Joel; and from his *kinsfolk,*10 Asaph, the son of Berechiah; and from the sons of Merari, their *kinsfolk,*10 Ethan the son of Kushaiah. 18. And with them, their brethren in the second order: Zechariah, Ben,*e* Jaaziel, Shemiramoth, Jehiel, Unni, Eliab, Benaiah, Maaseiah, Mattithiah, *Eliphalehu,*11 Mikneiah, Obed Edom and Jeiel, the gatekeepers. 19. The singers: Heman, Asaph and Ethan, (who were) to sound the bronze cymbals. 20. Zechariah, *Uzziel,*12 Shemiramoth, Jehiel, Unni, Eliab,

Apparatus, Chapter 15

a V, C: *knš.* L, AS: *'knš.*
b C, E, L, AS have "Shemaiah" after "Joel" (= MT).
V omits "Shemaiah."

c C, L, AS omit: "the sons of."
d C, L, AS: "who were the singers."
e C: "Bar."

Notes, Chapter 15

3V omits: "Shemaiah."
4MT: "sanctify yourselves."
5MT omits "the place which," though it is found in a few Hebrew MSS, LXX, Syr, Vg.
6MT: "you were not (present)."
7MT: "sanctified", see note 4.
8Lit.: "upon their shoulders with poles upon them."
9MT: "to appoint."
10MT: "his brethren."
11MT: "Eliphelehu."
12MT: "Aziel."

Maaseiah and Benaiah, who were to play lutes *accompanying young men singing praise with rich voices.*[13] 21. Mattithiah, *Eliphalehu,*[11] Mikneiah, Obed Edom, Jeiel and Azariah, who were to *offer praise* on lyres of eight strings.[14] 22. Chenaniah, the chief of the Levites who were in the *procession,*[15] *was to be in charge* of the bearer party,[15] for he was competent. 23. Berechiah and Elkanah were to be door-keepers at the *curtain where the ark was.*[16] 24. Shebaniah, Joshaphat, Nethanel, Amasai, Zechariah, Benaiah and Eliezer, the priests, were to blow the trumpets before the ark of *the Lord,*[2] while Obed Edom and Jehiah were also to be doorkeepers at the *curtain where* the ark *was.*[16] 25. So David, with the elders of Israel and the leaders of thousands, who were setting off to bring up the ark of the covenant of the Lord from the house of Obed Edom, (did so) joyfully. 26. While *the Lord*[2] was helping[17] the Levites who were carrying the ark of the covenant of the Lord, they sacrificed seven oxen and seven *lambs.*[18] 27. David was wearing a linen cloak, as were all the Levites who were[f] carrying the ark, the singers and Chenaniah, the leader of the bearer party, who[g] were the singers;[g] David was also wearing *a sleeved linen tunic.*[19] 28. So all Israel were bringing up the ark of the covenant of the Lord, with shouts of jubilation and with the sound of the ram's horn, with trumpets and cymbals, making[h] music with lutes and lyres. 29. As the ark of the covenant of the

Apparatus, Chapter 15

[f] C, L, AS omit: "who were."

[g-g] C omits.

[h] C, L, AS insert *d,* the relative pronoun before "making music," which may necessitate the insertion of a comma after "making music," giving, "with trumpets and cymbals sounding forth, with lutes and lyres." However, the change in meaning in the sentence would be minimal.

Notes, Chapter 15

[13]MT has *'l 'lmwt,* "with lyres according to Alamoth." "Alamoth," a technical musical term, traditionally associated with soprano voices (cf. *'lmh,* "young woman, virgin") (Braun, 184). There are two approaches to Tg. Chr's expansion. JL II, 367 regards *qlpwn'* as a melodious musical instrument, giving some such translation as "the sweet sound of melodious instruments of praise." MJ (1381) sees the clue as being in the root of *'lmwt,* namely, *'lm,* "young man," and interprets *qlpwn'* in this light, that the fine voices referred to in this Greek loan-word (*kalliphōnoi,* plural of the adjective *kalliphōnos,* "with fine voices") are the voices of young men, giving the translation above, or "bringing out the sweetness of young men's fine voices joined in praise." Le Déaut suggests: "with sweet and harmonious instruments (accompanying) the singing."

[14]Tg. Chr: Lit.: "to offer praise on lyres *on the eighth.*" MT: "to lead on lyres *on the eighth.*" MT: *'l hšmynyt,* lit.: "on the eighth" is found also in the heading to some Psalms, e.g., Psalm 6, but its meaning is uncertain: "on an instrument of eight strings"; "on the octave"?

[15]The word *mś'* may have a musical reference in MT, but Tg. Chr seems to interpret it in relation to the carrying of the ark.

[16]MT: "(doorkeepers) for the ark." For "curtain," Tg. Chr uses *prs',* which JL (II, 294) regards as borrowed from Greek *pharos.*

[17]Following E, C, L, AS, *s'yd* (though C actually has *s'yr*) instead of *s'wd* in V.

[18]MT: "rams."

[19]MT: "linen ephod." The ephod could be worn only by a priest, so Tg. Chr makes the necessary adjustment. Smolar and Aberbach (14) note the same procedure in Tg. 1 Sam 2:18 and 2 Sam 6:14 (the parallel verse to 1 Chr 15:27). For "sleeved tunic," Tg. Chr uses the word *krdwt,* borrowed from the Greek adjective *cheiridōtos* (Latin *chiridota*), "having sleeves" (MJ 664; JL I, 384).

Lord was coming to the city of David, Michal, the daughter of Saul, watched from a window and saw the king leaping and *offering praise,*[20] and she felt contempt for him in her heart.

CHAPTER 16

1. They brought in the ark of *the Lord*[1] and set it up in the middle of the tent which David had pitched for it. Then they offered whole burnt offerings and *sacrifices of holy things*[2] before *the Lord.*[1] 2. When David had finished offering up the whole burnt offering and the[a] *sacrifices of the*[a] *holy things,*[2] he blessed the people in the name of *the Memra of* the Lord, 3. and he distributed to all the people of Israel, both men and women, to each one loaf of bread, *one sixth of an ox*[3] and *one sixth of a hin of wine.*[4] 4. As well, he appointed some of the Levites as *singers*[5] before the ark of the Lord, that they might call to remembrance, give thanks and offer praise *before*[6] the Lord, the God of Israel. 5. Asaph was *at* the head; second to him was Zechariah, (then) Jeiel, Shemiramoth, Jehiel, Mattithiah, Eliab, Benaiah, Obed Edom and Jeiel, on *musical* instruments, lutes[b] and lyres, with Asaph sounding[c] the cymbals, 6. and Benaiah and Jahaziel, the priests, (sounding) the trumpets continually before the ark of the covenant of *the Lord.* 7. It was then, on that day, that

Notes, Chapter 15

[20]MT: "making merry"; cf. 13:8 and see note 14 in chapter 13, though Tg. Chr's change in 15:29 would remove some of the cause for the contempt Michal felt for David.

Apparatus, Chapter 16

[a] C omits the definite article.
[b] C omits "lutes."

[c] V: participle; C: infinitive. L, AS use the verb "to offer praise."

Notes, Chapter 16

[1]MT: "God."
[2]Tg. Jonathan and Tg. Chr use this phrase "sacrifices of holy things" for MT's *šlmym,* "peace offerings."
[3]MT: *'špr. BDB* (80) notes: "actual etym. and mng. unknown." Tg. Chr, following *b. Pes.* 36b and Rashi, splits the word into two syllables, *'š* (taken as related to the numeral "six") and *pr* "young bull, ox," giving the translation: "one sixth of an ox."
[4]MT: *'šyšh,* "raisin cake." Tg. Chr also links *'š* with *six* and, following *b. Pes.* 36b and Rashi, translates: "one sixth of a hin of wine."
[5]Or "those offering praise." MT: "ministers."
[6]MT: "to."

David *was appointed*[7] as head, to offer praise *before* the Lord with the assistance of Asaph and his brethren. 8. Offer praise[8] *before*[6] the Lord, call on his Name, make known his deeds among the peoples. 9. Offer praise *before* him, make music *before*[6] him, tell forth his wonderful works, all *of them.* 10. Glory in his holy Name; let the heart of those who seek *the Memra of* the Lord rejoice. 11. Seek *the Memra of* the Lord and his strength; *visit*[9] him continually. 12. Remember his wonderful works which he has done, his miracles, and the judgments of his mouth. 13. O offspring of Israel, his servant, sons of Jacob *whom he has chosen.*[10] 14. He is the Lord, our God; in all the earth are his judgments. 15. Remember his covenant for ever, the word which he commanded for a thousand generations, 16. which he made with Abraham, and *his* oath[11] to Isaac. 17. He confirmed it to Jacob as a decree, *and*[d] to Israel as an everlasting covenant, 18. saying: "To you[e] I shall give the land of Canaan, the share of your[e] inheritance," 19. when you were *a people*[12] few in number, insignificant, but *dwelling*[13] in it. 20. They went from people[14] to people,[14] and from a kingdom to another people.[14] 21. He allowed no one to oppress them, and on their account he rebuked kings. 22. "Do no injury to my *holy ones whom I have anointed with a good name,*[15] and to my prophets do no harm." 23. *Offer praise*[16] *before*[16] the Lord, all *the inhabitants of* the earth, from day to day proclaim his salvation. 24. Tell among the peoples his glory, among all the nations his wonderful deeds. 25. Because great is the Lord and much praised; he is feared above all *the angels.*[17] 26. Because all the *idols*[17] of the peoples are

Apparatus, Chapter 16

[d] E, L, AS omit "and" (= MT). V and C have "and."
[e] V preserves MT's use of the singular and plural forms respectively in the two occurrences of the second person in this verse, but C, E, L, AS make both forms plural.

Notes, Chapter 16

[7]MT is a little complicated, but the thrust is that on a certain day, David first (lit.: "at the head/beginning) appointed (*ntn*) that praise be offered to the Lord." In Tg. Chr David is appointed "at the head" (either as leader or at the beginning) to offer praise.

[8]Tg. Chr uses the same verb *šbḥ* to translate MT's "give thanks," *ydh*, and "sing," *šyr.*

[9]MT: "Seek his face." Tg. Chr: *qbylw 'pwy.* Lit.: "accept his face." In Talmudic usage this means "visit" (see JL II, 339). In modern Hebrew, this expression means: "to welcome, greet, meet" (see Le Déaut, I, 77 n. 6).

[10]MT: "his chosen ones."

[11]Tg. Chr: *qyym*, which means both "covenant" and "oath."

[12]MT: "men." Tg. Chr lit.: "a people of number," i.e., a people who could be numbered, i.e., few in number: the same basic idiom as in MT (cf. Gen. 34:30).

[13]MT: "sojourning." Tg. Chr's "dwelling," with a prefixed *waw* "but," suggests that we ought to take 18 and 19 together, starting a new "paragraph" at 20 and not at 19, as most English versions do.

[14]MT uses *'m, 'm,* and *gwy,* whereas Tg. Chr uses *'m* for all three words.

[15]MT: "my anointed ones."

[16]MT: "sing."

[17]MT: "gods." In 25, "gods" of MT seem to be given a certain status as "angels" in Tg. Chr (cf. Ps. 8), but in 26, immediately they are specified as "gods of the people," the more derogatory term "idols" is used. In the same verse yet another word for "gods" appears, from the root *dḥl.* The expansion "gods which are of no use" is a very good description of the Old Testament attitude to the gods of the nations and is a restatement of the basic meaning of the word used in MT: *'lylym,* "worthlessness."

gods[17] *which are of no use,* but the Lord made the heavens. 27. Splendor and glory are before him, strength and rejoicing are in his place. 28. Render[18] *before* the Lord, O families of *the* peoples, render[18] *before* the Lord glory and strength. 29. Render[18] *before*[6] the Lord the glory of his Name, bring *the* offering, come in before him *and*[f] worship *before* the Lord in the *splendors*[19] of holiness. 30. Tremble before him, all *the inhabitants of* the earth; but he *has* established the earth[20] so that it does not *tremble.* 31. Let *the angels on high*[21] rejoice, let *the inhabitants of* the earth[21] exult,[g][22] let them say among the peoples: "The Lord reigns." 32. Let the sea and its fullness roar, let *the trees of* the field exult and every *plant* that is in it. 33. Then let the trees of the thicket give a shout of joy before the Lord, for *he has appeared*[23] to judge *all the inhabitants of* the earth.[21] 34. Give thanks *before*[6] the Lord for he is good, because his *goodness*[24] is everlasting. 35. And say: "Deliver us, O God, our salvation,[25] gather us and rescue us from the peoples, that we may give thanks to your holy Name *and* find our glory[26] in your glory.[26] 36. Blessed be the Lord, the God of Israel, from *this* age until the age *to come.* And all the people said: "Amen; Praise *before*[6] the Lord." 37. And he left there before the ark of the covenant of the Lord, Asaph and his brethren, to render service continually before the ark, as each day required, 38. as well as Obed Edom and their sixty-eight brethren, while Obed Edom, the son of *Jeduthun*[h][27] and Hosah were to be gatekeepers; 39. and Zadok the priest and his brethren, the priests, (he left) before the tent of the Lord in the *synagogue*[28] which was at Gibeon, 40. to offer whole burnt offerings *before*[6] the Lord upon the altar of the whole burnt offering continually, morning and evening, and (to do) according to all that is written in the Law of the Lord which he imposed upon Israel. 41. With them were Heman and Jeduthun and the

Apparatus, Chapter 16

[f] "and" in V. Missing in C, E, L, AS (= MT).
[g] "and": C, L, AS (= MT). V omits.

[h] V and C: Jeduthun. L, AS: Jedithun (= MT).

Notes, Chapter 16

[18]Lit.: "Give."
[19]MT: singular.
[20]MT: "the earth is established." For MT's *tbl,* "world," Tg. Chr uses the normal word for "earth" (*'r'*). Note the word play at the beginning and end of the verse and how at the end Tg. Chr changes MT's "totter" to "tremble."
[21]MT: "the heavens." Tg. Chr does not allow heaven or earth to rejoice, but their inhabitants, human or angelic, are permitted to do so!
[22]V omits "and."
[23]MT: "comes."
[24]MT: "steadfast love," *ḥsd.*
[25]MT: "God of our salvation."
[26]An attempt to preserve the word play in Tg. Chr, which is not in MT, which reads: "and glory in your praise." In Tg. Chr noun and verb share the same root.
[27]MT: "Jedithun."
[28]MT: "high place." An attempt on the part of Tg. Chr to push the origins of the synagogue as far back into the distant past as possible.

rest of those chosen, who had been designated by name to give thanks *before*[6] the Lord, because his *goodness*[24] is everlasting. 42. With them Heman and Jeduthun *with* the trumpets and cymbals for those who were making music, and instruments of praise *before the Lord.*[29] The sons of Jeduthun *were put in charge of the gates.*[30] 43. Then all the people went off, each to his home, but David returned to bless *the people.*[31]

CHAPTER 17

1. Now when David[a] was settled[1] in his house, David said to Nathan, the prophet: "Here am I living in a house *which is covered with* cedar *paneling*[2] while the ark of the covenant of the Lord *dwells in a tent surrounded by*[3] curtains." 2. Nathan said to David: "Everything that is in your heart do, for *the Memra of the Lord is in support of you.*"[4] 3. That night there was a word of *prophecy from before the Lord with* Nathan,[5] saying: 4. "Go and tell my servant David: 'Thus has the Lord said: It is not you[b] who will build *before*[6] me the house *in which to cause my Shekinah* to dwell,[7] 5. for I did not *cause my Shekinah to* dwell in *a* house from the day that I brought up *my people*[c] Israel *from Egypt* until today, but *I caused my Shekinah to dwell from the* tent *of meeting to Nob, and from Nob to Shiloh, and*

Notes, Chapter 16

[29]MT: Lit.: "instruments of the song of God."
[30]MT: "at the gate."
[31]MT: "his house." Le Déaut: "David blessed the people again." Either translation raises the question as to how David was able to bless the people who had already gone "each to his home."

Apparatus, Chapter 17

[a] V: "David." C: "the king." L, AS: "King David."
[b] V has personal pronoun (= MT). Missing in C, L, AS.

[c] "My people" is missing in L, AS (= MT).

Notes, Chapter 17

[1]Lit.: "dwelt."
[2]MT: "of cedars."
[3]MT: "is under."
[4]MT: "God is with you."
[5]MT: "the Word of the Lord was to Nathan."
[6]MT: "for."
[7]Here and in the following verses in Tg. Chr the Lord does not dwell in...; rather, "he causes his Shekinah to dwell in...."

from Shiloh to the tent *at Gibeon.*[8] 6. *In every place where I caused my Shekinah to dwell,* wherever *my Shekinah*[9] traveled among *the sons of*[10] Israel, *do*[11] *you think it possible that* I ever spoke[11] with one of the judges of Israel whom I had commanded to look after my people, saying: "Why have you not built *before*[6] me a house *covered with* cedar *paneling?"'*[2] 7. Now, then, thus you will say to my servant David: 'Thus has the Lord of hosts said: I took you from the *sheepfold*[12] from behind the flock, so that you would be *king*[13] over my people Israel. 8. And *my Memra was in support of you*[14] everywhere you went, and I destroyed all your enemies from before you and I *made*[15] a reputation for you, a reputation as *good as* that of the great *fathers of the universe who have been* on the earth. 9. And I shall assign a place *prepared* for my people,[16] and I shall *establish*[17] them and they will dwell in their place,[d] and they will not be frightened any more and wicked men will never again harass them in the way that *they tormented them* formerly. 10. And[e] from the days that I appointed judges over my people Israel, I shattered[18] all your enemies and I have told you *that*[19] the Lord will establish a *kingdom*[20] for you. 11. And when your days are completed and[21] you must go to be[21] with your fa-

Apparatus, Chapter 17

[d] V, C: "in their place." L, AS: "in their places."   [e] L, AS omit "waw."

Notes, Chapter 17

[8]MT finishes the verse rather abruptly: "from tent to tent and from dwelling." It is assumed that "to dwelling" has dropped out, possibly through homoioteleuton. Tg. Chr uses this confusion as an opportunity to provide a "tent route map" for the wanderings of the Shekinah, which, one assumes from verse 1, is identified here with the ark of the covenant. Yet the fact that the Shekinah was present at Nob, whither the priests had fled after the fall of Shiloh, when in fact the ark was in the hands of the Philistines, may indicate that the Shekinah did not need the ark to guarantee its presence. It is puzzling that in the list of stopping places provided, Nob precedes Shiloh.

[9]MT: "I."

[10]MT: "all."

[11-11]MT: "did I speak a word?"

[12]MT: "pasture."

[13]MT: *ngyd*, "prince," "ruler."

[14]MT: "I was with you."

[15]MT: "I shall make," but LXX has "I made."

[16]Tg. Chr omits "Israel."

[17]MT: "plant."

[18]MT: "I shall subdue." Many English versions treat the *waw* at the beginning of verse 10 in MT as epexegetical, as it were an expansion of "formerly" in verse 9. This means that a comma is placed after "formerly," and the sentence ends after "Israel" midway through verse 10. The new sentence begins: "I shall subdue . . . and I declare . . ." (the first verb in MT is future). The thrust of MT is that from the time of the judges until the present day, Israel has been oppressed, but a brighter future lies ahead. Tg. Chr, however, puts a full stop after "formerly" in verse 9, gives *waw* its "and" force, and by changing the tense of the second verb ("I shall subdue" becomes "I shattered"), indicates that the period of the judges inaugurated a series of victories for Israel over her enemies.

[19]MT: "and."

[20]MT: "house."

[21-21]Lit.: "to go."

thers, I shall raise up *your son* after you, *your very own son,* [22] and I shall establish his kingdom. 12. It is he who will build for me *the sanctuary* house for *my name* [23] and I shall establish *the* throne *of* his *kingdom* [24] for ever. 13. I *shall love him as a father (loves) his son,* and he will be *cherished before me as* a son *(is cherished) by his father,* [25] and I shall not withdraw my *goodness* [26] from him as I withdrew it from *Saul, who reigned* before you. [27] 14. And I shall establish him *as a faithful one among my people* in my *sanctuary* house and in my kingdom for ever, and *the* throne of *his kingdom* [28] will be established for ever.'" 15. In accordance with all these words and in accordance with all this *prophecy,* [29] Nathan spoke [30] with David. 16. Then King David came and *lingered in prayer* [31] before the Lord, and he said: "*I am not worthy,* [32] Lord God, and *what* [33] is my house? (Yet) you have brought me thus far *that I am about to take possession of the kingdom.* 17. And this was a small thing *before you,* [34] O God;[f] you have spoken also about the house of your servant *for the world to come,* [35] and you *have let me see that I shall stand in the ranks of the mighty ones,* [36] O Lord God. 18. What more can David *say before* [37] you, *in that you have answered the request of* your servant *by honoring him,*[g][38] and you know your

Apparatus, Chapter 17

[f] C, L, AS: "Yahweh Elohim." V: "Elohim" (=   [g] L, AS: "me."
MT).

Notes, Chapter 17

[22]MT: "I shall raise up your seed after you, who will be from your sons." In Tg. Chr "your very own son" is (literally) "a son whom you will father."
[23]MT: "a house for me."
[24]MT: "his throne."
[25]MT: Lit.: "I shall be to him for a father, and he will be to me for a son." Tg. Chr is making clear how the divine fatherhood is to be understood (see also 22:10; 28:6). Any explicit suggestion of "fathering" is avoided; cf. Tg. Isa 64:7.
[26]MT: "steadfast love."
[27]MT: "from him who was before you."
[28]MT: "his throne."
[29]MT: "vision."
[30]Tg. Chr omits "thus" of MT.
[31]MT: "sat."
[32]MT: "Who am I?"
[33]MT: "who?"
[34]MT: "in your eyes."
[35]MT: Lit.: "to a distance" or "from afar."
[36]Most commentators regard MT here as almost unintelligible: "You look upon me as a man exalted." (?) Le Déaut suggests an alternative to Tg. Chr's translation: "You have made me fit to stand. . . ." At any rate, Tg. Chr regards it as underlining the promise of power already given to David through Nathan. For "mighty ones" (as in C), V has simply "men," which may be more in keeping with the 'dm of MT.
[37]MT: "to."
[38]MT: Lit.: "for honor your servant." Tg. Chr treats *lkbwd* as if it were *lkbd*: "to honor."

servant.*[h]* 19. O Lord, for the sake of your servant and according to*[i]* your *good pleasure*[39] you have done all this greatness*[j]* in making known *to your servant* all (these) great things. 20. O Lord, there is no one *who is* like you, and there is no God apart from you in*[k]* all that we have heard *and that has been spoken before us.*[40] 21. And who is like your people Israel, a people *unique and select*[41] in the earth, *for* whom *an angel sent from before the Lord appeared,*[42] to deliver a people to be his own, to make a name *for himself and to do for them* great and *mighty* deeds[43] by driving out *the* nations from before your people whom you had delivered from Egypt? 22. And you *established*[44] your people, Israel, as your own people for ever and you[45] became their God. 23. And now, O Lord, the word which you have spoken concerning your servant and concerning his house—let it be established for ever, and do as you have spoken. 24. Let it be established and your name magnified for ever:*[l46]* 'The Lord, *the Lord of* armies, *the Lord,* the God of Israel, *is*[47] the God for Israel.' And let the house of your servant, David, be established before you. 25. You,[48] *O Lord,*[49] have *informed*[50] your servant *saying: 'I shall set up a kingdom for you.'*[51] For this reason your servant has found *courage to speak in prayer*[52] before you. 26. And now, O Lord, you*[m]* are*[m]* the God *who*[53] has spoken this good thing concerning your servant. 27. And now you have begun to bless the house of your servant that it may be *enduring* for ever before you, for you, O Lord, have blessed and it will be blessed for ever."

Apparatus, Chapter 17

[h] L, AS: add "Yahweh Elohim."
[i] C: "in."
[j] E: *r'wt*, "good pleasure," for *rbwt*, "greatness."

[k] L, AS: "according to" (= many Hebrew MSS, LXX, Syr).
[l] E adds: "saying."
[m-m] L, AS omit.

Notes, Chapter 17

[39]MT: "heart."
[40]MT: "with our ears."
[41]MT: "one."
[42]MT: "for whom God went."
[43]MT: Lit.: "to make for you a name great and awesome deeds."
[44]MT: "gave" or "made." MT of 2 Sam 7:24 has "established."
[45]Tg. Chr omits "Yahweh."
[46]Tg. Chr omits "saying."
[47]Reading "is," with C, L, AS.
[48]Reading an initial "For," with C, L, AS, and MT.
[49]MT: "O my God."
[50]MT: "uncovered the ear of."
[51]MT: "to build a house for him."
[52]Lit.: "Your servant has found opening of the mouth (= courage to speak) to pray...." MT: "Your servant has found to pray...."
[53]MT: "and you."

CHAPTER 18

1. After this David struck down the Philistines and *a destroyed*[b1] them. As well he took Gath and its *villages*[2] from the hand of the Philistines. 2. He also struck down *the Moabites,*[3] and *the Moabites*[3] became slaves to David, bringing *tribute*[4] *and presenting* gifts.[5] 3. David also struck down *Hadarezer,*[6] the king of Zobah, in Hamath, when he went to establish [*v.l. to change*[c]] his *border*[7] at the river Euphrates. 4. David seized from him a thousand chariots, seven thousand horsemen, and twenty thousand infantry. David hamstrung all the chariots[8] but left a hundred chariots.[8] 5. *The men of* Aram of Damascus came to help *Hadarezer,*[6] the king of Zobah, and David *killed*[9] twenty two thousand *mighty* men[d] among *the Arameans.*[10] 6. David stationed *soldiers*[11] in Aram of Damascus, *and the Arameans*[10] became slaves to David, bringing tribute *and paying taxes.* Thus the Lord delivered David in every *place* that he went. 7. David took the shields of gold which were carried by[12] the servants of *Hadarezer*[6] and brought them to Jerusalem. 8. From Tibhath and from Cun, cities of *Hadarezer,*[6] David took a very large quantity of bronze; *from*[13] it Solomon made the sea of bronze, the pillars and the bronze vessels. 9. When Tou, the king of *Antioch,*[14] heard that David had *killed*[9] the entire army of *Hadarezer,*[6] the king of Zobah, 10. he sent Hadoram, his son, to

Apparatus, Chapter 18

[a] "and destroyed them": missing in C.
[b] L, AS: "shattered them" (root *tbr*).
[c] This alternative reading (which is the reading in Tg. 2 Sam 8:3) is found also in C as an alternative reading, but in E, L, AS it has become the reading. At the end of verse 3 in V, there is a stray line, unvocalized: "and he seized Hadarezer, the king of Zobah, at Hamath, when he went."
[d] V has "mighty men," but C, L, AS have "men," (though C vocalizes the word with "mighty men" in mind!).

Notes, Chapter 18

[1] MT: "subdued."
[2] MT: "daughters," i.e., dependent villages.
[3] MT: "Moab."
[4] Tg. Chr uses the word *prs*, borrowed (suggests JL II, 293) from the Greek *phoros*, "tax, tribute, gift."
[5] Tg. Chr uses the plural of *dwrwn*, borrowed from the Greek *dōron*, "gift" (MJ 289; JL I, 188).
[6] MT: "Hadadezer," but many MSS and the other main versions read "Hadarezer."
[7] MT: "to establish his power" (lit.: "hand").
[8] Unless the verb is being used in a metaphorical sense, one assumes that in the first instance at least, we should read "chariot horses"; see Tg. 1 Chr 19:18, note 27.
[9] MT: "struck down."
[10] MT: "Aram."
[11] MT seems to have lost some such word here. 2 Sam 8:6 has "garrisons." Tg. Chr uses the plural of *'strtywt*, borrowed from the Greek *stratiōtēs*, "soldier" (MJ 92; JL I, 46).
[12] Lit.: "which were upon. . . ."
[13] MT: "with."
[14] MT: "Hamath."

King David, to greet him[15] and to congratulate him, because he had *waged war*[16] against *Hadarezer*[6] and *killed*[9] him, for *Hadarezer*[6] had been at war with *Tou*,[17] along with all kinds of vessels of gold, silver and bronze *which he sent him.* 11. These also King David dedicated *before*[18] the Lord, with the silver and the gold which he had *captured*[19] from all the peoples, from Edom, and from Moab, and from the sons of Ammon, and from the Philistines and from *the Amalekites.*[20] 12. Abishai, the son of Zeruiah, *killed*[9] eighteen thousand *Edomites*[21] in the valley of salt. 13. He stationed *soldiers*[22] in Edom, and all *the Edomites*[21] became slaves to David, and the Lord delivered David in every *place* that he went. 14. So David reigned over all Israel, and *David* dispensed[23] justice and *truth*[24] to all his people. 15. Joab, the son of Zeruiah, *was put* in charge of the army, and Jehoshaphat, the son of Ahilud, was *put in charge of the official records.*[e][25] 16. Zadok, the son of Ahitub, and Abimelech,[f] the son of Abiathar, were *the leaders of the high priesthood*[26] and Shavsha[g] was the scribe. 17. Benaiah, the son of Jehoiada, *was*[27] *put in charge of the Great Sanhedrin and of the Little Sanhedrin, and he was making*

Apparatus, Chapter 18

[e] L, AS: singular.
[f] C has "Ahimelech" (= some Heb MSS, LXX, Syr, Vg).

[g] C, L, AS: *šyš*.

Notes, Chapter 18

[15] Lit.: "to ask for him in peace."
[16] MT: "fought."
[17] Lit.: "for a man making wars with Tou was Hadarezer," for MT's odd statement: "for a man of wars of Tou was Hadadezer."
[18] MT: "to."
[19] MT: "taken up."
[20] MT: "Amalek."
[21] MT: "Edom."
[22] MT: "garrisons"; see note 11 for word used.
[23] MT: "and he was doing/making."
[24] MT: "righteousness." Tg. 2 Sam 8:15 combines the two elements: "a judgment of truth and righteousness."
[25] MT: "recorder."
[26] MT: "were priests." Tg. Chr: "the *sagans* of the high priesthood." The *sagan* in later times was a priest of very high rank, in fact, "the captain of the Temple," with supreme charge of order in the Temple area. When the word occurs in the plural forms, it refers to the heads of the Temple police, lower in rank than the *sagan* but with the same kind of duties (see 2 Chr 24:11). Tg. Chr does not tell us who the supreme *sagan* was or indeed who the high priest was (see MJ 955; JL II, 144; Schürer II, 277–278).
[27-27] MT: "over the Cherethites and the Pelethites." On Sanhedrin, see 4:12, note 17; on Benaiah, see 11:22, note 47. The expansion here is based partly on the fact that the Cherethites and Pelethites, as David's bodyguard, must have been expert bowmen and slingers, and partly on the desire of the Targumist to give a "modern" designation to two groups of people, the meaning of whose original names had long since disappeared. Benaiah was already a "big name" and he is used here as a leading priestly figure to underline "the Talmudic concept that nothing of importance may be undertaken by a king or leader of the people without consulting the Urim and the Thummim" (Smolar and Aberbach, 24; and Tg. 1 Chr 11:22, note 47; 27:34, note 49; and *m. Yom.* 7:5).

inquiry through the Urim and the Thummin. It was at his command[28] *that the archers and slingers went*[h] *down*[h] *to battle.*[27] The sons of David *had the oversight of* the king's guard.[29]

CHAPTER 19

1. Now after this Nahash, the king of the sons of Ammon, died, and *Hanun,*[a][1] his son, became king in his place. 2. David said: "I shall show *kindness*[2] to Hanun, the son of Nahash, because his father showed *kindness*[2] to me." So David sent[b] messengers to express sympathy to him about his father. And David's servants came to the land of the sons of Ammon to Hanun to express sympathy to him. 3. The princes of the sons of Ammon said to Hanun: "*Do you really think that David is honoring*[3] your father *before you*[4] by sending men to sympathize with you?[5] Is it not rather to reconnoiter, overthrow and spy out the land that his servants have come to you?" 4. So Hanun took David's servants, shaved them and cut off their clothes *from* the middle[6] *as far as their private parts,*[c][7,8] and dismissed them. 5. Someone[9] came and told David[d] about the men's *problem,*[10] and he sent

Apparatus, Chapter 18

[h-h] Missing in C, L, AS.

Notes, Chapter 18

[28]Lit.: "by the Memra of his mouth."
[29]MT: "The sons of David were the chief ones at the hand (side) of the king." In Tg. Chr this becomes: "were sitting in the forefront (had the oversight) of the king's guard." Le Déaut suggests that *mṭr*, "guard," may be a corruption of *sṭr*, "side," which would be very much in line with MT's understanding of the situation.

Apparatus, Chapter 19

[a] Hanun, missing in C, L, AS (= MT).
[b] C: *šlḥ.* V, E, L, AS: *sdr.*

[c] V: "as far as the place of their shame." L and AS omit "the place of" (*byt*).
[d] Missing in C, L, AS.

Notes, Chapter 19

[1]Missing in MT but found in a few Hebrew MSS, Syr, and parallel passage, 2 Sam 10:1.
[2]Lit.: "I shall do goodness with" for MT's "I shall do *ḥsd,* steadfast loyalty with. . . ."
[3]Lit.: "Is it possible that David is honoring. . . ?" MT: "Is David honoring. . . ?"
[4]MT: "in your eyes."
[5]Lit.: "because he has sent to you sympathizers. . . ."
[6]MT: "in/at the middle."
[7]MT: "as far as the buttocks."
[8]Lit.: "as far as the place of their shame."
[9]Lit.: "they."
[10]Lit.: "matter, affair."

to meet them, for the men were thoroughly ashamed. The king said: "Stay at Jericho until your beards have grown and then come back." 6. When the sons of Ammon saw that they had *offended*[11] David, Hanun and the sons of Ammon sent a thousand *centenaria*[12] of silver to hire chariots and horsemen from Aram *which is on the Euphrates,*[13] from Aram *which is on* Maacah[14] and from Zobah. 7. So they hired thirty-two thousand chariots and the king of Maacah and his people, who came and encamped before Medeba, while the sons of Ammon mobilized from their towns and came to *wage war.*[15] 8. When David heard, he sent Joab with all the army *commanders and the companies of* the warriors.[16] 9. The sons of Ammon came forth and drew up in battle formation at the entrance to the city, while the kings who had come were on their own in the open country. 10. When Joab saw that *those making war were pressing* on him *from his* front and *from his* rear,[17] he selected some of all the young men *of*[18] Israel and drew up *battle* formation facing Aram. 11. And the remainder of the people he placed under the command of Abishai, his brother, and they drew up *battle formation* facing the sons of Ammon. 12. And he said: "If the *Arameans*[19] prove too strong for me, you will come to my rescue,[20] and if the sons of Ammon prove too strong for you, I shall rescue you. 13. Be strong and let us take courage for the sake of our people and for the sake of the cities of our God. And may the Lord do what is *right before him.*"[21] 14. Then Joab and the people who were with him drew near before Aram for battle, but they fled before him. 15. And when the sons of Ammon saw that *the men of* Aram had fled, they too fled before Abishai, his brother, and they entered the city. And Joab came to Jerusalem. 16. When *the men of* Aram saw that they had been defeated before Israel, they sent messengers and brought forth the Arameans[22] who were on the other side of the *Euphrates,*[23] with Shophach, the commander of *Hadarezer's*[24] army leading[25] them. 17. When this was reported to David, he mobilized all Israel,

Notes, Chapter 19

[11]MT: "made themselves odious to."

[12]MT: "talent(s)." For MT's "talent," Tg. Chr regularly uses *qntynr* (cf. Syriac *qantinara*), borrowed from the Latin *centenarium*, equivalent to one hundred thousand sesterces, "the weight of a *kikkar*" (= "talent"). (See Le Déaut I, p. 83 n. 4.) The sesterce was a small silver coin of the Romans. The weight factor inherent in "talent" is retained, e.g., in 1 Chr 29:7, where the plural of *qntynr* is used of both silver and gold (MJ 1389f. JL II, 371).

[13]MT: "Aram-Naharaim," usually thought of as Aram-of-the-two-rivers, i.e., the Tigris and the Euphrates.

[14]MT: "Aram-Maacah"; "a small Aramean kingdom not far from Damascus in Gaulanitis" (*ICC* 239).

[15]MT: "to battle" (noun).

[16]MT: "all the army, the warriors."

[17]MT: "the face of the battle was to him front and rear."

[18]MT: "in."

[19]MT: "Aram."

[20]Lit.: "you will be to me for a rescuer" (MT: "rescue, deliverance").

[21]MT: "good in his eyes."

[22]Lit.: "Aram."

[23]MT: "the river."

[24]MT: "Hadadezer"; see 18:3.

[25]Lit.: "before."

crossed the Jordan, advanced toward them and formed up facing[e26] them. David then drew up battle formation facing Aram, and they fought with him. 18. But *the men of* Aram fled before Israel and of *the men of* Aram David killed seven thousand chariots[27] and forty thousand infantry. He also *killed*[28] Shophach, the commander of the army. 19. When the servants of *Hadarezer*[24] saw that they had been defeated before Israel, they made peace with David and served him. So *the men of* Aram had no further desire to come to the rescue of the sons of Ammon.

CHAPTER 20

1. At the time of *the end*[a1] *of* the year, at the time when kings come forth *from their palace, during the days of the month of Nisan,* Joab led out the army of *conscripted troops,*[2] ravaged the land of the sons of Ammon and came and laid siege to Rabbah, while David remained in Jerusalem. Joab struck down Rabbah and destroyed it. 2. David took the crown of their king from his head and found it to weigh a *centenarium*[3] of *pure* gold. In it was *set* a precious stone *whose value*[4] was a

Apparatus, Chapter 19

[e] V: "to." C, L, AS: "against."

Notes, Chapter 19

[26]Lit.: "to them."
[27]One assumes "chariots" refers to the men in the chariots, or is a metaphorical sense intended?—"He destroyed seven thousand chariots." See 18:4, note 8.
[28]MT: "put to death."

Apparatus, Chapter 20

[a] V: *syp*: E, C, L, AS: *swp*:

Notes, Chapter 20

[1]MT: "turn." Tg. Chr goes on to specify the "turn" more exactly by giving the month, perhaps to avoid any confusion with a "turn of the year" in the autumn.
[2]MT has the rather puzzling *ḥyl ḥṣb*; lit.: "the strength of the army," or "the army of the army" (see also 2 Chr 26:13). Is this a reference to the crack troops of the army, or to a detachment of the army, or is it simply a rather roundabout way of saying "the army"? Here Tg. Chr translates it with "the camp of the *'wklwz*," a word borrowed, according to JL (I, 27) from the Greek *ochlos,* "crowd" (see 11:6, note 11). This word is translated sometimes by MJ (25) as "levy of troops"; hence the translation in the text above.
[3]MT: "talent"; see 19:6, note 12.
[4]Tg. Chr uses the plural of *tymy,* borrowed from Greek, "value, price, worth" (MJ 532; JL I, 300): *timē.*

centenarium[3] *of pure gold.*[5] *It was a lodestone which supported aloft*[6] *the gold setting*. It was (placed) on David's head, and he removed from the city a very large quantity of spoil. 3. He took away the people who were in it and sawed[7] them with saws and *threshing sledges with sharp iron teeth.*[b8] Thus David did to all the cities of the sons of Ammon. Then David and all the people returned to Jerusalem. 4. After this, war with the Philistines broke out[9] at Gezer. Then Sibbecai, *who was from Hushath,*[10] *killed*[11] Sippai *from the sons of Orphah,*[12] who was one[c] *of the warriors.*[d13] 5. Once again there was war with the Philistines. *David,*[14] *the son of Jesse—he was the pious man who awoke from his sleep in the middle of the night to offer praise before the Lord—killed* Lahmi, the brother of Goliath, *on the (same) day that he killed Goliath who was from Gath,*[14] and the shaft of his spear was like a weaver's beam. 6. There was another war at Gath, where there was a man of great

Apparatus, Chapter 20

[b] V and C have *sypwryn,* but V gives also a variant reading, *smpwryn,* which is in fact the reading of E, L, AS. Both MJ and JL regard these as alternative forms, both meaning "points, nails." In the translation above "sharp teeth" is used.

[c] V: "who was from the warriors." C, E, L, and AS: "who was from the sons of the warriors."
[d] C, E, L, AS add: "and they were defeated" (= MT).

Notes, Chapter 20

[5]This sentence is missing in V, possibly through homoioteleuton, but is found in C, E, L, AS. See also Tg. 2 Chr 23:11, note 13.

[6]Lit.: "in the air." For "air," Tg. Chr uses the word *'wyr',* borrowed from the Greek *aẽr,* "air" (JL I, 15; MJ 24?).

[7]MT: *wysr* may mean "and he sawed" (BDB 965) or "and he ruled" (*śrr*). 2 Sam 2:31 has *wysm:* "and he put (them to work)." Tg. Chr clearly understands it in the first sense in spite of its harshness (cf. Amos 1:3).

[8]MT: "with saws and sharp instruments of iron and saws."

[9]Lit.: "arose."

[10]MT: "the Hushathite."

[11]MT: "struck down."

[12]"Orphah," through association, may have come into this verse from verse 6, where the singular of "the Rephaim," viz., *hrp',* occurs. Alternatively, Tg. Chr may have wished to dispose of the idea of multiple parentage inherent in MT, and read: "from the sons of Rapha" (which, as in verse 6 has been corrupted into *'rph*), "one of the Rephaim" (which for Tg. Chr usually becomes "warriors").

[13]MT: "one of the descendants of the Rephaim; and they were subdued."

[14-14]MT: "Elhanan, the son of Jair (Qere. Kethibh *y'wr*) struck down Lahmi, the brother of Goliath, the Gittite." In MT Elhanan strikes down Lahmi. In Tg. Chr it is David who kills him.

i) In MT 2 Sam 21:19, Elhanan kills Goliath. But in 1 Sam 17:50 it is David who is the killer. In Tg. 2 Sam 21:19 the Targumist sets the record straight by stating that David killed Goliath. One can only assume that Tg. Chr, faced with Goliath's brother, Lahmi, the shaft of whose spear was like a weaver's beam (as with Goliath), felt that David should be responsible for his killing also. David's connection with the killing (as Le Déaut suggests, I, 85 n. 9) is further strengthened by the resemblance of his name to David's home town (Lahmi: *lḥmy*; Beth-lehem: *byt lḥm*).

ii) The nocturnal student emphasis in the expansion is thought to come: (a) from the word Yair (*y'yr*: Qere; Kethibh: *y'wr*), which is linked up with the Hebrew and Aramaic verb *'wr,* "to be awake," and this is in fact the verb used in the expansion "who awoke from his sleep ..." (b) from the Psalmist's nocturnal sessions of praise recorded in Ps 119:62. This verse, together with another "midnight verse" (Exod 11:4), provides the basis for a discussion in *b. Ber.* 3b, which mentions a self-playing harp hanging above David's bed, waking him at midnight, enabling him to study the Torah until dawn.

stature. [15] He had six fingers *on each hand* and six *(toes) on each foot—their total* twenty-four. [16] He, too, was a son of *Arapha,* [17] *one of the warriors.* 7. But when he sneered at Israel, Jonathan, the son of Shimea, David's brother, *killed* [18] him. 8. These were the *sons of Arapha* [19] in Gath, and they *were delivered* [20] into the hand of David and into the hand of his servants.

CHAPTER 21

1. *The Lord raised up* Satan [1] against Israel, and he incited David to number Israel. 2. So David said to Joab and to the leaders of the people: "Go, number Israel, from Beersheba to *Pameas* [2] and bring to me [a][3] the *total* number of them." [4] 3. But Joab said: "May the Lord increase his people by a hundred times as many as these! Does [5] not my lord the king *have authority over them?* Are they not all my lord's servants? [5] Why then does my lord demand this *thing?* And why should it become guilt upon Israel?" 4. But the king's word prevailed against Joab. So Joab went out and traveled through all Israel and *returned* [6] to Jerusalem. 5. Joab handed over to David the breakdown of the numbering of the people: in all Israel there were one million, one hundred thousand men who could draw the sword, while *the men of* Judah (amounted to) four hundred and seventy thousand men [b] who could draw the

Notes, Chapter 20

[15]Lit.: "a man of measure."
[16]MT lit.: "and his fingers, six and six, twenty-four."
[17]MT: "He too was born to the Rapha."
[18]MT: "struck down."
[19]MT: "born to the Rapha."
[20]MT: "fell."

Apparatus, Chapter 21

[a] C, E, L, AS have "that I may know" after "me" (=   [b] C: "warriors."
MT). V omits.

Notes, Chapter 21

[1]MT: "Satan stood up." Tg. Chr is making it clear that Satan does not exist as an independent entity, but that his actions are under God's control.
[2]Pameas or Paneas (modern Banias) is Tg. Chr's translation of "Dan." (MJ 1189; JL II, 273f.).
[3]V omits MT's: "that I may know."
[4]Lit.: "their total and their number" for MT's "their number."
[5-5]MT: "are they not, my lord, the king, all of them my lord's servants?"
[6]MT: "came."

sword.[7] 6. But he did not include[8] *the tribe of* Levi and *the tribe of* Benjamin among[c] them,[c] for the king's word was repugnant to Joab. 7. This matter was also displeasing *before the Lord,*[9] and he struck down Israel. 8. And David said *before the Lord*:[10] "I have sinned greatly by doing this thing. So now please forgive your servant's sin, for I have acted very foolishly." 9. Then the Lord spoke *with*[11] Gad, David's *prophet,*[12] saying: 10. "Go and speak to David, saying: 'Thus has the Lord said: "*One of* three things I am going to *lay upon* you.*[13] Choose*[d] one of them and I shall do it to you.'" 11. Gad came to David and said to him: "Thus has the Lord said: 'Take your choice:[14] 12. either three years of famine or three months *as an exhausted fugitive*[15] before your *adversary,*[16] with the sword of your enemy ruthlessly pursuing you, or three days of *killing by* the sword *from before*[17] the Lord while pestilence in the land[e18] ravages through the whole territory of Israel.' Now consider what word I am to bring back to the one who sent me." 13. David said to Gad: "*If I choose famine, those of the house of Israel will say: 'David's storehouses are full of grain, so it's of no concern to him if the people of the house of Israel die of famine.' If I choose battle and taking to flight from before my adversaries, those of the house of Israel will say: 'David is a mighty warrior*[f] *and an outstanding soldier,*[19] *so it's of no concern to him if the people of the house of Israel fall killed by the sword.' Oh,* how deep is my distress! Let me then *be given over*[20] into the hand of *the Memra of* the Lord, for his mercy is great, but let me not *be given over*[20] into the hand of *the sons of* man." 14. So the Lord sent[21] *the* pestilence throughout Israel, and seventy thousand men of Israel fell. 15. Then *the Memra of the Lord*[22]

Apparatus, Chapter 21

[c] Missing in C, L, AS.
[d] V, L, AS: *brwr.* C: *bḥr.* Both words mean the same: "choose."
[e] AS adds: "and the angel."

[f] C, L, AS omit *gbr',* but by the vocalization C omits "*the warrior,*" and it is not clear which *gbr'* is omitted by L and AS!

Notes, Chapter 21

[7] Lit.: "drawers of the sword." With regard to the number of men in Israel who could draw the sword, MT has "a thousand thousand and a hundred thousand" = 1,100,000. Tg. Chr has "a thousand and a hundred thousand" = eleven hundred thousand = 1,100,000.
[8] Lit.: "count."
[9] MT: "in the eyes of God."
[10] MT: "to God."
[11] MT: "to."
[12] MT: "seer."
[13] MT: "Three things I am going to spread out before (lit.: upon) you." Some Hebrew MSS and MT 2 Sam 24:12 have "impose" (*nwṭl* for *nṭh*).
[14] Lit.: "Take for yourself."
[15] MT: "being swept away."
[16] MT: plural.
[17] MT: "of."
[18] Tg. Chr omits: "and the angel of the lord."
[19] Lit.: "lord of the battle."
[20] MT: "fall."
[21] Lit.: "gave."
[22] MT: "God."

sent *the* angel *of the pestilence*[g] to Jerusalem to destroy it. When he was destroying it, *he*[23] observed *the ashes of the binding of Isaac which were at the base of the altar, and he remembered his covenant with Abraham which he had set up with him on the mountain of worship; (he observed) the sanctuary-house which was above, where the souls of the righteous are, and the image*[24] *of Jacob which was engraved on the throne of glory,* and he repented *in himself*[25] of the evil *which he had planned*[26] *to* do. So he said to the destroying angel: "*You* have had enough.[27] Now *take*[28] Abishai, their leader, from among them, and stop your striking down the rest of the people."[28] And an angel *sent from before* the Lord[29] was standing on the threshing floor of *Arwan,*[h][30] the Jebusite.[31] 16. David lifted up his eyes and saw the angel of

Apparatus, Chapter 21

> [g] V: "pestilence" (*mwtn'*). C, L, AS: "death" (*mwt'*).   [h] V, C: *'rwwn.* E, L, AS: *'rnwn.*

Notes, Chapter 21

[23]MT: "The Lord."

[24]Tg. Chr uses the plural form of *yqwn,* "icon, image," borrowed from the Greek *eikōn* (MJ 59; JL I, 25). Though the plural form is used here, the context suggests that a singular meaning is intended.

[25]Lit.: "in his Memra"; here *Memra* is used as a reflexive pronoun.

[26]Lit.: "said."

[27]MT: "Enough"; see also verse 27.

[28-28]MT: "stay your hand."

[29]MT: "the angel of the Lord."

[30]MT: "Ornan."

[31]The *Aqedah* ("binding") of Isaac has been a central theme in Jewish thinking on the relationship between God and man. In Gen 22 Isaac is bound, to be offered as a sacrifice on Monut Moriah. God stays Abraham's hand as he is about to kill his son; a ram is offered in his place. Isaac is delivered, and Abraham is assured of many descendants through whom the world will be blessed. According to 2 Chr 3:1, it was on this mountain that Ornan had his threshing floor, which became the site of the Temple.

The main part of our expansion is the result of Tg. Chr's attempt to fill the gap between the two verbs in MT 1 Chr 21:15: "the Lord *saw* and he *repented....*" Tg. Chr is concerned to mention those things the Lord saw which led to a change of mind. He saw (though the verb used is stronger than merely "seeing": "to observe carefully, consider, take note of"):

i) "The ashes of the Aqedah": the ashes, one assumes, of the ram which was sacrificed in place of Isaac. In the *Mekilta* of Exod 12:13 he saw the blood, in *b. Ber.* 62b, he saw the ashes. According to *PRE* 31, the ashes of the ram were the foundation on which stood the inner altar where the expiatory sacrifice was made once a year on the Day of Atonement. The sight of the ashes recalled the covenant made with Abraham on the mountain. Neither MT nor the Targums of Gen 22 refer to God's promise to Abraham as a covenant, but the covenant element is present in the swearing of the oath in Gen 22:16. In Tg. Ps.-J. of Lev 26:42, three covenants are mentioned—one with Jacob, one with Isaac on Mount Moriah, and one with Abraham "between the pieces" (Gen 15:17). The failure to mention Abraham in connection with Mount Moriah may indicate only that the emphasis had moved away from Abraham's obedience to Isaac's non-passive role in the incident.

ii) "The heavenly sanctuary": Tg. Ps.-J. Gen 28:17 gives a simple description of it: "This place is not common, but the sanctuary of the name of the Lord, the proper spot for prayer, set before the gate of heaven and founded beneath the throne of glory." There was thought to be a close correspondence between the earthly sanctuary and the heavenly sanctuary (cf. Tg. 2 Chr 6:2), some indeed, giving the distance between them, e.g., *Gen. R.* 69:7: 18 miles.

Two items of interest appeared in this sanctuary:

a) the souls of the righteous. (Here we find Naboth later on in Tg. 2 Chr 18:20). In *b. Ḥag.* 12b there is a list of seven heavens, and in the seventh are found "the souls of the righteous and the spirits and the souls which are yet to be born." The discussion links up with 1 Sam 25:29, whose Targum states that "the souls of my master will be hidden in the treasury of eternal life before the Lord our God."

the Lord standing, *suspended in mid-air,* between earth and heaven, with his drawn sword in his hand, aimed at Jerusalem. David fell down with *the scribes[i] and* the elders, who were *girdled and* dressed in sackcloth, and *they prostrated themselves* upon their faces. 17. Then David said *before the Lord:*[32] "Was it not I who gave the order[33] to number the people? I am the one who has sinned and acted in such an evil way. But these *people, who are like* sheep *in the hand of the shepherd,* what have they done? O Lord, my God, let now[j] your *blow*[34] be upon me and upon my father's house, but upon your people let there be no pestilence."[35] 18. Then an *angel sent from before the Lord*[36] told Gad to tell David that David should go up and erect an altar *before*[37] the Lord on the threshing floor of *Arwan*[k30] the Jebusite. 19. So David went up *in accordance with*[38] the word of Gad which he had spoken in the name of the Lord. 20. When *Arwan*[k30] turned round he saw the angel; his four sons[l39] were hiding *from before the angel,* and *Arwan*[k30] was threshing wheat. 21. As David approached *Arwan,*[k30] *Arwan*[k30] looked and saw David, and he left the threshing floor and bowed down to *the king*[40] with his face on the ground. 22. David said to *Arwan:*[k30] "Give me the site of the threshing floor that I may

Apparatus, Chapter 21

[i] E omits.

[j] V and C: *kdwn.* L and AS: *k'n.*

[k] In verse 18, V, C: *'rwwn.* E, L, AS: *'rnn* (= MT); see

also note *h* above, and see verses 20, 21, 22, 23, 24, 28, where V, C, E, L, AS all have *'rwwn;* (22: *'rwn*).

[l] C, L, AS: "with him" (= MT). V omits.

Notes, Chapter 21

b) the image/likeness of Jacob on the throne of glory. We find a reference to this in Tg. Ps.-J. Gen 28:12: "Come, see Jacob ... whose image is fixed to the throne of glory." See also Tg. Lam 2:1; *Gen. R.* 68:12; *PRE* 35.

After God's change of mind, Abishai becomes the leading character in the second part of the expansion. He was Joab's brother, one of David's leaders, chief of the three (1 Chr 11:20-21). In 1 Chr 21:15 God's instruction to the destroying angel is "Enough": (*rb*). Tg. Chr then interprets this word as "chief" and introduces Abishai in that role: Abishai, who in later Jewish tradition was regarded as a very righteous man. Tg. Chr feels that the destroying angel must finish his work, but instead of allowing him to wipe out the rest of the people, Abishai is to take their place, in much the same way as the ram in Gen 22 took the place of Isaac. This is an echo of *b. Ber.* 62b, where "R. Eleazar said: The Holy One, blessed be he, said to the angel: Take a great man (*rab*) among them, through whose death many sins can be expiated for them. At that time there died Abishai ... who was (singly) equal in worth to the greater part of the Sanhedrin."

In *PRE* 43, Rabbi Simeon gives a different interpretation: "Only Abishai ... fell amongst the Israelites, for he was equal in his good deeds and his knowledge of the Torah to the seventy thousand men. . . ," suggesting that Abishai's death had sufficed for the whole populace, based on the fact that in verse 14, when MT speaks of seventy thousand *men,* the singular form of the noun is used: "man" (*'yš*), as is often the case with certain nouns when used with a numeral. (For the *Aqedah,* see Robert Hayward, "The Present State of Research into the Targumic Account of the Sacrifice of Isaac," *JJS* 32 [1981] 127–150.)

[32] MT: "to God."

[33] Lit.: "said."

[34] MT: "hand."

[35] Lit.: "let it not be for a pestilence."

[36] MT: "the angel of the Lord."

[37] MT: "to."

[38] MT: "by" (*k* in Tg. Chr for *b* in MT).

[39] V omits "with him" of MT.

[40] MT: "David."

build in it *ᵐ* the altar *before*³⁷ the Lord—give it to me at full price—that the pestilence may be withdrawn from the people." 23. *Arwan*ᵏ³⁰ said to David: "Take it for yourself; and let my *master*⁴¹ the king do what is *proper before him.*⁴² Look! I have given oxen*º* for the whole burnt *offering,*⁴³ the threshing sledges *to be cut up* for the wood *of the arrangement,* and the wheat for the cereal offering. I have given everything." 24. King David said to *Arwan:*ᵏ³⁰ "No, but I shall indeed buy it at full price. For I shall not take *from* what is yours for *the name of* the Lord, to offer up a whole burnt offering which cost me nothing." 25. So David gave *Arwan*ᵏ³⁰ *the price of* the site, six hundred *selas*⁴⁴ of gold by weight. 26. Then David built there *an* altar to *the name of* the Lord and offered up whole burnt offerings and *sacrifices of holy things.*⁴⁵ He *prayed before*⁴⁶ the Lord, and he *accepted his prayer*⁴⁷ in the fire *which came down* from heaven upon the altar of the whole burnt offering. 27. Then the Lord said to the *destroying* angel: "*You have had enough!*"⁴⁸ So he returned his sword to its sheath. [*v.l. to its scabbard*].*ᵖ*⁴⁹ 28. At that time, when David saw that the Lord *had accepted his prayer*⁵⁰ at the threshing floor of *Arwan*ᵏ³⁰ the Jebusite, he offered sacrifices there. 29. The tent of the Lord which Moses had made in the wilderness and the altar of the whole burnt offering were at that time in the *sanctuary which was*⁵¹ at Gibeon. 30. But David *was* unable to go before it to seek *instruction from before the Lord,*⁵² for he was frightened of the sword of an angel *sent from before* the Lord.³⁶

Apparatus, Chapter 21

ᵐ E: *byt.* Others *byh* (= MT).

ⁿ C: "my people."

º V: "oxen." C, L, AS: "the oxen" (= MT).

ᵖ Variant reading found in V and C. In C it is introduced by *l yn* = "in Greek."

Notes, Chapter 21

⁴¹MT: "lord."

⁴²MT: "good in his eyes."

⁴³MT: plural.

⁴⁴MT: "shekels." "Sela" is the usual translation in Targums for "shekel." The coins were made of gold, silver, or bronze, and the value of the coin was determined by the value of the metal.

⁴⁵MT: "peace offerings."

⁴⁶MT: "He called to."

⁴⁷MT: "he answered him."

⁴⁸Cf. 21:15. In 27 the expression is not in MT.

⁴⁹The variant reading in V (and in C) is simply an alternative word for the word just used. The alternative word is *tyqh,* borrowed from the Greek *thēkē,* "sheath, scabbard" (MJ 1665; JL II, 536).

⁵⁰MT: "answered him."

⁵¹MT: "high place." An attempt by Tg. Chr to avoid any suggestion that the altar of the whole burnt offering should ever have been located at an improper place.

⁵²MT: "to seek God."

CHAPTER 22

1. Then David said: "This is *the place where it is fitting that the sanctuary* house of the Lord *should be built,*[1] and this is *the*[2] altar *which is fitting for* the whole burnt offering for *those of the house of* Israel. 2. And David gave orders[3] to bring together the strangers who were in the land of Israel, and he organized stonecutters to cut hewn stones for building the *sanctuary* house of *the Lord.*[4] 3. David also prepared a large quantity of iron for nails to fasten together[a5] the doors of the gates, and more bronze than *it was possible* to weigh, 4. And cedar trees beyond number, for the Sidonians and the Tyrians had brought large quantities of cedar trees to David. 5. David had said: "Solomon, my son, is young and gentle, and the *sanctuary* house which is to be built to *the name of* the Lord should be so *majestic* that it can be magnified to the height for the name *of the Lord* and that it may become an object of praise in all lands. I shall therefore make preparations for it." Thus David made extensive preparations for it before his death. 6. Then he summoned Solomon, his son, and instructed him to build *the sanctuary* house[6] to *the name of* the Lord, the God of Israel. 7. David said to Solomon, his[b7] son: "I had it in my heart to build *the sanctuary* house to the name of the Lord, my God. 8. But a word *of prophecy from before* the Lord[8] came to me, saying: 'Blood in plenty you have shed and great wars you have fought.[9] So you *are not permitted* to build *the sanctuary* house[10] to my name, for you have shed much blood on the earth before me. 9. But[11] a son will be born to you; he will be a man of rest, and I shall give him rest from all his enemies on every side, for Solomon *will be*[12] his name and I shall give Israel peace and quiet in his days. 10. It is he who will build *the sanctuary* house[6] to my name. He will be *cherished before me like* a son[13] and I shall *love* him *as a*

Apparatus, Chapter 22

[a] E: *lypwpy',* "clamps."

[b] C, L, AS follows Qere: "My son." V follows Kethibh: "his son."

Notes, Chapter 22

[1] MT: "This is the house of the Lord God."
[2] MT: "an." The definite article in MT may have disappeared through haplography.
[3] MT: "said."
[4] MT: "God."
[5] MT: "and for clamps."
[6] MT: "a house."
[7] V follows Kethibh. Qere is "my son."
[8] MT: "The word of the Lord."
[9] Lit.: "made."
[10] MT: "You will not build a house."
[11] Lit.: "behold."
[12] Missing in V, L, AS, but present in MT and C.
[13] MT: "He will be to me for a son." For Tg. Chr's translation of this phrase and the next, see 17:13.

father, [14] and I shall establish for ever the throne of his kingdom over Israel.'
11. Now, my son, may *the Memra of* the Lord be *in support of you,* [15] may you prosper and build the *sanctuary* house of the Lord, your God, as he has spoken concerning you. 12. But may the Lord give you intelligence and understanding that he may *appoint* you [16] *as king* over Israel, so that you may keep the law of the Lord, your God. 13. Then you will prosper if you are careful to practice the statutes[c] and the ordinances which the Lord commanded Moses for Israel. Be strong and resolute! Don't be afraid! And don't give up! [17] 14. Yes! Even when I was miserable *and hungry* I made preparations for the *sanctuary* house of the Lord: one hundred thousand *centenaria* [18] of gold, a million *centenaria* [18] of silver, bronze and iron that could not be weighed—there was so much of it. Wood and stone also I have provided—to them you must add. 15. You have also a large labor force: [19] hewers, stonemasons, carpenters and all kinds of experts in various crafts. [20] 16. As for gold, silver, bronze and iron—it's beyond *calculation.* [21] So arise and get on with it, [22] and may *the Memra of* the Lord be *in support of you.*" [23] 17. Then David gave orders to all the leaders of Israel to help his son, Solomon. 18. "Is not *the Memra of* the Lord, your God, *in support of you?* [24] Will he not give you rest on every side? [25] For he has *delivered* [26] into my hand *all* the inhabitants of the land, and the land has been subdued before the Lord and before his people. 19. So now, apply your heart and soul to inquire *from before* [27] the Lord, your God. Arise and build the sanctuary *house* of the Lord your God, so that you can bring into[d] it[d] the ark of the covenant of the Lord and the sacred vessels of *the Lord* for the house which is to be built to the name of the Lord." [28]

Apparatus, Chapter 22

[c] C, L, AS add: "of the Lord."   [d] C omits.

Notes, Chapter 22

[14] MT: "I (shall be) to him for a father."
[15] MT: "May the Lord be with you."
[16] MT: "that he may give you charge."
[17] Lit.: "be broken."
[18] MT: "talents."
[19] Lit.: "with you are workers in abundance."
[20] Lit.: "and every skilled man in every work."
[21] Lit.: "there is no calculation or number." MT: "there is no number."
[22] Lit.: "and do."
[23] MT: "May the Lord be with you."
[24] MT: "with you."
[25] Or: "He will give you rest. . . ."
[26] MT: "given."
[27] MT: "To seek."
[28] MT: "God."

CHAPTER 23

1. When David was old and full[1] of days, he made Solomon, his son, king over Israel. 2. Then he gathered together all the leaders of Israel, with the priests and the Levites. 3. They *numbered*[a][2] the Levites, from thirty years old and upward; the number of their males, on a head count, was thirty-eight thousand. 4. Of these, twenty-four thousand *were appointed*[3] supervisors,[4] in charge of the work of the *sanctuary* house of the Lord, six thousand leaders and judges, 5. four thousand gatekeepers and four thousand offering praise *before*[5] the Lord with *musical* instruments *made*[b][6] for offering praise. 6. David split them up into sections corresponding to the sons of Levi: Gershon, Kehath and Merari. 7.[c] To *the sons of Gershon:*[d][7] Laadan and Shimei. 8. The sons of Laadan, *who was appointed* head:[8] Jehiel, Zetham and Joel— three. 9. The sons of Shimei: Shelomith,[9] Haziel and Haran— three. These were the heads of the clans for *the house of* Laadan. 10.[e] And the sons of Shimei: Jahath, Zina, Jeush and Beriah. These were the sons of Shimei— four. 11. Jahath *was appointed* head and Ziza the second, but Jeush and Beriah did not have many sons, so they were reckoned as a clan *and assigned* to one duty. 12.[f] The sons of Kehath: Amram, Izhar, Hebron, and Uzziel—four. 13. The sons of Amram: Aaron and Moses. Aaron was set apart that he might consecrate most holy things, [10] he and his sons for ever; they were to offer up *sweet-smelling* incense before the Lord, to serve him and to pronounce blessings in his name for ever. 14. But Moses,

---

Apparatus, Chapter 23

[a] V and C: "they numbered the Levites." L and AS: "The Levites were numbered" (= MT).

[b] V: "they made." C, E, L, AS: "which I have made" (= MT).

[c] E omits verse 7.

[d] C, L, AS: "To Gershon."

[e] E omits verse 10.

[f] E omits verse 12.

Notes, Chapter 23

[1]"Full" is not quite adequate to bring out the "satisfied" nuance in *śbʿ*; perhaps "replete with."

[2]MT: "The Levites were numbered."

[3]Following C, L, AS. "Were appointed" missing in V. Not in MT.

[4]MT: "to supervise."

[5]MT: "to."

[6]MT: "I have made." Perhaps the suggestion is that David is the speaker outlining the duties and divisions of the Levites (see *BHS*, proposals at 4a and 5a). V, however, has in mind a more general "make." Lit.: "which they made for offering praise." But see *b* in Apparatus.

[7]MT: "the Gershunite(s)."

[8]MT suggests that Jekiel was head. Tg. Chr, however, by inserting "who was appointed head" after "Laadan," has promoted Laadan.

[9]Tg. Chr follows Qere. Kethibh: *šlmwt*.

[10]This could also be translated as: "to consecrate him as most holy" = "to be consecrated as most holy."

the prophet of the Lord,[11] his[g] sons were reckoned among[12] the tribe of Levi. 15.[h] The sons of Moses: Gershom and Eliezer. 16. The sons of Gershom: Sheboel[i][13] *was appointed* head; *he is Jonathan, who was appointed a false prophet, but he repented in his old age and David put him in charge of the treasuries.* 17. The sons of Eliezer were Rehabiah, (who) *was appointed* head. Now Eliezer had no other sons, but *because of the merit of Moses,* the sons of Rehabiah became exceedingly numerous—*more than sixty myriads.*[14] 18. The sons of Izhar: Shelomith *was appointed* head.[15] 19. The sons of Hebron: Jeriah the head, Amariah the second, Jahaziel the third, Jekameam the fourth. 20. The sons of Uzziel: Micah[j][16] the head, Isshiah the second. 21.[k] The sons of Merari: Mahli and Mushi; the sons of Mahli: Eleazar and Kish. 22. Eleazar died, having no sons, only daughters; the sons of Kish, their *father's brother,*[17] married them. 23.[l] The sons of Mushi: Mahli, Eder and Jeremoth—three. 24. These were the sons of Levi according to their clans, heads of clans according to their *number,*[18] (going) by the number of individual names of those,[19] from twenty years old and upward, who were[19] to carry out the

Apparatus, Chapter 23

[g] C, L, AS: "and his sons."
[h] E omits verse 15.
[i] V: *šbw'l.* C: *šwb'l* (= MT 1 Chr 24:20).

[j] C: *myk'.*
[k] E omits verse 21.
[l] E omits verse 23.

Notes, Chapter 23

[11]MT: "the man of God."

[12]Lit.: "were called/named upon."

[13]MT: "Shebuel." Judg 18:30 tells of Gershom's son, Jonathan, who, with his sons, acted as priest to the Danites, using an image in the worship. In 1 Chr 23:16 only one son of Gershom is mentioned, Shebuel, so Tg. Chr identifies him with Jonathan, especially as Shebuel is called "the chief." Jonathan's role as idolatrous priest seems to have brought him the title of false prophet, but in due course Jonathan (= Shebuel) repented, and David put him in charge of the treasuries (26:24). This verse in Tg. Chr mentions his repentance but adds a further reason for his financial appointment—that he was meticulous (agitated, concerned) about money. Other reasons are suggested elsewhere—that when David saw that the only reason why he was an idolatrous priest was to enable him to live, he thought such a man must be worthy of confidence (Ginzberg, IV, 51). (Ginzberg also notes that after Solomon had sacked him, he returned to his old ways, but repented and became so pure that God gave him the spirit of prophecy!) *b. B.B.* 110a gives another reason for David's choice: "... because he saw that he had an exceptional liking for money." However, *b. B.B.* sees the connection between the two names thus: "because he returned to God with all his heart," seeing in Shebuel two roots: *šwb,* "to return," and *'l,* "God."

[14]The verb "to become numerous" in this verse, in Hebrew and Aramaic, is *rbh.* The same verb is used of the little group of the sons of Israel in Egypt (Exod 1:7): they became numerous, the grand total that left Egypt eventually reaching six hundred thousand. And the children of Moses through Eliezer and through Rehabiah also reached six hundred thousand—in fact, that figure was passed, "more than sixty myriads." *b. Ber.* 7b brings these two verses together (Exod 1:7 and 1 Chr 23:17) and also quotes the final figure of Exod 12:37.

[15]MT: "Shelomith the head."

[16]C, L, AS: add "was appointed as."

[17]MT reads: "the sons of Kish, their brethren...." The antecedent of "brethren" is "sons," and when "brethren" is interpreted as "kinsfolk" there is no problem. Tg. Chr, however, regards "Kish" as the antecedent, involving an inevitable change to "the sons of Kish, the brother of their father."

[18]MT: "their musters."

[19]MT: singular, though many MSS have the plural.

work for the service of the *sanctuary* house of the Lord. 25. For David had said: *"The Memra of* the Lord, the God of Israel, has given rest to his people and *has caused his Shekinah to dwell*[20] in Jerusalem for ever. 26. So it is not *at all fitting* that the Levites should carry the tent *of the Lord,* and all its vessels for its service." (27. For by the words of David, *which he spoke prophetically at the end,*[m][21] these were the number of the sons of Levi from twenty years old and upward.) 28. "For their *place of* duty[22] is to be at the side of the sons of Aaron for the service of the *sanctuary* house of the Lord, (to be responsible) for the courtyards, the chambers, the purification[n] of every holy thing, the carrying out of the service of the *sanctuary* house of the Lord, 29. the shewbread, the flour[o] for the cereal offering, the unleavened *spongy cakes,*[23] (bread baked on) the pan, the mixed bread[24] and all dry measures and sizes; 30. to take up their position[25] every morning to offer thanks and praise *before*[26] the Lord, and likewise in the evening, 31. and *whenever* whole burnt offerings are presented *before*[26] the Lord on the Sabbath *days,* at *the beginnings of* the months and at the appointed festivals, according to the number[p] prescribed for them, continually before the Lord. 32. Thus they will keep the charge of the tent of meeting, the charge of the sanctuary[27] and the charge of the sons of Aaron, their brethren, for the service of the *sanctuary* house of the Lord."

Apparatus, Chapter 23

[m] V: "at the end." C, L, AS: plural. JL (I, 283) "at the last times."

[n] V: *dkwt.* C: *dkwwt':* "affairs concerning Levitical cleanness" (MJ 307).

[o] C, L, AS add "and."

[p] C: "numbers."

Notes, Chapter 23

[20]MT: "dwelt" or "has taken up residence."

[21]Lit.: "which he prophesied and spoke at the end" for MT's: "(with) the last (words)."

[22]Lit.: "the place of their camp."

[23]Tg. Chr uses: *spwgyn,* plural form of word borrowed from the Greek *spoggos,* "sponge." Here "sponge-cake"; MT has the word *rqyq:* "thin cake" (*BDB* 956); JL I, 48, but MJ (95 and 1012) thinks the Greek word is "of Semitic origin."

[24]MJ (1442) describes it as "pulp of flour mixed with hot water and oil."

[25]Lit.: "to stand."

[26]MT: "to."

[27]MT: *qdš:* "holiness, holy thing, holy place." One could also translate the corresponding Aramaic word which appears in the text, *qwdš',* as "holy thing(s)."

CHAPTER 24

1. As for the sons of Aaron, their divisions[1] (were as follows). The sons of Aaron: Nadab and Abihu, Eleazar and Ithamar. 2. Nadab and Abihu died in the presence of their father, and as they had no *male* children, Eleazar and Ithamar took over (their) service.[2] 3. David, with Zadok of the sons of Eleazar and Ahimelech of the sons of Ithamar, divided them according to their number, for their service. 4. As the sons of Eleazar were found to have more *leading warriors*[3] than the sons of Ithamar, he divided them up—sixteen heads of clans for the sons of Eleazar and eight clans for the sons of Ithamar. 5. They divided[a] them by lot, all alike, for there were holy officials and officials *who were serving before the Lord*[4] among both the sons of Eleazar and the sons of Ithamar. 6. *Moses,* the *great* scribe, *who is called* Shemaiah,[5] the son of Nethanel, from *the tribe of* Levi,[6] recorded them, *and the document was read* before the king, the nobles, Zadok the priest, Ahimelech the son of Ebiathar, and the heads of the clans of the priests and[b] of the Levites;[b] one clan which was taken *eight times* for *the watch of* Eleazar, and that which was taken was taken *sixteen times* for[c] Ithamar. 7. The first lot fell[8] to Jehoiarib, the second to Jedaiah, 8. the third to Harim, the fourth to Seorim, 9. the fifth to Malchijah, the sixth to Mijamin, 10. the seventh to Hakkoz, the eighth to Abijah, 11. the ninth to

---

Apparatus, Chapter 24

[a] V = C (consonantally). E, L, AS have singular: "he divided them."

[b-b] C, L, AS omit.
[c] C, L, AS add: "the watches of."

Notes, Chapter 24

[1]Following C (= MT). Tg. Chr (apart from C, which has plural) actually has "their division."

[2]MT: "acted as priests." Tg. Chr uses the verb *šmš,* "to serve, minister"; it is often used in the sense of "to serve as priests."

[3]MT: "leading men" (lit.: "heads of the men"), though some MSS, LXX and Vg have "heads of the warriors" (*gbwrym*).

[4]MT: "officers of the sanctuary and officers of God." "Sanctuary" could also be translated as "holiness," i.e., "officers of holiness," "holy officers." Tg. Chr chooses the second option.

[5]In Tg. 1 Chr 24:6, the scribal emphasis is strong. (i) Moses is described as "the Great Scribe," a term used in Tg. Song 1:2, where the Lord is blessed because he "hath given us the law by the hand of Moses, the Great Scribe, a law inscribed upon the two tablets of stone. . . ." (ii) He is called by the name of the scribe who is recording the details of the organization of the sons of Eleazar and Ithamar, Shemaiah, the son of Nethanel. This man's name is used—as with the six names given to Moses by Bithiah in Tg. 1 Chr 4:18—to heap further virtue on the great leader: Shemaiah (in which is found the root *šm',* "to hear," and the abbreviated form of the divine Name, *yh*) "because God heard his prayer" (one assumes, for deliverance in Egypt), and the son of Nethanel (in which is found the root *ntn,* "to give," and *'l,* "God": *God* gave him the law), "because he was a son to whom the Torah was given from hand to hand" (*Lev. R.* 1:3).

[6]MT: "from the Levite(s)."

[7]In line with verse 4. MT states: "one clan was taken for Eleazar and one [reading *ḥd* for *ḥz* with a few Hebrew MSS, LXX and Vg] was taken for Ithamar."

[8]Lit.: "went out."

Jeshua, the tenth to Shecaniah, 12. the eleventh to Eliashib, the twelfth to Jakim, 13. the thirteenth to Huppah, the fourteenth to *Jeshebab,*[d9] 14. the fifteenth to Bilgah, the sixteenth to Immer, 15. the seventeenth to Hezir, the eighteenth to Happizzez, 16. the nineteenth to Pethaiah, the twentieth to Jehezkel, 17. the twenty-first to Jachin, the twenty-second to Gamul, 18. the twenty-third to Delaiah, the twenty-fourth to *Mauziah.* 19. These were their *numbers*[e10] for their service when going into the *sanctuary* house of the Lord, as prescribed for them by Aaron their father, as the Lord, the God of Israel, had commanded him. 20. For the remainder of the sons of Levi: for the sons of Amram, Shubael; for the sons of Shubael, *Jehediah;* 21. for Rehabiah: for the sons of Rehabiah, Isshiah the leader; 22. for *the family of Izhar,*[f11] Shelomoth;[g] for the sons of Shelomoth,[g] Jahath; 23. the sons of Jeriah: Amariah the second, Jahaziel the third, *Jokmeam*[12] the fourth; 24. the sons of Uzziel, Micah; for the sons of Micah, Shamor;[h13] 25. the brother of Micah, Isshiah; for the sons of Isshiah, Zechariah; 26. the sons of Merari: Mahli and Mushi; the sons of Jaaziah, Beno; 27. the sons of Merari for Jaaziah: Beno, Shoham, Zaccur and *Ibrai;*[i14] 28. for Mahli, Eleazar who had no sons; 29. for Kish, the sons of Kish, Jerahmeel; 30. the sons of Mushi: Mahli, Eder and Jerimoth. These were the sons of the Levites according to their clans. 31. They too, alongside their brethren, the sons of Aaron, cast lots before king David, Zadok, Ahimelech and the heads of the clans of the priests and the Levites. The most senior member of each clan and his youngest brother were treated alike.

Apparatus, Chapter 24

[d] V: *yšbb.* C, L, AS: *yšb'b* (= MT).
[e] V and C: plural. L and AS: singular (= MT).
[f] V: "For the family of Izhar." C: "For Izhar." L, AS: "For the Izharite(s)." (= MT).

[g] C, L, AS: "Shelomith."
[h] V: *šmwr* (Kethibh). C, L, AS: *šmyr* (Qere).
[i] C: "Ibri" (= MT).

Notes, Chapter 24

[9] MT: "Yesheheab."
[10] MT: singular.
[11] MT: "For the Izharite(s)."
[12] MT: "Yekameam."
[13] V follows Kethibh.
[14] MT: "Ibri."

CHAPTER 25

1. David and the army commanders set apart for the cultic service the sons of Asaph, of Heman and of Jeduthun, who were to prophesy with lyres, lutes and cymbals. The number of the men who performed this *service* according to their service was[1] (as follows): 2. for the sons of Asaph: Zaccur, Joseph, Nethaniah and *Ashreelah;*[2] the sons of Asaph were under the direction[3] of Asaph, who prophesied[4] *by the Holy Spirit and was appointed head,* under the direction[5] of the king. 3. Of Jeduthun, the sons of Jeduthun: Gedaliah, Zeri, Jeshaiah, Hashibiah and Mattithiah, six, under the direction of their father Jeduthun, who prophesied[4] with the lute in thanksgiving and praise *before*[6] the Lord. 4.[a] For Heman, the sons of Heman: Bukkiah, Mattaniah, Uzziel, Shebuel, Jerimoth, Hananiah, Hanani, Elyatha, Giddalti, Romamti-Ezer, Joshbekashah, Mallothi, Hothir, Mahazioth. 5. All these were the sons of Heman, the king's *prophet,*[7] who was to sound the *ram's* horn[8] with words of *prophecy from before the Lord.*[9] The Lord had given Heman fourteen sons and three daughters. 6. They were all *put in charge of* the *songs* under the direction[5] of their father, in the *sanctuary* house of the Lord,[10] with cymbals, lutes and lyres for the service of the *sanctuary* house of *the Lord*[11] under the direction of the king *and* Asaph and Jeduthun and Heman. 7. Their number, along with their brethren, who were trained to sing praises *before*[6] the Lord, all competent men, was two hundred and eighty-eight. 8. They cast lots, each

Apparatus, Chapter 25

[a] E omits verse 4.

Notes, Chapter 25

[1]MT: Lit.: "Their number, the workmen for their service."
[2]MT: "Asarelah."
[3]Lit.: "under the hands of." MT: "under the hand of."
[4]MT: participle. Tg. Chr: perfect.
[5]Lit.: "under the hand of." MT: "under the hands of."
[6]MT: "to."
[7]MT: "seer."
[8]MT: "to lift up (his) horn" can mean (i) to exalt him (cf. 1 Sam 2:1); (ii) to sound the horn. Tg. Chr prefers (ii) and puts the issue beyond doubt by using the shophar, "ram's horn," rather than the more general word for "horn" used by MT (*qeren*). In his expansion on 1 Sam 2:1, Tg. Sam refers to the involvement of Heman and his fourteen sons in the exaltation of Hannah's horn.
[9]MT: "with words of God." RSV translates the Hebrew of this part of 1 Chr 25:5 as: "according to the promise of God to exalt him."
[10]MT: "They were all under the direction of their father in the song (music) of the house of the Lord. . . ."
[11]In MT there is a pause here, and the next clause is usually translated as "under the direction of the king (were) Asaph, Jeduthun and Heman." By inserting "and" before "Asaph," Tg. Chr alters somewhat the "chain of command." LXX also inserts "and" before "Asaph."

watch in the presence of *the other,* [12] both small and great, *scribe* [13] along with pupil. 9. The first lot, which was for Asaph, fell to Joseph; the second Gedaliah: he, with his brethren and his sons, were twelve. 10. The third Zaccur, his sons and his brethren, twelve. 11. [b] The fourth to *Yezer,* [c][14] his sons and his brethren, twelve. 12. The fifth Nethaniah, his sons and his brethren, twelve. 13. The sixth Bukkiah, his sons and his brethren, twelve. 14. The seventh Jisreelah, his sons and his brethren, twelve. 15. The eighth Jeshaiah, his sons and his brethren, twelve. 16. The ninth Mattaniah, his sons and his brethren, twelve. 17. The tenth Shimei, his sons and his brethren, twelve. 18. The eleventh Azarel, his sons and his brethren, twelve. 19. The twelfth to Hashabiah, his sons and his brethren, twelve. 20. For the thirteenth, Shubael, his sons and his brethren, twelve. 21. For the fourteenth, Mattithiah, his sons and his brethren, twelve. 22. For the fifteenth, to *Jerimoth,* [d][15] his sons and his brethren, twelve. 23. For the sixteenth, to Hananiah, his sons and his brethren, twelve. 24. For the seventeenth, to Joshbakshah, his sons and his brethren, twelve. 25. For the eighteenth, to Hanani, his sons and his brethren, twelve. 26. For the nineteenth, to Mallothi, his sons and his brethren, twelve. 27. For the twentieth, to *Eliathah,* [e][16] his sons and his brethren, twelve. 28. For the twenty-first, to Hothir, his sons and his brethren, twelve. 29. For the twenty-second, to Giddalti, his sons and his brethren, twelve. 30. For the twenty-third, to *Mahaziah,* [f][17] his sons and his brethren, twelve. 31. For the twenty-fourth, to Romamti-Ezer, his sons and his brethren, twelve.

Apparatus, Chapter 25

[b] E omits verses 11–31.
[c] V and C: "Yezer." L and AS: "Yizri" (= MT).
[d] V and C: *yrymwt.* L and AS: *yrmwt* (= MT).

[e] V and C: *'ly'th.* L and AS: *'lyth* (= MT).
[f] V: *mḥzyh.* C, L, and AS: *mḥzy' wt* (= MT).

Notes, Chapter 25

[12] Lit.: "watch in the presence of watch." MT omits the second "watch," but it is found in some Hebrew MSS and LXX.
[13] MT: "expert/master."
[14] MT: "Yizri."
[15] MT: "Jeremoth."
[16] MT: *'lyth,* but see verse 4, where it is: *'ly'th.*
[17] MT: "Mahazioth."

CHAPTER 26

1. As for the divisions of *the* gatekeepers. For the *sons of Korah:*[1] Meshelemiah, the son of Kore, from the sons of Asaph. 2. Meshelemiah had sons: Zechariah, the first-born, Jediael the second, Zebadiah the third, Jathniel the fourth, 3. Elam the fifth, Jehohanan the sixth and Eliehoenai the seventh. 4. Obed Edom also had sons: Shemaiah the first-born, Jehozabad the second, Joah the third, Sacar the fourth, Nethanel the fifth, 5. Ammiel the sixth, Issachar the seventh and *Peuelethai*[a][2] the eighth, for *the Lord* had blessed him *because of the ark of the Lord which was in his house when it had been brought and left in his house. He shared in the honor of seeing*[3] *eighty-one*[b] *of his sons and*[4] *grandsons leaders of the Levites.*[5] 6. To his son Shemaiah sons were[6] born who exercised authority in their *clans,*[7] for *the* warriors *were leaders.*[8] 7. The sons of Shemaiah: Othni, Rephael and Obed *Edom;*[c][9] his brethren who were *army commanders,* were Elihu and Semachiah. 8. All these were of the sons of Obed Edom, who, with their sons and their brethren, were mighty warriors, with adequate strength for the service; sixty-two belonging to Obed Edom. 9. Meshelemiah had sons and brothers, eighteen mighty warriors. 10. *Hotah,*[d][10] of the sons of Merari, had sons. *Shamri*[e][11] was the head, for, though he was not *the* first-born, his father had appointed him head; 11. Hilkiah the second, Tebaliah the third, and Zechariah the fourth. All the sons and brethren of Hosah were thirteen. 12. These, the divisions of the gatekeepers, the heads of *the warriors,*[f][12] had the responsibility, alongside their brethren, of offering service in the *sanctuary* house of the Lord. 13. They cast lots for each gate, according to their

Apparatus, Chapter 26

[a] V: *pwlty.* C, L, AS: *p'wlty.*
[b] E, C, L, and AS have "eighty-two."
[c] V, L, AS: "Obed Edom." C: "Obed Edom Elzabad." MT: "Obed Elzabad."

[d] V: "Hoṭah." C, L, AS: "Hosah" (= MT).
[e] V: "Shamri." C: "Shimri" (= MT).
[f] V: The consonants of "men," but the vocalization of "warriors." C has "men."

Notes, Chapter 26

[1] MT: "The Korahite(s)."
[2] MT: *p'lty.* V: *pwlty.*
[3] Lit.: "He (the Lord) imparted to him honor and he (Obed Edom) saw. . . ."
[4] Reading "and" with E, C, L, AS.
[5] See 13:13, 14 for full details of how God's blessing resulted in a household of eighty-one. In 26:5 there is a new element: the eighty-one become leaders of the Levites.
[6] MT: singular.
[7] MT: singular though a few Hebrew MSS have plural.
[8] MT: "for they were warriors."
[9] MT: "Obed Elzabad."
[10] MT: "Hosah." In verse 11, Tg. Chr has "Hosah."
[11] MT: "Shimri."
[12] MT: "men." Tg. Chr has the consonants of "men" but the vocalization for "warriors."

clans, small and great alike. 14. The lot for the east (gate) fell to Shelemiah. They cast lots also for his son Zechariah, a wise counselor,[g] and his lot came out for the north (gate). 15. For Obed Edom the south (gate) and the *thresholds*[13] for his sons. 16. For Shuppim and Hosah the west (gate), as well as the gate *which had been erected*[14] on the upward path *facing the sanctuary house; each watch faced the other. 17. On the east there were six Levites, on the north four each day, on the south four each day, and two each[h] for the *thresholds.*[13] 18. *Facing outward*[15] on the west there were four at the road, two *facing outward.*[15] 19. These were the divisions of the gatekeepers for the sons of *Korah*[16] and the sons of Merari. 20. As for the Levites: Ahijah was in charge of the treasuries[17] of the *sanctuary* house *of the Lord*[18] and[i] of the treasuries[17] of the holy things. 21. The sons of Ladan, the sons of *Gershon*[19] belonging to Ladan, the heads of the clans of Ladan, *from the house[j] of Gershon,*[19] *Jehiel.*[20] 22. The sons of *Jehiel,*[20] Zetham and Joel his brother, were in charge of the storehouses of the *sanctuary* house of the Lord. 23. For *Amram,*[21] *Izhar,*[22] *Hebron*[23] and *Uzziel:*[24] 24. and Shebuel,[25] *that is Jonathan, the son of Gershom, the son of Moses, returned to the fear of the Lord. When David saw that he was meticulous about money, he appointed him* superintendent of the treasuries.[26] 25. His brothers by Eliezer: Rehabiah his son, Jeshaiah his son, Joram

Apparatus, Chapter 26

[g] C prefaces the expression with *yw'ṣ,* the word used in MT for "counselor." It may be that he thought of it as a proper noun.
[h] E: "twelve."

[i] C omits, thereby putting the two areas of operation in apposition to each other.
[j] C: "sons."

Notes, Chapter 26

[13] MT: "storehouses." Le Déaut thinks that Tg. Chr reads MT *'spym* as *spym* = "thresholds."

[14] MT: "the gate of Shalleketh." This name is found only here. Vg translates (*š lkt*): *quae duxit.* Tg. Chr may have thought of an origin in the root *šlk,* "to throw, cast."

[15] There is uncertainty about the exact meaning of the Hebrew word *parbar,* which in Tg. Chr has become "facing outward": perhaps "a road, other outside area, or room adjacent to the Temple" (Braun, 249). MJ (1213) lists one explanation of the word: *par,* "running" (from *pr'*) *bar,* "outside." In Tg. Chr the word has been split into two also: *par* becomes *kl'py* (MJ 645: abbreviation for *kwwn l' py*), "directed towards," and *br',* "outside." *b. Zeb.* 55b understands the *parbar* to be "a small passage behind the place of the Mercy Seat"; there were two of them. "What does *le-par bar* mean?"—said Rabbah son of R. Shila: "As one says, 'facing without.'" This word is found in 2 Kgs 23:11 with a slightly different spelling (*parwar*), but in Tg. Kgs it appears simply in a plural form.

[16] MT: "the Korahite(s)."

[17] Tg. Chr uses the plural of *tsbr':* "storehouse, treasury," borrowed from the Greek *thesauros* (JL II, 547). MJ 1682 believes the Greek word is of Semitic origin.

[18] MT: "God."

[19] MT: "the Gershunite(s)."

[20] MT: "Jehieli."

[21] MT: "the Amramite."

[22] MT: "the Yizharite."

[23] MT: "the Hebronite."

[24] MT: "the Uzzielite."

[25] MT: *šb'l.* V: *šbw'l.*

[26] See comments on 23:16.

his son, Zicri his son, and *Shelomith*[27] his son. 26. This *Shelomith*[27] and his brothers were[k] in charge of all the sacred treasuries[l28] which David the king and the heads of the clans and[29] the commanders of thousands[30] and the hundreds and the army commanders had consecrated. 27. Some of the spoil from the wars[31] they consecrated for the support of the *sanctuary* house of the Lord. 28. As well, all *the consecrated gifts*[32] which Samuel, the seer, Saul, the son of Kish, Abner, the son of Ner, and Joab, the son of Zeruiah had consecrated—all *the consecrated gifts*[33] were under the charge of Shelomith and his brethren. 29. For *the family of Yizhar,*[34] Chenaniah and his sons (were assigned) to external duties over Israel, as officials and judges. 30. For *Hebron,*[35] Hashabiah and his brothers, one thousand seven hundred mighty warriors,[36] were responsible for the oversight of Israel on the western side of the Jordan, for all the *service*[37] of the Lord and the service of the king. 31. For *the family of Hebron:*[38] Jedijah[m39] *was appointed* head of the *family of Hebron*[38] according to the clan genealogies. In the fortieth year of David's reign search was made and mighty warriors[36] were[n] *found*[40] among them at Jazer of Gilead. 32. His brothers, two thousand seven hundred mighty warriors,[36] were heads of clans and David the king placed them in charge of the *tribe of Reuben,*[41] the *tribe of Gad*[42] and the half-tribe of *Manasseh*[43] for every matter relating to *the Lord*[44] and the king.

Apparatus, Chapter 26

[k] C, L, AS add: "appointed."
[l] V, C: "the treasuries of holiness." L, AS: "the treasuries of the holy things" (= MT).

[m] C, L, AS: "Jerijah" (= MT). Some Hebrew MSS have "Jedijah."
[n] C, L, AS: "were found." V: "he found."

Notes, Chapter 26

[27]Tg. Chr follows Qere, with some Hebrew MSS, LXX(L), Syr, Vg.
[28]MT: Lit.: "treasuries of the holy things." V: "treasuries of holiness."
[29]To translate as "for" (*l* in both MT and Tg. Chr) makes little sense. I have translated as "and," following most EVV.
[30]MT: "the thousands."
[31]Lit.: "From the wars and from the spoil."
[32]Lit.: "everything which had been consecrated."
[33]MT: "everyone who was consecrating."
[34]MT: "the Yizharite(s)."
[35]MT: "the Hebronite(s)."
[36]There are times when "capable men" might have been a better translation than "mighty warriors," but for the sake of consistency we have kept to the latter.
[37]MT: "work."
[38]MT: "The Hebronite(s)."
[39]MT: "Jerijah," the difference of one letter. "d" and "r" are very similar in shape and could be easily confused.
[40]V: "he found." Translation follows C, L, AS.
[41]MT: "in charge of the Reubenite(s)."
[42]MT: "the Gadite(s)."
[43]MT: "the Manassite(s)."
[44]MT: "God."

CHAPTER 27

1. This is the list of the Israelites,[1] the heads of clans, commanders of thousands[2] and the hundreds and their officials, who served the king in everything relating to the divisions which came and went month by month throughout all the months of the year, each division consisting of twenty-four thousand. 2. In charge of the first division for the month of *Nisan*[3] was Jashobeam the son of Zabdiel. With[4] his division were twenty-four thousand. 3. A member of the family of Perez,[5] *he was appointed* chief of all the army commanders for the first month. 4. In charge of the division for the month[a] *of Iyyar*[6] was Dodai, *of the family*[7] *of Ahoah:*[8] Mikloth was the leader of his division. With his division were twenty-four thousand. 5. The third army commander for the month *of Sivan,*[9] Benaiah, the son of Jehoiada, the priest, *was appointed* head. With his division were twenty-four thousand. 6. This Benaiah was a warrior *alongside*[10] the thirty and in command of the thirty. (In) his division was Ammizabad his son. 7. The fourth, for the month *of Tammuz,*[11] was Asahel, the brother of Joab, and his son Zebadiah *was appointed* after him. With his division were twenty-four thousand. 8. The fifth, for the month *of Ab,*[12] was the commander Shamhuth, *who was from the family of Izrah.*[13] With his division were twenty-four thousand. 9. The sixth, for the month *of Elul,*[14] was Ira, the son of Ikkesh, *who was from Tekoa.*[15] With his division were twenty-four thousand. 10. The seventh, for the month *of Tishri,*[16] was Helez, *who was from the*

Apparatus, Chapter 27

[a] C, L, AS: "for the second month of Iyyar."

Notes, Chapter 27

[1] Lit.: "the children of Israel according to their numbers" (MT: "number").
[2] MT: "the thousands."
[3] MT: "for the first month."
[4] To translate *'l* here and in the following verses as "upon" would be quite out of place. The meaning "with," as suggested by Braun (257), in line with *BDB* (755, II, 4C), is more appropriate.
[5] Lit.: "From the sons of Perez."
[6] MT: "for the second month."
[7] Reading *mzr 'yt (for mdr'yt)* with E, C, L, AS.
[8] MT: "Dodai, the Ahohite."
[9] MT: "for the third month."
[10] MT: "of."
[11] MT: "for the fourth month."
[12] MT: "for the fifth month."
[13] MT: Lit.: "Shamhuth, the Izrah."
[14] MT: "for the sixth month."
[15] MT: "the Tekoite."
[16] MT: "for the seventh month."

family of Pelen,[17] of the sons of Ephraim. With his division were twenty-four thousand. 11. The eighth, for the month *of Marcheshvan,*[18] was Sibbecai, *who was from the family of Hushai,*[19] of *the house of Zerah.*[20] With his division were twenty-four thousand. 12. The ninth, for the month *of Chislev,*[b21] was Abiezer, *who was from Anathoth,*[22] of *the tribe of Benjamin.*[23] With his division were twenty-four thousand. 13. The tenth, for the month *of Tebeth,*[c24] was Mahrai, *who was from Netophah,*[25] of *the family of Zerah.*[20] With his division were twenty-four thousand. 14. The eleventh, for the eleventh month *of Shebat,* was Benaiah, *who was from Pirathon,*[26] of the sons of Ephraim. With his division were twenty-four thousand. 15. The twelfth, for the twelfth month *of Adar,* was Heldai, *who was from Netophah,*[25] of *the family of* Othniel. With his division were twenty-four thousand. 16. Over the tribes of Israel: For the *tribe of Reuben,*[27] the officer in charge was Eliezer, the son of Zichri; for the *tribe of Simeon,*[28] Shephatiah, the son of Maacah; 17. for *the tribe of* Levi, Hashabiah the son of Kemuel; for *the house of* Aaron, Zadok; 18. for *the tribe of* Judah, Elihu, one of David's brothers; for *the tribe of* Issachar, Omri, the son of *Micah;*[d29] 19. for *the tribe of* Zebulun, Ishmaiah, the son of Obadiah; for *the tribe of* Naphtali, Jerimoth, the son of Ariel; 20. for the sons of Ephraim, Hoshea the son of Azaziah; for the half tribe of Manasseh, Joel, the son of Pedaiah; 21. for the half-*tribe* of Manasseh, *which was* in Gilead, Iddo, the son of Zechariah; for *the tribe of* Benjamin, Jaasiel, the son of Abner; 22. for *the tribe of* Dan, Azarel, the son of Jeroham. These were the commanders of the tribes of Israel. 23. David did not take a count of those who were twenty years old or under, for the Lord had promised to make Israel as numerous as the stars of the heavens. 24. Joab, the son of Zeruiah, began to number *Israel,* but he was *unable to* complete *the numbering before* anger came upon Israel because of it[30] *and many*[31] had

Apparatus, Chapter 27

[b] L, AS: "for the ninth month of Chislev."
[c] L, AS: "for the tenth month of Tebeth."

[d] C: "Michael" (= MT). L, AS: "Micah" (= V).

Notes, Chapter 27

[17]MT: "Helez, the Pelonite."
[18]MT: "for the eighth month."
[19]MT: "Sibbecai, the Hushathite."
[20]MT: "of the Zerahite(s)."
[21]MT: "for the ninth month."
[22]MT: "the Anathothite."
[23]MT: "of the Benjaminite(s)."
[24]MT: "for the tenth month."
[25]MT: "the Netophathite."
[26]MT: "the Pirathonite."
[27]MT: "for the Reubenite(s)."
[28]MT: "for the Simeonite(s)."
[29]MT: "Michael."
[30]MT: "but he did not complete (it), and anger came upon Israel because of it."
[31]Lit.: "they."

died from the pestilence. So the number was not entered *as* a number *in*[e] the chronicles of king David.[32] 25. Azmaveth, the son of Adiel, was in charge of the treasuries of the king's *house,*[f33] while Jonathan, the son of Uzziah, had charge of the storehouses[34] which were in the country, the towns, the villages and the towers. 26. Ezri, the son of Chelub, was in charge of the farm workers who were responsible for tilling the soil. 27. Shimei, *who was from Ramathah,*[35] was in charge of the vineyards, while Zabdi, *who was from Sapham,*[36] was in charge of *what was produced* in the vineyards[37] for the wine cellars. 28. Baal-Hanan, *who was from Geder,*[38] was in charge of the olive and sycomore trees which were in the Shephelah; Joash was in charge of the *oil.*[39] 29. Shirtai,[40] *who was from Sharon,*[41] was in charge of the cattle grazing on *the plain;*[42] Shaphat, the son of Adlai, was in charge of the cattle in the valleys. 30. Obil, the *Arab,*[43] was in charge of the camels; Jehdeiah, *who was from Maron,*[44] was in charge of the she-asses. 31. Jaziz, the Hagrite, was in charge of the flocks. All these were the officials responsible for king David's property. 32. Jonathan, David's uncle, was a counselor; he was an intelligent man and a scribe; and Jehiel, the son of Hachmoni, looked after[45] the king's sons. 33. Ahitophel was a counsellor to the king and Hushai, the *Urchite,*[46] was the king's close friend.[47] 34. *When war was imminent,*[48] *advice was sought from* Ahitophel *and, following Ahitophel's advice, inquiry was made from the Urim and the Thummin through* Jehoiada, the son of Benaiah, *the head of the Sanhedrin, the*

Apparatus, Chapter 27

[e] C: "as in the number of." E, L, AS: "in the number of."   [f] V: "the king's house." C, L, AS: "the king" (= MT).

Notes, Chapter 27

[32]MT: "So the number was not entered in the number of the chronicles of king David."

[33]MT: "the king."

[34]MT uses the same word as in the first part of the verse: "treasuries." MJ (34) suggests "storekeepers," JL (I, 63) "magazines."

[35]MT: "the Ramathite."

[36]MT: "the Shiphmite."

[37]Lit.: "the work which was in the vineyards," for MT: "that which was in the vineyards."

[38]MT: "the Gederite."

[39]MT: "the oil stores."

[40]MT: "Shitrai," but Qere is "Shirtai," followed by Tg. Chr, some Hebrew MSS, LXX(B), and Syr.

[41]MT: "the Sharonite."

[42]MT: "in Sharon"; cf. 5:16.

[43]MT: "the Ishmaelite."

[44]MT: "the Meronothite."

[45]Lit.: "he was with."

[46]MT: "the Archite."

[47]"close friend," to bring out the nuance of the word used in V and C for MT's *r'*, "friend, companion": *šwšbyn',* "the friend of the bridegroom, intimate companion." E, L and AS used the more general *ḥbr'*: "friend, companion."

[48]Lit.: "When they had to go out to war."

superintendent of the priests, and through Abiathar, *the chief priest. After[g] consulting the Urim and the Thummin, they went forth to battle—the armed troops, the archers and the slingers, under the command of* Joab, the commander of the king's army. [49]

CHAPTER 28

1. David assembled[a] at Jerusalem all the leaders of Israel: the tribal leaders, the commanders of the divisions who served the king, the commanders of thousands[1] and the commanders of the hundreds, the officials who were in charge of all the property and livestock which belonged to the king and to his sons, along with the leaders,[2] the mighty men and all the courageous *warriors.* 2. King David stood up on his feet and said: "Listen to me,[3] my brethren and my people, *my brethren the[b] house of Israel, and my people, the proselytes who are in their towns.[4]* It was my heart's desire to build a resting-place for the ark of the covenant of the Lord, and for the footstool *of the throne of the glory of the Lord,[5]* and I made preparations to build (it). 3. But the *Memra of the Lord[6]* said to me: 'You will not build a *sanctuary* house for my Name, for you are a fighting man[7] and you have shed blood.' 4. Yet the Lord, the God of Israel, chose me out of all *my* father's house to be king

Apparatus, Chapter 27

[g] V and C: *mn d.* L, AS: *mn btr d.*

Notes, Chapter 27

[49]MT: "after Ahitophel, Jehoiada, the son of Benaiah, and Ebiathar, and Joab was the commander of the king's army." Tg. Chr uses the names of the people in this verse, and the functions and activities elsewhere associated with them, to show that the army of God's people does not go forth to war without first seeking divine guidance, at the highest level, through God-appointed people and procedures (see 11:22, note 47; 18:17, note 27).

Apparatus, Chapter 28

[a] V and C: *knš.* E, L, AS: *'knš.*   [b] C, L, AS: "all the house of Israel."

Notes, Chapter 28

[1]MT: "the thousands."
[2]MT: "eunuchs" or "officials." MT uses the same word (*śr*) six times to describe the "leaders" and *srys,* "eunuch," once. Tg. Chr uses the same word (*rbn'*) to describe all seven groups.
[3]Lit.: "accept from me" for MT "hear me."
[4]An example of what Le Déaut calls "exégèse extensive," where synonymous expressions are each given a different interpretation.
[5]MT: "of the feet of our God": a clear avoidance of anthropomorphism.
[6]MT: "God."
[7]Lit.: "a man making wars" for MT "a man of wars."

over Israel for ever, for it was *the tribe of* Judah which he chose as ruler, and within the house of Judah, *my* father's house, and among my father's sons he *chose*[8] me to be king over all Israel. 5. And from all my sons—for the Lord gave me many sons—he has chosen my son Solomon to sit upon the throne of the kingdom of the Lord *that he should be appointed* over Israel. 6. He said to me: 'Your son, Solomon, is the one who will build my *sanctuary* house and my courts, because I have chosen him, *to love him that he should be before me beloved as a son* and I shall be to him *like* a father.[9] 7. I shall establish his kingdom for ever if he continues resolutely to carry out[10] my commandments and my judgments as (he does) today.' 8. So now, *before*[11] all Israel, the assembly of the Lord, and *before the Memra of the Lord,*[12] observe and seek out all the commandments of the Lord, your God, so that you may possess the good land and pass it on as an inheritance to your sons after you for ever. 9. And you, Solomon, my son, acknowledge the God of your father and serve *before*[c] him with a perfect heart and a willing soul, for the Lord searches out all *the desires of* the hearts and discerns all the imaginations of the thoughts. If you seek him, he will be found by you *whenever you seek his fear and seek him.* But if you forsake him, he will reject you for ever. 10. Take note[13] then that *the Memra of the Lord* has chosen you to build *the* house for the sanctuary. Be strong and act!" 11. Then David handed over to his son, Solomon, the plan of the entrance hall, its houses, its storerooms,[14] its *staircases,*[15] its inner bedrooms[16] and the place of atonement. 12. As well as the plan of everything that, by (the guidance of) the Spirit *of prophecy which was* with him,[17] was *thought necessary* for the courts of the *sanctuary* house of the Lord and for all the surrounding rooms, for the treasuries of the *sanctuary* house of *the Lord*[18] and for the treasuries of the sacred things; 13. for the divisions of the priests and the Levites, for all the work of the service *for*[19] the *sanctuary* house of the Lord and for all the vessels which were used in the

Apparatus, Chapter 28

[c] V: *qwmwy.* C, E, L, AS: *qdmwy.*

Notes, Chapter 28

[8]MT: "took delight in." Tg. Chr uses the same word for this verb and for MT's verb "to choose," used twice earlier in the verse.

[9]MT: Lit.: "for me for a son and I shall be to him for a father" (see 17:13; 22:10).

[10]Lit.: "if he will be strong to do ..."

[11]MT: "in the eyes of."

[12]MT: "in the ears of our God."

[13]Lit.: "See!."

[14]Reading with C, E, L, AS: *qwrṭwrwhy.* V has *qwrṭwhy.*

[15]MT: "upper rooms."

[16]Tg. Chr uses the plural of *qytwn*, "bedchamber," borrowed from the Greek *koitōn* (MJ 1357; JL II, 357).

[17]MT: "the plan of everything which was in the spirit with him." This enigmatic phrase "in the spirit with him" may mean (i) "what was in his mind" (e.g., RSV) or (ii) that the Spirit was prompting him (e.g., NIV). Tg. Chr develops the latter approach and it becomes "by the spirit of prophecy, which was with him...."

[18]MT: "God."

[19]MT: "of."

service of the *sanctuary* house of the Lord; 14. for the gold, with the weight of gold required for[d] all the vessels for every type of service, for all the silver vessels with the weight required for all the vessels for every type of service; 15. the weight for the golden lampstands and their lamps, the weight of gold for the lampstand and its lamps; for the silver lampstands, the weight for the lampstand and its lamps, according to the use of each lampstand; 16. the weight of gold for each of the shewbread tables[20] and the silver for the silver tables; 17. the forks, the sprinkling bowls and the libation vessels of pure gold, and the weight (of gold) for each of the golden dishes, and the weight (of silver) for each of the silver dishes; 18. the weight of refined gold for the altar of *sweet-smelling* incense, and for the model of the chariot, *like the model of the canopy with the representation of* the golden cherubim spreading *their wings*[21] and screening the ark of the covenant of the Lord. 19. All this is in a writing from the hand of the Lord. *It was* my responsibility to consider carefully[22] all the details of the plan. 20. Then David said to his son Solomon: "Be strong and take courage and get on with it![23] Do not be afraid! Do not be downhearted, for *the Memra of* the Lord God,[e] my God, is *in support of you.*[24] He will not leave you nor reject you until all the work of the service of the *sanctuary* house of the Lord is completed. 21. And here are the divisions of the priests and the Levites for all the work[f] of the *sanctuary* house of *the Lord;*[18] and with you in all the work will be everyone who is willing and skilled in every kind of service. As well, the leaders and all the people *will be ready to assist you*[25] in all your affairs.

Apparatus, Chapter 28

[d] C, L, AS insert "and" before "for."
[e] C omits.

[f] C: *pwlhn.* Others: *'bydt.*

Notes, Chapter 28

[20] Lit.: "for the shewbread tables, for each table."
[21] Tg. Chr supplies the obvious object for "spreading" which is missing in MT but is found in 2 Chr 5:8.
[22] MT: "he caused me to understand." I have taken *'ly* with what follows rather than with the preceding words.
[23] Lit.: "do."
[24] Lit.: "is with you."
[25] Lit.: "in your support." In MT this phrase is lacking and the following phrase is usually translated as "wholly at your command." Tg. Chr presents a more willing people all eager to assist the king in all his concerns.

CHAPTER 29

1. Then King David said to the whole assembly: "Solomon, my son, the one whom *the Lord* has chosen,[1] is young and[a] immature, and the task is great, for the *Palace*[2] is not for *the name of a son of* man but for *the name of the Memra of* the Lord God. 2. *With*[3] all my might I have made provision for the *sanctuary* house of my God—gold for the gold *work*, silver for the silver *work*, bronze for the bronze *work*, iron for the iron *work*, wood for the wood *work*, beryl stones, mounted stones, *emeralds*,[4] *embroideries*[5] and all sorts of precious *jewels*[6] and *marble*[7] stones in great quantities. 3. In addition, because I have such delight in the *sanctuary* house of my God, my personal fortune *of* gold and silver I have given for the *sanctuary* house of my God over and above all that I have (already) provided for the holy[b] house: 4. three thousand *centenaria*[8] of gold, of the gold of Ophir, and seven thousand *centenaria*[8] of refined silver with which to overlay the walls of the houses,[9] 5. *gold* for (whatever is) gold, and *silver* for (whatever is) silver[10] and for all the work which will be done by[11] the craftsmen. Whoever wishes to *present his offering*[12] today, *let him offer it before* the Lord." 6. Then the leaders of the clans, the leaders[c] of the tribes of Israel and the leaders of thousands[13] and the hundreds and those who were in charge of the king's work showed their willingness: 7. they gave towards the work of the *sanctuary* house of *the Lord*[14] five thousand

Apparatus, Chapter 29

[a] C, L, AS omit "and." The phrase could then be translated "an immature youth."

[b] L, AS: "sanctuary."
[c] C, L, AS: "heads."

Notes, Chapter 29

[1] Lit.: "Solomon my son, one, and the Lord (MT: "God") has chosen him."
[2] Loan word: see 9:18, note 17. MT: *byrh*: "citadel."
[3] MT: "according to."
[4] MT: "stones of antimony." Tg. Chr uses the plural of *'zmrgd',* "emerald," borrowed from the Greek *smaragdos* (MJ 38; JL I, 18 and 224). See also 1:9, note 29.
[5] MT: "variegated fabric."
[6] MT: "stones." Tg. Chr uses the plural of *mrglyt',* "gem." See 1:23, note 59.
[7] MT: "alabaster." Tg. Chr uses the plural of *mrmyr',* borrowed from the Greek *marmaros,* Latin *marmor* (MJ 844; JL II, 70).
[8] MT: "talents."
[9] LXX, Syr, Vg have the singular "house," even though MT and Tg. Chr have the plural. The different readings in Tg. Chr (V: *byt'y';* C: *byty';* L, AS: *btyy'* and E: *byt'*) may reflect an uncertainty as to the number of the word. Or, as plural, the word may be a general term for "buildings."
[10] Lit.: "For the gold, for the gold, and for the silver, for the silver" (= MT).
[11] Lit.: "by the hand of."
[12] MT: "Who will present himself willingly, to fill his hand today for the Lord?" Though the origin of the "filling the hand" expression is uncertain, it is used for setting apart a priest in his office. Here Tg. Chr interprets it as "to present an offering."
[13] MT: "the thousands."
[14] MT: "God."

centenaria[8] of gold, ten thousand *zuzin,*[d][15] ten thousand *centenaria*[8] of silver, eighteen thousand *centenaria*[8] of bronze and one hundred thousand *centenaria*[8] of iron. 8. Anyone who had *jewels*[e][16] gave them to the treasury of the *sanctuary* house of the Lord, into the keeping of Jehiel, *of the family of Gershon.*[17] 9. Then the people rejoiced[f] because these[18] had made the donations voluntarily, for they had given their voluntary donations wholeheartedly *before*[19] the Lord. King David also rejoiced greatly. 10. Then David blessed the Lord in the *sight*[20] of the whole assembly and David said: "Blessed are you, O Lord, the God of Israel, our father, from *this* age and to the age *to come.*[21] 11. Yours, O Lord, is the greatness, *for with great power you created the world,* and the might, *for you brought our fathers out of Egypt with many mighty acts and brought them across the sea, and you were revealed in* splendor *upon the mountain of Sinai, with bands of angels,*[22] *to give the law to* your *people. You gave* victories[23] *over Amalek, Sihon, Og and the kings of the Canaanites; in* the majesty *of your glory you caused the sun to stand still in Gibeon and the moon in the plain of Ajalon, until your people, the house of Israel, were avenged on those who hated them. For all these things are the works of your hand,* in heaven and on earth, *and you have authority over them and sustain everything which is in heaven and everything which is on earth.* Yours, O Lord, is the dominion *in the firmament,* and you are exalted above all *the angels that are in heaven and above all* those *who are appointed* as leaders[24] *on earth.*[25] 12. And the wealth *of the wealthy* and the glory *of kings and potentates are given to them* from before you and you have authority over all,[g] and[h] in your hand are might and power,[h] and in your hand is *the ability* to make great and to give strength to all. 13. And now, our God, we give you thanks and we praise your glorious Name. 14. For *what*[26] am I and *what*[26] are my

Apparatus, Chapter 29

[d] L, AS: *yrdyn* ?? Intended for *drkyn,* "darics," as MT ?

[e] C, L, AS: plural, where V uses singular, though probably in a collective sense.

[f] V: *hdy'w.* C: *śmḥw* (following Hebrew *śmḥw*), but C gives also a variant reading: *hdw* (= E, L, AS).

[g] L, AS add: "of them."

[h-h] C, L, AS omit.

Notes, Chapter 29

[15]MT: "darics." Daric was a Persian coin. The *zuz* was a silver coin worth a quarter-shekel.

[16]MT: "Stones." Tg. Chr: Lit.: "a jewel." See note 6.

[17]MT: "Jehiel, the Gershunite."

[18]Lit.: "they."

[19]MT: "to."

[20]MT: "eyes."

[21]MT: "from everlasting to everlasting."

[22]See Gal 3:19.

[23]MT: singular.

[24]MT: singular.

[25]A paean of praise embroidered around individual words in MT to Israel's God, Yahweh, who has shown himself Lord of creation and history by creating and sustaining the universe, by using it to redeem and assist his people, and by instructing, leading, and championing the cause of his people.

[26]MT: "who."

people that we should have sufficient resources to contribute in this way, for from *before* you *is* everything *given* and from *the blessing of* your hand *they*[i27] have given to you? 15. For we are sojourners with you and temporary residents, as were all our fathers; like the shadow *of a bird which flies in the air of the heavens,* so are our days upon the earth. There is no hope *for a son of man that he should live for ever.* 16. O Lord our God, *according to*[j] *all these numerous materials*[28] which we have provided, in order to build *for your glorious Name*[29] the *sanctuary* house *in which we can praise* your holy Name—they are from your hand and they all belong to you. 17. I know, O my God, that you test the heart and that you delight in noble[30] *deeds;* as for me, in the uprightness of my heart I have willingly contributed all these. And now, I have seen *that* your people,[k] who are present[31] here, *have come joyfully* to make their freewill offerings to you. 18. O Lord, the God of Abraham, Isaac and Israel, our fathers, keep this *freewill offering as* eternal *merit,*[32] to *direct the inclination of the thoughts of the heart* of your people, and prepare their heart to *fear*[33] you. 19. And to my son Solomon give a perfect heart that he may keep your commandments, your testimonies and your covenant, that he may do everything and build the *palace*[34] for which I have made provision." 20. Then David said to the whole assembly: "Bless, now, the Lord your God." And the whole assembly blessed *before*[35] the Lord, the God of their fathers and bowed down and worshiped *before*[35] the Lord and *before*[35] the king. 21. Then they offered sacrifices *of holy things before*[35] the Lord, and they offered up whole burnt offerings *before*[35] the Lord on the next day: a thousand oxen, a thousand rams, a thousand lambs, with their libations,[l] and sacrifices in abundance for all Israel. 22. And they ate and drank before the Lord that day with great joy, and they made Solomon, the son of David, king a second time, and they anointed *him* as *king before*[36] the Lord, and Zadok as *chief* priest. 23. So Solomon sat on the throne of the *kingdom,*[37] *by the authority*[38] *of the Memra of the Lord,* as king in place of his father David. He pros-

Apparatus, Chapter 29

[i] C, L, AS: "we" (= MT).
[j] C: "in all." L, AS: "all" (= MT).
[k] C, L, AS add: "we," though the two plural verbs in

the rest of the sentence remain in the third person.
[l] C adds "a thousand."

Notes, Chapter 29

[27] MT: "we."
[28] MT: "all this abundance."
[29] MT: "for you."
[30] Or "right," "just."
[31] Lit.: "who have been found."
[32] MT: "keep this for ever." For "merit" see also 2:55; 4:18; 8:33; 23:17.
[33] Lit.: "toward you."
[34] MT: "citadel." See 29:1 (note 2).
[35] MT: "to."
[36] MT: "to" or "for."
[37] MT: "the Lord."
[38] Reading *pm* or *pwm* with C, L, AS for *ps* of V.

pered and all Israel obeyed[39] him. 24. All the leaders and the warriors, as well as all the sons of King David, pledged their loyalty[40] to king Solomon, *to support him and to strengthen him in all his kingship.* 25. The Lord magnified Solomon greatly *before*[41] all Israel, and he bestowed on him kingly splendor *and great glory, the like of* which had not been on any king over *all*[m] Israel before him. 26. David, the son of Jesse, was king over all *those of* the house of Israel. 27. The length of his[n] reign[42] over Israel was forty years: in Hebron he had been king for seven years, and in Jerusalem he had been king for thirty-three *years.* 28. David[o][43] died in a good old age, rich[44] in years,[45] *with* wealth and honor, and *he set up* his son Solomon *as* king[46] in his place.[p] 29. The acts of King David, from first to last, you will find written[47] in the Acts of Samuel, the seer, and in the Acts of Nathan, the prophet, and in the Acts of Gad, the watchman, 30. with full details of his reign,[48] his power *and his work,* and the events which happened to him, to Israel and to all the kingdoms of the nations.

Apparatus, Chapter 29

[m] C, L, AS omit "all."
[n] C: "David's."
[o] V and C: "David." L, AS: "he" (= MT).

[p] V and C: "after him." L and AS: "instead of him." Both have the same meaning.

Notes, Chapter 29

[39] Lit.: "accepted from him."
[40] Lit.: "gave the hand under."
[41] MT: "to the eyes of."
[42] Lit.: "The days which he reigned."
[43] MT: "he."
[44] It is difficult to find one English word which brings out the meaning of the Aramaic (or Hebrew) word: "sated," "replete." See also 23:1; 2 Chr 24:15.
[45] Lit.: "days."
[46] MT: "and Solomon ... became king."
[47] Lit.: "Behold they are written."
[48] Lit.: "With all his reign. ..."

The Targum of Second Chronicles

Translation

CHAPTER 1

1. Solomon, the son of David, established himself over his kingdom, and *the Memra of* the Lord, his God,*[a]* was *in support of him*[1] and magnified him exceedingly. 2. Solomon spoke to all Israel, to the commanders of thousands[2] and the hundreds, to the judges and to every leader in all Israel, the heads of the clans. 3. Then Solomon, and the whole assembly with him, went to the *height*[3] which was at Gibeon, because the tent of meeting of *the Lord,*[4] which Moses, the servant of the Lord, had made in the wilderness, was there. 4. But the ark of *the Lord*[4] David had brought up from Kiriath Jearim after David had made preparations for it, for he had pitched a tent for it in Jerusalem. 5. And the bronze altar, which Bezalel, the son of Uri, the son of Hur, had made, he placed in front of the tent of the Lord, and Solomon and the assembly*[b]* consulted it.[5] 6. There, before the Lord, Solomon made offerings[6] upon the bronze altar which was in the tent of meeting, and he offered up upon it one thousand whole burnt offerings. 7. That night *the Lord*[4] *revealed himself*[7] to Solomon and said to him: "Ask for whatever you would like me to give you."[8] 8. Solomon said *before the Lord:*[9] "You showed great kindness[10] *to my*[11] father David, and you have set me up as king in succession to him.[12] 9. Now, Lord God, let your word *which you spoke* to *my*[11] father David be established, for it is you who have set me up as king over *Israel,* a people as numerous as the dust of the earth. 10. Give me, now, wisdom and knowledge, that I can go out and come in before this people, for who *is capable of* judging this great people of yours?"*[c]*

Apparatus, Chapter 1

[a] C, L, AS omit: "his God."
[b] E: "all the congregation," with a few Hebrew MSS, LXX (A), Syr, Vg.

[c] V follows exactly the order of MT: lit.: "your people, the this, the great." E, C, L, AS: "improve" on this as follows: "the people, the great, the this," i.e., "your great people."

Notes, Chapter 1

[1]MT: "with him."
[2]MT: "the thousand."
[3]Reading singular with C, where V has plural.
[4]MT: "God."
[5]"Him" is also a possible understanding of the pronoun. Tg. Chr, like MT, is ambiguous.
[6]MT: *wy'l,* which is Qal "and he went up" or Hiphil "and he caused to go up, sent up, offered up." If the latter possibility is chosen, an object (e.g., "offering") needs to be supplied, but sometimes in MT the verb is used in an absolute sense, i.e., without an object, e.g., 2 Chr 8:13, though in both those instances Tg. Chr provides an object. In 2 Chr 1:6 Tg. Chr has chosen the latter possibility but this time has not given us the specific object. Perhaps the Targumist felt it unnecessary, since an object is supplied with the same verb later in the sentence.
[7]MT: "appeared."
[8]Lit. in MT and TC: "ask what I shall give you."
[9]MT: "to God."
[10]MT: "you have done *hesed* with" = "you have shown steadfast love to. . . ." Tg. Chr "you have done great goodness with. . . ."
[11]Lit.: "the." MT: "my" as in 1 Chr 28:4; 2 Chr 6:4, 7, 10, 15, etc.
[12]Lit.: "in his place," "instead of him"; see 1 Chr 29:28.

11. And *the Lord*[4] said to Solomon: "In that this was *the thought that was* in your heart and you have not sought[d] wealth, property, honor and the *lives*[13] of those who hate you, nor have you asked even for long life,[14] but you have requested[15] for yourself wisdom and knowledge so that you will *be able* to judge my people over whom I have made you king, 12. wisdom and knowledge are[16] given you, and wealth, property and honor I shall give you, such as none of the kings who were before you had and the like of which those after you will not have." 13. So Solomon came to the *height* which was at Gibeon. *From there he went to* Jerusalem, *(to)* before the tent of meeting.[17] And he reigned over Israel. 14. Solomon gathered together chariots and horsemen. He had fourteen hundred chariots and twelve thousand horsemen, and these he stationed in the chariot towns, *apart from those that were*[18] with the king in Jerusalem. 15. *Solomon*[19] made[20] silver and gold *as common* in Jerusalem as stones, and cedars he made[20] as numerous as the sycamores that were in the Shephelah. 16. The horses which Solomon had were imported from Egypt, as[21] was *the food which* the king's merchants *sold, and they were unable to sell food except from the king,* at a (fixed) price.[21] 17. They would import[22] a chariot from Egypt at six hundred *selas of* silver and a horse at one hundred and fifty. In the same way, they acted as export agents for all the kings of the Hittites and the kings of Aram. 18. Solomon gave orders[23] for the building of a *sanctuary* house for the name of the Lord and a royal house for himself.

Apparatus, Chapter 1

[d] E, L, AS: *š'lt* : "you have asked for," using same verb as in MT; V and C use the corresponding form of the verb *tb'*, "to seek."

Notes, Chapter 1

[13]MT: singular.
[14]Lit. (as in MT): "many days."
[15]Same verb as preceding: *š'l*.
[16]MT uses singular of the passive participle.
[17]MT: "and Solomon came to the high place which was at Gibeon Jerusalem from before the tent of meeting." English translations often change "to" to "from," giving, e.g., "Solomon came from the high place which was at Gibeon, from before the tent of meeting, to Jerusalem." Tg. Chr resolves the difficulty by making it a two-stage journey. (i) He came to the high place which was at Gibeon; (ii) and from there to Jerusalem, *to* before the tent of meeting.
[18]MT: "and." By changing "and" into "apart from those that were," Tg. Chr has increased considerably Solomon's chariot force.
[19]MT: "the king."
[20]Lit.: "gave" (MT and Tg. Chr).
[21-21]MT: "and from Kue, the king's merchants were taking them from Kue at a price." In Tg. Chr, *mqwy* "from Kue" has twice become *mzwn*, "food." It would seem that Tg. Chr has read the first word, *mqwy*, as *mqwh*, "gathering of the merchants; fair; goods," and rendered it as *mzwn*.
[22]Lit.: "They were bringing up and bringing out."
[23]Lit.: "said." It could also be translated as "decided," "resolved."

CHAPTER 2

1. Solomon conscripted[1] seventy thousand men[a] (to act as) *load carriers*[2] and eighty thousand to quarry in the mountain, while three thousand six hundred overseers *were put* in charge of them. 2. And Solomon sent to Huram,[b] the king of Tyre, saying: "As you dealt with *my*[3] father David,[c] sending him cedars to build himself a house to live in, 3. now I am about to build a *sanctuary* house for the name of the Lord, my God, *to be dedicated* to him,[4] *to be a place prepared* for offering up before him sweet-smelling incense, for laying out *the* continual *bread,* and for whole burnt offerings morning and evening, on Sabbath *days,* at new moons, and on the fixed festivals of the Lord, our God: this *commandment* is laid upon Israel for ever. 4. The *sanctuary* house which I am building will be great, for our God is greater than all the *objects of worship of the nations.*[5] 5. And who would have the strength to build the *sanctuary* house for him, for the *lower* heavens, the *middle* heavens and the *upper* heavens are unable to contain him *because it is he who sustains all things by his powerful arm. The heavens are the throne of his glory and the earth a footstool before him, and the deep and the whole world*[d] *are sustained by the spirit of his Memra.*[6] So who am I that I should build him a house except to offer up (in it) sweet-smelling things before him? 6. So now, send me a man who is skilled in carrying out *work* in gold, silver, bronze and iron, in purple, crimson and blue fabrics, and who knows how to do engravings *in a clear script;*[e] (he will work) alongside the craftsmen who are with me in Judah and Jerusalem, whom *my*[3] father David has provided. 7. Send me also cedar, cypress and sandalwood timber from Lebanon, for *it has come to my knowledge*[7] that your servants are expert at

---

Apparatus, Chapter 2

[a] C: "strong men."
[b] C: "Hiram," with some Hebrew MSS, LXX, Syr, Vg.

[c] C, L, AS omit.
[d] E: "people" (*'m'* instead of *'lm'*).
[e] E: *štr,* "document."

Notes, Chapter 2

[1] Lit.: "counted."
[2] Lit.: "carriers of loads." MT uses one noun, *sbl,* "porter."
[3] MT: "my" but Tg. Chr: "the."
[4] MT: "to dedicate to him."
[5] MT: "than all the gods." Tg. Chr: lit.: "objects of fear," then, "objects of worship."
[6] MT: "for the heavens, and the heavens of heavens, cannot contain him." The word "heavens," used in MT three times in a hyperbolic way, becomes in Tg. Chr three heavens, each one higher than the one before, giving a great feeling of immensity and therewith an even stronger emphasis on the majesty and transcendence of the God who not only cannot be contained by these heavens but in fact sustains them and all things by the arm of his strength. This theme of God as Lord of heavens and earth has already been introduced by Tg. Chr in 1 Chr 29:11. See also Tg. Ps.-J. Deut 33:27.
[7] Lit.: "it has been revealed before me," which, Le Déaut notes, is the normal Targumic way of saying that God *knows* something. Here it is used of Solomon. MT: "I know."

cutting timber *from* Lebanon. You can rest assured that[8] my servants (will work) with your servants, 8. the intention being that they should provide[9] for me large quantities of timber, for the house which I am building will be great and magnificent. 9. Now, as for the cutters,[10] *that is,* for those who are cutting down the trees, I have provided twenty thousand cors of wheat, *as sustenance*[11] for your servants, and twenty thousand cors of barley along with twenty thousand baths of wine and twenty thousand baths of oil." 10. Huram,[f] the king of Tyre, replied in a letter which he sent to Solomon: "It is because the Lord loves his people that he has appointed[12] you over them." 11. Huram[f] went on to say:[13] "Blessed be the Lord, the God of Israel, who made the heavens and the earth, who gave to King David a wise son, endowed with intelligence and understanding, who is to build a *sanctuary* house for *the Name of* the Lord and a royal house for himself. 12. Now then, I have sent a skilled man, endowed with understanding, Huram[g] *the master,*[14] 13. the son of a woman of the daughters of Dan; *this woman's father belonged to the tribe of Naphtali, and she was married to a man of Tyre: so Hiram's*[15] father is a Tyrian.[16] He is skilled in carrying out *work* in gold, silver, bronze, iron, stone and wood, in purple, blue, linen and crimson fabrics, in[17] engraving *in a script which is both clear and engraved,* and *in imparting any skill*[17] that is given to him, along with your skilled men and the skilled men of my lord, David, your father. 14. So now, let my

---

Apparatus, Chapter 2

[f] C: "Hiram"; see *b* above.   [g] C, L, AS: "Hiram."

Notes, Chapter 2

[8]Lit.: "Behold."

[9]MT begins the verse with *wlhkyn* (Tg. Chr: *wl' tqn'*), "to provide, to prepare." It is difficult to translate the *Waw* by one word, as LXX also found. It renders: "they will come to prepare." *ICC* (323) regards it as *Waw* explicative. The translation above is an attempt to bring out this emphasis.

[10]Perhaps "the cutters" refers to the stone quarriers of 2:1 (in MT, the same verb, *hṣb*, is used in both cases). If so, the *Waw*, treated in the translation as a *Waw* explicative, "that is," should have simply the force of "and." Unfortunately, in verse 9 Tg. Chr uses twice the same verb "to cut" (*qt'*) for both groups, which is a different verb from that used by Tg. Chr in verse 1 (*psl*) and from that used in verse 7 (*qṣṣ*); in verse 7 the reference is specifically to cutting wood.

[11]MT: "wheat crushed." The word translated "crushed" (*mkwt*) may have been a misreading of *mklt*, "food," in 1 Kgs 5:25, which Tg. Kgs translates as *prnws*, which is the word used in Tg. Chr.

[12]MT: "given, placed, set."

[13]Lit.: "said."

[14]Often taken in Hebrew as a proper noun, Huram-Abi, which, if treated partly as a common noun, becomes "Huram, my father." In Tg. Chr this becomes "Huram, the great," which may be a reference to his status as the master craftsman (as in the translation) or, bearing in mind that Tg. Chr often translates Hebrew *'by,* "my father," as *'b',* "the father," may be an error for *'b':* "the Great" is *rb'*.

[15]MT: "his."

[16]Reading *ṣwr'h* with E, C, L, AS. The preceding expansion is an attempt to reconcile 1 Kgs 7:14 and 2 Chr 2:13. In MT both verses state that Hiram's father is a man of Tyre; in Kgs however, Hiram's mother is a widow of the tribe of Naphtali, while in Chr she is of the tribe of Dan. Tg. Chr's solution is that Hiram's mother was of Dan but her father was of Naphtali.

[17-17]MT: "in engraving all kinds of engraving and in designing any design. . . ."

lord send his servants the wheat, barley, oil and wine which he promised,[18] 15. and we shall cut timber from Lebanon, according to all your requirement, and we shall bring it for you as rafts *to* the sea *of* Jaffo,[19] and it will be your responsibility to bring[20] it up to Jerusalem." 16. Then Solomon took a census of all the immigrants who *were living* in the land of Israel, following the census which his father David had taken of them and there were found to be one hundred and fifty-three thousand six hundred. 17. He divided them *into groups:* seventy thousand *to carry loads on their shoulders,*[21] eighty thousand to quarry in the mountains, and three thousand as overseers to make the people work.

CHAPTER 3

1. Solomon began to build the *sanctuary* house of the Lord in Jerusalem, on the mountain of Moriah, *on the spot where Abraham had worshiped and prayed in the Name of the Lord. That place is the land of worship where all the generations worship before the Lord. There Abraham offered up his son Isaac as a whole burnt offering, but the Memra of the Lord delivered him and a ram was chosen to take his place. There Jacob prayed as he fled from before his brother Esau. There the angel of the Lord* appeared to David as he prepared *the altar* on the site which he *had bought from Orwan,* on the threshing-floor of Orwan[a][1] the Jebusite.[2] 2. He began to build *it in the month of Iyyar, which is* the second month, on the second[3] *day of the month,* in the fourth year of his reign. 3. These *are the measurements according*

Notes, Chapter 2

[18]MT: "said."
[19]MT: Lit.: "upon the sea Jaffo," i.e., "by the sea to Jaffo."
[20]Lit.: (MT and Tg. Chr) "And *you* will bring it. . . ."
[21]MT: "porters."

Apparatus, Chapter 3

[a] V and C: *'rwwn*; L and AS: *'rwn*; MT: *'rnn*.

Notes, Chapter 3

[1]MT: "Ornan."
[2]The word "Moriah" occurs in MT only in Gen 22:2 and 2 Chr 3:1. Tg. Chr cannot let this occasion pass without stressing the sanctity of the place as he recalls some of the crucial encounters some of the great ones of Israel had with God on that site: the Abraham–Isaac offering; Jacob's nocturnal sojourn (referred to, e.g., in *b. San.* 95b and *PRE* 35); the David-Orwan-Angel of the Lord meeting, which resulted in the purchase of the site for the building of the Temple.
[3]MT: "on the second," which most commentators regard as a dittograph. Tg. Chr, however, justifies its presence by adding "day of the month."

to which Solomon *laid its foundations*[4] *when he began* to build the *sanctuary* house of *the Lord:*[5] the length, by the old measurement *of ancient times,* was sixty cubits and *its* breadth twenty cubits. 4. The hall which was in front of the house—its length across the width of the house was twenty cubits;[6] its height was one hundred and twenty cubits. He overlaid it on the inside with pure gold. 5. The large house he covered with cypress *paneling,*[7] which he overlaid with fine gold, and he decorated it with *a design of* palm trees and chains. 6. He adorned[8] the house with precious stones, *set in gold*—gold of Parvaim.[9] 7. He overlaid the house, the beams,[10] the thresholds, its walls and its doors with gold, and he carved *the figure of* cherubs on the walls. 8. He also made the most holy place; its length, corresponding to the width of the house, was twenty cubits and its width twenty cubits: he overlaid it with six hundred *centenaria*[11] of fine gold. 9. The weight of the nails was fifty shekels of gold. The upper rooms also he overlaid with gold. 10. In the most holy place he made two cherubs of lily work,[12] and they overlaid them with gold. 11. The length of the wings of the cherubs was twenty cubits. One wing, of five cubits, touched the wall of the house, while the other wing, of five cubits, touched the wing of the *other*[b] cherub.[c][13] 12. The wing of the other[14] cherub, of five cubits, touched the wall of the house, and the other wing, of five cubits, joined the wing of

Apparatus, Chapter 3

[b] V and C: "one." E, L, AS: "other" (= MT).   [c] V: "cherubs." C, E, L, AS: "cherub" (= MT).

Notes, Chapter 3

[4]Tg. Chr uses a verb *bsys,* which in Pael means "to establish, found," based on the Greek noun *basis* (JL I, 103). MJ 179 makes no reference to Greek origin.

[5]MT: Lit.: "These are the founding of Solomon to build the house of God," usually interpreted as "This is the foundation which Solomon laid for building...." The word translated by *BDB* (414a) as "founding" is *hwsd,* which, according to J. M. Myers (AB II, 14), Tg. Chr takes "as an abbreviation for *hmdwt 'šr ysd,* "the measures which he fixed"; hence the translation above.

[6]Tg. Chr, which follows MT, is difficult and reads: "The hall which was in front of the length in front of the width of the house...." Various suggestions have been made about the resolution of the problem in MT, one of which is followed here. It is interesting to note that Tg. Chr, which often tries to resolve difficulties, makes no such attempt here.

[7]MT: "wood."

[8]Lit.: "He covered ... for adornment."

[9]For "set ... Parvaim," MT has: "the gold was the gold of Parvaim." Tg. Chr alters the emphasis somewhat. MT: "the gold" may refer to the gold of the previous verse; in Tg. Chr, however, it refers specifically to the gold in which the stones were set.

[10]Reading *mryšy'* (with E, L, AS) for *mdyšy'* in V, which arose from confusion of two letters of similar appearance, *d* and *r.* C has: *mryšyy'.*

[11]MT: "talents."

[12]MT is uncertain. LXX: "of wood." Vg: "sculpture work."

[13]V has "one cherubs"!

[14]Reading "other," even though Tg. Chr has "one" (= MT). It is assumed that the "one" mentioned here refers to the "one" at the end of the previous verse, which would be "the other."

the other[d][15] cherub.[13] 13. The wings of these cherubs had a complete spread of twenty cubits:[16] they (themselves) stood on their feet, with their faces pointing *inwards.*[17] 14. He made the curtain[18] of blue, purple, crimson and linen materials, and he worked on it *a design of* cherubs. 15. In front of the house he made two columns, thirty-five cubits long; on the top of each was a capital[19] of five cubits, *in the form of a lamp.*[e] 16. He made chains in *the place of atonement*[20] and placed them on the top of the columns. He also made one hundred pomegranates and set them on the chains. 17. He erected the columns in front of the temple, one on the right and one on the left. To the one on the right he gave the name Jachin, *because the kingdom of the house of David had established it;*[21] to the one on the left the name Boaz, *because of Boaz, the leader of the clan of the house of Judah, from whom have come forth all the kings of the house of Judah.*[22]

Apparatus, Chapter 3

[d] V, C, L, AS: "one." E: "other."

[e] V, C and E: *šrg'*, "lamp." L and AS: *sryg'*, "lattice work; net"; cf. 4:12 and MT and Tg. 1 Kgs 7:17.

Notes, Chapter 3

[15]"other," in the sense of the "first" cherub mentioned. MT has "other," but V has "one."

[16]Lit.: ". . . were extended for twenty cubits."

[17]MT: "toward the house."

[18]Tg. Chr uses the word *prgwd'*, "curtain, tunic," borrowed from the Latin *paragauda* (JL II, 286). MJ (1214) refers to the Latin word and a Greek word, but regards their origin as Semitic.

[19]Tg. Chr uses the word *qrwnt'*, "capital of a column," borrowed from the Greek *korunthos* (MJ 1414); *korōnis* (JL II, 389).

[20]MT: "in the inner sanctuary" (the *dbyr*).

[21]V has Aphel of *tqn*; therefore a transitive sense is expected, as in the translation, but the more appropriate reading would be that of C, Ithpaal, giving "the kingdom of the house of David had been established." At any rate, the expansion is based on the name Jachin (*ykin*, "he will establish"), from the root *kwn*, "to be firm, established."

[22]Boaz was Naomi's kinsman, who married Ruth, from whom came Obed, father of Jesse, father of David, the founder of the dynasty that in due course would provide all the kings of Judah.

CHAPTER 4

1. Then he made *the* bronze altar, twenty cubits long,[1] twenty cubits wide and ten cubits high. 2. He also made the molten sea, ten cubits[a] from edge to edge, making a complete circle; it was five cubits high and a *measuring* line[2] of thirty cubits went right round it. 3. Below it, going right round it, were figures of oxen, for ten[3] cubits, completely surrounding the sea; there were two rows of oxen, cast with it when it was cast. 4. It stood upon twelve oxen, three facing north,[4] three facing west, three facing south, and three facing east. The sea *was set* on top of them, and all their hindquarters (were) *inward.*[5] 5. It was a handbreadth thick, and its rim was shaped like a cup, *chiseled all round like*[6] a lily, holding three thousand baths *by the dry measure,* containing *two thousand baths by the liquid measure.*[7] 6. He also made ten basins and placed five on the right *of the basin which Bezalel had made,* and five on the left.[8] These were for washing; whatever was used[9] for the whole burnt offering was washed clean in them. *Bezalel's basin was for the sanctification of the chief priest,*[8] and the sea for the *sanctification*[10] of the priests. 7. He made the ten golden lampstands, in the manner laid down for them, and he placed them in the Temple, five on the right[b] and five on the left. 8. He made ten tables and set them up in the Temple, five on the right *of the table which Bezalel had*

Apparatus, Chapter 4

[a] Lit.: "ten in cubits" = V. E, C, L, AS omit *b* "in." It may be that V was influenced by the Hebrew statement of measurement, "ten in the cubit."

[b] E, C, L, and AS add: "of the lampstand which Bezalel had made." See note 8, and Exod 25:31.

Notes, Chapter 4

[1] "its length," etc.

[2] Lit.: "a cord, a measure" or "a cord of measure." MT: "a line."

[3] Following verse 2, "thirty" cubits would be more appropriate. Some commentators avoid the difficulty by translating "ten per cubit" (*'śr b'mh*), though they translate the same expression in previous verses as "x cubits." Tg. Chr's translation rules out any such approach: Tg. Chr reads "ten cubits." Is it possible to translate this as "every ten cubits"?

[4] Lit.: "their face to the north," etc. MT: "facing."

[5] MT: "to the house."

[6] MT: "flower of."

[7] This expansion is an attempt to reconcile the two thousand baths of 1 Kgs 7:26 with the three thousand of 2 Chr 4:5. Tg. Chr finds the solution in the difference between a "dry bath" and a "liquid bath": one dry bath = two-thirds of a liquid bath. The *bath,* in fact, was a liquid measure, used, e.g., to measure water, wine, oil; it was of the same capacity as an *ephah,* which was normally used to measure cereals. See *b. Erub.* 14b, where the explanation for the equation: "3000 'dry baths' = 2000 'liquid baths'" lies in the fact that with the dry measure, one third of the material is in a "heap" above the rim-level, which of course is impossible in dealing with liquids.

[8] With Exod 30:18-21 and 31:2 in mind, Tg. Chr ensures that Bezalel's bronze basin, made for use in the Tabernacle in the wilderness is not forgotten but is now flanked by the ten basins of MT 2 Chr 4:6, and used by the high priest exclusively. (See *m. Yom.* 3:3-6 and *b. Yom.* 31a and *b. Men.* 98b.)

[9] I have left this three word phrase imprecise, as it is in both MT and Tg. Chr. Lit.: "the works of the ..."

[10] MT: "the washing."

made[11] and five on the left; as well, he made one hundred flat golden bowls.[12]
9. He made the court of the priests and the large court and doors for the court;
these[13] doors he overlaid with bronze. 10. But the sea he placed at the right hand
side *of the house*[c][14] in the direction of the east, *toward the east but* facing south.
11. Then Huram[d] made the basins, the shovels, and the flat bowls. Thus *Huram*[d][15]
finished off *all*[e][16] the work which he had been doing for King Solomon in the *sanctuary* house of *the Lord*:[17] 12. the two columns, and the bowls and the two capitals
on top of the columns and the two pieces of latticework which were to cover the
two bowls of the capitals which were on top of the columns; 13. the four hundred
pomegranates for the two pieces of latticework, two rows of pomegranates for each
piece of latticework, to cover the two bowls of the capitals which were on top of the
columns. 14. He also made the stands,[18] and he made the basins upon the
stands;[18] 15. the one sea and the twelve oxen beneath it; 16. the pots, the shovels,
the forks, and all their utensils, Huram,[f] his *Master*,[g][19] made for King Solomon, for
the *sanctuary* house of the Lord, in polished bronze. 17. The king cast them in the
thick layers of *red clay*[20] in the *plains*[21] of the Jordan, between Succoth and
Zeredath.[22] 18. Solomon made all these vessels in very large quantities, for *there
was no limit* to the weight of bronze.[23] 19. Solomon made all the vessels which
were *in* the *sanctuary* house of *the Lord*,[17] and the golden altar and the tables upon
which was the bread of the presence, 20. the lampstands and their lamps of fine
gold, which were to be lit, as prescribed, before *the place of Atonement*,[24] 21. the
lilies, the lamps, and the tongs of *pure* gold, *everything completely* of gold;[25] 22. the
snuffers, the sprinkling bowls, the censers, and the firepans of fine gold, the main
door of the house *and* its interior doors leading to the most holy place, and the
doors of the house leading to the temple were of gold.

Apparatus, Chapter 4

[c] "of the house" is missing in C, L, AS.
[d] V: "Huram." C, L, AS: "Hiram."
[e] V: "all." C, L, AS omit (= MT).

[f] V: "Huram" (= MT). C, L, AS: "Hiram."
[g] E: *abwhy* "his father." (= MT).

Notes, Chapter 4

[11] See note 8 and Exod 25:23.
[12] Tg. Chr uses the plural of *pyyl*, "broad, flat bowl," borrowed from the Greek *phialē* (MJ 1162 and JL II, 262).
[13] Lit.: "their."
[14] "of the house" is not in MT, but it is found in a few Hebrew MSS, LXX, and 1 Kgs 7:39.
[15] V follows Qere.
[16] Missing in MT but found in some Hebrew MSS, LXX, Vg, and 1 Kgs 7:40.
[17] MT: "God."
[18] Tg. Chr uses the plural of *bsys*, "base, stand," borrowed from the Greek *basis* (JL I, 103. MJ 179 makes no reference to Greek origin). See also Tg. 2 Chr 3:3, where the verb *bsys* is used.
[19] MT: "his father."
[20] MT: "in the thickness of the ground," i.e., "in the clay ground."
[21] MT: singular.
[22] MT: "Zeredathah."
[23] MT: "for the weight of bronze was incalculable."
[24] MT: "before the innermost sanctuary" (*dbyr*).
[25] MT: "of purest gold."

CHAPTER 5

1. Thus all the work which Solomon did for the *sanctuary* house of the Lord was completed. Then Solomon brought in the consecrated gifts of his father David, and he placed the silver, the gold, and all the vessels in the treasuries of the *sanctuary* house *of the Lord.*[1] 2. When this was done, Solomon assembled in Jerusalem the elders of Israel and all the heads of the tribes, the leaders of the clans of the children of Israel, in order to bring up the ark of the covenant of the Lord from the city of David, which is Zion. 3. So all the men of Israel assembled before King *Solomon* at the Feast *of Booths,*[2] *which* is in the seventh month. 4. All the elders of Israel came and the Levites[a] took up the ark. 5. And they brought up the ark and the tent of meeting and all the sacred vessels that were in the tent; it was the priests *and*[3] the Levites who brought them up. 6. King Solomon and the whole congregation of Israel *who* met with him before the ark were *slaughtering and* sacrificing sheep and oxen in such large numbers that it was impossible to keep a tally[b] of them or to count them.[4] 7. The priests brought in the ark of[c] the covenant of the Lord to its place, to *the place of Atonement, which had been prepared for it in the middle of* the house,[5] to the most holy place, beneath the wings of the cherubs. 8. The cherubs spread out their wings[6] over the place where the ark was, and the cherubs provided a covering for the ark and its bolts[7] from above. 9. Now the bolts[7] were long *and stuck out* so that the tops of the bolts[8] were visible, *like two breasts,*[9] facing *the place of Atonement,*[10] but they could not be seen outside *the curtain. They*[11] are still there today. 10. There[d] was nothing *deposited* in the ark ex-

Apparatus, Chapter 5

[a] E: "the priests," as in 1 Kgs 8:3, MT and Tg.
[b] V: *skym*. C, L, AS: *skwm*.
[c] "of" is missing in V and C.

[d-d] In Codex Reuchlinianus of Tg. 1 Kgs 8:9, there is a marginal note labeled "Jerusalem Targum" containing a similar statement. (See A. Sperber II, 231).

Notes, Chapter 5

[1] MT: "God."
[2] See Lev 23:34.
[3] "and" is not in MT but is found in many Hebrew MSS, and the other Versions, and in 1 Kgs 8:4, MT and Tg.
[4] Lit.: "to which there was no total number and they were not counted because of largeness" for MT: "which were not numbered and were not counted because of largeness."
[5] MT: "to the inner sanctuary of the house."
[6] MT: "two wings" (dual).
[7] MT uses the plural of *bd,* "pole." Tg. Chr uses the plural of *ngr*, whose basic meaning is "bolt, bar."
[8] V omits "from the ark" of MT.
[9] See *b. Yom.* 54a and *b. Men.* 98a-b, which, in an attempt to explain why the ends of the poles did not damage the curtain and why they were not seen without, uses the following comparison: "They pressed against the curtain and bulged out as the two breasts of a woman" (*b. Men.* 98b), borrowing the picture from Song of Songs 1:13.
[10] MT: "the innermost sanctuary."
[11] MT: "it," though some MSS, LXX, Syr, and 1 Kgs 8:8 have "they."

cept the two tablets which Moses had placed *there after they had been broken because of the calf which had been made at Horeb*[d] *and the two other sound tablets upon which were engraved in a clear script the ten words. These are the tablets of the covenant* which the Lord made with the children of Israel when they came out of Egypt.[12] 11. Now when the priests came out of the holy place—for all the priests who were present *in the holy place* had sanctified themselves, *as none of them was involved in the guard duty of the house according to the division of the Levites*[13]— 12. the Levites who were singers,[14] according to all their *families*, Asaph, Heman and Jeduthun, their sons and brethren, dressed in linen *robes, were offering praise* with cymbals, lutes and lyres, standing on the east side *of the altar*, and with them up to one hundred and twenty priests blowing trumpets. 13. They were[15] *giving themselves* unitedly, trumpeters and singers, to sound forth in unison, to praise and give thanks to *the name of* the Lord, and when they raised the sound with trumpets and cymbals and musical instruments and with praise *before*[16] the Lord, for he is good, for his *goodness*[17] is everlasting, the *sanctuary* house was filled with a *thick black* cloud[18] in the *sanctuary* house of the Lord. 14. The priests were unable to stand to perform their service because of the cloud *of glory*, for the glory of the Lord had filled the *sanctuary* house of *the Lord*.[1]

Notes, Chapter 5

[12]MT of 2 Chr 5:10 raises questions: (i) Which two tablets of stone were placed in the ark—the original pair or the post-calf pair? See also 6:11; 32:31. (ii) "Which the Lord cut with the children of Israel"—What did the Lord cut? Tg. Chr answers these queries. In the ark were the broken tablets and the new tablets (Deut 10:1-5). In *b. B. B.* 14a-b there is a discussion on our verse or its parallel in 1 Kgs 8:9, and it is noted that the verse contains a limitation following a limitation: "there was *nothing* in the ark except. . . ." Such a limitation following a limitation intimates "the presence of something which is not mentioned," which in this case is twofold—the scroll of the Law and (later on in the discussion) the fragments of the broken tablets. (Another tradition in, e.g., *Sifre Num.* section 82 [Levertoff] suggests that the fragments were placed in a different ark which accompanied Israel into battle.) The answer to (ii) is: that which was cut was the covenant, bearing in mind that "to make a covenant" is often in Hebrew "to cut a covenant."

[13]MT: "without keeping to their divisions."

[14]Or "those offering praise."

[15]C: singular.

[16]MT: "to."

[17]MT: "steadfast love."

[18]Lit.: "a cloud of darkness."

CHAPTER 6

1. Then Solomon said: "The Lord *has chosen to cause his Shekinah* to dwell *in the city of Jerusalem,* in the *sanctuary house which I have built for the Name of his Memra, but* a thick black cloud *has concealed before him.*[1] 2. Yes! I have built a *sanctuary* house *before* you, a place *prepared as a residence for your Shekinah, and corresponding to the throne of the house* where you dwell, *which is* for ever *in the heavens."*[2] 3. Then the king turned round[3] and blessed the whole assembly of Israel[a] as the whole assembly of Israel stood. 4. He said: "Blessed be *the Name of* the Lord, the God of Israel, who *by his Memra*[4] made a decree[5] with *my*[6] father David, and by his *good will*[7] has confirmed it. For He said:[8] 5. 'From the day that I brought my people *Israel* out of the land of Egypt I have not chosen a town[b] *in which to cause my Shekinah to dwell*[9] nor have I chosen a man to be *king*[10] over my people Israel. 6. But I have chosen Jerusalem, *in which to cause my Shekinah to dwell,*[11] and I have chosen David to be *king* over my people Israel.' 7. Now it had been the intention[12] of *my*[6] father David to build a house for the Name of the Lord, the God of Israel. 8. But the Lord said to *my*[6] father David: 'Because it was your intention to build a house for my Name, you have done right that this was your intention.[13] 9. Nonetheless, it will not be you who will build the house, but *a son of whom you will be the father,*[14] he will build the house for my Name.' 10. The Lord has kept[c] his promise which he made.[15] I have succeeded *my*[6] father David[16]

Apparatus, Chapter 6

[a] C, L, AS: "the Lord." V, E: "Israel" (= MT).
[b] C, L, AS add: "from all the towns of Israel" (= MT).

[c] V has a variant reading: *wqyym* for *w'qym*: "He has established" for "He has set up." Scarcely any difference in meaning. E, L, and AS follow V; C follows V's variant reading.

Notes, Chapter 6

[1] MT: "The Lord has said that he would dwell (lit.: to dwell) in thick darkness."
[2] MT: "And I! I have built an exalted house for you, and a place for you to dwell in for ever." The earthly temple is a replica of the heavenly. See also Tg. 1 Chr 21:15.
[3] Lit.: "turned his face."
[4] Or: "who made a decree in his Memra," i.e., in himself. *b* can mean either "with" or "in."
[5] MT: "who spoke with his mouth."
[6] Following MT. Tg. Chr has "the."
[7] MT: "by his hands."
[8] MT: "saying."
[9] MT: "from all the tribes of Israel, in which to build a house, that my name should be there."
[10] MT: "leader"; "prince" (*ngyd*).
[11] MT: "that my name should be there."
[12] Lit.: "in the heart."
[13] Lit.: "in your heart."
[14] MT: "your son, who comes forth from your loins."
[15] Lit.: "his word which he spoke."
[16] Lit.: "I have arisen in the place of my father David."

and have taken my seat upon the *royal* throne of Israel, just as the Lord promised,[17] and I have built the *sanctuary* house for the Name of *the Memra of* the Lord, the God of Israel. 11. There I have placed the ark in which are *the tablets*[18] *of* the covenant of the Lord which he made with the children of Israel." 12. Then he stood in front of the altar of the Lord, facing the whole assembly of Israel, and he spread out his hands *in prayer.* 13. For Solomon had made the bronze platform and had placed it in the middle of the courtyard, *in the sacred enclosure;* it was five cubits long,[19] five cubits wide and three cubits high. He stood upon it, then knelt down upon his knees before the whole assembly of Israel, and he spread out his hands *in prayer* toward heaven. 14. He said: "O Lord, the God of Israel, there is no one *apart from*[20] you; *you are the* God *whose Shekinah dwells* in the heavens *above* and *who rules* over the earth *beneath,*[21] keeping covenant and *goodness*[22] with your servants who walk *in your ways and who worship* before you *with all the desire of their soul and* with all *the inclination of* their heart;[23] 15. who have kept what you promised to your servant David, *my*[6] father; *you decided, by your Memra, and by your will you brought it about,*[24] as it is this very day. 16. Now, O Lord, the God of Israel, keep to your servant David, *my*[6] father, the promise which you made to him[25] when you said: 'You will never lack a man before me to sit upon the *royal* throne of Israel, if only your sons will take heed to their *ways*[26] by walking in *the*[27] law as you have walked before me.' 17. So now, O Lord, the God of Israel, *do*[d28] let your words[29] be established which you spoke to your servant David. 18. *For who would imagine and who would consider that the Lord would indeed choose to cause his Shekinah to dwell in the midst of the sons of* man *who inhabit* the earth?[30] For *it is* utterly *impossible for* the *upper* heavens, *the middle* heavens, *and the lower* heavens to contain *the glory of your Shekinah, for you are the God who sustains everything,*

Apparatus, Chapter 6

[d] *kdwn* in V, but not in C, L, AS.

Notes, Chapter 6

[17]Lit.: "spoke."
[18]See 5:10 and 32:31.
[19]Lit.: "Its length, five cubits," etc.
[20]MT: "like."
[21]MT: "There is no God like you, in heaven and in earth."
[22]MT: "steadfast love."
[23]MT: "who walk before you with all their heart."
[24]MT: "You spoke with your mouth and with your hand you have fulfilled it."
[25]Lit.: "what you spoke to him."
[26]MT: singular.
[27]MT: "my law."
[28]To bring out the force of a second "now" in V (though not in MT), found as *n'* in a few Hebrew MSS, LXX, and Syr, and in 1 Kgs 8:26.
[29]MT: singular.
[30]MT: "For will God indeed dwell with man on the earth?"

the heavens and the earth and the depths and everything which is in them[31]—how much less this house which I have built! 19. Yet, turn[32] to the prayer of your servant and to his request, O Lord, my God, so that you may *accept* the *request*[33] and the prayer which your servant is praying before you. 20. That *there be good pleasure before you to protect*[34] this house day and night, the place where you promised *to cause your Shekinah to dwell;*[35] to *accept*[36] the prayer which your servant will pray *over*[37] this place. 21. *Accept the request*[38] of your servant and of your people Israel, who pray toward this place; *accept*[39] from heaven, the dwelling place of *your Shekinah,*[40] *accept*[39] *their prayer* and forgive[e] *their sins.* 22. If a man sins against his neighbor who insists that he swear an oath and *comes and makes him* take the oath before your altar in this house,[41] 23. you will *accept*[39] from heaven and execute[f] *judgment between them:*[42] judge your servants, bringing *retribution to the* sinner by bringing down his conduct[43] upon his head, and showing the righteous to be righteous by rewarding him according to his righteousness. 24. If, when your people Israel are defeated before *their* enemies[44] because they sin *before* you, they return *to your worship* and acknowledge your Name and pray and make request *from*[45] you in this house, 25. then you will *accept*[39] from heaven and forgive the sins[46] of your people Israel and restore them to the land which you gave to them and to their fathers. 26. When the heavens are prevented *from sending down*

Apparatus, Chapter 6

[e] V: *tštbq.* C: *tšbyq.* L, AS: *tšbq.*
[f] C, L, AS follow MT: "and you will do and judge," where V separates the two verbs and supplies an object for the first verb.

Notes, Chapter 6

[31]MT: "Behold the heavens and the heavens of the heavens cannot contain you." See 2:5 and note 6 in Chapter 2.
[32]Lit.: "And you will turn ..."
[33]MT: "to give heed to (lit.: to hear to) the cry."
[34]MT: "That your eyes may be opened toward this house." The anthropomorphism of MT is avoided, but the note of watchfulness contained in the "opened eyes" is made explicit.
[35]MT: "to the place where you have said to place your name."
[36]MT: "to give heed to (lit.: to hear to)."
[37]MT: "toward."
[38]MT: "Give heed to the supplications."
[39]MT: "You will hear."
[40]MT: "the place of your dwelling."
[41]Verse 22 is difficult in MT. Literally it reads as follows: "If a man sins against his neighbor and he (the neighbor) lifts up (reading *nś'* for *nš'*) against him an oath to cause him to swear and he (the sinner) enters the oath (supplying *b* before *'lh*; alternatively, "he comes and swears," supplying *waw* before *'lh*) before your altar in this house." Tg. Chr gives the following (literal translation on which the translation above is based): "If a man sins against his neighbor and he (the neighbor) has power over him to cause him to swear an oath, and he (the neighbor) comes and causes him to swear before your altar in this house."
[42]Lit.: "and do their judgment." MT: "and do."
[43]Lit.: "to give his conduct" (= MT).
[44]MT: "an enemy."
[45]MT: "before."
[46]MT: singular.

rain[47]—because they sin *before*[48] you—if they pray toward this place and acknowledge your Name *and* turn away from their *sins*[46] *because you accept their prayer,*[49] 27. then you will *accept*[39] *from* heaven and forgive the sin of your *servant*[50] and of your people Israel, when you teach them[51] the *right*[52] way in which they should walk, and you will give rain upon your land which you have given to your people for an inheritance. 28. When there is in the land *the distress that* famine *brings,*[53] when there is plague, blight, and mildew, when there is locust and grasshopper—for their enemies will harass them in the land of *their cities*[54]—whatever affliction or trouble there may be, 29. every prayer *and* every request which may be *in the mouth of* any member *of* your whole people Israel,[55] who knows his own particular affliction and pain—if he spreads out his hands *in prayer* toward this house, 30. then you will *accept*[56] from heaven, from the dwelling place of *your Shekinah,*[57] and you will forgive *their sins* and give to every man according to all his ways, *for he lays bare his heart before you,*[58] because *you are and there is no one apart from you, and before you* alone *are* the hearts of the sons of man *revealed,*[59] 31. in order that they may fear *from before* you by walking in *ways which are right before you*[60] all the days that they live as inhabitants of the land[61] which you gave to our fathers. 32. Likewise when *one from a son of peoples,*[62] who is not of your people Israel, comes from a distant land for the sake of your great Name, your powerful hand and your *uplifted*[63] arm—when they come and pray toward this house, 33. Then you will *accept*[39] from heaven, from the dwelling place *of your Shekinah,*[57] and act in accordance with everything which *a son of peoples*[62] may *pray before*[64] you, so that all the nations of the earth may know your Name, and to fear *from before* you like your people Israel, and to know that your Name has been called over this house which I have built. 34. When your people go forth to *wage* war against *their*[65] ene-

Notes, Chapter 6

[47]MT: "and there is no rain."

[48]MT: "to" ("against").

[49]MT: "you answer them."

[50]MT: plural.

[51]MT adds "toward."

[52]MT: "good."

[53]Lit.: "the distress of famine." MT has: "famine."

[54]MT: "gates." Syr: "in their land and in their cities."

[55]MT: Lit.: "which may be to any man and to all your people, Israel."

[56]MT: "you will hear."

[57]MT: "your dwelling place."

[58]MT: "whose heart you know."

[59]MT: "because you alone know the heart of the sons of man."

[60]MT: "in your ways."

[61]Lit.: "live upon the face of the land. . . ."

[62]MT: "the foreigner."

[63]MT: "stretched out."

[64]MT: "may call to."

[65]MT: "his."

mies by the way that you will send them, and they pray[g] *before*[66] you, *facing toward the way which leads to*[67] this city which you have chosen and the *sanctuary* house which I have built for your Name, 35. then you will *accept*[39] from heaven their prayer and their request and *avenge their humiliation.*[68] 36. When they sin *before*[66] *you*—for there is *no one of human kind*[69] who does not sin—and *your anger is directed against them*[70] and you *hand them over*[71] before *their enemies*[72] and their captors take them prisoner *and bring them into exile* to a land far away or close at hand; 37. if they bring back *your fear* to their heart, in the land to which they have been taken captive,[h][73] and turn and *make request*[74] (for mercy) from you in the land of their captivity, saying: 'We are guilty, we have behaved foolishly, we have sinned,' 38. and they return *to your worship*[75] with all their heart and with all their soul in the land of their captivity to which they have been taken captive, and pray *before you and direct their heart* toward *the way which leads to* their land[76] which you gave to their fathers, and the city which you chose and to the *sanctuary* house which[77] I have built for your Name, 39. then you will *accept*[39] from heaven, the[i] dwelling place *of your Shekinah,*[40] their prayer and their *request*[78] and *avenge their humiliation,*[68] and forgive your people who have sinned *before*[66] you. 40. Now, O my God, *may there be good will from before you,*[79] that your ears may be attentive[80] to *receive* the prayer of *those who set their heart to pray toward* this place.[81] 41. So now, arise, O Lord God, *dwell*[j] *in your Glory,*[82] you and the ark of

---

Apparatus, Chapter 6

[g] V: Imperfect Pael. L, AS also Imperfect. C: Participle Pael.

[h] V: Pael. C, L, AS: Ithpeel (= MT, which is Niphal).

[i] V omits *mn,* found in C, L, AS (= MT).

[j] *šry* (= V, E), but C, L, AS: *'l šdy* = "Arise, O Lord, God, El Shaddai."

Notes, Chapter 6

[66]MT: "to."

[67]Lit.: "the way facing." MT: "of."

[68]MT: "and do their justice." Tg. Chr gives a picture of a defeated and humiliated Israel not found in MT and reflecting perhaps later defeats.

[69]Lit.: "no son of man." MT: "man."

[70]Or "threatens them." MT: "you are angry with them."

[71]MT: "And you give them."

[72]MT: "an enemy."

[73]Lit.: "to which they have taken (them) captive" (= MT).

[74]MT: "and make supplication to"; cf. 6:24 and 7:14.

[75]MT: "to you."

[76]MT: "and pray toward their land." Lit.: "the way of their land."

[77]V has an additional redundant relative pronoun, *dy.*

[78]MT: plural, though a few Hebrew MSS and 1 Kgs 8:49 have the singular. See also verse 35 above.

[79]MT: "May your eyes be opened." See note 34, verse 20.

[80]Reading *ṣyyty* with E, C, L, AS for V's *ṣlty.*

[81]MT: "attentive to the prayer of this place."

[82]MT: "to your resting-place."

the glory of your strength;[83] let your priests, O Lord, God, be clothed with *garments of glory by* your salvation, and let your pious ones rejoice in (your) goodness.[84] 42. O Lord, God, do not turn away the face of your Anointed *Ones*[85] *without cause;* call to mind the acts of devotion of your servant,[86] David."

CHAPTER 7

1. When Solomon had finished praying, the fire came down *and spread* from heaven *over the altar* and consumed the whole burnt offering and the sacrifices *of holy things* and the glory of *the Shekinah of* the Lord filled the house. 2. The priests were unable to enter the *sanctuary* house of the Lord, for the glory of *the Shekinah of* the Lord filled the *sanctuary* house of the Lord. 3. All the children of Israel were watching as the fire came down *and spread over the house* and the glory of *the Shekinah of* the Lord *rested* upon the house; they bowed down on the pavement with *their* faces *on*[1] the ground, they worshiped and gave thanks *before*[1] the Lord, for he is good, for his *goodness*[2] is for ever. 4. Then the king and all the people offered sacrifice before the Lord. 5. King Solomon offered a sacrifice (consisting) of twenty-two thousand oxen and one hundred and twenty thousand sheep; and the king and all the people dedicated the *sanctuary* house of *the Lord.*[3] 6. The priests stood at their posts and the Levites *on their platform,*[4] with musical instruments, *offering praise before* the Lord—who *had brought* David *near in order* to appoint him king[5] *and who had caused the spirit of holiness to rest upon him* so that he might offer praise *before*[1] the Lord, for his goodness[6] is everlasting—*by means of the praise which* David *had offered* by their *hands,*[7] while, facing them, the priests blew *their trumpets* and all Israel (remained) standing. 7. Solomon consecrated the center of the court which was in front of the *sanctuary* house of the Lord,

Notes, Chapter 6

[83]Lit.: "of the glory of your strength."
[84]V has actually the plural form.
[85]MT: plural, but many Hebrew MSS and Versions have singular.
[86]Acts of devotion done by David or acts of devotion done to David (by God)?

Notes, Chapter 7

[1]MT: "to."
[2]MT: "steadfast love."
[3]MT: "God."
[4]Tg. Chr uses the word *dwkn*, "platform," borrowed from the Greek *docheion* (JL I, 16).
[5]MT: "which king David made" (the reference is to the instruments). It seems that Tg. Chr has taken the other translation possibility, "who made David king."
[6]MT: "steadfast love" (*ḥesed*).
[7]MT: "when David offered praise by their hand." The corresponding three words in Tg. Chr are found only in V.

for he offered[8] the whole burnt offerings and the fat portions of the sacrifices *of the holy things*[9] there, because the bronze altar which Solomon had made *was narrow and* could not hold the whole burnt offering, the cereal offering and the fat portions. 8. At that time Solomon kept[8] the festival for seven days *after he had celebrated*[8] *the seven days of the dedication of the house,*[10] and all Israel with him—a very large assembly—from the entrance of *Antioch*[11] as far as the *Nile*[12] of Egypt. 9. And on the eighth day they held[8] an assembly *before the Lord,* because they had celebrated[8] the dedication of the altar for seven days and the festival *of booths* for seven days. 10. On the twenty-third day of the seventh month he sent the people away to their tents; *they set off for their towns,* happy and contented in heart, because of *all*[13] the goodness which the Lord had done *to his servant*[14] David, *for it was due to his merit that the gates of the sanctuary house had been opened,* and to *his son* Solomon, *whose prayer the Lord had accepted and the Shekinah of the Lord had taken up residence in the sanctuary house,* and to his people Israel, *because their offerings had been accepted with good will and the fire had come down from heaven and had spread out over the altar and had consumed their sacrifices.*[15] 11. Thus Solomon finished the *sanctuary* house of the Lord and the royal palace;[16] *he accomplished* everything which Solomon had intended doing[17] in the *sanctuary* house of the Lord and in his own house, and he *did* (it) successfully.[18] 12. During the night the *Memra of* the Lord *was revealed*[19] to Solomon and said to him: "Your prayer *has been heard before me,*[20] and I have chosen this place *that it may become for me* a house for the sacrifice *of offerings.*[21] 13. Whenever I shut up the heavens *so that they send down no rain,*[22] and whenever I order the locust to eat up *the fruits of* the land, and when *I let loose the angel of death because of the sins of my people,*[23] 14. if my people, over whom my Name has been called, humble

Notes, Chapter 7

[8]Lit.: "made."

[9]MT: "the fat portions of the peace offerings" (*šlmym*).

[10]In 7:8 (MT) Solomon kept the festival (of Tabernacles) for seven days. When, then, did the dedication take place? 7:9 (MT) explains that the dedication took place during the preceding seven days. Tg. Chr inserts these details at 7:8. There is a hint of the reference to a second "seven days" in 1 Kgs 8:65, where MT states: "he kept the festival seven days and seven days." Tg. Kgs interprets this as "seven days the dedication of the house and seven days the festival." Modern commentators are not sure whether MT Chr is dependent on Kgs on this matter or vice versa.

[11]MT: "Hamath," see 1 Chr 13:5, note 7.

[12]MT: "Wady." See 1 Chr 13:5, where "Nile" is used for "Shihor."

[13]Not in MT, but found in some Hebrew MSS and Syr.

[14]Not in MT, but found in 1 Kgs 8:66.

[15]MT, in referring to three names, provides Tg. Chr with a neat three-point sermon outline, by which, in his expansion, he reminds them of God's goodness, of their kings' virtues (under God), and of their status as an "accepted people."

[16]MT: "the house of the king." Tg. Chr: "the house of the kingdom."

[17]Lit.: "which went up upon the heart of Solomon to do."

[18]Lit.: "he did and he succeeded." MT lacks "he did."

[19]MT: "appeared."

[20]The usual Targumic formula used when God hears something (Le Déaut I, 119 n. 4).

[21]MT: "this place for me as a house of sacrifice."

[22]MT: "and there will be no rain."

[23]MT: "and if I send pestilence among my people."

themselves *and do penitence* and pray and *seek mercy from before me*[24] and turn away from their evil ways, then I shall *accept* from heaven *their penitence,*[25] *I* shall *loose and* forgive[26] their *sins*[27] and I shall *bring healing to*[28] their land. 15. So now, *there will be good will from before my Memra*[29] *that I may incline my ear*[a] *to accept*[30] the prayer *which my people pray before* this place.[31] 16. And now, I have chosen *by my Memra* and I have consecrated this house *that I may cause my Shekinah to dwell* there[32] for ever, and *it will be my pleasure to do good there*[33] always. 17. As for you, *if*[34] *you will worship before me* and walk *in ways which are right* before me,[35] as your father David walked, and do as I have commanded you, and keep my statutes and my judgments, 18. I shall establish your royal throne, *something which*[36] I covenanted[37] with your father David, saying: 'You will not fail to have a man *sitting on my royal throne and* ruling over Israel.' 19. But if you turn away and forsake my statutes and my *judgments*[b][38] which I have set before you, and go and worship *idols of foreign nations*[39] and bow down to them, 20. I shall drive them out from upon my land which I gave them and this house which I have consecrated *so as to cause my Shekinah to dwell in it,*[40] I shall put far away from before me and I shall make it *proverbs*[41] and a byword among all the nations. 21. And this house, which was exalted, *will be desolate;* everyone who passes by it shall *cry out* and say:[42] 'Why did the Lord act in this way towards this land and this house?'

Apparatus, Chapter 7

[a] V: "my ear." C, L, AS: "ears" (= MT).
[b] V: "my judgment." C: "my commandments,"

pqwdyy. L, AS: pqwdy. MT: mṣwty ("my commandments").

Notes, Chapter 7

[24]MT: "and seek my face."
[25]MT: "then I shall hear from heaven."
[26]Le Déaut notes (I, 119 n. 6) that this is a characteristic paraphrase of the Palestinian Targum to indicate pardon. Tg. Onq. uses only one verb.
[27]MT: singular.
[28]MT: "heal."
[29]MT: "My eyes will be open"; see 6:20, 40; 7:15.
[30]MT: "and my ears attentive to."
[31]MT: "the prayer of this place."
[32]MT: "that my name may be there."
[33]MT: "and my eyes and my heart will be there."
[34]Reading 'yn "if" with C, L, AS. Missing in V.
[35]MT: "and walk before me."
[36]MT: "as."
[37]Both MT and Tg. Chr have "cut," but there is clearly a covenant allusion, and as "cut" is often used in the expression "to make (cut) a covenant," "covenanted" seems to be a better translation here.
[38]MT: "commandments."
[39]MT: "other gods."
[40]MT: "for my Name."
[41]MT: singular.
[42]MT: Lit.: "And this house which was exalted, everyone passing by it will be appalled and will say. . . ." Tg. Chr simplifies this considerably.

22. And they will say: 'Because they forsook *the worship of* the Lord, the God of their fathers, who had brought them out of the land of Egypt, and they laid hold of *the idols of the nations*[43] and bowed down to them and worshiped them. For this reason he brought upon them all this evil.'"

CHAPTER 8

1. At the end of twenty years (during) which Solomon had built the *sanctuary* house of the Lord and his own house, 2. Solomon (re-)built the towns which Huram had given Solomon, and he settled in them[1] the children of Israel. 3. Solomon went to *Hamatha*[2] *of* Zobah and *besieged it rigorously.*[3] 4. He rebuilt[4] Tadmor in the wilderness and all the store[a] cities[5] which he had built in *Hamatha.*[2] 5. He built Upper Beth-Horon and Lower Beth-Horon, fortified cities, *surrounded* with walls, doors, and bars, 6. and *Baalah,*[6] and all Solomon's store[a] cities,[5] and all the cities for[7] the chariots[b8] and the cities for[7] the horsemen[c8] and all the desire of *the heart of* Solomon, which he wanted *to do and* to build in Jerusalem, in Lebanon and in all the land of his dominion. 7. All the people who were left of the *Hittites,* the *Amorites,* the *Perizzites,* the *Hivites* and the *Jebusites,*[9] who did not belong to Israel, 8. those of their descendants[10] who were left after them in the land, whom the children of Israel had not wiped out, these Solomon *placed under tribute*[11]—(and that is the position) up to this day. 9. But there were

Notes, Chapter 7

[43]MT: "other gods"; cf. 7:19.

Apparatus, Chapter 8

[a] V: *byt 'wṣr'.* C, L, AS: *byt 'wṣry'.*
[b] V: *'rtkyh:* "his chariot." C: *'rtkyy':* "chariots." E, L, AS: *'rtky':* "chariots."

[c] V: *prṡyh:* "his horseman." C: *prṡyh:* "horsemen." E, L, AS: *prṡy':* "horsemen."

Notes, Chapter 8

[1]Lit.: "there."
[2]MT: "Hamath."
[3]MT: "and seized it." Tg. Chr (reading with C, Aphel of *tqp*): "he strengthened the siege against it."
[4]Lit.: "built" (= MT).
[5]Lit.: "the cities of the place of stores" ("the place of" missing in MT). See also verse 6.
[6]MT: "Baalath."
[7]Lit.: "of."
[8]Reading with C or E. See the Apparatus.
[9]In each of the gentilic nouns, MT has singular.
[10]Lit.: "sons."
[11]MT: "and he brought them up for a forced levy," i.e., "he made them a forced levy." Tg. Chr translates this as: "he made (lit.: gave) them bearers of tribute"; cf. Josh 17:13; 2 Sam 20:24; Gen 49:15; Deut 20:11.

some of the children of Israel whom Solomon[12] did not conscript for his work,[13] for they were the men *waging* war[14] and the commanders of his *warriors*[15] and the commanders of his chariot[d] force and his horsemen. 10. These were the commanders of the garrisons[16] which king Solomon had, two hundred and fifty, who kept the people in subjection. 11. Solomon brought up *Bithyah,*[17] Pharaoh's daughter, from the city of David to the *palace*[18] which he had built for her, for he said: "*It is not possible that a woman should rule* over me in the house of David,[19] king of Israel, for these (places) are holy, *and it is not right* that a woman should live *there after* the ark of the Lord has come into them." 12. After this Solomon offered up[e] whole burnt offerings *before*[20] the Lord upon the Lord's altar which he had built before the vestibule, 13. And, as each day required, he offered up[21] *the continual offering,* in accordance with the commandment of Moses, *and the additional offerings*[22] for the Sabbaths, for *the beginnings*[f] *of* the months and for the three annual

Apparatus, Chapter 8

[d] C, E, L and AS have the form of the third person masculine singular suffix normally attached to a plural noun, while V has the form of the third person masculine singular suffix normally attached to a singular noun—it may be that V is regarding the noun as a collective noun.

[e] V: *ysyq.* E, L, AS: *'syq.*
[f] C: "the commandment of Moses for the Sabbaths and the additional offerings for the beginnings . . ."

Notes, Chapter 8

[12] In MT this relative pronoun is rather awkward, and it is not found in a few Hebrew MSS, LXX, Syr, Vg, nor in the parallel verse in 1 Kgs 9:22. Though most commentators and translators ignore it, it is interesting that Tg. Chr retains it. If we retain it, then some such translation as that given above is necessary.

[13] Lit.: "Solomon did not give to be servants for his work."

[14] MT: "men of war."

[15] MT: "officers."

[16] At first sight Tg. Chr seems to follow *Kethibh* of Hebrew text "garrisons." The *Qere* "commanders" is the reading found in MT 1 Kgs 9:23. Both Tg. Chr and Tg. Kgs use the same word (borrowed from the Greek *'stṛtyg:* see 1 Chr 11:16, note 31). But as there is debate as to the meaning of this word (MJ : "garrison"; JL: "commander"), it is difficult to be certain which reading Tg. Chr is following.

[17] In MT 1 Chr 4:18, Bithyah is listed as Pharaoh's daughter, whose husband was Mered of the line of Caleb. In Tg. Chr she becomes the foster-mother of Moses, no doubt as a result of "the daughter of Pharaoh" reference. One can only assume that in 8:11, Tg. Chr, seeing "daughter of Pharaoh," supplies a name for her from 1 Chr 4:18 reference. Ginzberg (VI, 297) notes: "The daughter of Pharaoh (= Shishak), whom Solomon took as wife, is called Bithiah in Targum on 2 Chron. 8:11. This is very likely due to a confusion of Shishak's daughter with the one of his predecessor, the foster-mother of Moses. . . ."

[18] MT: "house." Loan word. See 1 Chr 9:18, note 17.

[19] MT: "My wife shall not live in the house of David." In MT "my wife" is *'šh ly* (lit.: "a wife to me"). In Tg. Chr the words are reversed, and the verb "to rule" introduced, giving: "a woman shall not rule over me" (*woman* and *wife* are the same word in Hebrew)—which seems a strange statement to come from the lips of the king of Israel. The suggestion seems to be that as both temple and king's palace are holy areas, only a man should have authority in such sacred areas, especially now that the presence of the ark has made them doubly sacrosanct.

[20] MT: "to."

[21] Lit.: "to offer up" (= MT). But in MT this verb has no specific object. Tg. Chr supplies all the necessary objects to fit in with each occasion mentioned.

[22] On certain occasions additional offerings (*musaphim*) were made. After the destruction of the Temple a "Musaph" service continued. The Talmud suggests this service was in use even in Temple times (see *b. Suk.* 53a).

festivals—at the Feast of Unleavened Bread, at the Feast of Weeks and at the Feast of Tabernacles. 14. Then, *as* David his father *had commanded,*[23] he appointed the divisions of the priests for their work, and the Levites for their duties to offer praise and service in the presence of the priests as each day required, and the gate-keepers in their divisions for each of the gates, for such was the commandment of David, *the prophet of the Lord.*[24] 15. And they did not disregard[g] the king's command in respect of the priests and the Levites *or*[25] with regard to any matter,[h] including the treasuries.[i] 16. So all the work of Solomon was accomplished *from*[26] the day that the foundation of the *sanctuary* house of the Lord was laid until *the day that* it was completely finished. The sanctuary house of the Lord was complete. 17. After this Solomon went to *Fort Tarngola*[27] and to Eloth, which is on the sea-coast in the land of Edom. 18. And Huram sent to him, through his servants, ships and skilled seafarers, who, along with Solomon's servants, came to Ophir and took away from there four hundred and fifty *centenaria*[28] of gold, and they brought *it* to King Solomon.

CHAPTER 9

1. Now when the queen of *Zemargad*[1] heard of Solomon's reputation, she came to test Solomon with *enigmatic* problems in Jerusalem, with a very large retinue and camels laden with spices, a large quantity of gold and *choice jewels.*[2] She came to Solomon and spoke with him about everything which was in her heart.

Apparatus, Chapter 8

[g] C, L, AS: *'dw,* also, "to turn aside."
[h] V: *md'm.* C, L, AS: *ptgm'* (no real difference of meaning).

[i] V: *tsbry'.* C, L, AS: *'wṣry'* (no real difference of meaning).

Notes, Chapter 8

[23] MT: "according to the ordinance of David his father."
[24] MT: "the man of God."
[25] MT lacks "or." The importance of *waw* (here translated "or") by V (only) makes the translation difficult. Without *waw,* "with regard to any matter" can be taken with what precedes, but the presence of *waw* forces one to separate what follows from what goes before.
[26] MT has "until."
[27] MT: "Ezion-Geber."
[28] MT: "talents."

Notes, Chapter 9

[1] MT: "Sheba." See Tg. 1 Chr 1:9, note 29. Zemargad: Based on the Greek *smaragdos,* "emerald."
[2] MT: "precious stone" (singular).

2. Solomon answered all her queries:[3] there was nothing hidden from Solomon which he did not tell her. 3. When the queen of *Zemargad*[1] saw the wisdom of Solomon and the *sanctuary* house which he had built, 4. the food of his table, the *dining arrangements* of his officials,[4] the bearing of his ministers and their apparel, his cup-bearers and their apparel, and *the way* in which he went up *in procession to the*[5] *sanctuary* house of the Lord, there was no spirit *left* in her anymore. 5. She said to the king: "The *report*[6] which I heard in my country about your words and wisdom is true. 6. But I did not believe their[a] reports[7] until I came and saw for myself.[8] Indeed, the half of the greatness of your wisdom was not told me: you have surpassed the report which I had heard. 7. Happy are your men! Happy are these your officials who wait upon[b9] you continually, listening to your wisdom. 8. Blessed be the Lord, your God, who *chose* you *that he might make you king so that you would sit upon the royal throne*[10] to be ruler *before*[11] the Lord, your God. Because[c] your[d] God loved Israel, in order to establish her for ever, he appointed you king over them, to exercise *true* judgment[12] and righteousness." 9. Then she gave the king one hundred and twenty *centenaria*[13] of gold, a very large quantity of spices[e] and *choice jewels.*[2] There were no spices such as those which the queen of *Zemargad*[1] gave to king Solomon. 10. As well as this, the servants of *Hiram*[14] and the servants of Solomon who brought gold from Ophir brought *almug*[f15] wood and choice *jewels.*[16] 11. From the *almug*[15] wood the king made stools,[17] *as a support*

Apparatus, Chapter 9

[a] C, L, AS: "the"; cf. 1 Kgs 10:7 and LXX of 2 Chr 9:6.
[b] V: *qwmk.* C: *qdmk.*
[c] V: *kd.* C: *byd.* L, AS: *bd.*

[d] C, L, AS: "the Lord your God."
[e] C, L, AS use the plural of noun, while V uses the singular. MT also uses the plural form.
[f] V, L, AS: "almug." C: "algum."

Notes, Chapter 9

[3] Lit.: "told her all her words."
[4] MT: "the seating of his servants." A reference to the splendor of the official banquet. *šhrwt',* from Aphel of *šhr,* one of whose meanings MJ (971) gives as "to recline around the table, to dine."
[5] MT: Lit.: "his roof chamber (by) which he went up to . . ." Tg. Chr: lit.: "his going up/procession which he went up to. . . ."
[6] Lit.: "word."
[7] Lit.: "words."
[8] Lit.: "my eyes saw."
[9] Lit.: "stand before."
[10] MT: "who delighted in you to place (lit.: give) you upon his throne."
[11] MT: "for."
[12] Lit.: "judgment of truth."
[13] MT: "talents."
[14] V and C follow Kethibh; Qere = Huram (= L, AS).
[15] MT: "algum," though some Hebrew MSS and 1 Kgs 10:12 have "almug."
[16] MT: "precious stone" (singular). Tg. Chr actually has: "and the jewels were choice. . . ."
[17] Commentators are unsure of the exact meaning of MT's *mslwt* in this context (see R. B. Dillard, 70). Tg. Chr uses a word which can mean "ascent, stool, path, step," but also complicates the issue by bringing in the expression "as a support." "Sockets" is a further possibility, but the value of the socket would depend on the quality of the wood. Le Déaut prefers "ramps."

for the *sanctuary* house of the Lord and for the king's house, and lyres and lutes for the *sons of Levi, who were to offer praise with them.* [18] Their like had not been seen before this in the land of *the house of* Judah. 12. King Solomon gave the queen of *Zemargad*[1] all she desired, [19] whatever she asked *of him,* apart from *what he had given her in exchange for* what she had brought to the king. Then she turned and set off for her own land, with her retinue. [20] 13. The weight of gold which came to Solomon annually[21] was six hundred and sixty-six *centenaria*[13] of gold, 14. not counting the *wages earned by the craftsmen and the tolls brought in by the merchants who*[g] *acted as carriers;*[g22] as well, all the kings of *the auxiliaries*[h23] and the governors of the land *who* brought *tribute of* gold and silver to Solomon. 15. King Solomon made two thousand round shields of *refined*[24] gold *which they spun like thread*: six hundred *selas* of gold[i] were used on[25] each shield, 16. and three hundred small shields of *refined*[24] gold *which they spun like thread*: three hundred *selas* of gold were used on[25] each shield. The king put them in the *summer–house of the kings.*[j26] 17. The king also made a large *ivory*[27] throne and overlaid it with pure gold. 18. The throne had six steps and a golden footrest *going right round* the throne, attached to it. There were arms on each side of *the seat,*[28] with two lions standing beside the arms, 19. and twelve lions standing there, on the six steps on each side. Nothing like it had been made for any of the *kingdoms.*[29] 20. All the

Apparatus, Chapter 9

[g-g] C, L, AS omit. E: "bringing tribute and all the kings of Arabia and the governors of the land bringing gold and silver to Solomon."

[h] C: *systwwt'.*
[i] C, L, AS: "refined gold."
[j] E has: "the house of the forest of Carmela."

Notes, Chapter 9

[18]MT: "for the singers." Tg. Chr ensures that praise is offered by the "correct" people.

[19]Lit.: "all her pleasure."

[20]MT: "she and her servants."

[21]Lit.: "in one year."

[22]Lit.: "the wages of the craftsmen and the commerce of the merchants who were carrying...," which is Tg. Chr's attempt (quite closely paralleled in Tg. 1 Kgs 10:15) to translate MT's: "the men of the traders (explorers?) and the merchants bringing...."

[23]MT: "Arabia." Smolar and Aberbach (96, 97) note that the same substitution made in Tg. 1 Kgs 10:15 may be a reference to the "prominent role played by Arab auxiliaries in the Roman Jewish war"; cf. Tg. Jer 25:20.

[24]MT: "beaten," *šḥwṭ.* Perhaps the following expansion "which they spun like thread" is also based on this word, *š* "which," *ḥwṭ* "thread."

[25]Lit.: "went up upon."

[26]MT: "the house of the forest of Lebanon," so called, no doubt, originally from the material used in its construction or from its appearance. For Tg. Chr (and for Tg. 1 Kgs 7:2; 10:17, 21) this has become "the house of the cooling of kings." Smolar and Aberbach (106f.) think the usage of this term reflects a Hellenistic-Roman background, where such structures had become common in aristocratic circles.

[27]Tg. Chr is very specific. Not just a "throne of ivory," "tooth" as in MT, but a "throne of ivory (tooth) of the elephant." See verse 21.

[28]MT: "the place of sitting." Tg. Chr "the place of the location of the sitting."

[29]MT: "for any kingdoms." Tg. Chr lit.: "for all the kingdoms."

drinking vessels of King Solomon were of gold[k] and all the vessels of the *summer-house of the kings*[126] were of pure[30] gold; there was no silver *in them, for silver* was regarded as of no value in the days of Solomon. 21. For the king had ships *which* sailed to *Africa,*[31] manned by Huram's men.[32] Once every three years the ships would arrive (from) *Africa,*[33] laden with gold and silver, ivory,[34] apes, and peacocks. 22. King Solomon surpassed all the kings of the earth in wealth and wisdom. 23. And all the kings of the earth sought *audience*[35] with Solomon, to hear his wisdom which *the Lord*[36] had put in his heart. 24. Each of them brought his gift *to Solomon,* items[37] of silver and items[37] of gold, *linen*[m] cloaks, *military* weapons, spices, horses and mules—*a fixed amount*[38] year by year. 25. Solomon had four thousand[n] stalls for horses and chariots, as well as twelve thousand horsemen; he stationed them in the chariot cities *apart from those who were*[39] with the king in Jerusalem. 26. He had authority over all the kings from the *Euphrates*[40] to the land of the Philistines and as far as the border of Egypt. 27. The king made silver in Jerusalem as *common as* stones, and cedars he made *as cheap* as the sycamores that were in the Shephelah—there were so many of them.[41] 28. Horses were imported for Solomon from Egypt and from all countries. 29. The rest of the acts of Solomon, from beginning to end[42]—are they not written in the records of Nathan, the prophet, and in the prophecy of Ahijah, *who was from Shiloh,*[43] and in the vision of Iddo, the *prophet,*[44] *who prophesied*[o] concerning Jeroboam, the son of Nebat? 30. Solomon reigned in Jerusalem over all Israel for forty years. 31. And Solomon slept with his fathers, and they buried him in the city of David, his father, and Rehoboam, his son, became king in his place.

Apparatus, Chapter 9

[k] C omits.
[l] L and AS: "king."
[m] E, L, AS: *dkyn*: "clean."

[n] C: "hundred."
[o] V, C, L, AS: plural. E: singular.

Notes, Chapter 9

[30] Lit.: "good." MT: "pure."
[31] MT: "Tarshish." But see 1 Chr 1:7 and 2 Chr 20:36.
[32] Lit.: "with the servants of Huram."
[33] Or "the African ships," as with C, L, AS. For "Africa," MT has "Tarshish."
[34] Lit.: "ivory (tooth) of elephant." Here (contrast verse 17), the word in MT is a different word for "ivory," *šnhbym.*
[35] MT: "the face of." Tg. Chr: "the inclining of the face of."
[36] MT: "God."
[37] Lit.: "vessels."
[38] MT has *dbr,* which in Tg. Chr becomes the more precise *gzyrt.*
[39] See 1:14.
[40] MT: "river."
[41] Cf. 1:15.
[42] Lit.: "the first and the last."
[43] MT: "the Shilonite."
[44] MT: "the seer."

CHAPTER 10

1. Rehoboam went to Shechem, for all Israel had come to Shechem to make him king. 2. When Jeroboam, the son of Nebat, heard—he was *living* in Egypt, where he had fled from before[a] King Solomon—Jeroboam returned from Egypt. 3. They sent and summoned him and Jeroboam, and all Israel came[b] and spoke *with*[1] Rehoboam, saying: 4. "Your father made our yoke hard; but now, *as for you,*[2] ease the hard service of your father and his severe yoke which he laid upon us, and we shall serve you." 5. He said to them: "*Wait for* three days[3] and (then) come back to me." So the people went away. 6. Then King Rehoboam consulted the elders who had stood *and served* before his father Solomon when he was alive, saying: "How do you advise (me) to reply to these people?" 7. And they spoke *with*[1] him, saying: "If you will be good to these people and show yourself well disposed to them, and[c] speak *with* them *right*[4] words,[c] they will be your servants for ever."[5] 8. But he rejected the advice of the elders which they had given him, and he consulted the young men who had grown up with him, who were standing *and serving* before him. 9. He said to them: 'What do you advise that we reply to these people who have spoken to me saying: 'Ease the yoke which your father placed upon us'? 10. The young men who had grown up with him spoke with him as follows: "Thus you will say to the people who have spoken with you, saying: 'Your father made our yoke severe, but you, ease it for us'—thus you will say to them: 'My *weakness* is *more powerful* than *my* father's *strength.*[6] 11. So now—*my* father placed a heavy yoke upon you, but I shall add to your *yokes;*[d7] *my* father chastised you with *rods,*[8] but I (shall chastise you)[e] with *whips.*'"[9] 12. So Jeroboam and all the people came to Rehoboam on the third day, as the king had spoken, saying: "Come back to me on

Apparatus, Chapter 10

[a] C omits.
[b] V, L, AS: plural. C: singular (= MT).
[c-c] C, E, L, AS omit.

[d] V, C: "Yokes." L, AS: "Yoke" (= MT).
[e] The words in brackets are understood by MT and V, but expressed in C, L, AS.

Notes, Chapter 10

[1]MT: "to."
[2]Not in MT, but found in a few Hebrew MSS and Vg and in 1 Kgs 12:4.
[3]Lit.: "Wait up to the time of three days." MT: "Yet three days."
[4]MT: "good."
[5]Lit.: "all the days."
[6]MT: "My little finger is thicker than my father's loins." Tg. Chr "the father" for MT "my father": also in next verse.
[7]MT: singular.
[8]MT: "whips."
[9]MT: "scorpions." Tg. Chr uses an Aramaic noun with a plural form, *mrgnyn,* "whips, scourges," borrowed from the Greek *maragna* (MJ 836; JL II, 66).

the third day." 13. The king *gave them a harsh answer,* [10] and King Rehoboam rejected the advice of the elders. 14. Following the advice of the young men, he spoke to them saying: "*My* [11] father made your *yokes* [d][12] severe, [f][13] but I shall add to it; *my* [11] father chastised you with *rods,* [8] but I (shall chastise you) with *whips.*" [9] 15. Thus the king did not *accept from* [14] the people, for it was an occurrence from *before the Lord,* [15] so that the Lord could establish his Word which he had spoken through Ahijah, *who was from Shiloh,* [16] *concerning* [17] Jeroboam, the son of Nebat. 16. When all Israel *saw* [18] that the king had not *accepted from* [19] them, the people replied to the king, saying: "What share do we have in David? *And* (what) inheritance [20] in the son of Jesse? Each of you to your *towns,* [21] O Israel! Now *rule over the men of* [22] your house, O David!" So all Israel went off to *their towns.* [21] 17. As for the children of Israel who were living [g] in the towns of *the house of* [h] Judah, Rehoboam ruled over them. 18. When King Rehoboam sent Hadoram, who had been *put* in charge of *those who were bringing tribute,* [23] the children of Israel hurled *stones* [24] at him, and he died. King Rehoboam, however, took urgent steps to climb up into a chariot, to flee to Jerusalem. 19. So *the house of* Israel has been in rebellion against the house of David up to this *very* day.

Apparatus, Chapter 10

[f] V: *tqyp.* C, L, AS: *yyqr.*
[g] V, C: "who living." E, L, AS: "who were living."

[h] V: "the towns of the house of." E, C, L, AS: "the towns of."

Notes, Chapter 10

[10]Lit.: "and the king returned harsh words" for MT: "and the king answered them harshly."

[11]MT: "my father." Tg. Chr: "the father."

[12]MT: singular.

[13]MT has "I shall make your yoke severe," but many Hebrew MSS and 1 Kgs 12:14 have "My father made. . . ."

[14]MT: "hear to," "listen to."

[15]MT: "from with God."

[16]MT: "the Shilonite."

[17]MT: "to."

[18]Lacking in MT, but present in many Hebrew MSS and the Versions and 1 Kgs 12:16.

[19]MT: "heard to," "listened to."

[20]MT: "and there is no inheritance."

[21]MT: "tents."

[22]MT: "see."

[23]MT: "the corvée." Smolar and Aberbach (100) note that though the corvée system still existed in Roman times, "it was not nearly as important or pervasive as the numerous monetary impositions and taxes which burdened the provinces of the Roman empire, all too often beyond their capacity." Hence the translation in Tg. 1 Kgs 12:18 and in Tg. Chr.

[24]MT: singular.

CHAPTER 11

1. Rehoboam arrived in Jerusalem and assembled the house of Judah and Benjamin, one hundred and eighty thousand *men, every one*[a] *of them* fighting men,[1] *in order to draw up battle lines*[2] with *the house of* Israel to restore the kingdom to Rehoboam. 2. Then a word of *prophecy from before* the Lord was *with*[3] Shemaiah, *the prophet of the Lord,*[4] saying: 3. "Say to Rehoboam, the son of Solomon, king of *the tribe of the house of* Judah, and *with*[5] all *the house of* Israel *who are* in Judah and Benjamin, saying: 4. 'Thus has the Lord said: "Do not go up and do not *make war*[6] with your brethren, *the children of Israel*; return, every one to his house, for this matter has come about *from before the Lord.""*[7] They *accepted*[8] the words of the Lord and turned back from marching against Jeroboam. 5. Rehoboam lived in Jerusalem and he built *fortified* towns[9] in *the land of the tribe of the house of* Judah. 6.[b] He built Bethlehem, Etam, Tekoa, 7. Bethzur, Soco, Adullam, 8. Gath, Mareshah, Ziph, 9. *Adoram,*[c][10] Lachish, Azeqah, 10. Zorah, Aijalon, and Hebron, which were in *the tribe of* Judah and in *the tribe of* Benjamin, as fortified towns. 11. He *repaired*[d] *the fortified towns*[11] and placed in them commanders and depots *full* of food, oil, and wine. 12. And in every one of the towns *he put* round shields and spears and made them exceedingly strong. Thus *the tribe of* Judah and *the tribe*[e] *of* Benjamin were his. 13. The priests and the Levites *who were* in all Israel made preparations to come to him from all their areas. 14. For the Levites left their common lands and their inheritances and went off to *the tribe of* Judah and to Jerusalem, because Jeroboam and his sons had *hindered* them *and had not allowed them to offer service before* the Lord.[12] 15. He had appointed his own "*priests*"[13]

Apparatus, Chapter 11

[a] V, C: *gbr gbr.* L, AS: *gbr gybr* ("mighty men").
[b] Verses 7-9 are missing in E.
[c] V: "Adoram." C, L, AS: "Adoraim" (= MT).

[d] C, L, AS add: "and strengthened," which is the verb used in MT.
[e] C omits "the tribe of."

Notes, Chapter 11

[1] MT: "chosen, maker(s) of war," becomes in Tg. Chr, literally: "men, every one makers of war."
[2] MT: "in order to fight."
[3] MT: "The word of the Lord was to."
[4] MT: "the man of God."
[5] MT: "to."
[6] MT: "fight."
[7] MT: "from with me."
[8] MT: "heard."
[9] MT: Lit.: "towns for siege."
[10] MT: "Adoraim."
[11] MT: "He strengthened the fortresses."
[12] MT: "had rejected them from acting as priests to the Lord."
[13] In the Old Testament *kmr* is used only for idol priests, though not all idol priests are given that title: *khn* is also used, e.g., in MT 2 Chr 34:5. Normally, however, when idol priests are referred to in Tg. Chr the word *kwmr'* is used and here translated "*priest.*" See, e.g., 13:9; 15:3; 23:17; 34:5. See Smolar and Aberbach, 36–38.

for the high places and for the demons and for the calves which he had made. 16. After them, those from *every tribe*[f][14] of Israel, who set their heart to seek *instruction from before* the Lord, the God of Israel, came to Jerusalem, to offer sacrifice *before*[5] the Lord, the God of their fathers. 17. They strengthened the kingdom of *the house of* Judah, and they gave support to Rehoboam, the son of Solomon, for three years, for they walked in the way of David and Solomon for three years. 18. Rehoboam took as his wife Mahalath, the *daughter*[15] of *Jeremoth,*[16] the son of David, *and*[17] *Abihail,*[18] the daughter of Eliab, the son of Jesse. 19. She bore him sons: Jeush, Shemariah, and Zaham. 20. After her he took Maacah, the daughter of Absalom, and she bore him Abijah, Attai, Ziza, and Shelomith. 21. Rehoboam loved Maacah, the daughter of Absalom, more than all his wives and concubines, for he had taken eighteen wives and sixty concubines, and he became the father of twenty-eight sons and sixty daughters. 22. Rehoboam appointed Abijah, the son of Maacah, as head, to be ruler *over*[19] his brothers, for *he intended to give him the kingship.*[20] 23. He *built*[21] and *repaired towns* and *put*[22] some of his sons *in charge of* all the districts of *the house of* Judah and Benjamin,[g] in all the fortified cities, and he gave them food in abundance and sought *to take* a multitude of wives.[23]

Apparatus, Chapter 11

[f] V: "every tribe." C, L, AS: "all the tribes" (= MT).   [g] C, L, AS omit "and Benjamin."

Notes, Chapter 11

[14]MT: "from all the tribes."
[15]Following Qere. Kethibh is "son."
[16]MT: "Jerimoth."
[17]Though "and" is missing in MT, most English Versions supply it, "the daughter of Jerimoth ... *and* of Abihail," thus making Abihail the mother of Mahalath. Tg. Chr inserts "and," but as well he inserts the object marker before "Abihail," thus making Abihail the second wife of Rehoboam, which raises a question as to the identity of "she" in verse 19 and the "her" in verse 20.
[18]MT: "Abihail" (*h*); Tg. Chr: "Abihail" (*ḥ*).
[19]MT: "*b*," which could be "over" or "among," though in the final analysis there is no difference in the outcome!
[20]MT: "for (*ki*) to make him king," as though some such verb as "to intend" had fallen out.
[21]MT: "and he acted wisely." *wybn*, from *byn*, "to understand, show discretion." Tg. Chr interpreted these consonants as from *bnh*, "to build": "and he built."
[22]MT: "and he distributed some of his sons to all the districts." The verb is *prṣ*, "to break through," but *BDB* suggests "distribute" as a meaning in this verse, "but dubious" (829).
[23]One assumes "for his sons," not for himself. Rudolph in *BHS* suggests "and he took for them wives."

CHAPTER 12

1. Now when the kingdom of Rehoboam *was established*[1] and he had become strong, he, and all Israel with him, forsook the law of the Lord. 2. In King Rehoboam's fifth year, because they had been unfaithful to *the Memra of* the Lord, *Sheshak,*[2] king of Egypt, came up against Jerusalem, 3. with twelve hundred chariots and sixty thousand horsemen, and it was impossible to count[3] the people who came with him from Egypt, Libyans, Sukkites, and Cushites. 4. He captured the fortified cities which *belonged* to Judah, and came[a] to Jerusalem. 5. Then Shemaiah, the prophet, came to Rehoboam and the commanders of Judah who had assembled in Jerusalem because of *Sheshak,*[2] and he said to them: "Thus has the Lord said: 'You have abandoned *my fear,*[4] I too *shall abandon*[5] you in to the hand of *Sheshak.*'"[2] 6. The commanders of Israel and the king humbled themselves and said: "The Lord is in the right." 7. *When it was revealed before the Lord*[6] that they had humbled themselves, a word *of prophecy* from *before* the Lord was *with* Shemaiah,[7] saying: "*My people*[8] have humbled themselves: I shall not destroy them, but I shall give them deliverance in a little while, and my anger will not *be a threat to*[9] Jerusalem by the hand of *Sheshak.*[2] 8. But they will become his slaves, *and*[10] they will know[11] (the difference between) my service[12] and the servitude of the kingdoms[b] of the countries." 9. Then *Sheshak,*[2] the king of Egypt, went up against Jerusalem. He carried off the treasures of the *sanctuary* house of the Lord along with the treasures of the king's house; he took all *the most desirable things*; he even carried off the golden shields which Solomon had made. 10. In their place King Rehoboam made round shields of bronze, which he committed to the care[13] of the officers in charge of the runners who were guarding the gate of the king's

Apparatus, Chapter 12

[a] C: "they came."

[b] L and AS: singular.

Notes, Chapter 12

[1] MT: "When Rehoboam had established his kingship." Tg. Chr presupposes *khkwn* for the *khkyn* of MT.
[2] MT: "Shishak."
[3] Lit.: "and there was no number to...."
[4] MT: "me."
[5] MT: "I have abandoned."
[6] MT: "When the Lord saw."
[7] MT: "The word of the Lord was with Shemaiah."
[8] MT: "They."
[9] MT: "will not be poured out upon."
[10] MT: "that."
[11] Reading *wyd'wn* (Imperfect) with C.
[12] MT uses *'bwdh* "service" twice. Tg. Chr, by using *pwlḥn,* "service" or "worship," for the first occurrence of the word and *šy'bwd,* "servitude," for the second, brings out more strongly the contrast between the service requested by the Lord and the servitude imposed by other regimes.
[13] MT: "hand."

house. 11. Whenever the king went in to the *sanctuary* house of the Lord, the runners would come in carrying them and then returning them to the hall of the runners. 12. When *he broke his heart,*[14] the anger of the Lord turned away from him, and *he did* not *resolve* to destroy and *to exterminate all the people.*[15] Indeed, to *those of the house of* Judah *he decided to bring* good fortune.[16] 13. So King Rehoboam established his authority in Jerusalem and reigned. For he was forty-one years old when he became king, and he reigned for seventeen years in Jerusalem, the city which the Lord had chosen out of all the tribes of Israel in which to *cause his Shekinah to dwell;*[17] and his mother's name was Naamah, the Ammonitess. 14. He did *what was* evil, for he did not set his heart to seek *instruction from before* the Lord. 15. The acts of Rehoboam, from beginning to end,[18] are they not written in the records of Shemaiah, the prophet, and Iddo, the *prophet,*[19] *in the book of the genealogy of the house of David,*[20] as are also the continual[21] battles *which took place between*[22] Rehoboam and Jeroboam? 16. And Rehoboam slept with his fathers, and he was buried in the city of David, and Abijah, his son, became king in his place.

CHAPTER 13

1. In the eighteenth year[a] of King Jeroboam, Abijah became king over *those of*[b] *the house of* Judah; 2. and he was king in Jerusalem for three years. His mother's name was Micaiah, the daughter of Uriel from *Gibeatha.*[1] *She was Maacah,*[c] the

Notes, Chapter 12

[14]MT: "When he humbled himself."

[15]MT: "so as not to destroy to extermination."

[16]MT's statement is rather ambiguous: "and also in Judah were good things." It seems to imply that in spite of Rehoboam's unfaithfulness and in spite of the devastation brought by invasion, there was still something worth while left in Judah. Tg. Chr makes it slightly less ambiguous by promising blessings ("good things") from the Lord.

[17]MT: "to place his name there."

[18]Lit.: "the first and the last."

[19]MT: "the seer."

[20]MT: "to enroll oneself by genealogy." Commentators are not sure what to do with this word. Williamson (249) thinks: "it could preserve an indication of a further source referred to by the Chronicler. . . ." Tg. Chr tells us exactly which source is being referred to.

[21]Lit.: "all the days."

[22]MT: "of."

Apparatus, Chapter 13

[a] V has an additional word, *šnyn,* "years."   [c] C: Micah.

[b] C omits "those of."

Notes, Chapter 13

[1]MT: "Gibeah."

daughter of *Absalom, but because she was a worthy woman her name was changed to the more excellent one of Micaiah. Her father's name was changed to Uriel who was from Gibeatha, so as not to recall the name of Absalom.*[2] Now there was war between Abijah and Jeroboam. 3. Abijah *harnessed*[3] *his chariot* and drew up battle *lines* with an army, mighty men *making* war,[4] four hundred thousand *young*[5] men, while Jeroboam drew up battle *lines* against him, with eight hundred thousand[5] men who were warriors. 4. Then Abijah stood up on the top of Mount Zemaraim, which is in the mountain *of the tribe of the house* of Ephraim, and he said: "*Accept from me,*[6] O Jeroboam, and all *the house of* Israel. 5. You should surely know that the Lord, the God of Israel, gave the kingship to David, *and he gave authority* over Israel *to him* for ever—to him and his sons—by a covenant of salt. *Just as it is impossible that the waters of the sea could ever be sweetened, so it is impossible that authority should ever pass from those of the house of David.*[7] 6. Yet Jeroboam, the son of Nebat, the servant of Solomon, son of David, rose up and rebelled against his master. 7. And worthless men, sons of *wickedness,*[8] rallied to him and set themselves up against Rehoboam, the son of Solomon, when Rehoboam was young and soft-hearted,[d] and he was unable to stand up to them.[9] 8. And now, you are proposing to challenge the kingship[10] *which, from before* the Lord, *was given* into the hand of the sons of David, and you are a multitude *of numerous peoples,*[11] and with

Apparatus, Chapter 13

[d] V has *rkyn,* "tender, soft," where C, L, AS have *rkyk,* "tender, soft, young."

Notes, Chapter 13

[2] In MT 2 Chr 12:16 and 13:2, Abijah is the son of Rehoboam, and Micaiah, the daughter of Uriel. In MT 1 Kgs 15:2 (and 2 Chr 11:20), Maacah is the daughter of Absalom. Tg. Chr suggests that the original names were Maacah and Absalom but that these names were changed to Micaiah and Uriel, and goes on to give reasons for these changes:

i) Maacah was an excellent lady, deserving of a better name, and what better name could be found than a name which has as its final component the divine Name, but which also glorifies God in its meaning: "Who is like Yah?" Tg. 2 Chr 15:16 seems to suggest that after the unfortunate incident of idol worship in which she, Maacah, was involved, when she repented of this, the name change took place.

ii) Absalom, David's rebellious son, is also given a new name, partly, Tg. Chr suggests, to get rid of a name which had such unfortunate associations; this name too has a divine component: Uriel—"El (God) is my light"—an important name in that this was the name of one of the four angels guarding the heavenly throne (*PRE* 4) who was also involved in the burial of Moses (Tg. Ps.-J. Deut 34:5).

[3] Tg. Chr uses the verb *tqs,* "to arrange, prepare (battle), harness" borrowed from the Greek *tassō* (JL I, 317); MJ 549 sees some influence from the Greek.

[4] MT: "mighty men of war."

[5] MT uses *bḥwr,* "chosen," a word often used to describe healthy young men. Tg. Chr chooses this meaning here, though he uses a different word, *'wlm':* "strong, young (men)." The second occurrence of the word in this verse in MT, Tg. Chr ignores: "eight hundred thousand (chosen or young) men, warriors."

[6] MT: "hear me."

[7] An appropriate expansion to follow a reference to "salt."

[8] MT: "Belial."

[9] Lit.: "and he did not strengthen himself before them."

[10] Lit.: "saying to strengthen yourselves before the kingship."

[11] MT: "a great multitude."

you are the golden calves which Jeroboam, *the son of Nebat,* made as *objects of worship*[e][12] for you. 9. But have you not driven out the priests of the Lord, the sons of Aaron, and the Levites, and made for yourselves "priests"[f][13] just like the peoples of the lands? Everyone who comes *to present his offering*[14] with a young bull and seven rams becomes a priest—*but not by the Memra of the Lord.*[15] 10. As for us, *the Memra of* the Lord is *in support of us, and he is* our God.[16] We have not abandoned *his fear,*[17] and the priests who serve *before*[18] the Lord are the sons of Aaron, and the Levites are occupied with their own duties.[19] 11. They offer *sweet-smelling incense before* the Lord,[20] whole burnt offerings every morning and evening; sweet-smelling incense, arranging the bread on a clean table, the golden lampstand whose lamps they have to light every evening. For we keep the charge of *the Memra of* the Lord, our God, but you have forsaken *his fear.*[17] 12. So take note![21] With us, at the head, is *the Lord,*[22] and his priests with alarm trumpets to sound a battle cry against you. O children of Israel, do not fight *before*[23] the Lord, the God of your fathers, for you will not succeed." 13. Now Jeroboam had sent an ambush party round, which was to come (at them) from their rear; thus they were facing *those of the house of* Judah, while the ambush party was behind them.[24] 14. When *those of the house of* Judah *looked around them,*[25] to their amazement they were being attacked[26] from both front and rear. They cried *before*[18] the Lord for help, while the priests sounded the trumpets. 15. Then the men of Judah raised the battle cry. When the men of Judah raised the battle cry, *the Memra of the Lord* shattered Jeroboam and all Israel before Abijah and *the house of* Judah. 16. The children of

Apparatus, Chapter 13

[e] C adds "God."

[f] E: *khny.* V, C, L, AS: *kwmryn.*

Notes, Chapter 13

[12]MT: "gods." Tg. Chr: Lit.: "fears," a word often used to describe gods. See 2:4, note 5.

[13]"idol priests"; see note at 11:15.

[14]MT: "to fill his hand," an expression usually regarded as meaning "to consecrate himself"; see 1 Chr 29:5; 2 Chr 29:31.

[15]Lit.: "apart from." MT: "a priest to no-gods."

[16]MT: "the Lord (is) our God."

[17]MT: "him."

[18]MT: "to."

[19]Lit.: "with work/service."

[20]MT has "they offer up to the lord whole burnt offerings. . . ." For "offer up" the verb *qṭr* is used and, normally when Tg. Chr sees this verb, he inserts a specific "incense" object—which makes the second reference to incense a few words later seem a little out of place.

[21]Bringing out the force of the "behold" (*h'*).

[22]MT: "God."

[23]MT: "with."

[24]Lit.: "from behind them."

[25]MT: "turned round."

[26]Lit.: "to them the battle."

Israel fled from before *those of the house of* Judah and the Lord *delivered*[27] them into their *hands.*[28] 17. And Abijah and his people inflicted on them heavy casualties.[29] From *those of the house of* Israel there fell, killed *by the sword,* five hundred thousand *young* men.[30] 18. So at that time the children of Israel were *defeated,*[31] while the children of Judah gained the upper hand because they had relied on *the Memra of* the Lord, the God of their fathers. 19. Abijah pursued Jeroboam and took towns from him: Bethel and its villages,[32] Jeshanah and its villages,[32] and Ephron[33] and its villages.[32] 20. Jeroboam did not regain power[34] during the days of Abijah. And the Lord *shattered* him,[35] and he died. 21. Abijah, however, grew stronger. He took for himself fourteen wives and became the father of twenty-two sons and sixteen daughters. 22. Now the rest of the acts of Abijah, both his ways and his words, are written in the Midrash of the prophet Iddo. 23. So Abijah slept with his fathers, and they buried him in the city of David, and Asa, his son, became king in his place. In his days the land *of Israel* had peace for ten years.

CHAPTER 14

1. Asa did *what was* good and *what was* proper[1] *before*[2] the Lord, his[a] God. 2. He did away with the *"altars"*[3] of *foreign peoples*[4] and the high places; he

Notes, Chapter 13

[27]MT: "gave."
[28]MT: "hand."
[29]Lit.: "struck them down a great striking."
[30]See note 5. In verse 17 the words for "young" and "men" are in the singular.
[31]MT: "humbled."
[32]MT: "daughters," i.e., dependent villages.
[33]Tg. Chr follows Kethibh.
[34]Lit.: "There was no power in Jeroboam again."
[35]MT: "struck him."

Apparatus, Chapter 14

[a] C: "God" (*'lhym*).

Notes, Chapter 14

[1]MT: "right."
[2]MT: "in the eyes of."
[3]In MT the word *mzbḥ* means "altar," be it an altar to the Lord or a heathen altar. Tg. Chr uses the Aramaic form of the word, *mdbḥʾ*, to refer to an altar to the Lord, while a heathen altar is *'gwr*, "a pile of stones," perhaps acquiring its name from Hos 12:12: "their altars also shall be like stone heaps." In this translation they will be in inverted commas: "altars." (See Smolar and Aberbach, 38–41, and JL I, 9.)
[4]MT: "of the foreigner."

smashed the standing stones[5] and cut down the Asherahs. 3. He told *those of the house of* Judah to seek *the fear of* the Lord, the God of their fathers, and to observe the law and the commandment. 4. He removed the high places and the *solar statues*[6] from all the towns of Judah, and the kingdom had peace under him. 5. He built fortified towns in Judah, for the land *of Israel* was at peace, and there was no one at war with him[7] during these years, for the Lord had given[b] him rest. 6. He had said to *those of the house of*[c] Judah: "Let us build these towns and put[8] walls around them, with towers, gates and bars, while the *inhabitants of the* land *are subdued* before us,[9] for we have sought *the fear of* the Lord, our God, we have sought *instruction from before him,* and he has given us rest on all sides." So they built successfully.[10] 7. Asa had an army made up of three hundred thousand from *those of the house of* Judah, carrying round shields and spears, and two hundred and eighty thousand from *those of the house of* Benjamin, carrying small shields and drawing bows. All these were mighty warriors. 8. Zera, the Cushite, came out against them with an army of a million[11] men and three hundred chariots, and he got as far as Mareshah. 9. Asa went out to confront him,[12] and they drew up battle lines in the valley of *Zephath,*[13] *which is* at Mareshah. 10. Asa *prayed before*[14] the Lord, his God, and said: "O Lord *God, apart from* you[15] there is no one to help the weak against the strong.[16] Help us, O Lord, our God, for we rely upon *your Memra,*[17] and it is *in the Name of your Memra*[18] that we have come against this horde *of people.* O Lord, you are our God, let no *son of* man have authority over you!" 11. Then the Lord defeated the Cushites before Asa and before *the house of* Judah, and the Cushites fled. 12. Asa and the people who were with him pursued them as far as Gerar, and so many of the Cushites fell that there was no possibility of their survival,[19] for they had been shattered before the Lord and before his

Apparatus, Chapter 14

[b] E: *šbq:* "had forgiven."

[c] C omits: "those of the house of."

Notes, Chapter 14

[5]MT: "The Massebahs," the pillars.
[6]MT: "incense altars." MJ (483) sees these as obscene statues devoted to the sun. Usual translation for *ḥmnym.*
[7]Lit.: "there was not with him war."
[8]Reading *nqyp* with C. V has first person singular.
[9]MT: "while the land is before us."
[10]Lit.: "They built and they succeeded."
[11]A thousand thousand.
[12]Lit.: "before him."
[13]MT: "Zephathah."
[14]MT: "called to."
[15]MT: "with you."
[16]Lit.: "to help between the strong and the weak." This could also mean that only God can help both the weak and the strong, i.e., that both strong and weak require his help.
[17]MT: "you."
[18]MT: "in your Name."
[19]Lit.: "that there was for them no deliverance that they should be preserved," which is Tg. Chr's translation of MT: "that there was not to them preservation of life."

army. They also took a huge quantity of booty. 13. And they *killed*[20] all *the inhabitants of* the towns around Gerar, for *fear*[d] *from before* the Lord[21] was upon them. They looted all the towns, for there was a large amount of plunder in them. 14. They also attacked *those who had herds,*[22] and they carried off many sheep and camels. Then they returned to Jerusalem.

CHAPTER 15

1. The spirit *of prophecy from before the Lord rested*[1] upon Azariah, the son of Oded. 2. He went out to meet[2] Asa and said to him:[a] *"Accept from me,*[3] Asa, and all Judah and Benjamin. *The Memra of* the Lord is *in support of you* so long as you *walk in his ways;*[4] if you seek *instruction from before* him, he will let himself be found by you *at the time of your distresses;* but if you abandon *his fear,*[5] he will abandon you. 3. It is a long time *since those of the house of* Israel *separated*[b] *from those of the house of Judah; they mistakenly followed Jeroboam; they did not worship* the true God *but bowed down to golden calves;*[6] they had no priest to teach *righteousness: instead, they had 'priests'*[7] *who offered up incense for the foreign cult but*

Apparatus, Chapter 14

[d] C: *phd' dyy* (= MT).

Notes, Chapter 14

[20]MT: "struck down."
[21]MT: "the dread of the Lord."
[22]Lit.: "the tents of their herds," which translates MT's "tents of cattle"—perhaps the tents of those who had cattle. J. M. Myers (II, 83) refers to the cognate word for "tent" in Arabic, which can also refer to the people (who live in the tents). Thus "possessors of cattle." Hence the translation above.

Apparatus, Chapter 15

[a] C omits "to him."

[b] The strange reading in C, *l' ytplgwn*, Le Déaut regards as arising from confusion in word division.

Notes, Chapter 15

[1]MT: "The Spirit of God was upon."
[2]Lit.: "before."
[3]MT: "hear me."
[4]MT: "The Lord is with you when you are with him."
[5]MT: "him."
[6]MT: "For a long time Israel was without the true God."
[7]I.e., idolatrous priests. See 11:15 and note 13.

did not concern themselves with the Law.[8] 4. But *when* in their distress they returned to *the worship of* the Lord, the God of Israel, and sought *instruction from before* him, he let himself be found by them. 5. *Because* in those times there was no peace for him who went out *into the country* or for him who came in *to the town*, for many were the disturbances[9] which affected[10] all the inhabitants of the lands. 6. They *formed factions,*[11] people *against* people, and town *against* town, for *the Memra of the Lord*[12] had thrown them into confusion with every kind of distress. 7. And as for you *who belong to the house of Judah:* Be strong; don't let your strength flag,[13] for *you* will receive a good reward for your work." 8. When Asa heard these words and the words of the prophecy *of* Oded the prophet, he took courage and removed [*v.l. he completely did away with*][c] the detestable idols from all the land of *the house of* Judah and Benjamin, and from the towns which he had captured from the hill country of *the house of* Ephraim, and he restored the altar of the Lord which was before the vestibule of the Lord. 9. Then he assembled all *the men of* Judah and Benjamin and the members of *the house of* Ephraim and of *the house of* Manasseh and of *the house of* Simeon who were living with them, for large numbers *of those who belonged to the house of* Israel had *settled with him*[d][14] when they saw that *the Memra of* the Lord, his God, was *in support of him.*[15] 10. They assembled *at* Jerusalem in the third month of the fifteenth year of the reign of Asa, 11. and on that day, *at the Feast of Weeks,*[16] they sacrificed *before*[17] the Lord some of the plunder *which* they had brought—seven hundred oxen and seven thousand sheep. 12. And they entered the covenant to seek *the fear of* the Lord, the God of their fathers, with all their *will*[18] and with all their soul. 13. And anyone who would not seek *from before* the Lord, the God of Israel, was to be *killed,*[19] both small and great, both man and woman. 14. They took an oath *before*[17] the Lord

Apparatus, Chapter 15

[c] Only in V.

[d] V: "his people." C: "with him." The translation above follows the latter.

Notes, Chapter 15

[8] MT: "no priest giving instruction, no law." Commentators differ as to whether these verses in MT refer to past or future. Some think of them as describing the period of the Judges. Tg. Chr regards them as a description of the Northern Kingdom and adapts them accordingly.

[9] Reading plural with Le Déaut, following the number of the related adjective.

[10] Lit.: "were upon."

[11] Reading *sy't'* (plural. C has singular), "bands," "factions"; V vocalizes as "help." MT has "they were crushed, people by people. . . ."

[12] MT: "God."

[13] Lit.: "Don't let your hands flop/be weakened."

[14] MT: "for large numbers from Israel had defected to him."

[15] MT: "that the Lord, his God, was with him."

[16] Le Déaut notes that this return to the covenant and the Law took place at the Feast of Pentecost and that at Qumran the Feast of Weeks was always celebrated on the fifteenth day of the third month.

[17] MT: "to."

[18] MT: "heart."

[19] MT: "put to death."

with a loud voice, with a ringing cry, with trumpets and rams' horns. 15. All *the men of* Judah rejoiced because of the oath, for they had taken it wholeheartedly, and with all their will they had sought *his fear.*[20] And he let himself be found by them, and the Lord gave them rest all around. 16. Even Maacah, the mother[e] of King Asa, he deposed from *being queen,*[21] because she had made *idols, so that she could indulge in obscene practices before the Asherahs.*[22] Asa cut down the *obscene idols,*[23] crushed them, burnt them *and cast them* into the Wady *of* Kidron. *Later,[f] when Maacah, his mother, had become upright again, he restored her name Micaiah, the daughter of Uriel, who was from Gibeatha, so that she would not remember her former name, and that he would not be disgraced by it.[f]*[24] 17. The high places however, did not cease entirely from *those of the house of* Israel. Even so, the heart of Asa was perfect all his days. 18. And he brought his father's holy things[25] and his own holy things[25] to the *sanctuary* house of *the Lord*[12]—silver and gold and vessels. 19. There was no *war*[26] until the thirty-fifth year of Asa's reign.

CHAPTER 16

1. In the thirty-sixth year of Asa's reign, *Baasa,*[a1] king of Israel, went up against *those of the house of* Judah. He built *Ramatha,*[2] to prevent anyone from going[3] out

Apparatus, Chapter 15

[e] E: "father."

[ff] Found in C under the heading: "Another reading."

Notes, Chapter 15

[20]MT: "him."
[21]MT: "lady," "queen mother."
[22]MT: "because she had made an abominable cult image for the Asherah."
[23]MT: "the abominable cult image."
[24]See 13:2, note 2.
[25]"Objects" or "offerings" no doubt are implied.
[26]Tg. Chr has : "ranks of war" or "battle lines" for MT's "war."

Apparatus, Chapter 16

[a] C: "Baasha" (= MT).

Notes, Chapter 16

[1]MT: "Baasha," but a few Hebrew MSS have "Baasa."
[2]MT: "Ramah." Lit.: "the Ramah," "the high place."
[3]Lit.: "so as not to allow (MT: give) one going out ..."

or coming in to Asa, king of *the tribe of the house of* Judah. 2. Asa brought out silver and gold from the treasuries of the *sanctuary* house of the Lord and *from* the king's house, and he sent to Bar[4]-Hadad, king of Aram, who was living in Damascus, with this message: 3. "There is a covenant between *me and you,*[5] and between my father and your father. Now look! I have sent you silver and gold. Go! Change[6] your covenant *which you have* with *Baasa,*[1] king of Israel, so that he may withdraw from me." 4. *Bar*[4]-Hadad *accepted from*[7] King Asa and sent the commanders of his armies to the towns of Israel; they struck down Ijon, Dan, Abel *from the West,*[8] and all the supply depots *which were in* the towns of Naphtali. 5. When *Baasa*[1] heard (this), he stopped building *Ramatha*[2] and suspended[9] his work. 6. Then King Asa brought all *the men of* Judah and they carried away the stones of *Ramatha*[2] and its timber, which *Baasa*[1] had used for building and with them he built *Gebishta*[b][10] and *Sacutha.*[11] 7. At that time the *prophet*[12] Hanani came to Asa, king of *the tribe of the house of* Judah, and said to him: "Since you have relied on the king of Aram and have not relied on *the Memra of* the Lord, your[c] God— because of this, the army of the king of Aram has escaped out of your hand. 8. Were not the Cushites and the Libyans a great army, with an enormous number[d] of chariots and horsemen, but because you relied on *the Memra of* the Lord, he delivered them into your hand? 9. For the eyes of the Lord survey the whole earth, to give his support to *the righteous,* whose heart is committed to him.[13] You have

Apparatus, Chapter 16

[b] E, C, L, AS: *gb't'* (= Tg. 1 Kgs 15:22), but C has an alternative reading: *gbyšt'* (= V).

[c] C, L, AS omit. They have *'lhym.*

[d] "an enormous number" in Tg. Chr is, literally, "very many." E, C, L, AS omit "very."

Notes, Chapter 16

[4]"Bar," to correspond to MT's "Ben," "son of."

[5]Lit.: "between my Memra and between your Memra." "Memra" is here doing duty for the personal pronoun.

[6]Hebrew uses a stronger word, *prr,* "to annul, break." The Targums seem to prefer the verb *šny,* "to change," e.g., Gen 17:14; Judg 2:1; Jer 14:21. M. Aberbach and B. Grossfeld (*Targum Onkelos to Genesis,* Denver, 1982, 103 n. 9) suggest that for a man to be capable of breaking or annulling a divine covenant "may have seemed derogatory to God's majesty." "Hence the use of the verb *šny,* in the Af'el form, to reduce the dimensions of the breach to a mere 'change' or 'alteration.'" In our verse, however, the covenant is between people: one may assume, then, that "change" became the standard translation for "break" with reference to all covenants. Of course, there is little difference between "changing" and "annulling" a covenant.

[7]MT: "listened to."

[8]MT: "Abel-Mayim." The Hebrew for the second word is *mym,* which could also have been understood as "from the sea" (*m ym*), i.e., "from the West." In 1 Kgs 15:20 and 2 Kgs 15:29, it is "Abel-beth-Maacah." Perhaps "Maacah" (*m'kh*) and "West" (*m'rb*) have become confused.

[9]Reading *baṭṭil* for *beṭil,* Pael for Peal.

[10]MT: "Geba."

[11]MT: *mṣph.* The meaning of the Hebrew word: "outlook point, watchtower" is reproduced in the Aramaic word *skwt.* The same change takes place in Tg. Gen 31:49.

[12]MT: "seer."

[13]Lit.: "perfect with him" (MT: "to him").

acted foolishly [*v.l. you have acted stupidly*]*ᵉ* in this matter, for from now on you will have wars to contend with." [14] 10. Asa was angry with the *prophet*[12] and put him in *prison,*[15] for *he was annoyed*[16] with him over this matter. At that time Asa also reduced some of the people to slavery.[17] 11. As for the acts of Asa, from beginning to end,[18] you will find they are written in the book of the kings of *the house of* Judah and of *the house of* Israel. 12. Asa became ill in the thirty-ninth year of his reign. He *went lame* in his feet, and his illness *became* very serious. But even when he was ill he did not seek *instruction from before* the Lord but (resorted to) physicians.[19] 13. So Asa slept with his fathers; he died in the forty-first year of his reign. 14. They buried him in his tomb which he had *made ready*[20] for himself in the city of David. They laid him on a couch which was full of spices and *all kinds of*[21] sweet-smelling aromas, *ointments* produced by[22] *the physicians.*[23] Then they burned for[24] him a huge fire *of sweet-smelling wood.*

CHAPTER 17

1. After him Jehoshaphat, his son, became king, and he strengthened himself against *those of the house of* Israel. 2. He stationed *forces*[1] in all the fortified cities of Judah and placed garrisons[2] in the territory of *the tribe of the house of* Judah

Apparatus, Chapter 16

ᵉ In E, C, L, AS, the variant reading in V has become the text.

Notes, Chapter 16

[14]Lit.: "there are with you lines of battles" (MT does not have "lines of").
[15]MT: "in the house of the stocks."
[16]Tg. Chr simplifies the rather clumsy "with anger" of MT.
[17]MT: "he grievously oppressed." Tg. Chr gives a very good appreciation of the verb.
[18]MT: "the first and the last."
[19]At first sight this word looks like "cures," but MJ (93) and JL (I, 47) give *'swwt'* also as a plural for *'sy',* "physician"; cf. the more normal form in verse 14.
[20]MT: "dug."
[21]Taking this phrase with "sweet-smelling aromas," in spite of the *Waw* "and" between them.
[22]Lit.: "the work of."
[23]MT: "the ointment mixers." The Hebrew of the second half of this sentence is difficult. With the help of *BDB*'s suggestions (955), it reads (literally) as follows: "... full of spices and (various) sorts mixed as ointment in an ointment mixture, the work of an ointment mixer."
[24]In the sense: "in honor of."

Notes, Chapter 17

[1]MT: "an army."
[2]Or "army commanders." The Hebrew word *nsyb* can have both meanings, as can the loan word here used to translate it. See 1 Chr 11:16, note 31.

and in the towns of Ephraim which Asa his father had conquered. 3. *In support of* Jehoshaphat was *the Memra of* the Lord,[3] for he walked in the earlier ways of David, his father, and did not seek *instruction from the idols.*[4] 4. For[5] he sought the God of his father and walked in his commandments—and not according to[a] the *evil* practices of *the house of* Israel. 5. So the Lord established the kingdom in his hand, and all *those of the house of* Judah brought gifts[6] to Jehoshaphat, and he had much wealth, *property* and honor. 6. His heart was lifted up *so that he walked* in ways *which were right before* the Lord,[7] and once more he removed the high places and the Asherahs from *those of the house of* Judah. 7. In the third year of his reign he sent (instructions) to his leading men, to Benhayil, to Obadiah,[8] to Zechariah, to Nethanel, and to Micaiah, to teach *the fear of the Lord* in the cities of Judah. 8. With them were the Levites: Shemaiah, Nethaniah, Zebadiah, Asahel, Shemiramoth,[9] Jehonathan, Adonijah, Tobiah, Tobadonijah, the Levites, and with them were the priests Elishama and Jehoram. 9. They taught among *those of the house of* Judah.[10] They had with them the book of the Law of the Lord, and they traveled around through all the towns of Judah and taught among the people. 10. Then the fear of the Lord came upon all the kingdoms of the countries which were round about Judah, and they did not *wage war*[11] with Jehoshaphat. 11. Some Philistines were bringing a gift to Jehoshaphat and an *offering of* silver[12] *and gold;* the Arabians too brought him flocks—seven thousand seven hundred rams and seven thousand seven hundred he-goats. 12. Jehoshaphat gradually became exceedingly powerful. In Judah he built castles[13] and store cities. 13. He had many rendering him service[14] in the cities of Judah and warriors,[b] fighting men,[15] in

Apparatus, Chapter 17

[a] E, L, AS: "in."

[b] C: "men."

Notes, Chapter 17

[3]MT: "The Lord was with Jehoshaphat."

[4]MT: "he did not seek the baals."

[5]The *ky* of MT becomes "for," "because" in Tg. Chr, though the "but" of EVV would be a more appropriate translation.

[6]Tg. Chr: singular, possibly in a collective sense, though MT itself uses a singular form of a different word, *mnḥh.* Tg. Chr uses the Greek loan word *dwrwn.* See 1 Chr 18:2, note 5.

[7]MT: "in the ways of the Lord."

[8]V's reading could suggest "his servant," though MT has clearly "Obadiah," as do C, L, AS.

[9]Following Qere. Kethibh is *šmrymwt.*

[10]MT: "They taught in Judah."

[11]MT: "fight."

[12]MT: "and silver (as) tribute" or "and silver, a load," i.e., a large quantity of silver. Tg. Chr takes the ambiguous word *mś'* and makes it into an "offering."

[13]Following *byrnyyt'* of C.

[14]MT: "He had much work in the cities of Judah." "Work" is a very wide term—property, (military) supplies, work in progress? Tg. Chr translated as *pwlḥn,* "service, worship"; perhaps "he had many rendering him service" is not too far wide of the mark. Le Déaut: "labor force," "manpower."

[15]Lit.: "making war." MT: "men of war, mighty warriors."

Jerusalem. 14. This was their number[c] according to their clans: for *the tribe of Judah*, commanders of thousands, Adnah was the chief and with him three hundred thousand mighty warriors. 15. *Alongside him*[16] was Jehohanan, the chief, and with him were two hundred and eighty thousand. 16. *Alongside him*[16] was Amasiah, the son of Zicri, who offered himself willingly *before*[d17] the Lord, and with him were two hundred thousand mighty warriors. 17. From *the tribe of Benjamin* were the mighty *warriors,*[18] Eliada, and with him two hundred thousand men *drawing* the bow and *holding* shields.[19] 18. *Alongside him*[16] was Jehozabad, and with him were one hundred and eighty thousand armed soldiers. 19. These were the men who served the king, apart from those whom the king had stationed[e20] in fortified towns, in all *the towns of* Judah.[21]

CHAPTER 18

1. Now Jehoshaphat had wealth and honor in abundance,[1] and he made an alliance, through marriage, with Ahab. 2. At the end of some years he went down to Ahab in Samaria. Ahab slaughtered[a] a large number of sheep and oxen for him and for the people who were with him, and he persuaded him to go up to Ramoth Gilead. 3. Ahab, king of Israel, said to Jehoshaphat, king of *the tribe of the house of* Judah: "Will you go with me to Ramoth Gilead?" He said to him: "*I am as you,*[b]

Apparatus, Chapter 17

[c] C, L, AS: "numbers."
[d] C: "to" (= MT).

[e] MT: "gave"/"placed." E, C, L, AS: *mny,* "placed, stationed." V has *msr,* "to hand over."

Notes, Chapter 17

[16] Lit.: "The one who dwelt near him." MT: "on his hand."
[17] MT: "to."
[18] MT: singular. MT makes Eliada the mighty warrior, along with two hundred thousand. Tg. Chr makes them all mighty warriors.
[19] MT: "armed with bow and shield."
[20] Reading *mny* with C.
[21] Tg. Chr's addition makes the last phrase awkward. Either all the towns in Judah were fortified, or we translate "in the fortresses in all the towns of Judah." Neither is very satisfactory.

Apparatus, Chapter 18

[a] E: *nsb.*

[b] V: *dykmtk.* E, L, AS: *dkmtk.* C: *dkwwth.*

Notes, Chapter 18

[1] Cf. 2 Chr 17:5.

and my people are as your people.[2] *Whatever happens* you in the battle *will happen me too."*[3] 4. Jehoshaphat said to the king of Israel: "Seek now this day the word of the Lord." 5. Then the king of Israel gathered the prophets together, four hundred men, and said to them: "*Is it right for us*[4] *to* go up to Ramoth Gilead[c][5] or shall I[d] desist?" They said: "Go up, and *the Lord will deliver*[6] it into the hand of the king." 6. Then Jehoshaphat said: "There *must surely be* another prophet here *who is in a correct relationship with* the Lord,[7] of whom we may inquire." 7. The king of Israel said to Jehoshaphat: "There is one other man from whom we may seek *the word of* the Lord. But I *loathe*[8] him because he does not prophesy *good things*[9] about me but always evil; he is Micaiah, the son of Imlah." But Jehoshaphat said: "Let not the king speak in this way." 8. So the king of Israel summoned a servant[e] and said: "Hurry up *and*[10] *fetch* Micaiah, the son of Imlah." 9. Now the king of Israel and Jehoshaphat, the king of *the tribe of the house of* Judah,[11] wearing *royal* robes, were sitting in *a circle, like a half* threshing-floor,[12] *one inquiring from the prophets of falsehood and the other seeking instruction from before the Lord and praying* at the entrance to Samaria, while all the prophets *of falsehood* prophesied *falsely* before them. 10. Then Zedekiah, the son of Chenaanah, *a prophet of falsehood,* made[f][13] *a likeness of the form of* iron horns and said: "Thus hath the Lord said: 'With these you will *kill the men of* Aram[14] until you have wiped them out.'" 11. Then all the prophets *of falsehood* prophesied *falsely* in the same vein,[15] saying: "Go up to

Apparatus, Chapter 18

[c] C, L, AS add: "for battle" (= MT). V omits.
[d] C: "we."

[e] V: *gww'wh*. C: *gwz'h*. E, L, AS: *gw'h*. All = "eunuch, servant."
[f] L, AS add: "for himself" (= MT). V and C omit.

Notes, Chapter 18

[2]MT: "like me, like you, and like your people, my people."

[3]MT: "and with you in the battle," a phrase which, like most modern translations, Tg. Chr expands to make it read more easily.

[4]MT: "Shall we. . . ?"

[5]MT: "for battle." V omits.

[6]MT: "and God will give."

[7]Lit.: "Is it possible that there is not still here a prophet who is legitimate before the Lord. . . ?" for MT's "Is there not still here a prophet to the Lord?"

[8]Reading Pael instead of Peal. MT: "hate."

[9]MT: singular (= C).

[10]Lit.: "to."

[11]Tg. Chr omits: "were sitting each upon his throne."

[12]MT: "in a threshing floor." Le Déaut notes the similarity to the seating arrangements of the Sanhedrin. See *m. San.* 4.3. "The Sanhedrin was arranged like the half of a round threshing floor so that they all might see one another."

[13]MT adds "for himself."

[14]MT: "you will gore Aram."

[15]Lit.: "thus."

Ramoth Gilead and be successful, and the Lord will *deliver*[16] it into the hand of the king." 12. The messenger[g] who had gone to summon *Micah*[17] spoke to him saying: "Look! The words of the prophets *of falsehood* are one *speech,*[18] *valued*[h] *and favorable before* the king.[19] So now, let your word be like (that of) one of them and speak *favorable words.*"[20] 13. *Micah*[17] said: "As sure as the Lord is alive, whatever my God says, that I shall speak." 14. He came to the king, and the king said to him: "Micah, *is it right that* we should go up to Ramoth Gilead to *wage* war or should I desist?" He said: "Go up[i][21] and be triumphant! They will be delivered into your *hands.*"[22] 15. The king said to him: "How many times must I put you on oath not to *prophesy*[23] anything concerning me except the truth in the Name of *the Memra of* the Lord?" 16. He said: "I saw all Israel *rolling*[j][24] *down* upon the mountains like sheep without a shepherd. And the Lord said: 'These have no masters. Let each return to his house in peace!'" 17. The king of Israel said to Jehoshaphat: "Did I not tell you that he would not prophesy good about me but *only* evil?"[25] 18. Then he said: "Pay attention! *Accept*[k] the *words*[l] of *the prophecy* of the Lord.[26] I saw *the glory of the Shekinah of* the Lord, sitting upon *the throne of his glory,*[27] with all the *armies*[28] of heaven standing *and serving from*[29] his right hand and *from*[29] his left. 19. The Lord said: 'Who will entice Ahab, the king of Israel, *and*[30] he will go up and *be cast down slain*[31] at Ramoth Gilead?' And he said: 'One was saying this and another was saying that.' 20. Then the spirit *of Naboth who was from Jezreel* came

---

Apparatus, Chapter 18

[g] V: *'zgdh.* C, E, L, AS: *'zgd'.*
[h] C: "good."
[i] V and C: singular. E, L, AS: plural (= MT).

[j] V: *mndryn,* "rolling down." C, E, L, AS: *mbdryn,* "scattered" (= MT).
[k] V, C, L, AS: singular. E: plural (= MT).
[l] V, L, AS: plural. C, E: singular (= MT).

Notes, Chapter 18

[16]MT: "give."
[17]MT: *mykyhw.*
[18]MT: "mouth."
[19]MT: "good to the king."
[20]MT: "good."
[21]V: singular. MT: plural.
[22]MT: singular.
[23]MT: "speak."
[24]MT: "scattered."
[25]Tg. Chr's faithfulness to MT must be noted here. He reproduces *l* before "evil." This *l* is not in Kgs, and many commentators on Chr (e.g., *ICC* and Rudolph) would like to be rid of it!
[26]MT: "hear the word of the Lord."
[27]MT: "his throne."
[28]MT: singular.
[29]MT: "on."
[30]MT: "that."
[31]MT: "and fall."

forth *from the chamber of the righteous*[32] and stood before the Lord and said: 'I shall lead him astray.' And the Lord said to him: 'How?' 21. And he said: 'I shall go forth and become a spirit of false *prophecy* in the mouth of all his prophets.' He said: 'You will lead astray and you will also have the ability *to lead them astray, but you will not have authority to return*[m] *and sit*[m] *among the righteous, because whoever speaks falsehood, it is impossible for him to have his abode among the righteous.*[33] *So* go forth *from my presence*[34] and do this.' 22. So now, behold, the Lord has put a spirit of false *prophecy* in the mouth of these prophets of yours,[n][35] and *it has been decreed from before the Lord to bring* evil upon you."[36] 23. Then Zedekiah, the son of Chenaanah, drew near, and struck *Micah*[17] on *his*[37] cheek and said: "At which *moment* was the spirit *of prophecy from before* the Lord *taken up* from me in order to speak with you?"[38] 24. *Micah*[17] said: "That you will discover on that day when you go into an innermost room, in order to hide yourself." 25. Then the king of Israel said: "Take *Micah*[17] and return him to Amon, the city governor, and to Joash, the king's son. 26. And say: 'Thus has the king said: "Put[39] this man in prison, feed him a restricted diet of bread and water[40] until I return in peace."'" 27. *Micah*[17] said: "If, in fact, you do return in peace, then *the will of* the Lord *is not in me and he* has not spoken *to me by the spirit of prophecy.*"[o][41] Then he said: "Hear, O peoples, all of them." 28. Then the king of Israel and Jehoshaphat, the king of *the tribe of the house of* Judah, went up to Ramoth Gilead. 29. The king of Israel said to Jehoshaphat: "I shall disguise[42] myself and go[42] into the battle, but you, wear your (normal) robes." So the king of Israel disguised himself and *went*[43]

Apparatus, Chapter 18

[m] C omits: "to return." L and AS: omit "to sit." Both words in Aramaic are very similar in appearance.

[n] V: *nbw'k.* C: *nby'n.* E, L, AS: *nby'yk.*
[o] V: *nbwth.* C, E, L, AS: *nbw't.*

Notes, Chapter 18

[32]Following the Lord's invitation for a volunteer to lead Ahab astray, MT tells us in 18:20 that "*the* spirit came forth. ..." As there is a definite article involved, the Rabbis felt obliged to identify the spirit, and justice demanded that the spirit of the one whom Ahab had so recently murdered should be the one who would now lead Ahab astray—the spirit of Naboth (*b. Shab.* 149b and *b. San.* 89a). Such an act, however, inevitably involved deceit and, as the next verse makes clear, this deceit (in line with Ps 101:7) automatically excluded Naboth from the congregation of the righteous (see *b. San.* 102b and 1 Chr 21:15, note 31).

[33]Marginal glosses dealing with Naboth in a way similar to the story in Tg. Chr are quoted in A. Sperber, II, 269.

[34]Lit.: "from with me."

[35]Reading *nby'yk* with E, L, AS.

[36]MT: "The Lord has spoken evil against you."

[37]MT: "the."

[38]MT: "Which way did the spirit of the Lord pass from me to speak with you?"

[39]Tg. Chr: singular. MT: plural.

[40]Lit.: "bread *in* restriction and water *in* restriction."

[41]MT: "then the Lord has not spoken by me." The literal translation in Tg. Chr of the second part of his sentence is: "and it has not been spoken by the spirit of prophecy with me."

[42]The two verbs used in Tg. Chr are in the Imperfect. MT has two infinitive absolutes, which here are usually translated as referring to the first person.

[43]MT: plural, but many Hebrew MSS and main Versions have the singular.

into the battle. 30. Now the king of Aram had ordered the commanders of his chariot force, saying: "*Make war*[44] with neither the small *nor* the great but only with the king of Israel." 31. So when the commanders of the chariot force saw Jehoshaphat, they said: "It's[*p*] the king of Israel." They surrounded him to *make war.*[44] But Jehoshaphat cried out and *the Memra of* the Lord came to his aid and *the Lord kept them at a distance*[45] from him. 32. When the commanders of the chariot force saw that it was not the king of Israel, they ceased following him.[46] 33. *Then Naaman, the army commander of the king of Aram,*[47] drew a bow *against him,*[48] *so as to fulfill the prophecy of Elijah from Teshub, and the prophecy of Micah, the son of Imlah,* and he struck the king of Israel between *the heart and the lobe of the liver,* at the place of *the joints* of *the coat of mail.*[49] He (Ahab) said to his driver: "Turn round,[50] and get me out of the *warriors'* lines,[51] for I have been wounded." 34. The *soldiers* continued fighting[52] that day, and the king of Israel *summoned his strength and remained standing*[53] in the chariot facing *the men of* Aram until the evening and he died as the sun was setting.

Apparatus, Chapter 18

[*p*] C, L and AS have: "but it's. . . ." The "but" is found in MT and Tg. 1 Kgs 22:32.

Notes, Chapter 18

[44]MT: "fight."

[45]MT: "distracted them" (*wysytm*). LXX presupposes *wysyrm*: "and he removed them," which seems to be what Tg. Chr also had in mind.

[46]Lit.: "they turned from after him."

[47]MT: "a man." The unknown man of MT becomes Syria's army commander, Naaman, who appears in the Elisha stories. See *Midr. Teh.* 78.11.

[48]MT: *ltmw,* "in his innocence," usually given the sense of "without definite aim," "at random." Tg. Chr is much more specific "against him," which suggests deliberate intent, and within the divine plan, to fulfill prophecy—that of Elijah (one assumes, as recorded in 1 Kgs 21:17 ff.) and that of Micaiah earlier in 2 Chr 18. This fulfillment of prophecy expansion is probably based on the Hebrew word already quoted, *ltmw,* which springs from the root *tmm,* which stresses completion, fulfillment, thus opening the door to the completing or fulfilling of prophecy. This prophetic reference is also found in a marginal gloss in Tg. 1 Kgs 22:34, quoted in A. Sperber, II, 270.

[49]MT: "between the scale armor and the breastplate." This is RSV's translation of a difficult phrase.

[50]Lit.: "turn to your rear" for MT's "turn your hand."

[51]Lit.: "the camp of those making war." MT: "the camp."

[52]Lit.: "Those making war went up" for MT: "the battle went up."

[53]MT: "was causing to stand" (Hiph), though most commentators follow Hophal of 1 Kgs 22:35: "was caused to stand," i.e., "was propped up."

CHAPTER 19

1. Jehoshaphat, the king of *the tribe of the house of* Judah, returned safely[a] to his home in Jerusalem. 2. But there came out to meet him[1] Jehu, the son of Hanani, the seer,[2] and he said to King Jehoshaphat: "*Is it right that you should have gone*[3] to the aid of the wicked and show your love for those who hate the Lord? Because of this, anger from before[4] the Lord is upon you. 3. However, there are some things in your favor,[b][5] for you removed the Asherahs from the land and you have set[c] your heart to seek *instruction from before* the Lord." 4. Jehoshaphat stayed in Jerusalem, but he went out again *to give instruction* among the people from Beersheba to the mountain of *the house of* Ephraim, and he brought them back to *the fear of* the Lord, the God of their fathers. 5. He also appointed judges in the land, in all the fortified cities of Judah, *from* city *to* city.[d][6] 6. He said to the judges, "Watch what you're doing! For you are acting as judges not *before*[7] the sons of man but *before*[7] *the Memra of* the Lord, and *his Shekinah dwells*[8] with you when you pass judgment. 7. So now, let the fear of the Lord be upon you, be careful how you act,[9] for *before*[10] the Lord our God there is neither *falsehood*[11] nor partiality nor acceptance of bribes." 8. In Jerusalem also Jehoshaphat appointed some of the Levites and priests and some of the heads of the clans of *the house of* Israel to take decisions[12] *before*[13] the Lord and to (act) in cases of litigation. Then they returned to Jerusalem. 9. He charged them saying: "Thus you will act, in the fear of the Lord, in faithfulness *and truth* and in sincerity of heart. 10. Every case which is referred

Apparatus, Chapter 19

[a] V: *lšlwm*. C, L, AS: *bšlwm* (= MT).
[b] E: *'bl ptgmyn tqnyn* (*'bl* is the same word as is used in Hebrew text).

[c] V: *kwynt'*. E, L, AS: *'tqnt'*. There is little difference in meaning.
[d] V: "from city to city." C, E, L, AS: "for city and city" (= MT).

Notes, Chapter 19

[1] Lit.: "to before him." MT: "to his face."
[2] V has *skwt*, "watchtower." Unless this is to be taken as a nickname, it would be better to follow E, C, L, AS and read *skw'h*, "seer, watchman" (= MT).
[3] While MT may imply a query as to the rightness of Jehoshaphat, Tg. Chr underlines it.
[4] It is of interest to see the Chronicler use a thoroughly Targumic expression.
[5] Lit.: "good things have been found with you."
[6] MT: "for city and city," i.e., for each and every city.
[7] MT: "for," "on behalf of."
[8] MT: "with you." Some commentators think *hw'* has dropped out through haplography. Tg. Chr supplies the subject without difficulty.
[9] Lit.: "take heed and do."
[10] MT: "with."
[11] MT: "unrighteousness."
[12] Lit.: "for judgment."
[13] MT: "of." MT seems to be making some distinction between "religious" and "civil" suits—"for the judgment of the Lord and for disputes." This distinction is blurred somewhat by Tg. Chr's inserting before "the Lord" the word "before."

to you by your brethren who live in their towns, *whether it has to do with a man who is guilty of a capital offense or a man who is innocent of a capital offense,*[14] whether it relates to the Law or to the commandment, the statutes and the judgments, you will caution them,[15] so that they*[e]* do not incur guilt before the Lord and there be anger upon you and your brethren. If you act in this way you will not incur guilt. 11. Look to[16] Amariah, the chief priest, *who is appointed* as your *chief* authority[17] in every matter which concerns the Lord, and *Zechariah,[f]*[18] the son of Ishmael, ruler of the house of Judah, in every matter which concerns the king; and the Levites will act as your officials.[19] Act firmly[20] and may *the Memra of* the Lord be *in your support* of *him who is* good!"[21]

CHAPTER 20

1. After this the sons of Moab and the sons of Ammon, together with some *Edomites who had allied themselves to* the Ammonites,[1] came against Jehoshaphat to *wage* war. 2. Word was brought*[a]* to[2] Jehoshaphat, saying: "A massive horde *of*

[e] C: "you."

[f] V and C: "Zechariah." L and AS: "Zebadiah" (= MT).

Notes, Chapter 19

[14]MT: "between blood and blood"; cf. Deut 17:8, though Ps.-J. interprets the expression differently than Tg. Chr. MT is usually regarded as making a distinction between murder and manslaughter. In Tg. Chr, if a man is innocent of a capital offense, the implication may be that he is guilty of a non-capital offense. An alternative translation could be: "a man who is liable to a death sentence or a man who is clear of a death sentence."

[15]Reading Aphel with C, rather than Peal with V. (Peal = "you will shine.")

[16]Lit.: "And behold."

[17]MT: "the chief priest (is) over you."

[18]MT: "Zebadiah," though a few Hebrew MSS, Syr, and Arabic have "Zechariah." In Hebrew, the names have a similar appearance.

[19]Lit.: "and (as) officials the Levites are before you."

[20]Lit.: "be strong and do."

[21]MT: "And may the Lord be with the good." But when "with" is replaced in Tg. Chr by "in your support," "the good" is left out on a limb and becomes "of the good." If that can be understood as "the good man," then the above translation is possible.

Apparatus, Chapter 20

[a] C has Ithpaal, perhaps under the influence of the preceding word.

Notes, Chapter 20

[1]MT: "together with some Ammonites."

[2]Lit.: "And they came and they told."

people has come against you from the *Western Region of* Aram[3] and already they are in the 'Thicket of Palms,'[4] that is, Engedi." 3. Jehoshaphat was *terrified,*[5] and he resolved[6] to seek *instruction from before* the Lord and decreed a fast[b] for all *the men of* Judah. 4. *The men of* Judah assembled to seek *mercy* from *before* the Lord: indeed they came from all the cities of Judah to seek *instruction from before* the Lord. 5. Then Jehoshaphat stood up in the assembly of *the house of* Judah in[7] Jerusalem, in the *sanctuary* house of the Lord in front of the new court. 6. And he said, "Lord, God of our fathers, are you not *the Lord,*[8] whose Shekinah is[c] in the heavens and you have authority over all the kingdoms of the peoples?[d] In your hand are strength and might, *and there is nothing apart from you,* and no *king is able to* stand *against* you.[9] 7. Did you not, O our God, *by your Memra,* drive out the inhabitants of this land from before your people Israel and give it for ever to *the sons*[10] of Abraham, your friend? 8. They settled in it and in it they built for you a sanctuary *house* for the name *of* your *Memra,* saying: 9. 'When there comes upon us evil,[e] *those who kill with* the sword,[11] pestilence and famine, we shall *pray*[12] before this *sanctuary* house and before you—for your *Shekinah*[13] is in this house— and we shall cry to you out of our distress and you will *accept*[14] *our prayer* and deliver *us.'* 10. And now, look what has happened:[15] the sons of Ammon and Moab, and the mountain of *Gabla,*[16] against whom you did not permit[17] *the house of* Israel to go *and wage war* when they came out of the land of Egypt, but they turned aside from them and did not wipe them out— 11. These very people[18] are repay-

Apparatus, Chapter 20

[b] C: *t'nyt.* E, L, AS: *t'nyt.* V: *t'ny.*
[c] E adds: "dwells."

[d] C: of the earth of the peoples."
[e] C seems to read *byšt,* "evil," as *bšt,* "in the year."

Notes, Chapter 20

[3]MT: "from beyond the sea, from Aram." One Hebrew MS has "from Edom," and most commentators are happy to accept this, but Tg. Chr is unaware of any problems.
[4]MT: *ḥṣṣwn tmr* (*tmr* = "palm") = Hazazon Tamar (place name), Hazazon of the Palm?
[5]MT: "afraid."
[6]Lit.: "he gave (set) his face."
[7]MT: "and," but a few Hebrew MSS and LXX have "in."
[8]MT: "God."
[9]MT: "and there is no one to withstand you."
[10]MT: "seed."
[11]MT omits "judgment."
[12]MT: "stand."
[13]MT: "name."
[14]MT: "hear."
[15]MT: "behold!"
[16]MT: "Seir."
[17]MT: "give."
[18]Lit.: "and behold they."

ing us *with evil*[19] by coming to drive us out from *our*[20] inheritance which you gave us to possess. 12. O our God, will you not *be avenged on*[21] them, for we do not have the strength *to stand up* before this massive horde *of people* who are coming against us? We just do not know what we should do, but *we have lifted up* our eyes to you."[22] 13. All *those of the house of* Judah were standing before the Lord, and with them their little ones *as well as* their wives and children. 14. Then, in the midst of the assembly, the Spirit of *prophecy from before* the Lord *rested* upon[23] Jahaziel, the son of Zechariah, the son of Benaiah, the son of Jeiel, the son of Mattaniah, a Levite from the sons of Asaph. 15. He said, "Listen, all *you men of* Judah and inhabitants of Jerusalem and King Jehoshaphat. Thus has the Lord said to you: 'Don't be afraid and don't be shattered from before this massive horde *of people,* for the battle *lines* are not yours but they are *before*[24] the Lord. 16. Tomorrow go down against them. Just now[25] they are climbing up the slope of *Odiquth-Kelila,*[26] and you will find them at the end of the wadi, opposite the wilderness of Jeruel. 17. There will be no need for you to *make* war[27] on this occasion. Be at the ready, stand up and see the deliverance of the Lord on your behalf, O Judah[g] and Jerusalem.' Don't be afraid and don't be shattered. Go forth to meet them tomorrow and *the Memra of* the Lord will be *in support of* you."[28] 18. Jehoshaphat bowed down, his face to the ground,[29] and all *the men of* Judah and the inhabitants of Jerusalem *bowed down*[30] before the Lord to worship *before*[24] the Lord. 19. Then the Levites, from the sons of *Qehath*[31] and from the sons of

Apparatus, Chapter 20

[f] C: "your" (= MT).

[g] C, L, AS: "O men of Judah..."

Notes, Chapter 20

[19]"With evil" is not in MT, but is found in a few Hebrew MSS.

[20]MT: "your."

[21]MT: "judge."

[22]MT: "our eyes are upon you."

[23]MT: "the spirit of the Lord was upon."

[24]MT: "to."

[25]MT: "Behold!"

[26]MT: "the slope of Ziz." (ṣyṣ in Hebrew is "flower, blossom"). JL (I, 11) thinks that Tg. Chr has taken two meanings of the Hebrew root ṣyṣ and set their Aramaic equivalents alongside each other. (i) A verb meaning "to look down." In Aramaic the corresponding verb is dyq, which in its Aphel form is 'wdyq (Odiq). (ii) ṣyṣ as a noun means "blossom" or "sparkle." It was used to describe the shining plate of gold, the holy crown ("crown" is klyl', Kelila). See Lev 8:9 and Tg. "The view of the crown" then would seem to be the meaning intended. E has 'ryqut blyl': The first word he sees as coming from the root yrq, "to be green," and the second meaning "mixture."

[27]MT: "to fight."

[28]MT: "The Lord will be with you."

[29]Lit.: "upon his face upon the ground," for MT: "face to the ground."

[30]Tg. Chr uses kr' twice in this verse, whereas MT uses a second verb which has probably a heavier stress on prostration.

[31]MT: "the Qehathites."

Korah,[32] stood up to offer praise *before*[24] the Lord, the God of Israel, with a very loud voice. 20. Early next morning they set out[33] for the wilderness of Tekoa, and as they were going out, Jehoshaphat stood up and said: *"Accept from me,*[34] *men of* Judah and inhabitants of Jerusalem! Put your trust in *the Memra of* the Lord, your God, *put your trust in his Law,*[35] put your trust in his prophets, and you will be successful." 21. Then he consulted the people and appointed those who *were to offer praise before*[36] the Lord, and as they went out ahead of the army, they were offering praise[h] in the splendor of holiness, saying, *"Offer praise before*[37] the Lord, for his *goodness*[38] is eternal." 22. As soon as they began (singing) hymns and offering praise, *the Memra of* the Lord laid ambushes for the sons of Ammon and of Moab and of the mountain of *Gabla,*[16] who had come[39] to *make war*[27] *with* Judah, and they were shattered. 23. The sons of Ammon and of Moab rose up against the inhabitants of the mountain of *Gabla*[16] in order to wipe them out and to destroy them utterly. When they had utterly destroyed the inhabitants of *Gabla,*[16] they *attacked* each other, with the same result.[40] 24. When *the men of* Judah reached the spot where they had a clear view of the wilderness,[41] they turned toward the *massed armies,*[42] and there they were, *dead* bodies lying on the ground: there were no survivors. 25. Jehoshaphat[i43] came *and proceeded*[44] to take their spoils. They found among them large amounts of property[45] *and possessions, dead* bodies, and

Apparatus, Chapter 20

[h] E, L, AS: *wmšbḥy.* This alters the structure of the sentence slightly and brings it more into line with MT. It would read thus: "he appointed those who were to offer praise before the Lord and those who were to offer praise in the splendor of holiness as they went out...."

[i] E, L, AS add "and his people" (= MT).

Notes, Chapter 20

[32]MT: "the Korahites."

[33]Lit.: "They rose early in the morning and set out..."

[34]MT: "hear me."

[35]"Put your trust in his law" replaces MT's "and you will be established." In making this change, Tg. Chr has lost the wordplay found here and in a slightly different form in Isa 7:8.

[36]MT: "singers to."

[37]MT: "Give thanks to."

[38]MT: "his steadfast love."

[39]Reading *'twn* with C, E, L, AS for V's *'rkwn.*

[40]MT: "they helped to destroy each other." Tg. Chr "they attacked each other, to destroy" or perhaps "they stirred themselves up to destroy one another."

[41]Lit.: "the watchtower (outlook) to the wilderness," referring perhaps less to a building than to some raised place where there was a clear view of the landscape. Such a place, of course, may have been given the name "Watchtower."

[42]Lit.: "the horde of the armies." MT: "the crowd."

[43]V omits "and his people."

[44]Lit.: "he rose up."

[45]MT: Lit.: "They found among them (i.e., among the spoils) large amounts and ..." or "They found on them (i.e., the corpses) large amounts and...." Either Tg. Chr improves his text by shifting "large amounts" or Tg. Chr confirms the suggestion that *bhm,* "among them," was originally *bhmh,* "cattle" (cf. LXX), represented in Tg. Chr by *nksyn.* The problem here is that Tg. Chr has also reproduced *bhm.*

precious vessels, which they carried off for themselves until they *could* carry no more. They spent three days taking *their* spoils, for there was so much. 26. On the fourth day they assembled in the Valley of *Birketha*, [46] for there they had blessed the Lord. This is why they called the name of that place the Valley of *Birketha* [46] up to this day. 27. Then all the men of Judah and Jerusalem returned, with Jehoshaphat *placed among their leaders*: [47] they returned to Jerusalem with joy, for the *Memra of* the Lord had given them joy because of their enemies. 28. With lutes, lyres, and trumpets they came to Jerusalem, to the *sanctuary* house of the Lord. 29. And the fear of *the Lord*[8] was upon all the kingdoms of the *earth* [48] when they heard that *the Memra of* the Lord had *waged war* [49] against the enemies of Israel. 30. Jehoshaphat's kingdom was at peace, and the *Memra of* his God[j] gave him rest on every side. 31. Thus Jehoshaphat reigned over *the men of* Judah. He was thirty-five years old when he became king, and he reigned in Jerusalem for twenty-five years. His mother's name was Azubah, the daughter of Shilhi. 32. He walked in the way of Asa, his father, and did not turn aside from it, doing what was right *before* [50] the Lord. 33. Except that the high places [51] did not disappear entirely; the people had not yet set their heart on *the fear of*[k] the God of their fathers. 34. The rest of the acts of Jehoshaphat, from beginning to end, [52] are to be found written in the Acts of Jehu, the son of Hanani, *who was appointed scribe* in charge of the book [53] of *the records of* the kings of *the house of* Israel. 35. After this, Jehoshaphat, the king of *the tribe of the house of* Judah, made an alliance with Ahaziah, the king of *the house of*[l] Israel, who *incurred guilt by being wicked.* [54] 36. He joined with him to build ships to go to Tarshish [55] *on the Mediterranean Sea;* [56] they built the

Apparatus, Chapter 20

[j] C, L, AS: "the Lord." V, E: "his God" (= MT).
[k] C, L, AS add: "the Lord."

[l] V: "the house of." C, L, AS: omit (= MT).

Notes, Chapter 20

[46]MT: "Berakah" = "blessing." Tg. Chr simply gives the Aramaic word for "blessing."
[47]MT: "at their head."
[48]MT: plural: "lands."
[49]MT: "fought."
[50]MT: "in the eyes of."
[51]There is an object marker in Tg. Chr before "the high places," leading us to expect a Pael form of *'tr*. Both V and C, however, point it as Peal, in which form it is normally intransitive. If we take it as transitive, the translation would then be: "They did not remove the high places," i.e., "the high places were not removed."
[52]Lit.: "the first and the last."
[53]MT: hophal of *'lh*: "which was taken up into (or inserted in) the book . . ." (*BDB* 750). Tg. Chr interprets this as "who was appointed scribe in charge of the book. . . ." The word used for "scribe" is *lblr*, borrowed from Latin *libellarius* (JL I, 401) or *librarius* (MJ 689).
[54]MT: "he acted wickedly to do," i.e., "he acted wickedly in so doing."
[55]MT: *tršyš*; Tg. Chr: *twrsws*. See 1 Chr 1:7, note 17.
[56]Lit.: "the Great Sea."

ships *at the fortress of Tarngola.* [57] 37. Then Eliezer, the son of *Dodaiah,* [m][58] from Mareshah, uttered this prophecy against Jehoshaphat: "Because you entered into an alliance with Ahaziah, *the Memra of* the Lord has ruined your efforts." The ships were wrecked and unable to go to Tarshish. [55]

CHAPTER 21

1. Jehoshaphat slept with his fathers, and he was buried with his fathers in the city of David, and his son Jehoram became king in his place. 2. He had brothers, sons of Jehoshaphat: Azariah, Jehiel, Zechariah, Azaryahu, Michael and Shephatiah. All these were the sons of Jehoshaphat, the king of Israel. 3. Their father had given them many gifts, of silver, gold and *splendid garments,* [1] and *they were given possession, by virtue of landed property,* [2] along with fortified towns in *the land of the house of* Judah. But the kingdom he had given to *his son* Jehoram, for he was the first-born. 4. When Jehoram had taken over [3] his father's kingdom and consolidated his own position, he killed all his brothers with the sword and some of Israel's nobles as well. 5. Jehoram [a] was thirty-two years old when he became king, and he reigned in Jerusalem for eight years. 6. He walked in the way of the kings of *the house of* Israel, as *the men of* [b] the house of Ahab had done, for his wife was

Apparatus, Chapter 20

[m] V and C: *dwdyhw.* L, AS: *dwdwhw* (= MT).

Notes, Chapter 20

[57]MT: "Eziongeber."
[58]MT: *ddwhw.*

Apparatus, Chapter 21

[a] C, L, AS omit.   [b] C omits "the men of" (= MT).

Notes, Chapter 21

[1]Lit.: "garments of glory."
[2]In *b. B.B.* 156b a case is cited where a man is not permitted to hand over gifts (of movable property) until he also hands over immovable property (land). His wishes cannot be carried out "until he transfers possession *on the basis of land*": *'d šyqnh 'l gb qrq'* (largely the same expression as we have in Tg. Chr). The reason for this limiting clause seems to have centered round the need to preserve a dying man from making an irrational, hasty decision. See also *b. B.M.* 11b.
[3]Lit.: "risen up upon."

Ahab's daughter, and he did *what was* evil *before*[4] the Lord. 7. *But there was no desire*[c] *from before*[5] the Lord to destroy the house of David, because of the covenant which he had made with David and because he had promised[6] to give *kingship*[7] to him and to his sons for ever. 8. In his days *the Edomites*[8] revolted, *and they freed themselves* from under the domination[9] of *the house of* Judah and appointed a king of their own.[10] 9. Then Jehoram went over,[11] along with his princes and all his chariots *which were* with him,[12] and *when* he arose during the night, he killed *the Edomites* who had *taken up their positions* all around him[13] and the chariot commanders. 10. So *the Edomites*[8] *who had freed themselves*[d] from under the domination[9] of *the house of* Judah have been in a state of revolt right up to this day. At that *same* time Libnah revolted *and freed itself* from under his domination,[9] because he had abandoned *the fear of* the Lord, the God of his fathers. 11. As well, he constructed high places in the mountains of Judah and *led astray*[14] the inhabitants of Jerusalem; he led astray also *those of the house of* Judah. 12. A letter[15] came to him from the prophet Elijah, saying: "Thus has the Lord, the God of your father David, said: 'Because you have not walked in the ways of Jehoshaphat, your father, nor in the ways of Asa, the king of *the tribe of the house of* Judah, 13. but you have walked in the *ways*[16] of the kings of *the house of* Israel, and have led astray *those of the house of* Judah and the inhabitants of Jerusalem, just as *those of* the house of Ahab led *them* astray,[e] and in addition you have killed your brothers, your father's *sons,*[f][17] who were better than you; 14. because of all

Apparatus, Chapter 21

[c] C: *r'wt'.* V, L, AS: *r'w'.*
[d] V: "Who had freed themselves ... revolted...."
C, L, AS: "The Edomites revolted and freed themselves...."

[e] V: *hykmh. d'ṭ'yw.* L, AS: *hykmh d'ṭ'w.* C: *hykmh d'ṭ'.*
[f] C, E, L, AS: "and your father's house."

Notes, Chapter 21

[4] MT: "in the eyes of."
[5] Tg. 2 Kgs 8:19 translated the same statement in MT: "But the Lord was not willing to ..." as "There was desire from before the Lord not to destroy...."
[6] Lit.: "said."
[7] MT: "lamp." See also 1 Chr 8:33, note 18, where "kingship" is compared to a lamp.
[8] MT: "Edom."
[9] Lit.: "hand."
[10] Lit.: "over them."
[11] Reading *'br* with C, L, AS for *'bd* of V.
[12] Reading "with him" in C instead of "his people" in V. The consonants are the same.
[13] MT: "he struck down Edom who surrounded him."
[14] MT: "seduced." In verse 11 Tg. Chr uses the same verb *ṭ''* to express two different Hebrew verbs.
[15] Tg. Chr uses the word *pyṭq'*, "tablet, letter," borrowed from the Greek *ptukton* or *ptuktion* (JL II, 260). MJ makes no reference to Greek origin.
[16] MT: singular.
[17] MT: "house," but LXX has "sons."

this, [18] *the Memra of* the Lord will let loose a great pestilence on your people and on your sons and on your wives and on all your possessions. 15. And you yourself (will be afflicted) with many illnesses, including a disease of your bowels, until your bowels protrude *from your body,* because of the disease *which will be prolonged for you for years to come.'*" [19] 16. Then *the Memra of* the Lord stirred up against Jehoram the spirit of the Philistines and the Arabs who are *on the borders* [20] *of the Africans.* [21] 17. They came up into *the land of the house of* Judah and *subdued* [22] it, and carried off all the possessions which were found that belonged to the king's house, as well as his sons and his wives. The only son left to him was Jehoahaz, [g] *who was* his youngest son. 18. After all this *the Memra of* the Lord smote him in his bowels with *diseases* [23] for which there was no cure. [h] 19. After some considerable time, when *he had a severe bout of diarrhea* for two days, his bowels protruded as a result of his illness and he died in intense agony. [24] But his people did not make a fire *of sweetly scented wood* in his honor [25] as had been made for his fathers. [26] 20. He was thirty-two years old when he became king, and he reigned for eight years in Jerusalem. He went *to the burying ground* unlamented, [27] and they buried him in the city of David but not in the graves of the kings.

Apparatus, Chapter 21

[g] C, L, AS: "Ahaziah." One Hebrew MS, LXX, and Syr also have "Ahaziah." Elsewhere (e.g., 22:1) he is known by this name. Both names (Ahaziah and Jehoahaz) are compounds of *Yahweh* and the verb "to seize" (*ḥz*), but written in reverse order, meaning: "Yahweh has seized."

[h] E: "physician."

Notes, Chapter 21

[18] Lit.: "Behold."

[19] Lit.: "the days upon the years." MT: "days upon days."

[20] MT: "on the hand of," i.e., near.

[21] "Africans," (MJ 108); "Phrygians," "Africans?" (JL I, 56). MT: "Cushites." See 1 Chr 1:5, note 4.

[22] MT: "broke through."

[23] MT: singular.

[24] Verse 19 in MT is difficult. MT reads in a literal translation: "To days from days (= after some considerable time) and about the time of the going out of the end for two days. . . ." Some take "end" with "two days," e.g., RSV: "at the end of two years"; some take it as a reference to the end of his life, e.g., *ICC:* "at the time when the end of his life came." Tg. Chr uses "end" to refer to the rectum and, linking "end" and "bowels," gives a frank and more detailed description of the unfortunate king's malady. The above translation is based on what seems to me to be the following literal translation: "And it came to pass for a time of days and years and when he was fulfilling his natural need in excess from his end for two days, his bowels protruded as a result of his illness and he died with grievous pains"; cf. JL II, 336f. and 378.

[25] Lit.: "for him."

[26] Lit.: "like the fire of his fathers."

[27] Lit.: "with no longing"; (see JL II, 404).

CHAPTER 22

1. Then the inhabitants of Jerusalem made Ahaziah, his youngest son, king in his place, for a (raiding) party which had come with the Arabs to the camp *of the Philistines and the Africans*[1] had killed all the older ones. So Ahaziah, the son of Jehoram, king of *the tribe of the house of* Judah, became king. 2. Ahaziah was forty-two years old when he became king. He reigned for one year in Jerusalem. His mother's name was Athaliah, the daughter of Omri. 3. He too walked in the ways of *the men of* the house of Ahab, for his mother acted as his adviser, leading him into sin.[2] 4. He did *what was* evil *before*[3] the Lord, *just as the men* of the house of Ahab *had done,* for after *his father died,*[4] they became his advisers, to his ruination.[5] 5. Moreover, he followed their advice and went with Jehoram, the son of Ahab, king of Israel, to battle against Hazael, the king of Aram, at Ramoth Gilead, and the Arameans[6] *mortally wounded*[7] Joram. 6. He returned to be healed in Jezreel, for the attackers had wounded him[8] at *Ramath,*[9] in his engagement with Hazael, the king of Aram. Now Azariah, the son of Jehoram, the king of *the tribe of the house of* Judah, came down to see Jehoram, the son of Ahab, in Jezreel, for he was ill. 7. *It was destined from before the Lord* that Ahaziah should come[10] to Joram. As soon as he arrived, he went out with Jehoram to Jehu, the son of Nimshi, whom *Elijah*[11] had anointed *by the authority of the Memra of the Lord,* to wipe out the house of Ahab. 8. When Jehu was executing judgment on the house of Ahab, he came across the princes of Judah and the sons of Ahaziah's brothers waiting upon Ahaziah, and he killed them. 9. Then he went in search of Ahaziah, and

---

Notes, Chapter 22

[1]In 21:16-17 Arabs and Philistines attacked Judah, carrying off all the royal sons, except Jehoahaz. In Tg. 2 Chr 22:1 the killers belong to a group which had come with the Arabs, not to the Judahite camp, but to the camp of the Philistines and the Africans, the latter being mentioned in Tg. 2 Chr 21:16 not as participants but simply as a map reference.

[2]Lit.: "was counseling him to incur guilt," for MT: "was his counselor to act wickedly."

[3]MT: "in the eyes of."

[4]MT: "his father's death."

[5]Lit.: "to destroy him."

[6]MT has lost the initial aleph, but the parallel verse in 2 Kgs 8:28 has the complete word.

[7]Tg. Chr has "killed" where MT has "struck down." As Joram reappears in verse 6 on his way for medical attention, Le Déaut's compromise is the best solution, as in the translation above. Tg. Chr translates *nkh,* "to strike down" with *qtl,* "to kill."

[8]In MT of verse 6 we have the conjunction *ky,* but we look in vain for a predicate: "for the wounds. . ."? Vg supplies one: "many." If we translate *hmkym* as "the wounders," we have the same problem. Many therefore follow some Hebrew MSS, LXX, Syr, and 2 Kgs 8:29 (cf. also 2 Kgs 9:15) and read *mn* for *ky:* "to be healed in Jezreel from the wounds. . . ." Tg. Chr has followed MT but seems to have understood *hmkym* as "the wounders." (Had it been "wounds," as in 2 Kgs, we would have expected *mht'* rather than *mhy'.*) However, the problem of the missing main verb in the sentence still remains. In the above translation I have omitted the relative pronoun following "the wounders/attackers"; this seems to give the best sense, even though there is no manuscript justification for it.

[9]MT: "Ramah."

[10]Lit.: "and from before the Lord was the destiny of Ahab to come . . ." for MT's "and from God was the downfall of Ahab to come."

[11]MT: "the Lord." While it was Elijah who was initially instructed to anoint Jehu (1 Kgs 19:16), it was Elisha (2 Kgs 9:1) who gave the final order for the anointing to "one of the sons of the prophets."

they seized him, hiding in Samaria. They brought*a* him to Jehu, and *he killed*[b][12] him. They buried him, for they said: "He was the son of Jehoshaphat who sought *the fear of* the Lord with all his heart." Thus there was no one belonging to the house of Ahaziah who had sufficient power *to seize*[13] the kingship. 10. When Athaliah, Ahaziah's mother, saw that her son was dead, she arose and *killed*[14] all the royal stock *who* belonged to *the men of* the house of Judah. 11. But Jehoshabeath, the king's daughter, took Joash, the son of Ahaziah, *whom Zibiah from Beersheba had borne to him,*[15] and she stole him away from the midst of the king's sons who were being *killed,*[16] and she put him and his nurse in *the Holy of Holies.*[17] Thus Jehoshabeath, the daughter of King Jehoram, the wife of Jehoiada the priest, because she was the sister of Ahaziah, hid him from before Athaliah so that she did not *kill*[18] him. 12. He remained[19] with them, hidden in the *sanctuary* house of the Lord for six years, while Athaliah was queen over the land *of Israel.*[c]

CHAPTER 23

1. In the seventh year Jehoiada took courage, and he took the commanders of hundreds—Azariah the son of Jeroham, Ishmael the son of Jehohanan, Azariah the son of Obed, Maaseiah the son of *Uzziah,*[a][1] and Elishaphat the son of Zichri—*and*

Apparatus, Chapter 22

> [a] V: *'tywhy.* E, L, AS: *'ytwhy.*
> [b] V: *qṭlyh* C, L, AS: *qṭlwhy.*
>
> [c] C, E, L, AS omit "of Israel" (= MT).

Notes, Chapter 22

[12]MT: "and they put him to death." The singular is found in a few MSS, LXX, Syr, Vg. But C, L, AS have the plural.

[13]MT: "for."

[14]MT: "and she spoke," *wtdbr.* As Williamson (314) suggests, this is either a mistake for *wt'bd* (most of the consonants are identical or similar in appearance), i.e., "and she destroyed," found in 2 Kgs 11:1, or "an example of the postulated root *dbr,* cognate with Akkadian *dabaru,* 'overthrow.'"

[15]See 24:1 and 2 Kgs 12:2.

[16]MT: "put to death."

[17]MT: "in a bedroom."

[18]MT: "put to death."

[19]MT and Tg. Chr: "and he was."

Apparatus, Chapter 23

> [a] V, E: *'wzyh.* C: *'dyh.* L, AS: *'dyhw* (= MT).

Notes, Chapter 23

[1]MT: "Adaiah."

he brought them into a covenant with him. 2. And they went around throughout Judah and gathered together the Levites from all the towns of Judah and the heads of the clans of Israel, and they came to Jerusalem. 3. And the whole assembly made a covenant with the king in the *sanctuary* house[b] of *the Lord.*[2] He said to them, "Look! The king's son will become king, just as the Lord spoke concerning the sons of David. 4. Now this is the thing which you will do: one third[c] of you— priests and Levites—arriving for Sabbath *guard duty,* (will make your way) to *the entrances of the palaces'*[d] *gate;*[3] 5. A third[e] (will take up position) at the king's house, and the (other) third[e] at the gate of the *warriors*[4]—*it is the gate of the school of the Sanhedrin,* while all the people will remain in the *court*[5] of the *sanctuary* house of the Lord. 6. No one may enter the *sanctuary* house of the Lord except the priests and the ministrants, the Levites. They may go in, for they are holy. All the people will keep the watch of the *sanctuary house of* the Lord. 7. The Levites will completely surround the king, each man with his *weapon*[5] in his hand. Anyone entering the *sanctuary* house of the Lord will be *killed.*[6] They will stay[7] with the king when he comes in and when he goes out." 8. The Levites and all *the men of* Judah did according to all which Jehoiada the priest had commanded. Each brought his men, those who were arriving for Sabbath *duty* along with those who were going off Sabbath *duty,* for Jehoiada the priest had not dismissed *his*[f8] divisions. 9. Then Jehoiada the priest gave the commanders of hundreds the spears, the shields and the round shields which belonged to King David and which were in the *sanctuary* house of *the Lord.*[2] 10. He stationed all the people, each man with his weapon in his hand, from the right-hand side of the house to the left-hand side of the house, at the altar and at the *sanctuary* house, *all* around the king. 11. Then they brought out the king's son and placed on him the *royal* crown *which David had taken from the head of the king of the sons of Ammon.*[9] *In it was a magnetic jewel,*[g10] in which

Apparatus, Chapter 23

[b] C omits, possibly through homoioteleuton—in Hebrew, "covenant" *(bryt)* and "in the house of" *(bbyt)* are similar in appearance.

[c] L, AS: *twlt'* (an alternative form of *tlt',* as in V). C: *plgwt.*

[d] E, L, AS: singular.

[e] L, AS: *twlt':* C: *tylt'* (alternative forms of *tlt',* as in V).

[f] L, AS: "the divisions" (= MT).

[g] Lit.: "a good stone, magnetic." "Magnetic" *(šyybh)* is missing in L and AS.

Notes, Chapter 23

[2]MT: "God."

[3]MT: "for gatekeepers of (or at) the thresholds." (See also 1 Chr 9:19, 22.) Tg. Chr uses the loan word *pltyry',* "palaces," for "thresholds." See 1 Chr 9:18, note 17.

[4]MT: "foundation." 2 Kgs 11:6 has *ṣwr,* which in Tg. Kgs becomes "protectors."

[5]MT: plural.

[6]MT: "put to death."

[7]MT: Imperative plural: "be" or "stay."

[8]MT: "the."

[9]See 1 Chr 20:2.

[10]See JL I, 5 and II, 442.

was clearly engraved the Great and Glorious Name; David had set it there by the Spirit of holiness. Its value was equivalent to the weight of a centenarium of gold. It was also a witness *to the house of David, that it would not fit*[11] *the head of any king unless he was of the line of David: it would be impossible for him to wear it. When the people saw that it fitted*[12] *the head of Jehoash, and that he was wearing the crown, they acknowledged that he was of David's line* and made him king immediately.[13] Jehoiada and his sons anointed him and said: "May the king *prosper in his reign!"*[14] 12. When Athaliah heard the sound of the people *shouting with delight*[15] and praising the king, she came to the people to the *sanctuary* house of the Lord. 13. She looked, and there was the king, standing on his *balcony*[16] at the entrance, with the nobles and the trumpets *in front of*[17] the king and all the people of the land rejoicing and blowing trumpets and *offering praise*[18] with musical instruments and directing the praise. Athaliah tore her garments and said: "Rebellion! Rebellion!" 14. Then Jehoiada the priest brought out the commanders of the hundreds, *who were appointed over* the troops,[19] and he said to them: "Bring her out from the ranks of (the soldiers who are stationed at) the entrances, into *the open;*[20] anyone who follows her is to be *killed*[21] by the sword." For the priest had

Notes, Chapter 23

[11]Lit.: "it would not be acceptable upon the head."

[12]Lit.: "accepted on," i.e., that it fitted.

[13]MT 1 Chr 20:2 tells of David's seizure of the crown of the king of the Ammonites: its weight was a talent of gold; in it was a precious stone, and it was placed on David's head. Now if a talent weighed approximately a half-hundredweight, David could be pardoned for not wearing the crown too often! The Rabbis also wondered if he ever wore it: one assumed that it was fit to rest on his head even if he didn't actually wear it; another suggested that the precious stone was a lodestone which held up the crown, giving the impression that, as he sat under it, he was indeed wearing it; another put forward the view that it wasn't a question of weight: rather, the precious stone was worth a talent of gold. The first speaker, however, emphasized the real significance of the crown as he looked at 2 Kgs 11:12, the parallel verse to 2 Chr 23:11, where we read: "They brought out the king's son and placed upon him the *crown* and the *testimony.*" He said: "It was a testimony to the house of David that whoever was eligible for the throne [the crown] fitted, but it would not fit anyone who was not eligible." This discussion, in *b. Ab. Zar.* 44a, is reflected in the expansions in Tg. 1 Chr 20:2 and 2 Chr 23:11, and the fact that the crown fitted the head of the king's son in the latter verse confirmed to the audience that Jehoash was indeed of the Davidic line and rightful king.

[14]MT: "May the king live."

[15]MT: "running."

[16]MT: "pillar," "column." Tg. Chr uses the word *'ṭwwn',* "balcony" (MJ 54); "pillar, column" (JL I, 45); with (according to JL) a Persian or, more likely, a Greek origin, perhaps *stulos, stēlē,* or *stoa.*

[17]MT: "beside."

[18]MT: "the singers."

[19]I have used "troops" instead of "army" (*ḥyl'*). "Army" suggests the whole defense force, while "troops" is less specific and can refer also to the local unit of soldiers on duty in the area. MT has *pqwdy hḥyl,* which, according to C. F. Burney (*Notes on the Hebrew Text of the Book of Kings,* Oxford, 1903, 311) commenting on 2 Kgs 11:15, can only mean "those of the army who were mustered," though Tg. Kgs interprets it exactly as Tg. Chr does.

[20]Lit.: "into the midst from the ranks of the entrances," for MT's: "to from the midst of the ranks." Something seems to have fallen out of MT after "to" (likewise in 2 Kgs 11:15). The word used for "ranks" (plural of *śdrh*) is found only here in MT Chr but occurs in 2 Kgs 11:15 and in 1 Kgs 6:9, in which latter place it is an architectural term of uncertain meaning. The word in Aramaic is *sdr,* "row, rank," and MJ (959) with Le Déaut, thinks in Tg. Chr of a "colonnade." "Peut-être le targumiste fait-il allusion à une sorte de péristyle" (I, 147); cf. JL II, 58.

[21]MT: "put to death."

said: "Do not *kill*[22] her *here lest she defile* the *sanctuary* house of the Lord."[23]
15. They gave her *ample room*,[24] and she went in *through*[25] the entrance of the
Gate of the Horses to the house of the king, and they *killed her*[22] there. 16. Then
Jehoiada made a covenant between *his Memra*[26] and all the people and *the Memra
of* the king, that they would be a people *serving before* the Lord.[27] 17. All the people came to the house of the Baal and broke it down; his *"altars"*[28] and his images
they smashed; and Mattan the *"priest"*[29] of the Baal they killed in front of the
"altars."[28] 18. Jehoiada appointed officials *in*[30] the *sanctuary* house of the Lord,
under the authority of the priests, the Levites,[h] whom David had divided up into
groups to be in charge of the *sanctuary* house of the Lord, to offer up whole burnt
offerings *before* the Lord—as written in the law of Moses—with joy and praise as
instructed by[31] David. 19. He stationed the gatekeepers at the gates of the *sanctuary* house of the Lord, so that no one who was unclean for any reason would enter.
20. Then he took the commanders of the hundreds and *the warriors*[32] and the leaders of the people and all the people of the land, and he brought down the king from
the *sanctuary* house of the Lord. They came through the middle of the upper gate
to the house of the king and seated the king[i] upon the royal throne. 21. And all the
people of the land rejoiced and the city was quiet. And Athaliah—they had *killed*[33]
with the sword!

Apparatus, Chapter 23

[h] C: "the priests and Levites." V, L, AS: "the priests,
the Levites" (= MT).

[i] C, L, AS: "him." V: "the king" (= MT).

Notes, Chapter 23

[22] MT: "put her to death."
[23] MT: "(in) the house of the Lord."
[24] MT: "and they placed to/for her two hands," which some (e.g., RSV) translate as "so they laid hands on her." It
may also suggest the idea of space: "and they made for her two hands," indicating space to move in (cf. Gen 34:21).
Tg. Chr: "a broad place."
[25] MT: "to." 2 Kgs 11:16 has *drk,* "way."
[26] Twice in this verse *Memra* has taken on the meaning of "self": In the first instance "between him," though in 2
Kgs 11:17 it is "between the Lord."
[27] MT: "for a people to the Lord," i.e., "the Lord's people."
[28] See 14:2, note 3.
[29] See 11:15, note 13.
[30] MT: "of."
[31] Lit.: "by the hand of."
[32] MT: "the nobles."
[33] MT: "put to death."

CHAPTER 24

1. Joash was seven years old when he became king. He reigned for forty years in Jerusalem. His mother's name was Zibiah from Beersheba. 2. Joash did what was right *before*[a1] the Lord all the days of Jehoiada the priest. 3. Jehoiada took two wives for him, and he became the father of sons and daughters. 4. After this Joash decided[2] to restore the *sanctuary* house of the Lord. 5. So he assembled the priests and Levites and said to them: "Go out to the cities of Judah and collect from all Israel as much silver as is required each year to repair the *sanctuary* house of *the Lord,* your God. But you must *speak*[b3] quickly." The Levites, however, were in no hurry. 6. Then the king summoned Jehoiada, *the treasury official*[4] *who had been appointed as* leader, and said to him: "Why is it that you have not required the Levites to bring from Judah and Jerusalem the *tent of meeting*[5] of Moses, the servant of the Lord and the assembly of Israel *with*[6] the tent of the testimony?" 7. For the wicked[7] Athaliah *and*[c] her sons had broken into the *sanctuary* house of *the Lord*[8] and as well had used[9] all the holy things of the *sanctuary* house of the Lord in the service of *the idols.*[10] 8. At the king's command[11] they made a box and set it outside the gate of the *sanctuary* house of the Lord. 9. They then sent a proclamation[12] throughout Jerusalem and Judah to bring in *before*[13] the Lord, *the tent of meeting*[5] of Moses, the servant of *the Lord,*[8] *which he had made to make atonement* for *the children of* Israel in the wilderness. 10. All the princes and all the

Apparatus, Chapter 24

[a] C: "in the eyes of" (= MT).
[b] V, C: "to speak" *(lmll'),* (= LXX). L, AS: "to the word" *(lmlt')* (= MT).

[c] L, AS omit "and" (= MT).

Notes, Chapter 24

[1] MT: "in the eyes of."
[2] Lit.: "it was with the heart of."
[3] MT: Lit.: "hurry to the word/matter," i.e., "hurry the matter along."
[4] *'mrkl'.* See 1 Chr 2:6, note 5.
[5] MT: "tax."
[6] MT: "with." Verse 6 in MT speaks of bringing a tax imposed by Moses. Tg. Chr speaks of bringing two tents. It is difficult to see the connection between the two texts.
[7] MT: "wickedness." *BDB* (958) "Athaliah, the (embodied) wickedness." Some emend MT "*mirshaath*" to "*marshaath*," "wicked."
[8] MT: "God."
[9] Lit.: "made."
[10] MT: "baals."
[11] Lit.: "and the king said and...."
[12] Lit.: "they caused to pass a proclamation." MT has *qwl* "voice." Tg. Chr has *krwz,* "a herald, public announcement." JL (I, 385) sees the origin of this word in the Greek *kērux.*
[13] MT: "to."

people gladly brought[14] *freewill offerings* and cast them into the box—*and there was no end (to them).*[15] 11. And when the box was brought by the Levites to those who had been appointed[16] by the king, and when they saw that there was a great deal of money *in the box,* the king's scribe[17] came, accompanied by *the high priest's second in command,*[18] *who had been appointed* head; they emptied the box, then took it and returned it to its place. Thus they did day after day and collected a large sum of money. 12. The king and Jehoiada gave it to *those*[19] who were involved in the work of the service of the *sanctuary* house of the Lord, for they were hiring masons and carpenters to renovate the *sanctuary* house of the Lord, as well as craftsmen in iron and bronze to repair the *sanctuary* house of the Lord. 13. Those *who* were involved in the work kept at it, and the repair work went forward in their *hands;*[20] they restored the *sanctuary* house of the Lord to its original state and reinforced it. 14. When they had finished they brought the remainder of the money before the king and Jehoiada, and[21] they made vessels for the *sanctuary* house of the Lord, vessels for the service, and *plates*[22] and dishes, and vessels of gold and silver. And they offered up whole burnt offerings continually in the *sanctuary* house of the Lord all the days of Jehoiada. 15. Jehoiada had reached a ripe old age when he died.[23] At his death he was one hundred and thirty years old. 16. They buried him with the kings in the city of David because he had kept the *commandments* in Israel and in so far as *the Memra of the Lord* and his *sanctuary* house were concerned.[24] 17. After Jehoiada died,[25] the princes of Judah came and bowed down to king *Joash and led him astray.* As a result the king *accepted their idols from them.*[26] 18. And they forsook the *sanctuary* house of the Lord, the God of their fathers, and served the Asherahs and the idols, and there was anger against *the men of* Judah and Jerusalem because of this sin of theirs. 19. He sent prophets among them to bring them back to the *worship of* the Lord, and they testified against them but they paid no heed. 20. Then the spirit of *prophecy from before* the Lord *rested upon* Zechariah, the son of Jehoiada, the priest, *when he saw the sin of the king and*

Notes, Chapter 24

[14]Lit.: "rejoiced and brought."

[15]MT: Lit.: "until completion," i.e., (*BDB* 478) "until all had given." Tg. Chr: "until there was no end," suggesting an unending stream of donors and gifts.

[16]In MT and Tg. Chr the word is singular, an abstract noun, but clearly with a plural reference.

[17]Tg. Chr: *lblr*! See 20:34, note 53.

[18]Perhaps "personal representative" would be a more appropriate translation here for *sgn,* "the sagan"; see 1 Chr 18:16, note 26.

[19]MT: singular, though it can be understood in a collective sense. Some Hebrew MSS and the Versions have the plural form.

[20]MT: singular.

[21]Tg. Chr omits "with it."

[22]MT: "and for offering up," i.e., for the sacrifices.

[23]Lit.: "and Jehoiada was old and full of days and he died."

[24]MT: Lit.: "for he had done good in Israel and with God and his house."

[25]MT: "after the death of Jehoiada."

[26]MT: "the king gave heed to them." MT suggests and Tg. Chr stresses that the princes helped to lead king Joash astray.

the people who were offering up incense on the altar to the image[27] *in the sanctuary house of the Lord, on the Day of Atonement, and preventing the priests of the Lord from offering the whole burnt offerings, the sacrifices, the daily offering and the additional offerings, as written in the book of the Law of Moses.* [28] He stood up opposite the people and said to them: "Thus hath *the Lord*[8] said, 'Why do you transgress the commandments of the Lord? You will not prosper. Because you have abandoned the *worship* of the Lord, he *will abandon*[29] you.'" 21. But they *rebelled*[30] against him and at the king's command hurled *stones*[31] at him in the court of the *sanctuary* house of the Lord. 22. Thus King Joash did not remember the kindness which Jehoiada his father had shown him, but killed his son; as *he neared* death,[32] he said: "*May it be revealed before the Lord! May it be avenged!* May he take account of it!"[33] 23. At the *end*[34] of the year *the armies of the Aramaeans*[35] came up against him; they came to Judah and Jerusalem and *killed*[36] all the leaders of the people from among the people, and all their spoil they sent to the king *at*[d37] Damascus. 24. Although the *armies of the Aramaeans*[35] had come with few men, yet the Lord delivered into their *hands*[38] a very great army, because they had forsaken *the fear of the Lord, the God of their fathers. So they executed judgment*[39] on Joash. 25. And when they had departed from him, leaving him very *badly* wounded,[40] his servants *rebelled*[30] against him *so that* the blood of the sons of Jehoiada the priest *might be*

Apparatus, Chapter 24

[d] L and AS have "of" (= MT). V and C omit *d*, "of": either we assume that it dropped out because of haplography, or we treat it as locative: "at Damascus."

Notes, Chapter 24

[27]Reading *pysl'* with C (V, L, AS have *psl'*).

[28]MT: "The Spirit of God clothed himself with Zechariah. . . ." Zechariah appears also in Tg. Lam 2:20 in the comment on the question: "Should priest and prophet be slain in the sanctuary of the Lord?"—"as they slew Zechariah, the son of Iddo, the high priest and faithful prophet in the house of Jehovah's sanctuary on the Day of Atonement, because he restrained you from doing evil before Jehovah?" (A. W. Greenup's translation in B. Grossfeld [ed.], *The Targum to the Five Megilloth*, New York, 1973; Greenup's translation, Sheffield, 1893.) As we have no record of the violent death of Zechariah, the son of Iddo, we must assume that the Zechariah mentioned in Tg. Lam is the son of Jehoiada. See also M. McNamara, *The New Testament and the Palestinian Targum to the Pentateuch* (second printing, Rome, 1978) 160–163.

[29]MT: "he has abandoned you."

[30]MT: "conspired."

[31]MT: singular.

[32]MT: "as he died."

[33]MT: "May the Lord see, and seek (retribution?)." The last two exclamations in Tg. Chr seem to be two different ways of expressing the thought contained in the final exclamation.

[34]MT: "turn."

[35]MT: "the army of Aram."

[36]MT: "destroyed."

[37]MT: "of."

[38]MT: "hand."

[39]Lit.: "they did acts of judgment."

[40]Lit.: "with many severe wounds."

avenged:[41] they slew him on his bed and he died, and they buried him in the city of David, but they did not bury him in the tombs of the kings. 26. Those who *rebelled*[30] against him were Zabad, the son of Shimeath, the Ammonitess, and Jehozabad, the son of Shimrith, the Moabitess. 27. His sons *had imposed* tax collectors[e] *on those of the house of Judah when* the *sanctuary* house of *the Lord* was being restored, *without any order from the king and the priests. They were killed in battle because of the sins of their father.*[42] And, behold, these are written *on the copy*[f43] of the book of the kings. Amaziah his son reigned in his place.

CHAPTER 25

1. When he was twenty-five years old, Amaziah became king and he reigned in Jerusalem for twenty-nine years. His mother's name was *Jehoadin*[a1] from Jerusalem. 2. He did what was right *before*[2] the Lord, only not with a perfect heart. 3. When his kingship was established,[3] he killed his servants who had *killed*[4] his

Apparatus, Chapter 24

[e] C: "who were among those imposing the tax."   [f] V, C: *pršgn.* E, L, AS: *ptšgn.*

Notes, Chapter 24

[41]MT: "because of the blood of the sons of. . . ."
[42]MT: "and his sons, and the large number of prophecies against him and the founding (restoration) of the house of God. . . ." *mś'* can mean either "a prophetic oracle" or "a tax." Both Kethibh and Qere take the first option. Kethibh: "and the large number of prophecies against him"; Qere: "may the prophecies against him increase." Tg. Chr takes the second option and uses it as the basis for an expansion in which Joash's sons are castigated for imposing unauthorized tax collectors on Judah and being killed in battle, not for this action but because of the sins of their father, some of which may have been the imposition of taxes in the first place.
[43]MT: "Midrash."

Apparatus, Chapter 25

[a] C: "Jehoadan" (= MT).

Notes, Chapter 25

[1]MT: "Jehoadan."
[2]MT: "in the eyes of."
[3]Lit.: "When the kingship was strong upon him."
[4]MT: "struck down."

father, the king. 4. But their sons he did not *kill,*[5] because[6] it is written in the law,[b] in the book of Moses, which the Lord commanded, saying: "Fathers will not die because of sons' *sins,* nor will sons die because of fathers' *sins.* Everyone[c7] will die because of his (own) sin." 5. Then Amaziah assembled *the men of* Judah, and he arranged[8] them by clans, under commanders of thousands and the commanders of the hundreds for all *the men of* Judah and Benjamin. He enlisted those[d] who were twenty years old and above, and he found that there were three hundred thousand young men,[9] fit for military service, carrying spear and shield. 6. He hired one hundred thousand mighty warriors from Israel for one hundred *centenaria*[10] of silver. 7. But *the prophet of the Lord*[11] came to him, saying: "O king, do not let the army of Israel come with you, because *the Memra of* the Lord *is not in support of* Israel,[12] all *the kingdom of the tribe of the house of* Ephraim.[13] 8. For if you go *with the tribe of the house of Ephraim,*[14] *the Lord*[15] will make you stumble[16] before the enemy,[17] for there is power in *the hand of the Lord*[18] to support or to cause to stumble." 9. Amaziah said to the *prophet of the Lord:*[11] "What, then, is to happen to the one hundred *centenaria*[10] of silver[e] which I have given *as hire charges* for the army of Israel?" The *prophet of the Lord*[11] said: "There is *strength before*[19] the Lord to give you more than this." 10. Then Amaziah separated off the army which had come to him from Ephraim, *and he gave them permission* to go back home.[20] But they were very angry[21] with *those of the house of*[f] Judah, and they returned home[20] in fierce anger. 11. Amaziah took courage and led out his people[22] to the Valley of Salt and struck down ten thousand sons of Seir. 12. The men[23] of Judah also cap-

[b] C omits: "in the law."
[c] C (in margin), L, AS: "but everyone" (= MT).
[d] C: "they were enlisted."

[e] C, L, AS omit: "of silver."
[f] C, L, AS omit: "those of the house of."

Notes, Chapter 25

[5]MT: "put to death."
[6]MT adds: "as."
[7]MT: "but everyone."
[8]Lit.: "appointed," "established," "set up."
[9]MT: *bḥwr,* see 13:3, note 5.
[10]MT: "talents."
[11]MT: "a man of God."
[12]MT: "is not with Israel."
[13]MT: "all the sons of Ephraim."
[14]MT is confusing here. "For if you go, act, be strong for the battle." Tg. Chr removes the confusion.
[15]MT: "God."
[16]Reading Aphel with C.
[17]MT: singular form; Tg. Chr: plural.
[18]MT: "with God."
[19]MT: "to."
[20]Lit.: "to their place."
[21]Reading Peal with C. Lit.: "their anger was very strong."
[22]Lit.: "he led his people and he went."
[23]Lit.: "sons."

tured ten thousand alive and brought them to the top of the rock; they hurled them
from the top of the rock, and they were all dashed to pieces. 13. The members of
the force whom Amaziah had prevented from accompanying him[24] into battle
spread out among the towns of Judah, from Samaria to Bethhoron; they *killed*[25]
three thousand of them and took a large amount of plunder. 14. Now after
Amaziah came from *killing*[26] the Edomites, *they*[27] brought the *idols*[28] of the sons
of *Gebal*;[29] he set them up as his own *objects of worship*,[30] worshiped before them
and offered up spices *before*[19] them. 15. The anger of the Lord grew strong against
Amaziah, and he sent him a prophet who said to him: "Why did you seek the
people's[g] *idols*[28] which did not deliver their own people from your hand?" 16. As
he was speaking with him, (the king) said to him, "*Am I right in thinking*[31] that
they[32] have appointed you to give counsel to the king? Stop! Why should they *kill*[33]
you?" Then the prophet ceased *prophesying* and said: "I know that *the Lord*[15] has
counseled to destroy you because you have done this and not *taken*[34] my counsel."
17. Then Amaziah, king of *the tribe of the house of* Judah, took counsel and sent to
Joash, son of Jehoahaz, son of Jehu, the king of Israel, saying: "*Come,*[35] let us look
at each other face *to face*[36] in battle." 18. Joash, the king of Israel, sent to Amaziah,
the king of *the house of* Judah, saying: "A thorn which was in Lebanon sent to a
cedar *which was* in Lebanon, saying: 'Give your daughter to my son as wife.' But a
wild beast which was in Lebanon passed by and crushed the thorn. *You did likewise
when you sent to me and hired a hundred thousand mighty warriors from those of
the house of Israel for a hundred centenaria of silver. Later you dismissed them without letting them go with you into battle. They were exceedingly angry that you sent
them away, so they spread out in the land of your kingdom and killed three thousand
of them and took a large quantity of booty.*[37] 19. You said *to yourself:*[38] 'See, I[h]

Apparatus, Chapter 25

[g] C: "peoples."   [h] C: "you have killed."

Notes, Chapter 25

[24]Lit.: "had returned from going with him."
[25]MT: "struck down."
[26]MT: "striking down."
[27]MT: "he."
[28]MT: "gods."
[29]MT: "Seir." In verse 11 "Seir" remained unchanged in Tg. Chr.
[30]MT: "gods" *('lhym)*. Tg. Chr uses the word for "objects of fear."
[31]MT: a simple question. Tg. Chr lit.: "Is it possible that. . . ?"
[32]MT: "we," though some Hebrew MSS have "they."
[33]MT: "strike you down."
[34]MT: "given heed to."
[35]Tg. Chr follows Qere "come." Kethibh is "to you."
[36]Lit.: "face in face." MT: "face."
[37]Tg. Chr ensures that the message of the parable as he understands it is set out in detail and applied to the current
situation; cf. Judg 9:15.
[38]Lit.: "in your Memra."

have *killed*[39] *the Edomites.'*[40] And your heart has *become proud*[i41] *upon you,* seeking glory for yourself. Now, stay at home! Why are you getting excited about evil, that will result in your *falling,*[42] you and all *the men of* Judah along with you?" 20. But Amaziah did not *accept,*[43] for it had come from *before the Lord*[44] in order to give them over into *his*[j] hand, because they had sought *the worship* of the *objects of worship*[30] of Edom. 21. So Joash, king of *the house of* Israel, went up, and at Beth Shemesh, which belongs to *the tribe of* Judah, he and Amaziah, king of *the tribe of the house of* Judah, saw each other face *to face*[36] in battle. 22. And *the men of* Judah were shattered before *the men of* Israel, and they fled, each to his *towns.*[45] 23. And Joash, the king of *the house of* Israel, seized Amaziah, king of *the tribe of the house of* Judah, the son of Joash, the son of Jehoahaz, in Beth Shemesh, and brought[46] him to Jerusalem, and he knocked down four hundred cubits of the wall of Jerusalem, from the Ephraim Gate to the Corner Gate. 24. And (he took) all the gold and silver, and all the vessels which were found in the sanctuary *house of the Lord,*[47] *which*[48] Obed Edom *had consecrated when David took the ark of the Lord from his house after the Philistines had returned it and the Lord had blessed him,* and the treasuries of the king's house and the sons of *the princes who were* hostages *with him.* Then he returned to Samaria. 25. Amaziah, son of Joash, the king of *the house of* Judah, lived for fifteen years after Joash, the son of Jehoahaz, the king of the *house of* Israel, *died.*[49] 26. Now the rest of the acts of Amaziah, the earlier ones *when he walked in the fear of the Lord,* and the later ones *when he turned aside from ways which were right before the Lord*—are *they*[50] not written in the book of the kings of *the house of* Judah and of *the house of* Israel? 27. From the time that Amaziah turned away from after *the worship of* the Lord, *they instigated a rebellion*[51] against him in Jerusalem, and he fled to Lachish. But they sent after him to Lachish, and there *they killed him.*[52] 28. And they bore him on horses, and they buried him with his fathers in the city of Judah.

Apparatus, Chapter 25

[i] C: *'ytrm.* L, AS: *'trm.* E: *'trwm.*   [j] C: "their hands."

Notes, Chapter 25

[39]MT: "struck down."
[40]MT: "Edom."
[41]Reading ithpalp. *'trrm* with MJ (1460) and Le Déaut (II, 137). MT: "your heart has lifted you up."
[42]Lit.: "and you will fall."
[43]MT: "hear."
[44]MT: "from God."
[45]MT: "to his tents."
[46]Reading *'yytyh,* with C.
[47]MT: "God."
[48]MT: "with Obed Edom." See 1 Chr 13:14.
[49]MT: "after the death of Joash, the son of Jehoahaz...."
[50]MT: "behold they." Targum presupposes *hm* rather than *hnm.* Cf. a few Hebrew MSS and 2 Kgs 14:18.
[51]MT: "made a conspiracy."
[52]MT: "put to death."

CHAPTER 26

1. All the people of *the house of* Judah took Uzziah—he was sixteen years old—and made him king instead of Amaziah his father. 2. It was he who built *Elath*[a][1] and restored it to *those of the house of* Judah after the king slept with his fathers. 3. Uzziah was sixteen years old when he became king, and he reigned for fifty-two years in Jerusalem. His mother's name was *Jecoliah*[2] from Jerusalem. 4. He did *what was* right *before*[3] the Lord according to all which his father Amaziah had done. 5. He was intent on seeking *instruction from before the Lord*[4] in the days of Zechariah, who gave instruction in the *fear of*[5] the Lord,[4] and so long as he sought *instruction from before* the Lord, *the Lord*[4] prospered him. 6. He went out and *made war*[6] with the Philistines and broke down the wall of Gath, the wall of *Gaza*[b][7] and the wall of Ashdod. As well, he built towns in Ashdod and among the Philistines. 7. *The Memra of the Lord*[4] helped him against the Philistines and against the Arabs who lived in *Gezer*[c][8] and *in the plain of Maon.*[9] 8. The Ammonites gave a gift to Uzziah, and his reputation spread until it *reached* Egypt[10] for he had become very powerful. 9. Uzziah built towers in Jerusalem, on the Corner Gate, on the Valley Gate and on *the Gate of* the *corners,*[d][11] and he fortified them. 10. He also built towers in the wilderness and dug many cisterns, for he had great *wealth,*[12] both in the Shephelah and on the *plains,*[e][13] (and he had) *those who tilled the fields with oxen,*[14] *and the grapes of the vineyards*[15] in the hill country, and on

Apparatus, Chapter 26

[a] C, L, AS: "Eloth" (= MT).
[b] E: "Yabneh" (= MT).
[c] C, L, AS: "Gerar." E: "Geder."

[d] E: singular. C, L, AS: *b'umny,* "and he went in with craftsmen and fortified them."
[e] C, L, AS: singular (= MT).

Notes, Chapter 26

[1] MT: "Eloth." 2 Kgs 14:22, LXX, Syr, Vg have "Elath."
[2] Tg. Chr follows Qere. Kethibh is *ykylyh.*
[3] MT: "in the eyes of."
[4] MT: "God."
[5] MT: "in seeing," "in the visions of"? *br't.* Tg. Chr presupposes *byr't,* "in the fear of," as in some Hebrew MSS, LXX, Syr.
[6] MT: "fought."
[7] MT: "Yabneh." Syr has "Gaza."
[8] MT: "Gur-Baal." *ICC* (449): "an unidentified place, and the reading is doubtful."
[9] MT: "and the Meunim." In Tg. Chr, *b'l* in a place name is sometimes replaced by *myšr,* "plain, valley," e.g., 1 Chr 14:11. It would seem that Tg. Chr has taken the "baal" from the place name "Gur-baal" and linked it up with the following word "Meunim," giving, finally, "the plain of Maon."
[10] MT: "the entrance of Egypt."
[11] MT: "the Angle," "the corner-buttress." Uncertain of the exact location, Tg. Chr simply calls it "the Gate of the Corners," using the same word as used for a previous gate. See Neh 3:19, 24.
[12] MT: "cattle."
[13] MT: singular.
[14] MT: "farmers."
[15] MT: "vinedressers."

Carmel, for he loved *agriculture.*[16] 11. Uzziah had military detachments,[17] fighting soldiers[18] *and* combat ready troops, organized in detachments, according to the total number of their muster operated by *Jeiel,*[19] the scribe, and Maaseiah, the commander, under the direction of Hananiah, one of the king's officers. 12. The total number of the heads of the clans of the mighty warriors was two thousand six hundred. 13. Under their command was a powerful army of three hundred and seven thousand five hundred fighting soldiers,[20] of great strength, supporting the king against the *enemies.*[f][21] 14. Uzziah provided for them, for the whole army, shields, spears, helmets,[22] coats of mail, bows and sling stones. 15. In Jerusalem, *through the work of* a skilled craftsman, he made cleverly designed devices,[23] *hollow towers,* to be (placed) on the towers and on the corners, from which they could aim arrows and *hurl* huge stones. His reputation spread far afield, for he was marvelously helped until he became strong. 16. As soon as he was strong he became so arrogant[24] that he brought about his own ruin. He showed disloyalty to *the Memra of* the Lord, his God; he entered the temple of the Lord to make an offering upon the altar of *sweet-smelling* incense. 17. After him went Azariah, the priest, with whom were eighty priests of the Lord, courageous men. 18. They confronted King Uzziah and said to him: "You do not have *authority,* Uzziah, to make an offering of *sweet-smelling* incense before the Lord, for that belongs to the priests, the sons of Aaron, who have been consecrated, to offer up *sweet-smelling* incense. Leave the sanctuary, for you have shown disloyalty, and there will be no honor for you in (offering) *incense before* the Lord."[25] 19. Uzziah became angry. He had a censer in his hand to present an offering, but when he became angry with the priests, leprosy spread over his forehead in the presence of the priests, in the sanctuary *house* of the Lord, above the altar of incense. 20. Azariah, the priest, *who had been appointed* head, and all the priests, turned toward him and behold his forehead was leprous.[26] They tried to get him out quickly, and he too hurried to get out, for *the Memra of* the Lord *had brought the affliction* upon him.[27] 21. King Uzziah was leprous until

Apparatus, Chapter 26

[f] C, L, AS: singular (= MT).

Notes, Chapter 26

[16]MT: "land." Tg. Chr: "the service of the land."

[17]MT: singular.

[18]MT: singular. Lit.: "a maker of war," though a few MSS have "makers of war," i.e., "fighting soldiers."

[19]Following Qere. Kethibh is *y'w'l.*

[20]Lit.: "makers of war."

[21]MT: singular.

[22]Tg. Chr uses the plural of *qwls',* "helmet," borrowed from the Greek *koros* (JL II, 364). MJ 1329 makes no reference to Greek origin.

[23]MT: "he made contrivances, the invention of inventive men" (*BDB* 364).

[24]Lit.: "his heart became haughty."

[25]MT: Lit.: "and it will not be to you for honor from the Lord God."

[26]Lit.: "he was leprous in his forehead."

[27]MT: "for the Lord had smitten him."

the day of his death. He lived as a leper in the *Leprosy House outside Jerusalem, for he had been separated from the men of his house because of what had been decreed concerning him in* the sanctuary *house* of the Lord.[28] Jotham, his son, was *appointed* over the king's house, judging the people of the land. 22. The rest of the acts of Uzziah, the former, *before he committed his offense and became a leper,* and the latter, *after he had become a leper,* Isaiah the prophet, the son of Amoz, has recorded them. 23. Uzziah slept with his fathers, and they buried him with his fathers in the burial field which belonged to the kings, for they said: "He is a leper." And Jotham his son became king in his place.

CHAPTER 27

1. Jotham was twenty-five years old when he became king, and he reigned for sixteen years in Jerusalem. His mother's name was Jerushah, the daughter of Zadok. 2. He did what was right *before*[1] the Lord according to all that Uzziah his father had done, except that he did not come into the temple of the Lord. But the people still acted corruptly. 3. It was he who built the upper gate of the *sanctuary* house of the Lord and carried out extensive building work on the *inner* wall of *the palace.*[2] 4. He also built towns in the hill country of *the house of* Judah, and *in the strongest fortresses*[3] he built castles and towers. 5. He *made war*[4] with the king of the sons of Ammon and subdued them; the sons of Ammon gave him that year one hundred *centenaria*[5] of silver, ten thousand cors of wheat and ten thousand of barley. The sons of Ammon gave him this (amount) in the second year and in the third. 6. So Jotham became strong, for *the Lord had established his kingdom because* he had established his ways before the Lord, his God. 7. Now the rest of the acts of Jotham and all his *battle-encounters*[6] and his behavior,[7] behold they are written in the book of the kings of *the house of* Israel and Judah. 8. He was twenty-five years old when he became king, and he reigned in Jerusalem for sixteen years. 9. And Jotham slept with his fathers, and they buried him in the city of David. And Ahaz his son became king in his place.

Notes, Chapter 26

[28]MT: "as a leper in a free (isolated) house, for he was cut off from the house of the Lord." In Tg. Chr he is also cut off from Jerusalem, perhaps in line with Lev 13:46, "in a habitation outside the camp."

Notes, Chapter 27

[1]MT: "in the eyes of."
[2]MT: "the Ophel." MT uses the loan word *pltyryn*. See 1 Chr 9:18, note 17.
[3]MT: "in the wooded areas."
[4]MT: "he fought."
[5]MT: "talents."
[6]Lit.: "the lines of his battle" for MT's "his battles."
[7]Lit.: "his ways."

CHAPTER 28

1. Ahaz was twenty years old when he became king, and for sixteen years he reigned in Jerusalem. He did not do what was right *before*[1] the Lord, like David his father. 2. He walked in the ways of the kings of *the house of* Israel and even made molten images for the baals. 3. It was he who offered up incense in the valley of Bar Hinnom and *made* his sons *pass*[a2] *through the fire. Of them, however, the Memra of the Lord rescued Hezekiah, because it had been revealed before the Lord, that from him three righteous men were destined*[3] *to come forth, Hananiah, Mishael, and Azariah, who were determined*[3] *to hand over their bodies to be thrown into the midst of the furnace of burning fire for the sake of the great and glorious Name, and they were rescued from the fire. First of all, Abraham was rescued from the burning of the furnace of fire of the Chaldeans, into which Nimrod had cast him because he would not serve his idols. Secondly, Tamar was rescued from the burning of the fire of Judah's tribunal when he had said: "Take her out and let her be burned!" Thirdly, Hezekiah, the son of Jotham,*[b] *was rescued from the burning of the fire when his father threw him into the valley of Bar Hinnom, on the altars of Topheth. Fourthly, Hananiah, Mishael, and Azariah were rescued from the furnace of burning fire of Nebuchadnezzar, the king of Babylon. Fifthly, Joshua, the son of Jehozadak, the chief priest, was rescued when the wicked Nebuchadnezzar threw him into the furnace of burning fire along with Ahab, the son of Kolaiah and Zedekiah, the son of Measeiah, the prophets of falsehood: they were burned in the fire, but Joshua, the son of Jehozadak, was rescued because of his merits.*[4] *But Ahaz acted wickedly* in ac-

---

Apparatus, Chapter 28

[a] V, L, AS: *"br.* C: *'b'r* (= *MT*).   [b] V, E: "Jotham." C, L, AS: "Ahaz" (= 2 Chr 28:27).

Notes, Chapter 28

[1]MT: "in the eyes of."

[2]MT: "he burned" *(wyb'r).* One Hebrew MS, LXX, Syr, and 2 Kgs 16:3 presuppose *wy'br,* "and he caused (his sons) to pass (through the fire)."

[3]Tg. Chr uses the plural form of *'tymws,* "ready, determined, destined," borrowed from the Greek *etoimos* (MJ 42 and JL I, 22).

[4]The basis for this expansion is twofold. (i) Fire—and those who have passed through it (or been burned in it. See Apparatus, note *a*). (ii) The existence of Hezekiah. If Ahaz burned his sons and Hezekiah became king, then he at least of the sons must have been rescued. This provides Tg. Chr with the opportunity to give a list of personalities who suffered a similar fate and experienced a similar deliverance (cf. list of famines given in Tg. Ruth 1:1), with reasons for the deliverance:

—Abraham, who refused to worship Nimrod's idol: Tg. Ps.-J. Gen 11:27; see also note on Nimrod Tg. 1 Chr 1:10.

—Tamar, who was more righteous than her father-in-law Judah. See Frg. Tg. Gen 38, where the three witnesses provided by God to rescue her from the fire are in fact Daniel's three friends, Hananiah, Mishael, and Azariah.

—Hezekiah, who (earlier in the expansion) was rescued so that he could be the progenitor of Daniel's three friends: see *b. San.* 63b. Topheth is not specifically mentioned in connection with Ahaz, but it does appear in Josiah's reform (2 Kgs 23:10) as a place where human sacrifice was prevalent. (A similar comment on Hezekiah is found in a marginal gloss in Codex Reuchlinianus of Tg. 2 Kgs 16:3: A. Sperber II, 306.) Daniel's three friends were ready to suffer death rather than renounce their faith (see Dan 3 and *PRE* 33).

cordance with the abominations of the peoples whom the Lord had driven out from before the sons of Israel. 4. He sacrificed and made offerings *of sweet-smelling things* on the high places, on the hills and under every *leafy*[5] tree. 5. So the Lord his[c] God *delivered*[6] him into the hand of the king of Aram, and they *killed some of his troops*[7] and took a large number of captives from him and brought them *to* Damascus. He was *delivered*[8] also into the hand of the king of Israel, *who inflicted a great slaughter on his forces.*[9] 6. Pekah, the son of Remaliah, killed among *the men of* Judah one hundred and twenty thousand in one day, all of them brave men, because they had forsaken *the fear of* the Lord, the God of their fathers. 7. And Zichri, a warrior of *the house of* Ephraim, slew Maasiah, the king's son, and Azrikam, the leader *who had been put in charge of the palace,*[10] and Elqanah, the king's *right-hand man.*[11] 8. The sons of Israel captured two hundred thousand of their kinsfolk—women, sons and daughters. As well, they took from them a large quantity of plunder, and they brought the plunder to Samaria. 9. Now there was a prophet of the Lord there whose name was Oded; he went out to meet the army as it came to Samaria and he said to them: "Look! It was because of the anger of the Lord, the God of your fathers, against *the men of* Judah that he *delivered*[12] them into your *hands,*[13] but you have killed them in anger *which*[d] has reached up to heaven. 10. And now these same[14] sons of Judah and Jerusalem you are planning to subjugate as your male and female slaves. Surely a guilt *offering*[e] *is required* from you as well? *You have incurred guilt in the matter of the battle,*[15] before the Lord, your God. 11. So now, *listen to* me[16] and restore the prisoners whom you have cap-

Apparatus, Chapter 28

[c] C omits "his."
[d] C omits "which."

[e] V: *qrbn.* C, E, L, AS: *qrb'.*

Notes, Chapter 28

—Joshua, son of Jehozadak (Zech 3), along with two named false prophets (Jer 29:21-22). Nebuchadnezzar decides to use fire to test the truth of the statements of these prophets. But the pious Joshua is allowed to accompany them into the furnace, in the hope that his merit will save all three. His merit saves himself ("a brand plucked from the burning," Zech 3:2), but is unable to rescue the false prophets (see *b. San.* 93a and *PRE* 33).

[5] MT: "flourishing."
[6] MT: "gave."
[7] MT: "and they struck him down."
[8] MT: "given."
[9] MT: "and he struck him a great blow."
[10] MT: "the leader of the house." Tg. Chr's "palace" is a loan word, *pltyryn*; see 1 Chr 9:18, note 17.
[11] MT: "the second of the king." Tg. Chr uses the word *'rqbt',* MJ (73) "a high dignitary in Persia"; the same word, in a slightly different form, describes the relationship of Joseph to Pharaoh in Ps.-J. Gen 41:44. See also JL (I, 34 and 70). MJ notes that this word has also come into Greek, *argapetēs.*
[12] MT: "gave."
[13] MT: "hand."
[14] Lit.: "the."
[15] Lit.: "Surely also you, with you an offering of guilt." MT is also awkward: "Surely also you, with you offenses." The thrust seems to be: "You are just as guilty as your brethren." Tg. Chr expands a little further, explaining exactly where the guilt has been incurred.
[16] MT: "hear me."

tured from your kinsfolk, for the anger of the Lord is vehement[f] against you." [17]
12. Then some of the heads of the sons of Ephraim, Azariah the son of Johanan, *the son of*[g][18] Berechiah, the son of Meshillemoth, Hezekiah, the son of Shallum,[h] Amasa the son of Hadlai confronted those who were coming from the campaign[19]
13. and said to them: "Do not bring the prisoners here, for you are proposing to make us guilty *before*[20] the Lord, *to bring wrath upon us,* to increase our sin and our guilt, for our guilt is great, and the vehemence[i] of the anger is against Israel." 14. So the *armed* soldiers left the prisoners and the spoil[j] before the commanders and the whole assembly. 15. Then the men who had been designated by name arose and took the prisoners, and from the spoil they clothed all those among them who were naked; they gave them clothes[21] and footwear,[21] food[21] and drink;[21] they washed them and transported on donkeys everyone who was unsteady, and they brought them to Jericho, the city of the palms, beside their brethren. Then they returned to Samaria. 16. At that time king Ahaz sent to the *king*[22] of Assyria for help.[23] 17. *The* Edomites had come again and had *killed*[24] some of (the people of) Judah and had carried off prisoners. 18. And *the* Philistines had spread out among the towns of the Shephelah and the south which belonged to *the tribe of* Judah and had captured Beth Shemesh and Aijalon and Gederoth and Soco and its common land,[25] and Timnah and its common land,[25] and Gimzo and its common land,[25] and they had settled there. 19. For the Lord had humbled Judah because of Ahaz, the king of *Judah,*[k][26] for *those of the house of* Judah *had given up the worship of the Lord*[27] and had acted unfaithfully against *the Memra of* the Lord. 20. Then *Tiglath*[28] Pilneser, the king of Assyria, came against him[l] and harassed him, but did not give him support. 21. Because Ahaz had plundered[29] the *sanctuary* house

---

Apparatus, Chapter 28

[f] V: *tqyp.* C, L, AS: *tqwp.* The latter reading, a noun instead of an adjective, is much closer to MT.
[g] V: *br.* Lacking in E, C, L, AS (= MT).
[h] E: "Uzziah."

[i] V, C: *tqwp* (= MT). L, AS: *tqyp.* Contrast note *f.*
[j] E, L, AS add: "which they had captured."
[k] C: "Israel" (= MT).
[l] C adds: "and he came."

Notes, Chapter 28

[17] MT: "for the burning of the anger of the Lord is upon you."
[18] Not in MT. Has arisen possibly through dittography, under the influence of the first two letters of the next word.
[19] Lit.: "army."
[20] MT: "to."
[21] In each case, MT and Tg. Chr use the causative form of the appropriate verb.
[22] MT: "kings," though one Hebrew MS has singular.
[23] Lit.: "to help him."
[24] MT: "struck down."
[25] MT: "its daughters," which Tg. Chr normally translates as "its villages."
[26] MT: "Israel," but some Hebrew MSS and the Versions have "Judah."
[27] MT: "for he had let things go in Judah."
[28] MT: "Tilgath," though many Hebrew MSS have "Tiglath."
[29] Lit.: "divided," "divided off," "siphoned off," "plundered."

of the Lord and the house of the king and the princes and had given (it) to the king of Assyria: but it was of no help to him. 22. During the time that he was being harassed he continued to act unfaithfully against *the Memra of* the Lord, did that King Ahaz. 23. And he sacrificed to the *idols*[30] of Damascus who had *killed some of his forces.*[31] And he said: "As the *idols*[30] of the kings of Aram are helping them, to them I shall sacrifice and they will help me." But they became a stumbling block to him and to all *m* Israel. 24. Then Ahaz brought together *all* the vessels of the *sanctuary* house of *the Lord,*[32] and he cut up the vessels of the *sanctuary* house of *the Lord,*[32] and he closed the doors of the *sanctuary* house of the Lord, and he made for himself *"altars"*[33] in every corner in Jerusalem. 25. And in every town that belonged to *the tribe of* Judah he made high places to offer up *sweet-smelling things to idols of foreign peoples,*[34] and he caused anger *before* the Lord, the God of his fathers. 26. Now the rest of his acts and all his ways, from beginning to end,[35] behold they are written in the book of the kings of *the house of* Judah and Israel. 27. And Ahaz slept with his fathers, and they buried him in the city *of*[36] Jerusalem, for they did not bring him to the graves of the kings of *the house of* Israel. And Hezekiah,[37] his son, became king in his place.

CHAPTER 29

1. Hezekiah became king when he was twenty-five years old, and he reigned for twenty-nine years in Jerusalem. His mother's name was Abijah, the daughter of Zechariah. 2. He did what was right *before*[1] the Lord, according to all which David, his father, had done. 3. He, in the first year of his reign,[2] in the first month,

Apparatus, Chapter 28

m C, L, AS add: "the sons of."

Notes, Chapter 28

[30]MT: "gods."
[31]MT: "who were striking him down."
[32]MT: "God."
[33]See 14:2, note 3.
[34]MT: "to other gods." See 7:19.
[35]Lit.: "the first and the last."
[36]MT: "in."
[37]MT: *yḥzqhyw.* Tg. Chr: *ḥzqyh.*

Notes, Chapter 29

[1]MT: "in the eyes of."
[2]Lit.: "when he reigned."

opened the doors of the *sanctuary* house of the Lord and repaired them. 4. He brought in the priests and the Levites and assembled them in the east square. 5. Then he said to them: "*Accept from me,*[3] Levites! Now, *be ready and* consecrate yourselves and consecrate the *sanctuary* house of the Lord, the God of your fathers, and bring out the abomination from the sanctuary. 6. For our fathers acted treacherously and did what was evil *before*[1] the Lord, our God; they forsook him and turned their faces away from the dwelling place of the Lord, and they *turned to him*[4] their back. 7. They also shut the doors of the vestibule and put out the lamps; they did not offer up *sweet-smelling* incense, they did not offer up the whole burnt offering in the holy place to the God of Israel. 8. And the anger of the Lord was upon *the men of* Judah and Jerusalem, and *they*[a][5] gave them over to trembling, to despair and to *devastation,*[6] as you see with your eyes. 9. And behold! Our fathers fell, *killed* by the sword, and our sons, our daughters, and our wives are in captivity because of this. 10. Now, it is in my heart to make a covenant *before*[7] the Lord, the God of Israel, that the vehemence of his anger may turn away from us. 11. My sons, now don't be slack, because the Lord has chosen you to stand before him, to serve him and to be before him, serving and offering up *sweet-smelling* incense." 12. Then the Levites arose: Mahath, the son of Amasai, and Joel, the son of Azariah, of the sons of *Qehath*;[8] of the sons of Merari, Kish, the son of Abdi, and Azariah, the son of Jehalelel; of *the sons of Gershon,*[9] Joah, the son of Zimmah, and Eden, the son of Joah; 13.[b] of the sons of Elizaphan, Shimri and *Jeiel*;[10] of the sons of Asaph, Zechariah and Mattaniah; 14. of the sons of Heman, *Jehiel*[11] and Shimei; of the sons of Jeduthun, Shemaiah and Uzziel.[12] 15. They gathered their brethren together, consecrated themselves and came, in accordance with the commandment of the king, by the words of the Lord, to purify the *sanctuary* house of the Lord. 16. The priests entered right into the interior of the *sanctuary* house of the Lord[13] and brought out everything unclean[14] that they found in the temple of

Apparatus, Chapter 29

[a] V: "they." C, L, AS: "he" (= MT).   [b] E omits verses 13 and 14.

Notes, Chapter 29

[3]MT: "hear me."
[4]MT: "they gave."
[5]MT: "he."
[6]MT: "hissing." See also Jer 29:18.
[7]Reading *qdm*, "before," with E, L, AS. MT: "to."
[8]MT: "the Qehathite."
[9]MT: "of the Gershunite."
[10]Tg. Chr follows Qere. Kethibh is *y'w'l.*
[11]Tg. Chr follows Qere. Kethibh is *yhw'l.*
[12]Following C (= MT). V has "Aziel."
[13]MT has: "to purify (it)."
[14]Lit.: "all the uncleanness."

the Lord, to the court of the *sanctuary* house of the Lord, and the Levites took it, to bring it outside to the Wadi Kidron. 17. On the first (day) of the first month, *Nisan,* they began to consecrate, and on the eighth*c* day of the month they came to the vestibule*d* of the Lord and they consecrated the *sanctuary* house of the Lord for *a period of* eight days, and on the sixteenth day of the month *of Nisan* they finished. 18. Then they came inside, to Hezekiah the king, and said: "We have purified the whole *sanctuary* house of the Lord and the altar of the whole burnt offering and all its vessels, and the table of the laying out and all its vessels. 19. All the vessels which Ahaz*e*[15] *made unclean*[16] *and abominable before the idols of foreigners* when he was king, when he was unfaithful to *the Memra of the Lord,* we have prepared *them* and *we have hidden them and set apart others in their place,*[17] and behold, *they are* in front of the altar of the Lord." 20. Then King Hezekiah rose early and assembled *all*[f] the commanders of the city, and he went up to the *sanctuary* house of the Lord. 21. And they brought seven oxen and seven rams and seven lambs and seven young he-goats for the sin offering, *to make atonement* for the kingdom, for the sanctuary and for *the men of* Judah. And he told the sons of Aaron, the priests, to offer (them) up upon the altar of the Lord. 22. Then they slaughtered *the oxen,* and the priests received the blood *for the altar*[g] and they splashed it against the altar; they slaughtered the rams and they splashed the blood against the altar; they slaughtered the lambs and they splashed the blood against the altar. 23. They brought forward the he-goats of the sin-offering before the king and the assembly, and they laid their hands upon them. 24. The priests slaughtered them and with their blood they *purified* the altar[18] in order to make atonement for all Israel, for the king had commanded that the whole burnt offering and the sin offering *should be made* for all Israel. 25. He stationed the Levites in the *sanctuary* house of the Lord, with cymbals and lutes and lyres, in accordance with the commandment of David and of Gad, the *prophet*[19] of the king, and Nathan the prophet, for the commandment was by *the Memra of* the Lord, through his prophets. 26. The Levites stood with the instruments of *praise of* David, and the priests with the trumpets. 27. Then Hezekiah*h* gave the order to offer up the whole burnt offering upon the

Apparatus, Chapter 29

c C: "second."
d E, L, AS : "temple."
e C, L, AS have "king Ahaz" (= MT).

f C, L, AS omit "and" (= MT).
g V: "for the altar." Missing in C, L, AS (= MT).
h C, L, AS: "Hezekiah the King."

Notes, Chapter 29

[15]V omits "king."
[16]MT: "rejected."
[17]MT: "We have prepared and we have consecrated." In *b. Ab. Zar.* 54b there is this comment: "'*Have we prepared*' means that we have stored them away and '*sanctified*' means that we have substituted others for them." Tg. Chr has followed this closely, except that he has left the "we have prepared them" intact, unless we take the following *Waw* as epexegetical.
[18]MT: "they made a sin offering on the altar."
[19]MT: "seer."

altar; and when the whole burnt offering began, the praise of the Lord began *with* [20] the trumpets and with the accompaniment of the instruments of *music* of David, the king of Israel. 28. The whole assembly bowed down[i] and *he who uttered* the song was offering praise, and they were sounding the trumpets, all of them *together* until the whole burnt offering was finished. 29. When the offering up of *the whole burnt offering* was finished, the king and all who were to be found *there* [21] bowed down and worshiped. 30. Then Hezekiah the king and the commanders told the Levites to offer praise *before* [22] the Lord *in accordance* with the words of David and Asaph the seer, and they offered praise until *they were possessed of great* joy, [23] and they bowed down and worshiped. 31. Then Hezekiah answered and said: "Now you *have presented your offering before* the Lord; [24] draw near and bring sacrifices and *the* thank offerings to the *sanctuary* house of the Lord." The assembly[j] brought sacrifices and *the* thank offerings,[j] and everyone whose heart was well disposed *was bringing* whole burnt offerings. 32. The *total of the* number of the *whole burnt offerings* [25] which the assembly brought was: seventy oxen, one hundred rams, and two hundred lambs. All these were for the whole burnt offering *before* [22] the Lord. 33. *The sacrifices of* the holy things were six hundred oxen and three thousand sheep. 34. However, the priests were few and were unable to skin [26] the whole burnt offerings, and their brethren the Levites assisted them until they had finished the work and until the priests had sanctified themselves, for the Levites were more conscientious in sanctifying themselves than the priests. 35. As well, (there were) large numbers of the whole burnt offerings, with the fat of *the sacrifices of holy things* [27] and with the libations for the whole burnt offering. Thus the worship of the *sanctuary* house of the Lord was restored. 36. Hezekiah and all the people rejoiced because *the Lord* [28] had restored to the people *the desire of their heart,* for the thing had happened suddenly.

Apparatus, Chapter 29

[i] E: *mstgdyn.* C, L, AS: *mšbḥyn.*   [j-j] C omits.

Notes, Chapter 29

[20]MT: "and."
[21]MT: "with him."
[22]MT: "to."
[23]Lit.: "until they rejoiced with great joy."
[24]MT: "You have filled your hand to/for the Lord," usually translated in English versions as "you have consecrated yourselves to the Lord." See 1 Chr 29:5, note 12.
[25]MT: singular.
[26]Tg. Chr omits "all."
[27]MT: "with the fat of the peace offerings."
[28]MT: "God."

CHAPTER 30

1. Then Hezekiah sent to all Israel and Judah and, as well, he wrote letters to *those of the house of* Ephraim and Manasseh, to come to the *sanctuary* house of the Lord in Jerusalem to keep the Passover *before*[1] the Lord, the God of Israel. 2. The king, his commanders, *all Israel* and all the assembly in Jerusalem had taken counsel *to intercalate the month of Nisan,*[2] *and* to keep the Passover in the *month of Iyyar, which is the* second month. 3. For they had not been able to keep the *Passover in Nisan*[3] because the priests had not sanctified themselves *so that they would be purified* in sufficient numbers[a] *for the work of the offerings,* and the people had not been able to assemble in Jerusalem. 4. The matter was right *before*[4] the king and *before*[4] the whole assembly. 5. So they took the decision to have a proclamation made[5] throughout all Israel from[b] Beersheba to *Pameas,*[6] to come to keep the Passover *before*[1] the Lord, the God of Israel, in Jerusalem, because the greater part *of the assembly* had not kept *the Passover in Nisan, at its proper time,* as it had been written. 6. Then the runners, with the letters from the hand of the king and his commanders, went[7] throughout all *the house of* Israel and Judah, and *by*[8] the king's command, saying: "Sons of Israel, return to *the fear of* the Lord, the God of Abraham, Isaac, and Israel, and he will *restore*[c][9] those who have escaped, who have been left to you from the *hands*[10] of the kings of Assyria. 7. Do not be like your fathers and like your brethren who acted unfaithfully against *the Memra of* the Lord,

---

Apparatus, Chapter 30

[a] V: *bmyst.* C, L, AS: *km(y)st:* "according to the number required."

[b] C: "From Dan to Beersheba and to Pameas."

[c] E, L, AS: "he will return to . . ." (= MT). C is confusing at this point, as he seems to have written *lwt,* "to," as *yt* (object marker), but has also retained the intransitive verb "return," *ytwb.*

Notes, Chapter 30

[1]MT: "to."

[2]Reading "to intercalate" with E, L, and AS. A shortage of priests and people at the proper Passover time had resulted in its non-celebration, and arrangements are made for a late festival. Because of the difference between the solar and the lunar calendars, it was necessary to add an extra month approximately every three years. This "leap month" was usually added after the twelfth month Adar, and known as "second Adar," immediately before Nisan. Here, however, it would seem that the intercalated month is a "second Nisan." There is a long and complicated discussion on the issue in *b. San.* 12a-b, and one of the reasons put forward for Hezekiah's prayer for forgiveness in verse 18 is given as follows: "Why then did Hezekiah implore divine mercy?—Because only an Adar can be intercalated and he intercalated a Nisan in Nisan." (For intercalation and a detailed account of its operation see *PRE* 8 and Schürer I, Appendix III, 587–601.)

[3]MT: "to keep it at that time."

[4]MT: "in the eyes of."

[5]See 24:9, note 12.

[6]MT: "Dan." See 1 Chr 21:2, note 2.

[7]Reading plural with E, C, L, AS.

[8]MT: "according to."

[9]MT: "that he may return to."

[10]MT: singular.

the God of their fathers, *and they[d] handed them over to those who hated them*, and *they[d]*[11] gave them up to desolation, as you see. 8. Now, therefore, do not stiffen your neck like your fathers; *stretch out* the hand *and return* to *the fear of* the Lord,[12] and come to his sanctuary *house* which he consecrated for ever. Serve *before* the Lord your God and he will *turn away* from you the vehemence of his anger.[e][13] 9. For when you return *to the fear of* the Lord, your brethren and your sons, *he will give* them mercy[14] before those who have captured them, and he will return[15] *by his Memra to restore them* to this land, for gracious and merciful is the Lord, your God; he will not take up *his Shekinah*[16] from *among* you if you return to *his fear*.[17] 10. So the runners were passing from city to city in the land of *the house of* Ephraim and *in[f] the house of* Manasseh and as far as Zebulun, but they were laughing at them and mocking them. 11. Only some from *the tribe of* Asher, and from *the tribe of* Manasseh, and from *the tribe of* Zebulun humbled themselves and came to Jerusalem. 12. Also among *those of the house of* Judah *there was good will from before the Lord*[18] to give them one heart to carry out the commandment of the king and the commanders, *in accordance with*[19] the word of the Lord. 13. So they assembled *in* Jerusalem—a great number of people—to keep the festival of Unleavened Bread in the second month—a very large assembly. 14. They arose and did away with the *"altars"*[20] which were in Jerusalem, and all *the places where sweet-smelling things were offered up*,[21] they did away[g] with *the idols* and threw them into the Wadi *of* Kedron. 15. Then they slaughtered the Passover on the fourteenth day of the second month, and the priests and the Levites humbled themselves and consecrated themselves and brought whole burnt offerings into the *sanctuary* house of

---

Apparatus, Chapter 30

[d] L, AS: "he."
[e] C, L, AS: "and the vehemence of his anger will turn away from you" (= MT).
[f] C, L, AS: "of."

[g] By its position in C, E, L, and AS, this verb is linked to the preceding phrase, giving the translation: "and they did away with all the places where sweet-smelling spices were offered up. . .," which would be more in keeping with the sentence order in MT.

Notes, Chapter 30

[11] MT: "he."

[12] MT: "give a hand to the Lord."

[13] MT: "that the vehemence of his anger may turn away from you."

[14] MT: "your brethren and your sons for mercy," normally translated, e.g., J. M. Myers, "your brothers and your sons will be dealt with mercifully." Tg. Chr has "your brothers and your sons he has given (in this context as prophetic perfect, 'he will give') for mercy," which seems to imply: "he will ensure that your brothers and sons are treated mercifully."

[15] Following L and AS. V and C have the Aphel transitive form.

[16] MT: "face."

[17] MT: "him."

[18] MT: "The hand of God was."

[19] MT: "by," though some MSS and LXX have "in accordance with."

[20] See 14:2, note 3.

[21] MT: "all the incense altars" (*BDB* 883).

the Lord. 16. They stood upon their platform, as was appropriate to them in accordance with the law of Moses, *the prophet of the Lord;*[22] the priests were splashing the blood (which they received) from the *hands*[23] of the Levites. 17. Because many in the assembly had not consecrated themselves, the Levites were *put* in charge of the slaughtering of the Passover *lambs*[24] for every *man* who had not been purified, so that he might consecrate *himself before*[25] the Lord. 18. For many of the people, *and some of those of the house* of [26] Ephraim, *some of those of the house of* Manasseh, *some of those of the house of* Issachar, *and some of those of the house of* Zebulun had not been purified, but they had eaten the *first* Passover, but not in accordance with what was written; *then they came back to keep the second Passover in accordance with that which was written,*[27] for Hezekiah had prayed for them, saying: "May the Lord, who is good, forgive[28] *the people who have erred.*" 19. *For*[29] he had set his heart to seek *the fear of* God, the Lord, the God of *[h]* his fathers. [30] *"May he not take account of the sins of the people who have not kept the Passover as prescribed, (namely), to eat the holy flesh in a state of purity."*[31] 20. Then the Lord *accepted the prayer of*[32] Hezekiah and healed the people. 21. The children of Israel who were to be found in Jerusalem kept the festival of Unleavened Bread seven days with great joy, with the Levites and the priests offering praise *before*[25] the Lord each day with instruments of *praise*[33] *before*[25] the Lord. 22. Hezekiah spoke encouragingly to all*[i]* the Levites *in whom there was* good understanding *before* the Lord,[34] and they ate *the sacrifices of the holy things of* the set festival*[j]* for seven days, offering *the sacrifices of the holy things*[35] and giving thanks *before*[25] the Lord,

Apparatus, Chapter 30

[h] C, L, AS: "the Lord, God, the God of. . . ."
[i] C, L, AS omit.

C, L, AS: plural.

Notes, Chapter 30

[22]MT: "the man of God."
[23]MT: "hand."
[24]MT has the plural of *psḥ,* "passover," which here in the plural has come to mean "Passover lambs." Tg. Chr has: "the lamb of the Passover."
[25]MT: "to."
[26]Instead of the four occurrences in Tg. Chr of "some of those of the house of," MT has an initial "a great number from" before "Ephraim," which refers also to the three following tribal names: "a great number from Ephraim, Manasseh, etc."
[27]See Num 9:11.
[28]In MT verse 18 stops in midair, leading to the suggestion that the verse division here is artificial. Tg. Chr, however, accepts the verse division and supplies his own object.
[29]MT: "all" or "everyone."
[30]In MT this sentence is either (i) a parenthesis extolling Hezekiah's piety, or (ii) a continuation of Hezekiah's prayer. If (ii), then "he" refers to "the people": "for they have set their heart. . . ."
[31]MT: "and (though?) not according to the purification of the sanctuary."
[32]MT: "gave heed to."
[33]MT: "strength."
[34]MT: "who displayed great skill for the Lord."
[35]MT: "sacrifices of peace offerings."

the God of their fathers. 23. All the assembly took counsel to have *a festive meal after the Passover* for seven more days; so they held *the festive meal* for seven days *with* joy. 24. For Hezekiah, the king of *the tribe of the house of* Judah, set aside for the assembly one thousand oxen and seven thousand sheep, and the commanders set aside for the assembly one thousand oxen and ten thousand sheep, and the priests consecrated themselves in large numbers. 25. Then all the assembly of *the house of*[k] Judah rejoiced, with the priests and the Levites and all the assembly who had come from *those of the house of* Israel, and the strangers who were coming from the land of Israel and those who were dwelling in Judah. 26. And there was great joy in Jerusalem, for since the days of Solomon, the son of David, the king of Israel, there *had* not *been*[36] the like of this in Jerusalem. 27. Then the priests,[l] the Levites, stood up and blessed the people, and *their prayer was accepted*[37] and their prayer entered the dwelling *place of the Shekinah* of his holiness, the heavens.

CHAPTER 31

1. When they had finished all this, all *the men of* Israel who were present[1] went out to the cities of Judah, and they broke the pillars and cut down the Asherahs and demolished the high places and the *"altars"*[2] from all *the house of* Judah and *from* Benjamin and *from*[3] Ephraim and Manasseh, *until they had destroyed them.*[4] Then all the sons of Israel returned to their cities, each one to his inheritance. 2. Then Hezekiah appointed the divisions of the priests and of the Levites *according to their service,* in their divisions, each according to his service, with reference to both the priests and the Levites, for the whole burnt offering and for the sacrifices of the holy things, to minister and to give thanks and to offer praise at the gates of the

Apparatus, Chapter 30

[k] C omits "the house of."

[l] C, L, AS add "and."

Notes, Chapter 30

[36] The verb does not appear in MT, but it is found in a few Hebrew MSS and in the Versions.
[37] MT: "it was heard with regard to their voice."

Notes, Chapter 31

[1] Lit.: "found."
[2] See 14:2, note 3.
[3] MT: "in."
[4] MT: "completely."

camps of the Lord.[5] 3. The king's share, *which he gave* from his possessions, was for the whole burnt offerings, for the whole burnt offerings of morning and evening and *whole burnt offerings* for *the additional offerings*[6] *of* the sabbaths, and for the *beginnings of the* months, and for the appointed times, according to what is written in the law of the Lord. 4. He told the people, the inhabitants of Jerusalem, to give the share of the priests and of the Levites in order that they might be strong in the law of the Lord. 5. When the matter[a] became known, the sons of Israel brought great quantities of the firstfruits of grain, of wine and oil and *date* honey and all the produce of the field,[b] and they brought in abundance the tithe of everything. 6. The children of Israel and Judah who were living in the cities of Judah, they too brought the tithe of oxen and sheep, and the tithe of the holy things which had been consecrated *before*[7] the Lord their God, and they placed them in piles. 7. In the month *of Siwan,*[8] piles began to build up, and in the month *of Tishri*[c][9] they were finished. 8. Then Hezekiah and the commanders came and saw the piles, and they blessed the Lord and his people, *the house of* Israel. 9. Then Hezekiah inquired of the priests and Levites about *the matter of* the piles. 10. And Azariah, *who was appointed* head *over those of* the house of Zadok,[10] said to him, and he said: "From the time that they began *to set aside* an offering to bring to the *sanctuary* house of the Lord, they have eaten their fill and have had plenty left over,[11] for *the Memra of* the Lord has blessed his people; and that which has been left over—*look!* it is[12] this mass *of good things.*" 11. Then Hezekiah gave orders[13] *that* chambers *be prepared*[d][14] in the *sanctuary* house of the Lord. And they prepared them. 12. And they faithfully brought the offering and the tithe *of*[15] the holy things, and Conaniah, the Levite, *was appointed* as officer-in-charge of them, with Shimei his brother *his* second-in-command. 13. Jehiel, Azaziah, Nahath, Asahel, Jerimoth,

Apparatus, Chapter 31

[a] E: *pytqwn,* but JL (II, 310) regards it as a corruption of *ptgm'.*

[b] E: "land," "ground."

[c] C, L, AS: "in the seventh month of Tishri."

[d] C: "to prepare chambers" (= MT).

Notes, Chapter 31

[5]See also 1 Chr 9:18, 19.

[6]See 8:13, note 22.

[7]MT: "to."

[8]MT: "the third month."

[9]MT: "the seventh month."

[10]MT: "the chief priest, of the house of Zadok." Tg. Chr has dropped "the priest" and made Azariah head of those of the house of Zadok.

[11]Lit.: "(they are) eating and being satisfied and leaving over in abundance." Hebrew infinitives absolute have become participles.

[12]The Hebrew object marker *'t* has become *'yt,* "(there) is."

[13]MT: "said."

[14]MT: "to prepare."

[15]MT: "and."

Jozabad, Eliel, Ismachiah, Mahath, and Benaiah were appointed under Conaniah and his brother Shimei, by the warrant of king Hezekiah and Azariah the officer-in-charge in the *sanctuary* house of *the Lord.*[16] 14. Kore, the son of Imnah, the Levite, (was put in charge of) *the east gate,*[17] to look after the freewill offerings *which they were bringing before the Lord,*[18] to allocate the offering *before*[19] the Lord, and the most holy things. 15. At his *side,*[20] giving faithful service,[21] were Eden, Miniamin, Jeshua, Shemaiah, Amariah, and Shecaniah, in the towns of the priests, distributing to their brethren, in the divisions, to great and small alike, 16. apart from those who were enrolled by genealogy, males from three years old and upward, everyone who was entering the *sanctuary* house of the Lord, to attend to their daily duty, for their service in their *watch,*[22] according to their *division.*[e22] 17. And *with regard to*[23] those who were enrolled by genealogy: the priests, according to their fathers' houses, *and* the Levites from twenty years old and upward, in their watch, by their divisions. 18. They were enrolled with all their little ones, their wives, their sons and their daughters, the whole assembly for in their devotion they consecrated themselves *to* holiness. 19. And with regard to the sons of Aaron, the priests, who were in the fields in the area of the common land of their towns, in each of the towns were men who were designated by name, to distribute shares to every male among the priests and to all who were enrolled by genealogy among the Levites. 20. Hezekiah did thus[f24] throughout all *the towns of* Judah, and he did *what was* good,[25] and *what was* right,[25] and *what was* true[25] before the Lord his God. 21. And every work which[g26] he undertook in the service of the *sanctuary* house of *the Lord*[16] and in the law and in the commandment, seeking *from before the Lord* his God, with all his heart he did it—and prospered.

Apparatus, Chapter 31

[e] C: "divisions."
[f] C, L, AS: *kd'* "thus"; V, E: *khd'* "together."

[g] C, E, L, AS: *šry.* V: *šrw.*

Notes, Chapter 31

[16]MT: "God."
[17]MT: "the gatekeeper for the east," i.e., "keeper for the east gate."
[18]MT: "the freewill offerings of God."
[19]MT: "of."
[20]MT: "hand."
[21]Lit.: "with faithfulness."
[22]MT: plural.
[23]Tg. Chr faithfully reproduces the *'t* (object marker) of MT, but it is difficult to find the verb. *ICC* (483) regards it as a late usage; see also *BDB* (484): "and hence may be rendered *as regards.*" In MT an infinitive construct follows it: "with regard to the registration of the priests." Tg. Chr reproduces this as "with regard to those who were enrolled—the priests. . . ."
[24]Reading *kd',* "thus," with C, L, AS.
[25]MT: "the good and the right and the true."
[26]Reading "he" with C.

CHAPTER 32

1. After these things and these acts of faithfulness *which Hezekiah had done, when the Lord decided in his Memra to bring Sennacherib, the king of Assyria, and his armies against the land of Israel, so that he could smash the Assyrians in the land of the house of Judah, and crush*[a] *their forces on the mountains of Jerusalem, and give over all the booty and the spoil into the hand of Hezekiah and his people who were in Jerusalem, behold, then* Sennacherib,[1] the king of Assyria, came *with camps so numerous as to be beyond calculation, and settled in the land of the tribe of* Judah, and he stationed *his forces* around the *fortified towns,* and he said *in his Memra to make them his.*[1] 2. Hezekiah saw that Sennacherib had come and that it was his *intention to wage* war[2] against Jerusalem. 3. He consulted his commanders and his warriors (with a view) to stopping up the waters of springs[3] that were outside the city; and they supported him. 4. A great crowd of people assembled, and they stopped up all the springs and the wadi that was flowing through the midst of the land *of Israel,* saying: "Why should the kings of Assyria come *here* and find plenty of water?" 5. And he took courage and built all the wall which was broken down, and he brought up towers upon *it,*[4] and outside the wall another *wall,*[b] and he strengthened the *rampart*[c][5] (of) the city of David; as well, he made weapons *of war* in great numbers, and shields. 6. He *appointed*[6] commanders over the people, *capable of drawing up* battle *lines* and gathered them to him in the square at the gate of the city and spoke *very* encouragingly to them,[7] saying: 7. "Be strong and bold: do not be afraid nor shattered from before the king of Assyria and from before all the horde *of invaders* who are with him, for *in our support* there are many

Apparatus, Chapter 32

[a] C: *l'šš.* There is a verb *'šyš,* "to fortify," but the meaning does not fit the context in verse 1.

[b] C omits.
[c] E has "all the rampart." L and AS add "of."

Notes, Chapter 32

[1-1]MT: "Sennacherib, the king of Assyria, came in Judah and encamped against the fortified towns and he said to break them (and take them) to himself." There are echoes in the expansion in verse 1 of the Gog-Magog episode in Ezek 38–39: the contrast between God's intentions and the intention of the invader, a contrast highlighted by the twofold use of the expression "in his Memra," Memra here being almost the equivalent of the personal pronoun. The invader has said "in his Memra" that he will make the cities his own: God has decided "in his Memra" to smash the invading forces on the mountains of Jerusalem. As in Ezek, the invading forces are massive, and the spoil of the enemy will be enjoyed by the intended victims. As in Ezek, God is in absolute control, and the defeat of the enemy will be his work alone, with Israel not having to fight a battle.

[2]MT: Lit.: "and his face for war."

[3]Tg. Chr omits definite article.

[4]MT: "and he brought up upon the towers." Tg. Chr "improves" this text by changing "upon" to "upon it." Cf. Vg.

[5]MT: "Millo."

[6]MT: "gave battle commanders over the people."

[7]MT: "he spoke to their heart." Tg. Chr: "he spoke consolations to their heart." Hence the "very" in the translation.

more than *the people who are* with him.[8] 8. *In his support* is the *power* of flesh,[9] but *in our support*[10] is *the Memra of* the Lord our God, to help us and to wage our[d] wars." And *all* the people put their trust in the words of Hezekiah, king of *the tribe of the house of* Judah. 9. After this, Sennacherib, the king of Assyria, sent his servants to Jerusalem—he *was besieging*[11] Lachish and all his *officers*[12] were with him—to Hezekiah, the king of *the tribe of the house of* Judah, and to all the *men of* Judah who were in Jerusalem, saying: 10. "Thus has Sennacherib, the king of Assyria, said: 'On what are you depending, as you sit under siege in Jerusalem? 11. Is not Hezekiah leading you astray so that he may *hand* you *over*[13] to die by famine and thirst, saying: "The Lord, our God, will deliver us from the hand of the king of Assyria"? 12. Is not this the Hezekiah who did away with his high places and his *altars*[14] and said to *those of the house of* Judah and to *the men of* Jerusalem, saying: "Before one altar you will worship, and upon it you will slaughter and upon it you will offer up *sweet-smelling things*"? 13. Do you not know what I have done, I and my fathers, to all the peoples of the lands? Was there ever the slightest *possibility* that the *idols* of the peoples of the lands would be able to rescue[15] their land from my hand?[e] 14. Who among all the *idols*[16] of these nations whom my fathers destroyed was able to rescue his people from my hand, that your God should be able to rescue you from my hand?[f] 15. So now, do not let Hezekiah mislead you, do not let him *advise*[17] you in this way, and do not believe *his Memra,*[18] for no *idol*[19] nor people nor kingdom has been able to rescue his people from my hand[e] and from the hand[g] of my fathers. How much less will your God rescue you from my hand!'"[e] 16. And his servants spoke further (words of) *revolt* against *the Memra of* the Lord God and against Hezekiah, his servant. 17. And he wrote letters to *cause shame before*[20] the Lord, the God of Israel, and to speak *rebellion*[h] against him, saying: "Like the *idols*[16] of the peoples of the lands who did not de-

---

Apparatus, Chapter 32

[d] C omits.
[e] C, E, L, AS: "hands." V: "hand" (= MT).
[f] E, L, AS: "hands."

[g] C, L, AS: "hands."
[h] C: "rebellions."

Notes, Chapter 32

[8] MT: "for with us more than with him."
[9] MT: "with him is an arm of flesh."
[10] MT: "with us."
[11] MT: *l*, "at, against."
[12] MT: "staff."
[13] MT: "to give you" (= C).
[14] See 14:2, note 3.
[15] MT: "Were the gods of the peoples of the lands ever at all able to rescue...."
[16] MT: "gods."
[17] MT: "entice."
[18] MT: "him."
[19] MT: "god."
[20] Lit.: "for shame before." MT: "to bring contempt to."

liver their people from my hand,*g* so the God of Hezekiah will not deliver his people from my hand."*g* 18. Then they shouted in a loud voice *in the language of the sanctuary house*[21] to the people *who were* in Jerusalem, who were on the wall, *with the intention* of[22] frightening them and upsetting them so that they might capture the city. 19. And they spoke about[23] *the Lord,* the God *whose Shekinah dwells in*[24] Jerusalem, *in the same way as they spoke* about the *idols*[16] of the peoples of the land, the *works*[25] of the hands of the *son of* man. 20. Then Hezekiah the king and Isaiah, the son of Amoz the prophet, prayed about this and they cried *toward* heaven. 21. Then *the Memra of* the Lord sent *the* angel *Gabriel,*[i] and *during the night of the Passover he destroyed with a molten stream of fire and burnt up their breath within them.*[j][26] He destroyed every mighty warrior and officer and commander in the camp of the king of Assyria, and he returned shamefacedly to his land. He entered the house of his *idols*[27] and *his sons, of whom he was the father,*[28] cast him down there, *killed* with the sword. 22. Thus the Lord delivered Hezekiah and the inhabitants of Jerusalem from the hand of Sennacherib, the king of Assyria, and from the hand of all *the people,*[k] and he *gave them security*[29] on every side. 23. Many brought[30] a gift *before*[31] the Lord[l] to Jerusalem and precious objects[m] to Hezekiah, the king of *the tribe of the house of* Judah, and he was exalted *before*[32] all the nations after this. 24. In those days Hezekiah became ill to *the point*

Apparatus, Chapter 32

[i] C: "Michael and Gabriel." L, AS: "Michael Gabriel."
[j] C: "their bodies"(?).

[k] C, E, L, AS do not have "the people" (= MT).
[l] For V's "before the Lord," C, L, AS have "to the sanctuary house of the Lord."

Notes, Chapter 32

[21]MT: "(in) Judean."

[22]MT: "to."

[23]MT: "to" or "against."

[24]MT: "the God of."

[25]MT: singular, though one Hebrew MS and LXX have plural.

[26]MT: "sent an angel." An unnamed angel in MT receives the name "Gabriel" in Tg. Chr. Some attribute the destruction to Michael. C, L, AS have the best of both worlds by mentioning the two angels. The destruction took place on the first night of Passover, "the night of miracles." "The view that many important events in the history of the patriarchs and that of Israel took place during the first night of Passover is very old. . ." (Ginzberg, V, 221, and see also Le Déaut's note 6 in I, 167). Gabriel's flowing molten fire burnt up their breath but, one assumes, left their bodies intact. There is a similar reference in Tg. Ps.-J. Lev 10:2, where the fire from the Lord penetrated the nostrils of Aaron's sons, Nadab and Abihu, "and burned their breath without destroying their bodies" (see *b. San.* 94a and 95b).

[27]MT: "gods."

[28]MT: Lit.: "some of those who came forth from his loins." In Tg. Chr "there" could also be taken with the previous verb, giving the translation "*and his sons, whom he had fathered* there, cast him down."

[29]MT: "And he led/guided them." Though *nhl* sometimes implies an element of rest, the suggested reading in MT is *wynḥ lhm,* "and he gave them rest" (= LXX); cf. 1 Chr 22:18.

[30]MT: participle. E, C, L, AS also participle.

[31]MT: "to."

[32]MT: "to the eyes of."

of death,[33] and he prayed *before*[31] the Lord, who decided[34] *by his Memra to heal him and to add fifteen years to the days of his life, for it had been decreed by heaven to shorten the days of his life,*[35] and he gave him the sign. 25. *The Lord* did not make return to Hezekiah *in accordance with the due reward*[n] *of his deeds,*[36] for his heart had become haughty and wrath was upon him and upon all *the men of* Judah and Jerusalem.[o] 26. But Hezekiah humbled himself *from*[37] the haughtiness of his heart, he and the inhabitants of Jerusalem, and the anger of the Lord did not come upon them during the days of Hezekiah. 27. Now Hezekiah had very great wealth and honor. He made for himself treasuries for silver, for gold, for precious *jewels,*[38] for ointments, for shields and for all (kinds of) desirable objects, 28. storehouses *and granaries* for the produce of grain and wine and oil; and stables[39] for all kinds of cattle, and flocks for[p] the stables.[39] 29. He provided towns for himself and herds of sheep and oxen in abundance, for *the Lord*[40] had given to him very great possessions. 30. It was this Hezekiah who stopped the outlet of the waters of Upper Gihon, and he directed them *and brought them in channels* underneath to *the valley of*[41] the city of David. And Hezekiah had success in all his works. 31. So too, in the (incident concerning) the *interpreters*[42] *of* the commanders of *the king of* Babylon *who had been sent*[43] to him to inquire about the wonder which had happened in the land, *to see the two tablets of stones which were in the ark of the covenants*[q] *of the Lord where Moses had placed them along with the two tablets of stones which had been broken because of the sins (connected with) the calf which they had made in Horeb: the Memra of the Lord allowed him to show them without his suffering any*

Apparatus, Chapter 32

[m] For "precious objects," C, L, AS have *tpnwqyn,* "delicacies."

[n] E: *twšlḥt*: "mission, command," caused by confusion of *m* and *ḥ*.

[o] C, L, AS: "the inhabitants of Jerusalem."

[p] E, C, L, AS: "and."

[q] C, E, L, AS: "covenant" (singular).

Notes, Chapter 32

[33]Lit.: "until he reached to die."

[34]Lit.: "and he said." MT: "and he said to him."

[35]MT Chr makes no reference to Hezekiah's prolongation of life, but 2 Kgs 2:1-6 and Isa 38:1-6 provide the background.

[36]MT: "Hezekiah did not make return according to the benefit (done) unto him." Tg. Chr's translation has reversed the thrust of MT, which suggests that Hezekiah had failed to show appreciation for the benefit he had received, whereas with Tg. Chr it is God who, in his mercy, does not repay Hezekiah in accordance with the (evil) deeds he has done.

[37]MT: "in." LXX=Tg. Chr.

[38]MT: "stone." Loan word: see 1 Chr 1:23, note 59.

[39]Tg. Chr uses the plural of *'sṭbl',* "stable, stall," borrowed from the Latin *stabulum* (JL I, 45). MJ (89) gives meaning as "colonnade-like walk."

[40]MT: "God."

[41]MT: "west of."

[42]MT: "ambassadors."

[43]MT: "had sent" (active).

injury,[44] because he was testing him to know all *that was* in his heart. 32. And the rest of the acts of Hezekiah and his acts of devotion, behold they are written in the *prophecy*[45] of Isaiah the prophet, the son of Amoz, in the book of the kings of *the house of* Judah and[r] Israel. 33. Hezekiah slept with his fathers, and they buried him in the ascent of the tombs of the sons of David; and all *the men of* Judah and the inhabitants of Jerusalem did him honor at his death. Manasseh, his son, became king in his place.

CHAPTER 33

1. Manasseh was twelve years old when he became king, and he reigned for fifty-five years in Jerusalem. 2. He did what was evil *before*[1] the Lord, according to the abominations of the peoples whom the Lord had driven out from before the children of Israel. 3. He rebuilt all the high places which his father Hezekiah had demolished and set up the *"altars"*[2] to the baals and made Asherahs and bowed down to all the *armies*[3] of heaven and worshiped[a] them. 4. He built the *"altars"*[2] *and set up a carved image* in the *sanctuary* house of the Lord, (of) which the Lord had said: "In Jerusalem *I shall cause my Shekinah to dwell*[4] for ever." 5. He built *the* "altars"[2] to all the *armies*[3] of heaven in the two courts of the *sanctuary* house of the Lord. 6. He caused his sons to pass through the fire in the valley of Bar

Apparatus, Chapter 32

[r] L, AS add "the house of."

Notes, Chapter 32

[44]MT: "God left him." "The wonder" is not specified in MT Chr, but the assumption is that the reference was to the sun's moving backward in 2 Kgs 20:11. The fact that there is no "and" between "in the land" and "to see" would indicate that Tg. Chr regarded the contents of the ark as the wonder in question. See 5:10, note 12.
[45]MT: "vision."

Apparatus, Chapter 33

[a] C: *'bd, served.*

Notes, Chapter 33

[1]MT: "in the eyes of."
[2]See 14:2, note 3.
[3]MT: "army."
[4]MT: "my name will be."

Hinnom, and *he consulted cloud-augurs, diviners, and sorcerers,*[5] and he made lying oracles and apparitions of the dead. He did much that was evil *before*[1] the Lord to stir up anger *before* him.[6] 7. He placed[b] the image of the figure which he had made *in his likeness*[7] in the *sanctuary* house of *the Lord,*[8] of which *the Lord* had said to David and to Solomon his son: "In this house and in Jerusalem, which I have chosen from all the tribes of Israel, *I shall cause my Shekinah to dwell* for ever *and ever.*[9] 8. And I[10] shall not any more *send into exile the people, the house of* Israel,[11] from upon the land which I set up *through*[12] your[c] fathers, only if they will observe to do all that I commanded them with regard to all the law and the covenants[13] and the judgments (given) through Moses." 9. But Manasseh led *the men of* Judah and the inhabitants of Jerusalem astray to do[d] more evil than the peoples which the Lord had destroyed from before the children of Israel. 10. Then the Lord spoke *with*[e][14] Manasseh and *with*[e][14] his people *and warned them through the prophet,* but they paid no heed. 11. Then the Lord brought against them the commanders of the army of the king of Assyria. They secured Manasseh with *manacles,*[15] bound him with *chains of* bronze,[16] and took him to Babylon. 12. *Then the Chaldaeans made a bronze mule and bored many small holes in it. They shut him up inside it and lit a fire all around it.* When he was in distress, *he sought (help) from all his idols which he had made, but there was no help forthcoming, for there is no profit in them.*[17]

Apparatus, Chapter 33

[b] C, E, L, AS: *'qym,* "he set up."
[c] C, E, L, AS: "their."

[d] C, L, AS: "and he did."
[e] C, L, AS: "to" (= MT).

Notes, Chapter 33

[5]MT: "he practiced soothsaying and he practiced divination and he practiced sorcery." Three verbs each in perfect tense.

[6]MT: "to provoke him," i.e., "to stir up his anger."

[7]Tg. Chr uses the word *dywqn,* "image, likeness," borrowed from Greek, MJ 297: "a reverential transformation of *'yqwn*" (= *eikōn*); JL I, 170, made up of *duo* and *eikōn.*

[8]MT: "God."

[9]MT: "I shall place my name for ever."

[10]Reading *'wsyp,* "I shall add," with C, E, L, AS, for *tsyp,* "you will add."

[11]MT: "remove the foot of Israel."

[12]Lit.: "by the hand of." MT: "for."

[13]MT: "statutes."

[14]MT: "to."

[15]MT: "hooks." Tg. Chr uses the word *kyrwmnyky,* "handcuffs, manacles," borrowed from the Greek *cheiromanikēs* (MJ 636), or *cheir* + *manikēs,* (JL I, 362).

[16]MT: "two bronzes," i.e., "bronze fetters."

[17]MT: "When he was in distress, he entreated the Lord, his God. . . ." In MT Chr, the Assyrians are the agents through whom the Lord punishes Manasseh—they take him captive; in his distress he cries to God; God hears him and returns him to his land. In the expansion in verse 12, Tg. Chr gives details of the distress suffered by Manasseh; it is ironic that for the man who "caused his sons to pass through the fire in the valley of Bar Hinnom" (33:6), a similar fate lay in store. Tg. Chr, anxious to stress the point that idols are worthless, does not record the soliloquy given, e.g., in *PRE* 43 and *Ruth R.* 5, 6, where Manasseh outlines his gradual yet speedy discovery that his idols are useless and that only the Lord can rescue him.

Then he changed his mind and prayed before the Lord his God, and humbled him-self greatly from before *the Lord,* the God of his fathers. 13. He prayed *before*[14] him. *Immediately all the angels who had been put in charge of the entrances to the gates of prayer which are in heaven went forth and, because of him, closed all the en-trances to the gates of prayer which are in heaven, and all the windows and openings of heaven, so that his prayer would not be accepted. But immediately the mercy of the Lord of the universe prevailed, whose right hand is stretched out to receive*[18] *the sin-ners who return to his fear and who break the inclination of their heart by repen-tance, and he made an opening and a gap in the heavens beneath the throne of his glory.* He heard his prayer, he accepted his request, *he shook the universe by his Memra, the mule was shattered, and he came out from there. Then there went forth a wind from between the wings of the cherubim; it blew him by the decree of the Memra of the Lord,* and *he returned* to Jerusalem to his kingdom. And Manasseh knew that the Lord was God, *who had worked with him these signs and wonders. He returned with all his heart before the Lord and forsook all the idols and no longer served them.*[19] 14. After this he built *the*[20] outer wall for the city of David *from the valley* of [21] Gihon in the wadi to the entrance to the gate of the *fishmongers,*[22] and he continued it round the *palace*[23] and raised it very high. Then he placed army commanders in all the fortified cities *which were* in *the house of* Judah. 15. He did away with the *idols of the nations*[24] and the figure from the *sanctuary* house of the Lord and all the *"altars"*[25] which he had built on the mountain of the *sanctuary* house of the Lord and in Jerusalem, and he cast them outside the city. 16. He

Notes, Chapter 33

[18]Reading Pael with E and C: "to receive."

[19]MT: "He prayed to him, he granted his entreaty, and heard his request and returned him to Jerusalem to his kingdom. And Manasseh knew that the Lord was God." In MT Chr and Tg. Chr, God looks with favor on those who repent (1 Chr 23:16; 2 Chr 7:14; 2 Chr 12:12). In MT the story of Manasseh's repentance is one of the unexpected high points of the book. In the expansion at 33:13, Tg. Chr sees the incident as an illustration of "Grace Abounding" to the chief of sinners—that in spite of Manasseh's well-documented evil past, in spite of opposition from the angels, God's mercy prevailed, and Manasseh received forgiveness and restoration. The expansion has two bases: (i) "And he was entreated," i.e., God responded to his entreaty: *wy'tr. b. San.* 103a, however, refers to an alternative reading found in a few Hebrew MSS, *wyḥtr,* "and it was dug," i.e., a hole was dug (from *ḥtr,* "to dig"), and it was through that hole that Manasseh's prayer reached heaven. The word used in Tg. Chr for "opening" is, in fact, *mḥtrt'.* (ii) MT has *wyšybhw:* "And he returned him (to Jerusalem)." At first glance, it seems that Tg. Chr has departed from MT in his translation: "And he returned him (to Jerusalem)." Tg. Chr takes these consonants *wyšybhw* and vocalizes them dif-ferently, giving the translation: "and it (the wind) blew him," using the Hiphil of the Hebrew verb *nšb,* "to blow, cause to blow" (cf. Ps 147:18). This he translates into Aramaic, using the cognate Aramaic verb *ntb.* He then adds "and he returned to Jerusalem," but this time does not use the cognate Aramaic verb *twb,* "to return." On Manasseh's repentance, see further *Ruth R.* 5, 6 and *PRE* 43, where, in a chapter on "The Power of Repentance," the Manasseh incident is used as an illustration. We see the outworking of this repentance in the verses following in chapter 33.

[20]MT: "an."

[21]MT: "from the west of."

[22]MT: "fishes."

[23]MT: "The Ophel." Tg. Chr uses loan word. See 1 Chr 9:18, note 17.

[24]MT: "the gods of the foreigner."

[25]See 14:2, note 3.

built[26] the altar of the Lord and sacrificed upon it sacrifices, the sacrifices of holy things and of the thanksgiving, and he told *those of the house of* Judah to serve the Lord, the God of Israel. 17. However, the people were still sacrificing on the high places, but only to *the name of the Memra of* the Lord, their God. 18. Now the rest of the acts of Manasseh, and his prayer *which he prayed before the Lord* his God,[27] and the words of the *prophets*[28] who spoke *with*[29] him in the name of *the Memra of* the Lord, the God of Israel, behold they *are written* in the Acts of the kings of *the house of* Israel. 19. And his prayer *which he prayed before the Lord* and *how the Lord accepted his prayer*[30] and all his sin and infidelity, and the sites on which he built the high places and set up the Asherahs and the images *and* his humbling himself[31]—behold, they are written in the Acts of Hozai. 20. Manasseh slept with his fathers, and they buried him *in* his house, and Amon his son became king in his place. 21. Amon was twenty-two years old when he became king, and he reigned for two years in Jerusalem. 22. He did what was evil *before*[32] the Lord, as Manasseh his father had done, and Amon sacrificed to all the images which Manasseh his father had made, and he served them. 23. But he did not humble himself before the Lord, as Manasseh his father had humbled himself, but this Amon caused sin to abound.[33] 24. His servants *rebelled*[34] against him and *killed* him[35] in his house. 25. But the people of the land *killed*[36] all those who had *rebelled*[34] against Amon the king, and the people of the land made Josiah his son king in his place.

CHAPTER 34

1. Josiah was eight years old when he became king, and he reigned for thirty-one years in Jerusalem. 2. He did what was right *before*[1] the Lord and walked in the

Notes, Chapter 33

[26]Following Qere *wybn*, Kethibh is *whkn*. The Qere is found in many Hebrew MSS, Syr.
[27]MT: "his prayer to his God."
[28]MT: "seers."
[29]MT: "to."
[30]MT: "and how his entreaty was granted."
[31]MT: "before he humbled himself."
[32]MT: "in the eyes of."
[33]Lit.: "multiplied guilt."
[34]MT: "conspired."
[35]MT: "put him to death."
[36]MT: "struck down."

Notes, Chapter 34

[1]MT: "in the eyes of."

ways[a] of his father David, and did not turn aside to the right or to the left. 3. In the eighth year of his reign—he was still a youth—he began to seek *instruction from before the Lord,* the God of David, his father, and in the *sixteenth*[2] year he began to purify Judah and Jerusalem from the high places and the Asherahs and the carved images and the molten images. 4. In his presence they broke down the *"altars"*[3] of the *idols,*[4] and the solar statues[5] which were above them he cut down, and the Asherahs, the carved images and the molten images he smashed and crushed to powder, and scattered it over the graves *of*[6] those who had offered sacrifice to them. 5. The bones of the *"priests"*[7] he burned upon their *"altars,"*[8] and he purified Judah and Jerusalem. 6. And in the cities of *the house of* Manasseh, of *the house of* Ephraim and of *the house of* Simeon, and as far as *those of the house of* Naphtali, in *the place of their devastation*[9] round about, 7. He broke down the *"altars,"*[3] and the Asherahs and the images which he crushed[10] in order to grind[b] them to powder, and all the solar statues[5] he cut down in all the land of Israel. Then he returned to[c] Jerusalem. 8. In the eighteenth year of his reign, *when he had purified*[11] the land and the *sanctuary* house, he sent Shaphan, the son of Azaliah, and Maasaeiah, the governor of the city, and Joah, the son of Jehoahaz, *who was placed in charge of the book of the records,*[12] to repair the *sanctuary* house of the Lord his God. 9. They came to Hilkiah, the great priest, and they gave him the money which had been brought into the *sanctuary* house of *the Lord,* which the

Apparatus, Chapter 34

[a] C: singular.
[b] C: *l'dq'* (Aphel): meaning unchanged.

[c] C: "he dwelt in."

Notes, Chapter 34

[2] MT: "twelfth." L, AS agree with MT. Is the reading represented by V and C an error of transcription—there is a certain similarity of the consonants—or does it represent a different tradition? Le Déaut (I, 171f. note 2) suggests that Tg. Chr in the second numeral in the verse (sixteenth) is thinking of the king's age, not of his reign. Thus his beginning to seek instruction and his first reform attempts took place in the same year, the eighth year of his reign, i.e., in the sixteenth year of his life.

[3] See 14:2, note 3.

[4] MT: "baals."

[5] See 14:4, note 6.

[6] Tg. Chr "tidies up" MT, which lacks "of."

[7] See 11:15, note 13.

[8] Following Qere. See 14:2, note 3.

[9] MT here is difficult and several emendations have been suggested, one of which is "their ruins" (see *ICC* 504). This is how Tg. Chr understood his text.

[10] MT: "he crushed," which could have been translated by *'dq.* Instead, V, L, and AS give *'dq,* absent in JL, but given the meaning "to stick to, seize" by MJ. I have retained MT's emphasis in the translation. C omits the word but leaves a blank space, which DW fills with *'dq.*

[11] Tg. Chr's rendering of an enigmatic infinitive, "to purify."

[12] MT: "Jehoahaz the recorder."

Levites, the keepers of the *palace,*[13] had collected from the *hands* of *the house of* Manasseh and Ephraim and from all the rest of *the house of* Israel and from all *the men of* Judah and Benjamin. Then they returned[d][14] to Jerusalem. 10. And they gave it into the hand of *those*[15] who were engaged in the work who had been put in charge in the *sanctuary* house of the Lord, and those who were engaged in the work, who were working in the *sanctuary* house of the Lord, gave it *to provide what was necessary*[16] and to repair the house. 11. They gave it to the carpenters and the masons to buy hewn stones and timber *to make beams, to provide joints*[17] *and to put a roof* on the houses[e] which the kings of *the house of* Judah had destroyed. 12. The men were working diligently at the work. Over them were appointed Jahath and Obadiah, the Levites, of the sons of Merari, and Zechariah and Meshullam of the sons of *Qehath*[18] who were *to offer praise,*[19] and the Levites with everyone who was expert[f] on instruments of praise. 13. And (they were) in charge of the burden bearers *and* were supervising all those[20] who were doing the work[g] *and* (who were seeking) *to offer service,*[21] and some of the Levites were scribes, *disciplinarians,*[22] and gatekeepers. 14. Now when they brought out the silver which had been brought[h] into the *sanctuary* house of the Lord, Hilkiah the priest found[i] the book of the Law of the Lord *which had been given* through Moses. 15. Hilkiah answered and said to Shaphan the scribe: "The book of the Law I have found in the *sanctuary* house of the Lord, *hidden and wrapped up.*"[23] Hilkiah gave the book to Shaphan. 16. Then Shaphan brought the book to the king, and he gave a further report to the king, saying: "All that has been entrusted to the *hands*[24] of thy servants they are doing."

Apparatus, Chapter 34

[d] V and E follow Qere, "and they returned to Jerusalem." C, L, AS prefer Kethibh: "the inhabitants of Jerusalem."

[e] C, E, L, AS: "the house." V: "the houses" (= MT).

[f] C: "instructing."

[g] C: "the great work."

[h] C: "was being brought" (= MT).

[i] C, L, AS: "brought out," presupposing the same Hebrew consonants as "found" (*mṣ'*).

Notes, Chapter 34

[13]MT: "threshold." Tg. Chr uses the word *plṭyn,* "palace," borrowed from the Greek *palation* and the Latin *palatium* (MJ 1160 and JL II, 269); cf. *plṭyryn,* 1 Chr 9:18, note 17. For this expression in MT, "keepers of the threshold," Tg. 2 Kgs 22:4 uses the word *'mrkly.* See 1 Chr 2:6, note 5.

[14]V follows Qere. Kethibh is "the inhabitants of Jerusalem."

[15]MT: "him," though many MSS have plural.

[16]MT: "to restore."

[17]MT: "timber for clamps and to lay beams."

[18]MT: "of the Qehathites."

[19]MT: "to supervise."

[20]MT: singular.

[21]MT: "for every kind of service."

[22]MT: "officials."

[23]According to Le Déaut (I, 173, note 6), the technical term for withdrawing from the public use and reverently laying aside a sacred text which, for whatever reason, was no longer usable.

[24]MT: "hand."

17. They have emptied out[j] the silver which was found in the *sanctuary* house of the Lord and have given it into the *hands*[24] *of the scribes* who were appointed, and into the *hands*[24] of those who are engaged *in* the work. 18. Shaphan the scribe reported[k] to the king, saying: "Hilkiah, the priest, has given me *the* book." And Shaphan read from[25] it before the king. 19. When the king heard the words of *the book of* the Law, he tore his garments. 20. And the king commanded Hilkiah and Ahikam, the son of Shaphan, and Abdon, the son of Micah, and Shaphan the scribe, and Asaiah the king's servant, saying: 21. "Go, and seek *instruction from before* the Lord on my behalf *and on behalf of my whole kingdom* and on behalf of *all* who remain in Israel and in Judah, with regard to the words of the book which has been discovered, for great is the anger of the Lord which has *come upon*[26] us because our fathers did not keep the *words*[27] of the Lord*[l28]* according to all that is written in this book." 22. Then Hilkiah and *those* who *were with* the king went to Huldah the prophetess, the wife of Shallum, the son of Tokhath,[29] the son of *Hasdah,*[m30] who looked after the *king's* garments; she lived in Jerusalem, *in the house of instruction,*[31] and they spoke to her thus. 23. She said to them: "Thus has the Lord, the God of Israel, said: '*Go!* Say to the man who sent you to me: 24. Thus has the Lord said: Behold, I am about to bring evil upon this place and upon its inhabitants, all *the oaths of* the curses which are written in the book which they have read before the king of *the tribe of the house of* Judah. 25. Because they have abandoned *my fear,*[32] and have offered up *sweet-smelling things* to *the idols of the peoples*[33] in order to cause anger *before* me[34] with all the works of their hands, my anger has *reached*[35] this place and it has not *passed* by.'[36] 26. And to the king of *the tribe of the house of* Judah who sent you to seek *instruction from before* the Lord, thus you will say to him: Thus has the Lord, the God of Israel, said: '(As to) the words which you have heard: 27. Because your heart was softened[37] and you

Apparatus, Chapter 34

[j] DW has *ṭqysw,* "counted"; cf. Tg. 2 Kgs 22:4, 9, where the same loan word is used.
[k] C: *ḥwy,* "told"; cf. Tg. 2 Kgs 20:10.

[l] C, L, AS add: "to do" (= MT).
[m] V: "Hasdah" (= a few Hebrew MSS and Brian Walton's Syriac); C, E, L, AS: "Hasrah" (= MT).

Notes, Chapter 34

[25]Lit.: "in."
[26]MT: "been poured out upon."
[27]MT: singular.
[28]Tg. Chr omits "to do."
[29]Tg. Chr follows Qere.
[30]MT: "Hasrah."
[31]MT: "in the second (quarter)"; see 1 Chr 5:12, note 20.
[32]MT: "me."
[33]MT: "other gods."
[34]MT: "to provoke me to anger."
[35]MT: "is poured out upon."
[36]MT: "will not be quenched."
[37]Lit.: "melted." MT: "tender."

humbled yourself before *the Memra of the Lord*[38] when you heard his words against this place and against its inhabitants and (because) you humbled yourself *from* before me and tore your garments and wept before me, *before me* also *it has been heard,* the Lord *has said.*[39] 28. Behold I am about to gather you to your fathers, and you will be gathered to your grave in peace, and your eyes will not look on[40] all the evil which I am about to bring upon this place and upon its inhabitants.'" Then they brought back word to the king. 29. The king sent and assembled all the elders of Judah and Jerusalem. 30. And the king went up *to* the *sanctuary* house of the Lord, and all the men of Judah, the inhabitants of Jerusalem, the priests, the Levites and all the people both great and small, and he read *before them*[n41] all the words of the book of the covenant which had been found in the *sanctuary* house of the Lord. 31. The king stood on his *balcony,*[42] and he made the covenant before the Lord, to follow *the fear of* the Lord and keep his commandments, his testimonies and his statutes with all his heart and with all his soul, and perform the words of the covenant which were written in this book. 32. Then he caused all those who were present[43] in Jerusalem and Benjamin to stand, and the inhabitants of Jerusalem did according to[44] the covenant of *the Lord,*[45] the God of their fathers. 33. Josiah did away with all the abominations from all the lands which belonged to the children of Israel, and he *compelled*[o46] all those who were present in *Jerusalem*[p47] to serve the Lord their God. All his days they did not cease from following *the worship of* the Lord, the God of their fathers.

Apparatus, Chapter 34

[n] V, C: *qwmyhwn.* E, L, AS: *qdmyhwn.*

[o] E: "he caused to serve/do" (= MT).

[p] E, C, L, AS: "Jerusalem" (= MT).

Notes, Chapter 34

[38]MT: "God."

[39]MT: "Also I have heard, an oracle of the Lord."

[40]Following E, C, L, AS, who have a Peal "see" for V's Ithpeel "be seen, appear."

[41]MT: "in their ears."

[42]MT: "standing place." Tg. Chr uses the loan word *'stwwn'.* See 23:13, where the word is used to translate "pillar" or "column," the subject also being the king. (In 30:16 and 35:10 the same Hebrew word is used as in 2 Chr 34:31 but is translated in Tg. Chr by another Greek loan word, meaning "platform" or "pulpit": *dwkn'.* In these two instances the personalities involved are priests and Levites.) The same loan word is used also in the parallel verse in Tg. 2 Kgs 23:3 for Hebrew "pillar." Smolar and Aberbach (107) regard this "identification of the Biblical Temple 'pillars' with the Hellenistic *stoa,* 'portico, colonnade,' which was indeed a feature of Herod's temple" as particularly anachronistic.

[43]Lit.: "found."

[44]Reading "according to" with C, E, L,AS (= MT), where V has "in," though V's reading "in the covenant" may be an echo of the same expression found in the parallel verse of MT 2 Kgs 23:3.

[45]MT: "God."

[46]MT is rather awkward here: "and he caused to serve all who were present in Israel to serve the Lord. . . ." Tg. Chr removes the clumsiness somewhat by using a stronger verb for the first occurrence: "he compelled."

[47]MT: "Israel."

CHAPTER 35

1. Josiah kept *the* Passover *before*[1] the Lord in Jerusalem, and they slaughtered the Passover (sacrifice) on the fourteenth day of the month *of Nisan.*[2] 2. He appointed the priests in their watches and encouraged them in the service of the *sanctuary* house of the Lord. 3. He told the Levites who were teaching[3] *the people of* the whole *house of* Israel who were consecrated[4] to *the name of* the Lord: "Put[5] the holy ark in the house which Solomon, the son of David, the king of Israel, built; you have no *authority* to carry it upon your shoulders.[6] Now, serve the Lord, your God, and his people, *the house of* Israel. 4. Make preparations,[7] according to your clans, by your divisions,[a] *as Moses commanded, and as* David, the king of Israel *wrote,*[8] and *according to*[9] the written document of Solomon, his son. 5. Stand in the sanctuary *house* according to the divisions[a] of the clans for your brethren, the sons of the people, and the division[b] of the clan of the Levites. 6. And slaughter the Passover and sanctify yourselves and make preparations for[10] your brethren, to do *as the Lord spoke*[11] through Moses." 7. Then Josiah set aside for the sons of the people lambs and he-goats from the flock, all of them as Passover offerings for everyone who was present,[12] to the number of thirty thousand, as well as three thousand oxen, *for the sacrifices of the holy things of the festival;* these came from the king's possessions. 8. His princes also set aside a freewill offering[c] for the people, the priests and the Levites. Hilkiah, Zechariah, and Jehiel, the administrators of the *sanctuary* house of *the Lord,*[13] gave to the priests, for Passover offerings, two

Apparatus, Chapter 35

[a] Though the translation has "divisions," V actually uses the singular form. C uses the plural form.

[b] C also uses the plural form here.

[c] V: *nsbt*. C, E, L, AS: *ndbt*. Both words mean "freewill offering."

Notes, Chapter 35

[1] MT: "to."

[2] MT: "the first month."

[3] Tg. Chr follows Qere.

[4] MT uses the adjective "holy": Tg. Chr uses the verb. As the plural form is used in both texts, the "who" refers to the Levites. It is also possible to translate the particle *d,* "who," as "that": "that they should consecrate themselves" (cf. LXX).

[5] Lit.: "give."

[6] MT: Lit.: "it is not to you a burden carrying on the shoulder." Tg. Chr retains the singular form, "shoulder."

[7] Tg. Chr follows Qere in using Hiphil/Aphel (*hkynw*); cf. Syr. "Prepare ..."—we expect a following object; the only object available is "your clans": (cf. verse 6). Kethibh is *hkwnw,* "be prepared, prepare yourselves." The translation above settles for a grammatical half-way house! The form in Tg. Chr could also be Ithpaal, but the vocalization does not support this.

[8] MT: "in the document of David," though some Hebrew MSS have "according to."

[9] MT: "in," though two Hebrew MSS, Syr, and Vg have "and according to."

[10] Or "prepare your brethren"; see note 7.

[11] MT: "according to the word of the Lord."

[12] Lit.: "found."

[13] MT: "God."

thousand six hundred (lambs and he-goats) and three hundred oxen. 9. And Conaniah, Shemaiah, and Nethanel, his brothers, and Hashabiah, Jeiel, and Jozabad, the chiefs of the Levites, set aside for the Levites, for Passover offerings, five thousand *sheep* and five hundred oxen. 10. So the service was prepared, and the priests stood on their platform [14] and the Levites in their divisions, according to the king's command. 11. They slaughtered the Passover. The priests splashed *the blood*[15] (received) from their hands while the Levites did the skinning. 12. And they set aside the whole burnt offering(s) with the intention of giving them [16] to the sons of the people, according to their clans, so that they could offer them *before*[1] the Lord, as is written in the book of Moses. And so they did *until the morning.*[17] 13. They *roasted*[18] the Passover with fire as prescribed, and they boiled *the sacrifices of* the holy things in pots and cauldrons and cooking vessels,[d] and they distributed[19] them to all the sons of the people. 14. After this they made preparation for themselves and for the priests, for the priests, the sons of Aaron, *were busy* offering up the whole burnt offering and the fat portions until night time; so the Levites made preparation[e] for themselves and for the priests, the sons of Aaron. 15. And the singers, the sons of Asaph, were on their *stand,*[f][20] according to the commandment of David and Asaph and Heman and Jeduthun, the *prophet*[g][21] *of* the king, and the gatekeepers were at each gate; they did not have to neglect[22] *any of* their duties, for their brethren, the Levites, had made preparation for them. 16. So all the service of *the worship of* the Lord was prepared on that day, to keep the Passover and offer up *the whole burnt offering*[23] on the altar of the Lord, in ac-

Apparatus, Chapter 35

[d] V has *mylwmy*. It is generally agreed that the correct reading is *mylwsy*, "cooking vessels."
[e] V: Aphel; C, L, AS: Pael. No difference in meaning.
[f] Lit.: "the place of their standing." E omits "the place of."

[g] L, AS: "the prophets," which would suggest the need to have a comma after David, "and Asaph and Heman and Jeduthun (were) the prophets of the king."

Notes, Chapter 35

[14] See 34:31; note 42.
[15] Not in MT, omitted perhaps through homoioteleuton: *(hdm) mydm.*
[16] MT: "to give them to groups" has become in Tg. Chr: "with their gift(s)." The thrust in MT seems to be that certain parts of the whole burnt offering were set aside to give them to family representatives to present to the priest for burning. It is difficult to interpret "with their gifts" in this context. The best solution seems to be that of C where the text (*bmyhbwthwn*, which in V is *bmwhbwthwn*), could be translated as "with (the intention of) giving them...."
[17] MT: "to the cattle," though some Hebrew MSS and LXX have "to the morning." Using only the consonants, *lbqr* can mean (i) "to the cattle," or (ii) "to the morning." Tg. Chr has followed the latter.
[18] MT: "boiled," unless we can regard *bšl* as also meaning "roasted"; cf. Dillard 285, note 13a.
[19] Tg. Chr lacks the note of haste in distribution, indicated in MT by the use of the causative form of the verb "to run."
[20] MT: "at their post" or "their place of standing." Tg. Chr gives us this in two words.
[21] MT: "seer."
[22] Lit.: "turn aside from."
[23] MT: "whole burnt offerings."

cordance with the commandment of king Josiah. 17. And the children of Israel who were found *faithful before the Lord* kept the Passover at that time *in the evening,* and the festival of Unleavened Bread for seven days. 18. No Passover *which was* like it had been kept in Israel since the days of Samuel the prophet; none of the kings of *the house of* Israel had celebrated the Passover like that which Josiah had kept, with the priests and the Levites and all *the men of* Judah and *the house of* Israel who were found *to be faithful*[24] and the inhabitants of Jerusalem. 19. This Passover was kept in the eighteenth year of the reign of Josiah. 20. After all this, when Josiah had set the *sanctuary* house of the Lord in order, *Pharaoh the Lame,*[25] the king of Egypt, came up *to wage war*[26] at Carchemish, *which is* on the Euphrates, and Josiah went out to meet him. 21. But he sent messengers to him, saying: "What have I to do with you, O king of *the tribe of the house of* Judah? It is not against you *that I have come up to wage war—for* you *are attacking me* this day[27]— but against the house with which I am at war.[28] *My idol*[29] has said that I should hurry! *So now,* stay away *from me* and from *my*[h] *idol*[29] which is with me, lest it destroy you." 22. *And when he heard how he mentioned his idol he did not turn back,* and Josiah did not turn his face from him. But he disguised himself in order to *wage war*[26] with him, *and he made battle preparations with weapons of war.* But he did not *accept*[30] the words of *the Lame One, who had spoken about his idol.*[31] So he came to *wage war*[26] in the plain of Megiddo. 23. *Because Josiah had not sought instruction from before the Lord and had gone to wage war in the plain of Megiddo, the Lord of the universe punished him:*[32] the archers *took aim and* shot *their arrows*

Apparatus, Chapter 35

[h] C, L, AS: "the." In V and C both occurrences of "idol" in verse 21 seem to be plural, but the fact that they are construed with a singular verb would indicate that the pattern of *Elohim* in the Hebrew text of this verse (plural in form but regarded as singular) is being followed.

Notes, Chapter 35

[24]Lit.: "in faithfulness."

[25]MT: "Necho." In appearance at least, the word used in the Hebrew for Necho, *nkw* or *nkh*, resembles the Hebrew verb *nkh*, "to smite," one form of which means "smitten, lame." This title, "the lame one" in Aramaic *(ḥgyr')* is normally given to this Pharaoh, e.g., 2 Kgs 23:29; Jer 46:2.

[26]MT: "to fight."

[27]Tg. Chr makes a commendable effort to make sense of a Hebrew text which is not in a happy state. Lit.: "Not against you, you (nominative) today." The Versions supply some verb of *coming* to fill the gap after the first "you," and Tg. Chr provides the rather isolated *you* (nominative) with a verb, "to attack."

[28]Lit.: "against the house of my war."

[29]MT: "God."

[30]MT: "listen to."

[31]MT: "from the mouth of God." At this point Tg. Chr does not wish to accept that God could have spoken through Necho.

[32]Tg. Chr goes out of the way to explain how such a good king could have come to such an abysmal end, and is forced to conclude that in spite of his reforming zeal, his arrogance in taking a momentous decision without reference to God brought terrible consequences. Tg. Lam 1:18 also regards this failure to seek instruction as a serious lapse, though it adds the further stricture on Josiah that he had done what he had not been commanded to do—all as a prelude to Josiah's acknowledgment that the Lord is righteous, "for I have transgressed his Word."

at king Josiah and the king said to his servants: "Move me away for I am badly wounded." 24. Then his servants moved him out of the chariot and transported him on his second chariot and brought him to Jerusalem. *There*[i] he died and he was buried in the tombs of his fathers. All *the men of* Judah and Jerusalem were in mourning for Josiah. 25. Jeremiah uttered a *great* lament for Josiah. Speaking it with him were all *the leading men and ladies of quality,*[33] *and they have been repeating* their laments[33] for Josiah up to this day. And they made them a *worthy*[j] decree for Israel *that they should mourn for Josiah in their laments.* Behold they are written *in the book which Baruch wrote, at Jeremiah's dictation,* in the laments. 26. Now the rest of the acts of Josiah, and *all* the kindly acts *which he did,* according to what is written in the law of the Lord, 27. his acts, the first ones, *which he did in his childhood,* and the last ones, *which he did in his youth, and all the judgments which he gave from the day that he became king when he was eight years old, being still a youth, to the eighteenth year, while still young, when he began to restore the sanctuary house of the Lord: all these he presented to the Lord of judgment from his own resources; and how he purified the house of Israel and Judah from all uncleanness:* behold these are written in the book of the kings of *the house of* Israel and of *the house of* Judah.

CHAPTER 36

1. Then the people of the land took Jehoahaz, the son of Josiah, and made him king in Jerusalem, in place of his father. 2. Jehoahaz was twenty-three years old when he became king, and he reigned for three months in Jerusalem. 3. The king of Egypt removed him *from his throne* in Jerusalem, and he imposed taxes on *the inhabitants of* the land *of Israel* of one hundred *centenaria*[1] of silver and one *centenarium*[2] *of* gold. 4. The king of Egypt made his brother Eliakim king over

Notes, Chapter 35

[33]MT: "and all the male and female singers have spoken in their laments. . . ." "Male and female singers" = *šrym* and *šrwt*. A slight change of consonant gives *śrym* and *śrwt*, "leading men and ladies of quality." This is the reading Tg. Chr has followed. The word Tg. Chr uses for "ladies of quality" is the plural (V gives the singular and C the plural) of *mṭrwnyt*, borrowed from the Latin *matrona* (MJ 769f. and JL II, 30).

Notes, Chapter 36

[1]MT: "talents"; see 1 Chr 19:6, note 12.
[2]MT: "talent."

Judah and Jerusalem and changed his name to Jehoiakim, but Joahaz*a* his brother, *the Lame One,*[3] took and brought him to Egypt. 5. Jehoiakim was twenty-five years old when he became king, and he reigned for eleven years in Jerusalem and he did *what was* evil *before*[4] the Lord, his God. 6. Nebuchadnezzar, the king of Babylon, came up against him and bound him *with manacles,*[5] with *chains of* bronze,[6] to carry him off to Babylon. 7. Some of the vessels of the *sanctuary* house of the Lord Nebuchadnezzar brought to Babylon and placed them in his *palace*[7] in Babylon. 8. Now the rest of the acts of Jehoiakim and his abomination *and* what he did, and *the sin* which was laid to his charge[8]—behold, they are written in the book of the kings of *the house of* Israel and of *the house of* Judah. And Jehoiachin, his son, reigned in his place. 9. Jehoiachin was eight years old when he became king, and he reigned for three months and ten days in Jerusalem and he did *what was* evil *before*[4] the Lord. 10. At the *end*[9] of the year King Nebuchadnezzar sent and brought him to Babylon with *all*b that was precious in the *sanctuary* house of the Lord, and he made his brother Zedekiah king over *those of the house of* Judah and Jerusalem. 11. Zedekiah was twenty-one years old when he became king, and he reigned for eleven years in Jerusalem. 12. He did *what* was evil *before*[4] the Lord his God and did not humble himself from before Jeremiah the prophet, *who prophesied to him* from the mouth of *the Memra of* the Lord. 13. He also rebelled against King Nebuchadnezzar, who had caused him to take an oath by *the Memra of the Lord,*[10] and he stiffened his neck and strengthened *the inclination of* his heart so as not to return[11] to *the fear of* the Lord, the God of Israel. 14. Likewise, all the leaders of the priests and the people became more and more unfaithful,[12] following all the *horrible* abominations of the peoples; and they defiled the *sanctuary* house of the Lord which he had consecrated in Jerusalem. 15. The Lord, the God of their fathers, sent to them, *that they might return,* by his*c* messengers, whom he sent to them regularly from the beginning,[13] because he had compassion on his people and

Apparatus, Chapter 36

a C, L, AS: *yhw'hz.* V: *yw'hz* (= MT).   *c* E: "their."
b C, E, L, AS lack "all."

Notes, Chapter 36

[3] MT: "Necho"; see 35:20, note 25.
[4] MT: "in the eyes of."
[5] No corresponding word in MT. For "manacles," a loan word, see 33:11, note 15.
[6] MT: "with two bronzes," i.e., fetters of bronze.
[7] MT uses the normal word for "palace, temple," *hykl.* Tg. Chr prefers the Greek–Latin derivative, *plṭyryn.* See 1 Chr 9:18, note 17.
[8] MT: "and what was found against him."
[9] MT: "turn."
[10] MT: "God."
[11] MT: "from returning."
[12] Lit.: "multiplied to act unfaithfully."
[13] Lit.: "rising early and sending," following the Hebrew idiom.

dwelling place, *the residence of the Shekinah of his holiness.*[14] 16. But they kept laughing at the messengers of *the Lord* and treating his words with contempt and mocking his prophets until the anger of the Lord arose against his people until there was no remedy. 17. So he brought up against them the king of the Chaldaeans, and he killed their young men with the sword in the house of their *sanctuaries,*[15] and he did not spare young man or maiden, old man or *leader*[16]—all of them he *delivered*[17] into his hand. 18. And all[d] the vessels of the *sanctuary* house of *the Lord,*[10] both large and small, *he delivered into his hand,* as well as the treasuries of the *sanctuary* house of the Lord and the treasuries of *the house of* the king and his nobles. All of these he brought to Babylon. 19. Then they burned the *sanctuary* house of *the Lord* and broke down the wall of Jerusalem and burned all its palaces with fire, and all its precious vessels (they gave over) to destruction. 20. And he took into exile to Babylon the remnant[e] *that remained* from *those killed by* the sword,[f] and they became servants to him and to his sons, until *the time that* the kingdom of Persia took control.[18] 21. To fulfill the word of *the prophecy from before* the Lord *from* the mouth of Jeremiah: "Until the land enjoyed its periods of rest." All the days *that the land of Israel was devastated*[19] it had a period of *rest,* to complete[g] seventy years. 22. In the first year of Cyrus, the king of Persia, *when* the word of *the prophecy of* the Lord by the mouth of Jeremiah *was* fulfilled,[20] the spirit *of the power of* the Lord *was given*[h] *to* Cyrus,[21] the king of Persia, and he had proclamation[22] made throughout all his kingdom, and as well *he sent it* by letter, saying: 23. "Thus has Cyrus, king of Persia, said: 'All the kingdoms of the earth *the Memra of* the Lord, the God of heaven, has *handed over*[23] to me and he has commanded me to build for him a *sanctuary* house in Jerusalem, which

Apparatus, Chapter 36

[d] C: "also."
[e] C: *šywr',* also means "remnant."
[f] C: "from the death of the sword."
[g] C omits "to complete."

[h] C: "came," perhaps through confusion between two words "was given" and "came," where many of the consonants are similar in appearance.

Notes, Chapter 36

[14]MT: "his dwelling-place."
[15]MT: singular.
[16]MT: "senior citizen."
[17]MT: "gave."
[18]Lit.: "reigned."
[19]MT: "all the days of the devastation."
[20]MT: "that the word of the Lord by the mouth of Jeremiah might be accomplished."
[21]MT: "the Lord stirred up the spirit of Cyrus."
[22]Cf. 2 Chr 24:9; 30:5, and see Chapter 24, note 12.
[23]MT: "given."

is in *the tribe of* Judah. Whoever is among you of all his people, may the *Memra of the Lord* be *in his support*[24] and let him go up!'"[25]

Notes, Chapter 36

[24]MT: "May the Lord, his God, be with him."

[25]The translation above omits *d'yt bynyh*. The latter word especially is difficult to fit in. Le Déaut's suggestion that we read *d'ytr'y* is much more reasonable, giving some such translation as: "Whoever among you who volunteers (to go up) of all his people, may the *Memra of* the Lord. . . ."

INDEXES

BIBLICAL TEXTS
Hebrew Bible

Genesis

2:7	62
2:8	62
2:11	37, 41
2:19	62
6:12	46, 47
10:1	41
10:2	36
10:3	36
10:4	37
10:8	38
10:9	38
10:10	38
10:14	38
11:1-9	39
11:10-26	41
14:20	41
15:13	74
15:17	116
22	116, 117
22:2	146
22:16	116
34:21	201
34:30	102
35:22	64
36:39	44, 45
38	41
38:2	46
38:7-10	46
38:7	46
38:9	46, 47
38:10	46
38:24	41
46:12	46
46:13	72
46:24	73
46:43	59
49:3	64
49:4	64
49:8-12	64
49:15	161

Exodus

1:7	122
1:15-21	50
11:4	113
12:37	122
13:17	74
22:23	96
24:5	64
25:23	150
25:31	149
30:18-21	149
31:2	149
32:25-29	64
34:16	46

Leviticus

8:9	191
21:9	41
11:29-31	88
13:46	211
21:9	41
25:3	47
25:4	47

Numbers

9:11	221
11:16	59
21:27-30	72
23:24	151
24:21	54
25:14	47
26:19	46
26:48	73
26:49	73
31:8	43

Deuteronomy

3:9	67
7:3	46
10:1-5	152
17:8	189
20:11	161
23:4	48, 76

Joshua

2:6	61
2:12	61
7:24	47
7:25	47
7:26	47
9:15	61
9:23	61
9:26	61
9:27	79
11:17	65
12:4	65
13:3	95
13:5	65
13:17	65
13:22	43
15:15	54
15:33	71
17:11	71
17:13	161
20:8	71

Judges

1:11	54
1:16	54
6:34	92
9:15	207
11:16	55
13:25	52
14:1	48
18:30	122
19	77
20	77
20:48	77

1 Samuel

2:1	126
9:1	78
15	85
17:12	50
17:50	113
22	85
28:6	85
31:9	84

2 Samuel

2:8	84
2:9	84
2:31	113
3:2	55
3:39	59
5:18	97
5:20	65
6:6	24, 96
7:24	107
8:6	108
8:18	89
9:6-13	82
10:1	110
17:25	49, 52
19:24-30	82
20:24	161
21:17	78
21:19	113
23:11	21
23:29	89
23:35	90
23:37	90
24:1	21
24:12	115

1 Kings

2:19	62
5:11	47
5:25	145
6:9	200
6:18	82
7:14	21, 145

Apocrypha and Pseudepigrapha

New Testament

Septuagint

Peshitta

Vulgate

TARGUMS
Targum Onqelos

Targum Pseudo-Jonathan

RABBINIC LITERATURE

Tosefta

Mishnah

Babylonian Talmud

Palestinian Talmud

Ta'anith		Yebamoth		Sotah	
68b	53	9c	48, 76	17a	48

Midrashim

Sifre Numbers

24ff	50
73	55
82	152

Genesis Rabbah

6:4	40
13:4	41
27:8	47
37:1	36, 37
37:2	38
37:6	39
37:7	39, 40
37:8	40
44:18	74
62:5	94
63:4	43
68:12	117
69:7	116
70:19	43
73:4	45
82:4	49
82:7	56
85:6	48
85:10	41
97	64

Exodus Rabbah

1:17	49, 50
20:11	74

27:3, 6	43
40:4	50

Leviticus Rabbah

1:1	60
1:3	12, 13, 24, 124
6:6	64
9:1	47
9:2	78

Numbers Rabbah

6:1	47
13:2	65
20:24	47
21:3	62

Ruth Rabbah

2:1	12, 61
2:2	61
4:1	48
5:1	87
5:6	230, 231

Esther Rabbah

7:13	43

Pesikta Rabbati

14:9	47

Mekilta de Rabbi Ishmael
Exodus

12:13	116
15:9	24

Pirke de Rabbi Eliezer

4	173
7	62
8	62, 219
22	47
31	116
33	212, 213
35	117, 146
43	117, 230, 231
47	62
48	74

Midrash Psalms

9:11	48
37:1	41
59:4	56
76:3	41
78:11	187

JEWISH WRITERS
Josephus

Antiquities		**Jewish War**	
I:46	39	VI :438	41
I:179-81	41		

Philo

De Abrahamo		**Legum Allegoriae**	
235	41	3:79-82	41

Pseudo-Philo

Lab.

IV 7	38
V 1	40
VI 1-4	40

AUTHORS